D1452994

Loyalty and Liberty

American Countersubversion from World War I to the McCarthy Era

ALEX GOODALL

UNIVERSITY OF
ILLINOIS PRESS
Urbana, Chicago,
and Springfield

Library of Congress Cataloging-in-Publication Data
Goodall, Alex (Alexis Vere)
Loyalty and liberty : American countersubversion from World War I
to the McCarthy era / Alex Goodall.
pages   cm
Includes bibliographical references and index.
ISBN 978-0-252-03803-7 (hardback) —
ISBN 978-0-252-09531-3 (e-book)
1. Anti-communist movements—United States—History—
20th century. 2. Radicalism—United States—History—20th century.
3. Political persecution—United States—History—20th century.
4. United States—Politics and government—1919–1933.
5. United States—Politics and government—1933–1945. I. Title.
E743.5.G63   2013
320.973'0904—dc23   2013023557

Contents

Acknowledgments

This book would never have been completed without the support, encouragement, and advice of many people over several years.

I am particularly indebted to those who have read sections of this work or work on which this was based and provided invaluable comments and suggestions, particularly Tony Badger, Jonathan Bell, Owen Dudley-Edwards, Patrick Flack, Hannah Greig, Nick Guyatt, Michael Heale, Andrew Hemingway, Fabian Hilfrich, Rhodri Jeffreys-Jones, Michael Kimmage, Nelson Lichtenstein, Robert Mason, Dan Matlin, James Patterson, Kirsten Phimister, Mark Roodhouse, Markku Ruotsila, Jonathan Sanders, Ben Schiller, Anthony Szynkaruk, John Thompson, Stephen Tuck, and the eagle-eyed Annette Wenda. At the University of Illinois Press, my particular thanks to Laurie Matheson and her fantastic team for their unwavering support, enthusiasm, and diligence.

I would also like to express my appreciation to the master and fellows of Trinity College, Cambridge; to my colleagues at York, who have provided such a productive and collegial environment in recent years; and to the fantastic students who have taken my various courses on countersubversion, antiradicalism, and anticommunism: a perpetual source of enthusiasm, not to mention unconscious guinea pigs for my ideas.

A researcher is naturally indebted to staff at archives, libraries, and research institutions, and though in this case there are too many to name individually, my particular thanks must go to the administrators of the various funds that have supported my research: including the Sara Norton Fund, Faculty of History, University of Cambridge; the Rouse Ball Research Fund Committee, Trinity College, University of Cambridge; the British Academy; the Gilder Lehrman Institute of American History, New York; and the Eccles Centre for North American Studies at the British Library, the last two granting me fellowships.

Finally, for providing friendship, assistance, references, dissent, tea, transport, conversation, and in certain instances something approaching a second home, huge thanks to Emily Critchley, Joe Crespino and his wonderful family, Steve Huot and Ana Maria Piedrahita, Robin Vandome and Lorna Cheyne, Kate Dossett, Jessica Gibbs, Ed Holberton, George Lewis, Chris Renwick, Mary Sarotte, and Sandra Scanlon. Anyone having written a book, especially one long in gestation, will know that it is not possible to do so without the forbearance of those around them. In my case, they certainly forbore, so thanks are due most of all to my dear friends in London, Cambridge, Leeds, Edinburgh, and elsewhere, and to my family.

Loyalty and Liberty

Introduction

The fear of subversion has been a persistent theme in the history of the United States of America. We most commonly associate it with the divisions, investigations, and accusations of the McCarthy era, but in the first half of the twentieth century warnings about the dangers of conspiracy were already being expressed with volume.[1] In response, the state and various private-sector groups sought to police the political conduct of the American people. Between World War I and the McCarthy era, countersubversive campaigns were launched against immigrants, racial, ethnic and religious minorities, radicals, reformers, and antiwar activists—who, it was claimed, were aligned with enemy states and conspiring to undermine the American political order. Campaigns ranged from efforts to discipline, punish, or exclude alleged subversives to ritualistic affirmations of nationalism by self-styled "100 percent Americans." While usually expressed within the bounds of the law, some of these actions were extrajudicial and violent, and often they resulted in the mistreatment of people who had little association with the crimes of which they were accused. These campaigns, the central subject of this book, formed the prehistory of McCarthyism and its successor movements and directly contributed to the emergence of the modern domestic security state.[2]

Yet the United States also witnessed sustained waves of opposition to political repression. Countersubversion was inherently problematic in a democratic regime, since it required surveillance, the centralization of power, censorship, propaganda, and controls over political advocacy as well as criminal action. These activities were deeply alien to American traditions of decentralized governance, and as a result countersubversives faced tenacious resistance. Although the clearest opposition came from the largely left-of-center civil liberties movement that emerged explicitly to challenge the politics of loyalty after World War I, radicals, liberals, and conservatives alike shared a deep commitment to the freedoms of expression, organization, and assembly enshrined in the Constitution and saw political policing as the province of European monarchies and empires.[3] What Michael Kazin has called the "populist persuasion" infused American identity across the political spectrum with a "profound outrage with elites who ignored, corrupted and/or betrayed the core ideal of American democracy: rule by the common people." As Woodrow Wilson put it, Americans swore faith to a flag, but this was "a flag of liberty of opinion, as well as of political liberty in questions of organization."[4]

Although historians have generally sought to understand it solely in terms of authoritarian tendencies in American life, the history of countersubversion was therefore shaped by *two* powerful and often conflicting impulses: the desire to ensure, coercively if necessary, the commitment of the people to the nation, and the countervailing urge to preserve the freedoms that made the nation worth defending in the first place—in short, between loyalty and liberty. Efforts to pass laws, build institutions, and launch campaigns against supposed subversive influences were viewed with ambivalence. Periods of repressive excess were followed by backlash and retrenchment, while memories and myths of past misdeeds endured to influence the present. Hailed as heroes in the moment, countersubversives were demonized in retrospect when their apocalyptic warnings did not come to pass, and as caricatures they served to strengthen resistance to the very policies they had advocated. In liberal histories written during the Cold War, countersubversion even came to exemplify a kind of psychosociological aberration. Unable to cope with modernity, countersubversives supposedly expressed a form of "political hysteria" or a "paranoid style" of politics out of tune with the rational, liberal norms of American society.[5] To Stanley Coben, nativists resembled "Melanesian and Papuan groups in the South Pacific" in placing their nonrational, communal loyalties over procedural rights, while campaigns for engineering purity through forced Americanization echoed in their fantasies of security Sioux beliefs that Ghost Dancers would be invulnerable to bullets.[6] This was a particularly ironic characterization, since countersubversives believed they were defending civilization against barbarism.[7] To their critics, countersubversives had come to resemble the demons they claimed to be fighting.

In recent years, the analysis of countersubversion and related fields has been conducted on more measured terms. As Alan Brinkley and Leo D. Ribuffo point out, radical populists and their supporters in the Depression era voiced, however incoherently, meaningful concerns over the relationship between the individual and the state, the effect of industrialization, and the challenges of modern international relations that were often integrated into the mainstream either at the time or later.[8] Historians on both the Right and the Left have since pointed out that many of the conflicts between countersubversives and their targets were not expressions of displaced anxieties and political hysteria but genuine clashes between groups with diverging interests and worldviews.[9] Others have stressed that efforts to limit the space for dissent were promoted not only by businessmen, segregationists, and nativists, but also by people who described themselves as liberals, progressives, and even radicals.[10] Indeed, recent scholarship has challenged simple distinctions between conservative and liberal thought in America altogether, showing how classically liberal arguments were used by both groups for distinctive ends.[11] This book suggests such intellectual exchanges were particularly extensive in the interwar period due to the absence of clear ideological lines between the two major parties. This points us to a politics of countersubversion that was multiple, contested, and evolving. Ideas crossed political boundaries and were used to promote both continuity and change, a point that perhaps helps to explain why countersubversive politics can have exerted such influence even as the United States was dramatically expanding the reach of its democracy.

This book seeks to examine how conflicting impulses for loyalty and liberty shaped the politics of countersubversion between World War I and the McCarthy era. By examining the ways this intellectual problem manifested in various historical contexts, one uncovers a history of fits and starts rather than simple, linear progression: waves of growth in political policing followed by undercurrents of reform. Although there is much truth in Regin Schmidt's assertion that the history of political surveillance in the interwar period was one of institution building and lawmaking, this was not a simple or unidirectional process. Importantly, the distinctive character of these institutions and laws was conditioned by American political culture.[12] The contradictory effort to retain historic freedoms while simultaneously limiting them is what gave American countersubversion its distinctively American character: populist, legalistic (if not always legal), voluble, and partisan, rather than simply bureaucratic, dull, and authoritarian or militant and genocidal.

In line with Larry Ceplair's call for a "neutral taxonomy" of the field, countersubversives are herein defined simply as those people who argued it was necessary to defend the political system from covert threats: that is, as participants in an ongoing political debate rather than representatives of a predetermined social group with normative characteristics.[13] However, to make sense of the complex ways in which countersubversion operated, the book does draw together three broad strands of countersubversive politics: antiradicalism, antifascism, and anticommunism. Although members of each strand often differed on many details, they did tend to share some basic concerns and assumptions. Antiradicals generally saw the principal danger to the American political system as coming from revolutionary leftists working among marginal or oppressed social groups supposedly aligned with Germany, Russia, or Mexico. Led by businessmen, religious groups, fraternal organizations, conservative union leaders, and politicians from both major parties, antiradical politics came to the fore in World War I, when prowar liberals and socialists broke with the radical Left and engaged uneasily with right-wing nationalists in efforts to strengthen the disciplinary state. Antifascism, by contrast, concerned itself with dangers to American democracy from the radical Right and capitalist elites, particularly following the Nazi seizure of power. It reflected the shift of politics leftward after the Great Depression, as liberals and radicals joined forces to build a welfare state and imagine the possibilities of racial and industrial democracy. Finally, anticommunist countersubversives argued that the worldwide communist movement was attaining a dangerous influence in American life by infiltrating the state, seizing control of the union movement, and agitating otherwise contented racial minorities against the existing social order. Although anticommunist fears of racial and industrial insurgency owed much to older strains of antiradicalism, they offered a sharp new emphasis on the state rather than the social periphery as the principal source of subversion.

As the first part of the book shows, although initially powered by a desire to preserve liberal ideals of democratic consent, social harmony, and progress, with its basically hostile orientation toward peripheral social groups antiradicalism quickly came to operate as a conservative defense of class and social privilege. In seeking to avoid the kind of big-state politics it associated with the national enemy, Germany, the administration of Woodrow Wilson—the first to grapple with the question of federal political repression on a sustained basis—developed a hybrid approach to countersubversion that, while centralizing powers in some areas, elsewhere radically derogated authority to the citizenry. Federal efforts to promote countersubversive politics were presented as investigations, legal prosecutions, and enlightened educational campaigns rather than more overt forms of coercion. And instead of building large police bureaucracies, both Wilsonian Democrats and prowar Republicans encouraged the kind of private-sector voluntary activism that supposedly marked out American popular democracy from the statist regimes of Europe. The government would coordinate and encourage local actors rather than interceding in people's lives directly. Since this kept "the people" at the heart of political life, it would ensure loyalty without risking tyranny—at least in theory.

In practice, despite the high-minded rhetoric, prowar countersubversives willfully obscured the distinction between dissent and sedition in order to prosecute antiwar protesters under laws created to deal with foreign espionage, and the supposed distinction between "educational" and "investigative" campaigns and "propaganda" proved to be illusory. Lacking both accountability and expertise, the public responded to the government's calls to action by targeting local rivals, punishing presumed violators of social norms, and bringing the impromptu tortures of the frontier back to the heartland of America. With little conspiracy to be found, loyalty campaigns quickly took on the class-based, gendered, and racial perspectives of their authors. By the time of the Red Scare in 1919, claims to be acting in the higher national interest had come to reflect a deep class division between American workers and their employers, especially in manufacturing industry.

In the short term, the effort to fight radical influence generated support for the war and crushed left-wing politics. In the process, countersubversives helped erect a barrier between reformers and revolutionaries that had rarely been policed during the Progressive Era and engineered support for a raft of new policies ranging from the restriction of immigration to the prohibition of alcohol. However, it also produced an antiauthoritarian backlash and a restitution of constitutionalism at a time when similar dynamics in other countries were undermining the political order entirely. Federally sponsored political repression generated fears of creeping tyranny, while popular vigilantism generated divisive social tensions. Over time a different conception of Americanism was reasserted: one that focused on continental isolation, the rule of law, and the decentralization of power as the United States' true heritage. This alternative was sufficiently powerful that under the Republican administrations of the 1920s, the federal government was obliged to retreat from countersubversive crusading almost completely.

The constraints on federal political repression that resulted from this backlash formed a perfect expression of the quixotic character of democratic countersubversion, for they in turn made it harder to justify countersubversive politics to the public. Instead of a disciplined national organization led by congressmen and Justice Department bureaucrats, the 1920s saw private-sector countersubversives forced to operate without the crucial coordinating influence of government. As Skocpol, Ganz, and Munson have shown, the popular image of voluntarist networks as effectively self-reliant—in their words, "tiny, local and disconnected from government"—fails to acknowledge the degree to which the state remained the cynosure even in the American system of distributed governance.[14] Without federal bureaucracies or a strong partisan motor behind their efforts, lacking investigative competence, and driven by transparently self-interested motives, antiradicals increasingly came to be seen as either deluded, malevolent, or both. By the time of the Great Depression, antiradicalism had become a widespread joke; many alliances had collapsed, and their chief advocates had become laughingstocks.

The second part of the book examines this troubled phase of countersubversive history. Chapter 4 shows how the structure of national politics militated against the building of a sustained national countersubversive movement in the twenties, then details the private-sector networks that were forced to lead the charge against presumed radical subversion instead. Chapter 5 examines the efforts by such "professional patriots" to sustain the country's hostile posture toward Russia (and Mexico) by uncovering covert Soviet activities in the Western Hemisphere and highlights the problems of expertise and ideology that produced an almost complete failure to do so. Meanwhile, chapters 6 and 7 focus on the central role of countersubversive ideas in industry—as revealed through one of the most visible, influential, yet contradictory personalities of the interwar period, Henry Ford—and in the churches. Both cases highlight the way in which established elites struggled to maintain the coherence of their countersubversive arguments in the face of economic and social crisis.

The early years of the Depression thus witnessed a decisive challenge both to the voluntarist approach that had dominated from 1917 to 1929 and to antiradical claims that the chief threat to American security came from small left-wing organizations and peripheral social groups. The Depression divided businessmen and amplified workers' voices. Populists, socialists, and liberals used fears of revolution to push for reform instead of reaction, arguing that the best way of dealing with extremism was by addressing its causes, which meant poverty, oppression, prohibition, racism, and social exclusion. And, believing that the historic failures of countersubversion stemmed from an excess of populism and a lack of expertise, President Franklin Delano Roosevelt returned to the Bureau of Investigation the powers to investigate political extremism that had been taken from it during the 1920s. In this way, efforts were made to reconcile the competing impulses of loyalty and liberty on new terms. Opponents of loyalty crusading had formerly argued that the relentless pursuit of security distracted people from pressing questions of domestic injustice; now, inequality itself was seen as a driver of subversion.

For many liberals, the crisis opened the possibility of constructive engagement with left-wing radicals and the Soviet Union, and by the mid-1930s elements of the Left and center-Left had begun working together in shared campaigns to reform American industrial life and fight for racial democracy.[15] To many, the real threat to American security seemed to come from the Right, not the Left—either from capitalist elites who used police forces and private armies to repress workers or from populist groups who sought to promote divisive racial and religious agendas as "100 percent Americanism." As politics polarized and fascism became a threatening presence on the world stage, reformers thus adopted the rhetoric of countersubversion that had previously been aimed at them and redirected it toward the Right.

The third part of the book shows how smears, innuendo, congressional investigations, and allegations of foreign influence, all countersubversive tactics that had been pioneered by antiradicals, were put in reverse. Presenting fascism as the unmasked face of monopoly capitalism, antifascists highlighted affinities between American businessmen and Nazi Germany in order to cast doubt on the former's commitment to democracy. Both groups, they argued, were expressions of a "totalitarian" politics that sought to subject by force the rights of the masses to the dictates of a self-interested elite. Facing accusations of fascism, disloyalty, and anti-Semitism, conservatives were forced to distance themselves from potential allies on the radical Right and defend their patriotic credentials in what became little short of a mirror image of McCarthyism.

In making such claims, antifascists sought, with no small degree of success, to redefine American liberty in terms of industrial and racial democracy rather than freedom of contract or freedom from government. They encouraged the state to intervene in areas that had previously been considered off-limits, and at their most radical they even argued that the security of the nation could be guaranteed only with the end of capitalism altogether. Unlike many parts of the world, the Depression crisis witnessed no serious challenge to the American political order. Indeed, because of these efforts, democracy was strengthened and citizens bound more tightly together. Yet this was in no small part dependent upon a widespread countersubversive fear that revolution and dictatorship were the only alternatives to reform: a recognition that exceptionalism was a status to be fought for, liberty a condition to be engineered, rather than either being a gift of Providence.

In the 1930s, then, despite the nation remaining comparatively secure, accusations of fascism and communism were traded with growing ferocity. But rather than highlighting the inherent difficulty of distinguishing legitimate political disagreements from seditious conspiracy, these attacks strengthened the urge to deploy the language of countersubversion against opponents in what effectively became a rhetorical arms race. Even when individual countersubversives were discredited, ideological conflict between Left and Right tended to push forward the politics of countersubversion in much the way pistons in an engine drive a vehicle through space.

As a result, just as antifascists had diverted countersubversive methods to reformist purposes, in the late 1930s and 1940s the anticommunist politics of the emerging conservative coalition co-opted the fear of fascism for new ends. Conservatives transformed antifascist language by depicting *both* Nazi Germany and Soviet Russia as totalitarian states, redefining the word to downplay the Left's concern with the class-state nexus and focusing instead on tyrannical state power in general—a characteristic, they believed, also of the New Deal. The power of this antistatist critique lay in the new way it reconciled the imperatives of countersubversion with the enduring ideal of liberty. Arguments that had previously been used to resist the growth of political policing now seemed to justify attacks on liberals in government. Formerly painful divisions between the conservative and progressive wings of the Republican Party (GOP) were reduced, and conservative elites found new allies among classes that had once viewed them with suspicion. This formed part of the long shift in the twentieth century of populist politics from the Left to the Right, as the welfare and regulatory state replaced trusts, monopolies, and corporations as the perceived source of tyranny in American life.

In the postwar era, Americans would continue to argue about whether they supported or opposed big government. Anticommunists on the Right would echo their antiradical predecessors in encouraging private-sector groups to purge disloyalty from their local communities while asserting their "intimacy with the people," as Buckley and Bozell said of McCarthy.[16] But despite the Main Street rhetoric, the new anticommunists sought to co-opt liberal institutions of federal power rather than challenge their existence. Since the later 1930s, conservatives had consistently supported new laws to expand Department of Justice powers and defended intrusive congressional investigations as a vital tool for the preservation of liberty. Indeed, they even began to argue that liberal disloyalty could be seen in a lack of willingness under Roosevelt and Truman to enforce the laws and use the institutions that in many cases liberals had themselves constructed. Far from the Wilson era, when politicians relied upon local actors to police a decentralized regime, the bureaucratic state had emerged as both a source of repression and a venue in which such repression could take place. Countersubversive politics had come to resemble a snake set upon swallowing its own tail.

At virtually every stage of the history of American countersubversion, campaigns to enforce political loyalty saw self-interested actors exploit public fears for personal benefit. Yet despite this persistent failure to develop a politics of countersubversion that could draw a clear line between legitimate and illegitimate dissent, by midcentury most Americans had come to accept the basic need for a degree of state-based political repression. The war against fascism and the success of the New Deal fatally weakened the nineteenth-century order of broad liberal latitude, local governance, and lax political monitoring, just as it decisively shattered the possibility of American isolation from the world. Memories of anti-German campaigns in World War I, antiradical campaigns in the interwar years, the destruction of the anti-interventionist movement during the Second World War, and of course McCarthyism were assembled into an array of conflicting narratives of victimhood, many of which continue to be reprised today. Yet despite this troubled history, most Americans accepted that the federal state had at least some role to play in managing extremism.

This book seeks to explain how a country with a long-standing hostility to the centralization of power and a strong disposition to associate activist government with tyranny gradually reconciled itself to a domestic security state that matched the national security state projecting American power overseas during the Cold War. In one sense, this story forms part of a larger transition throughout the world from the classically liberal states of the nineteenth century to the Leviathan regimes of the twentieth. The new systems that emerged in most democratic nations matched tighter restrictions on speech, action, and organization with new commitments to positive freedoms brought about through government action and energetic civil rights lobbies that vigilantly monitored countersubversive institutions for signs of excess and partiality. But as much as this story was repeated in other countries, countersubversion in the United States was shaped by a distinctive tradition in which politicians and leading public figures were consistently forced to reconcile their countersubversive instincts with the trends of decentralized governance that were assumed to mark out the New World from old Europe. The political ideologies of McCarthy, Goldwater, Wallace, and Reagan, which all variously combined discordant elements of antigovernment populism, social conservatism, and state-based political authoritarianism, owe much to this earlier history. As a number of contemporary scholars have pointed out, the modern conservative movement did not begin with the backlash to the sixties. It persisted under the radar throughout the era of the supposed liberal consensus, stemming from the unresolved conflicts of the interwar years. In many ways, then, the same fractious conflicts over the meaning of national loyalty and the promise of American liberty that are the subject of this book can be traced through to the present.[17]

PART I

The Revolutionary Challenge

1

Policing Politics

The Origins of Federal Countersubversion

President Woodrow Wilson and his supporters presented the decision to join the war in Europe as the beginning of a great coming together—a moment when, faced with existential threats, the inhabitants of the towns, cities, and countryside would bind themselves as one in a shared commitment to liberty and independence. "As a nation we are united in spirit and intention," Wilson declared in his December 1917 State of the Union address, eight months into the war. "I hear the voices of dissent," he acknowledged. "I also see men here and there fling themselves in impotent disloyalty against the calm, indomitable power of the Nation." But they "do not touch the heart of anything. . . . They may safely be left to strut their uneasy hour and be forgotten."[1]

The dominant, progressive-nationalist tradition to which Wilson belonged held that a shared sense of national purpose, especially in times of crisis, transcended narrow divisions of politics, wealth, color, place of origin, and sex.[2] As Herbert Croly, the foremost prophet of progressivism, had written in 1909, "We may distrust and dislike much that is done in the name of our country by our fellow-countrymen; but our country itself, its democratic system, and its prosperous future are above suspicion." But as powerful as this rhetoric of unity was, it did not describe American life in 1917. Americans were deeply divided over the decision to go to war, with a large minority unwilling to be sent to die in a conflict they did not support and did not think necessary. Wilson knew it: many had voted for his reelection in 1916 precisely to avoid such an engagement overseas. Few Americans signed up voluntarily after Congress declared war, millions refused to register for the draft that was implemented soon after, and thousands absconded rather than face being called up. In the South, three state governors were forced to request federal troops to suppress deserter-led insurrections.[3] Newspapers reported Americans fleeing across the border to

Mexico, while thousands of recently naturalized citizens gave back their papers rather than follow orders to enlist. In the North, millions of ethnic Irish, German, and Eastern Europeans opposed a conflict that saw the United States ally with Britain, France, and Russia. From coast to coast, sporadic antidraft marches and demonstrations bubbled up, occasionally surging into violence and bloodshed. As a minister in North Carolina wrote in a letter to his local representative, "Many mothers are desperate, and the thought of an unjustifiable, useless war to be backed up by CONSCRIPTION of our boys into a fight of which they do not approve, and the expenditure of sums, such as the world has never heard of, for War, of the PEOPLE's money, has spread like a Pall all over our country."[4]

Advocates of war found themselves in a double bind: forced to strain their resources and ingenuity to manage an undercurrent of anti-interventionism that had the power to derail the war effort, yet committed to a nationalist mythology that held as axiomatic the belief that "the people" were both united behind the government and free to speak—that the war was being waged to save democracy and that dissenters were so rare that they could be "safely left to strut their uneasy hour and be forgotten." As historian Merle Curti notes, "Former struggles by and large involved the civilian population only in minor ways. Now war required mass morale, support, and participation. Hence patriotism could hardly be left to casual education, to chance." But if patriotism was not left to chance, then how could it be said to reflect the natural will of the people? Only power would allow the United States to "sustain righteousness, justice, and the golden rule by drawing the sword against the enemy of these virtues."[5] But would not the application of power undermine the democratic values the war was supposedly being fought for?

This was not just a problem of ideology or political rhetoric; it was also a question of law. Although the United States prior to World War I had witnessed many forms of intolerance, rarely had these been translated into federal laws or institutional mechanisms capable of large-scale political policing. The classically liberal and anticolonial constitutional system strictly limited the power of the federal government to control the loyalty of its citizens. Washington was permitted to wage war to protect the nation and raise troops to put down rebellions, but it was forbidden from restraining the political utterances of its people more generally. The Bill of Rights strictly controlled the federal state's authority to interfere with individual freedoms, even in times of crisis, and correctly anticipating the potential for abuse the founders had tightly regulated the power of the state to prosecute people for treason.[6] Over time these principles had become articles of faith for the vast majority of American citizens. Most remembered the one marked instance of their violation—the Alien and Sedition Acts of 1798—as an aberration: "the very memory of which," declared turn-of-the-century constitutional historian Francis Newton Thorpe, "is to this day intolerable to thousands of Americans."[7] Virtually no treason cases were brought to trial in the nineteenth century, while broader federal restrictions on the political liberties of white citizens were effectively nonexistent. Not without controversy, Abraham Lincoln had suspended habeas corpus during the Civil War, but he did so using the clauses regarding the suppression of a domestic insurrection, which clearly did not apply to Wilson's foreign war of choice. Even after the defeat of secession, efforts to prosecute leaders of the Confederacy for treason came to naught.

In this sense, the radical critic Max Eastman was right when he said, "In nations as well as individuals, hysteria is caused by inner conflict, and the United States on entering the First World War suffered a violent attack of this disease."[8] The problematic domestic response to the war reflected a crisis of a dominant liberal ideology that sought to reconcile an idealistic commitment to free expression and autonomous action with a perceived need to engineer national unity. It was the depth of the divisions among Americans, combined with the strength of the desire to deny that such divisions existed, that gave wartime repression its fire and fury. In different contexts, countersubversives over the next thirty years would face variations upon the same question: how to reconcile the ideal of the United States as a free and open nation with growing pressures to engineer the loyalty of the people.

The idea of subversion allowed the supporters of war to get round these two, interrelated, problems of jurisprudence and rhetoric. In ideological terms, by defining dissenters as "subversive"—that is, as individuals whose actions served to weaken the foundations of the Republic—it was possible to present opponents of war as essentially unpatriotic and un-American: if not "un-American" in strictly legal terms, then at least metaphorically, such that the abstract image of a unified nation could be preserved. Only those who supported the war were truly American, ran the circular argument, and therefore the American nation remained united in its support of the war. Meanwhile, from a legal perspective, the idea of subversion could be used to designate a new, broad category of criminal behavior of sufficient gravity that the federal government's responsibility to guarantee the republican form of government gave it a mandate to act, but that, unlike treason, was not strongly regulated by the Constitution. By calling for the creation of new crimes short of treason, it would therefore be easier both to get laws passed by Congress and to put them swiftly into action.[9]

There was another obvious advantage for the Wilson administration to managing domestic dissent on countersubversive grounds: the term *subversive* itself is extremely hard to define. It can encompass both covert operations conducted by agents of foreign powers and acts of domestic sedition by citizens with radical or revolutionary objectives. There is a fine line between sedition and dissent, and if much of the American public and political elite were doubtful about the merits of limiting the political freedoms of patriotic citizens, there was little opposition to hunting foreign enemies on American soil. *Subversion* as a catch-all term, then, helped to hitch the protests of dissenting Americans to the professional activities of foreign conspirators.

Certainly, on the eve of American entry into the war, there was little doubt that Germany had been intervening in the Western Hemisphere, both in the United States and in its sphere of influence. The Treasury Department's Secret Service had uncovered a range of plots, and the State Department had for a generation been reporting on German diplomatic efforts to displace American influence in Central America and the Caribbean. Most famously, the decision to go to war followed the interception of a telegram from German foreign minister Arthur Zimmerman to Mexican president Venustiano Carranza proposing that if Mexico kept the United States tied up on its southern frontier, Germany would return to Mexico all the territory it had lost during the nineteenth century.

In matters of counterespionage, the United States remained a woefully nineteenth-century nation. The federal government had few agencies with the capacity to investigate foreign covert operations and virtually no legal mechanisms to prosecute agents if caught. Following a suspicious explosion of munitions in July 1916, Congress permitted the Department of Justice's Bureau of Investigation, barely eight years old, to look into such threats, and to assist its staff was expanded from one hundred to three hundred persons.[10] The population of the United States had recently exceeded a hundred million. It seemed hard to deny that new measures to identify, monitor, and if necessary eliminate foreign conspiracy were needed.

Many of the most frightening rumors of foreign conspiracy, however, turned out to be either exaggerated or untrue.[11] The real problem the Wilson administration faced in mobilizing for war was not German conspiracy but opposition among its own people. In this sense, the lack of a clear distinction between espionage and sedition was not a problem for the administration; it was of vital utility. It was precisely this lack of clarity that allowed Wilsonians to take measures designed to combat foreign agents and turn them against Americans. As Brett Gary notes, a growing awareness of the power of propaganda to influence popular behavior was crucial to this occlusion, since concern over the power of hidden forces to shape public opinion allowed countersubversives to present diffuse affinities between the thinking of antiwar activists and covert agents as signs of conspiracy.[12] The absence of evidence showing any direct links between dissenters and the German enemy was explained away on the grounds that the conspiracy was covert, while similarities in goals and rhetoric were used as circumstantial evidence to prove the existence of that which was otherwise hidden. Though unsubstantiated, this argument was also largely unfalsifiable.

Faced with overriding claims of national security, qualms about the central-ization of authority were therefore pushed aside in favor of a sweeping coun-tersubversive campaign to mobilize a sometimes sullen and intransigent popu-lation behind America's first total war. The president set the tone of coercive patriotism and conspiratorial thinking, and both parties and all branches of government followed up with vigor, generating a climate of repression that quickly came to pervade all aspects of American life. With a solid bloc of sup-port among southern Democrats and conservative Republicans, along with more variegated support in Democratic areas of the North, the administration amassed a formidable array of wartime countersubversive powers, permitting long prison sentences for people caught passing information to the enemy, draft dodging, opposing conscription, and eventually speaking out against the war or even defaming the Constitution, government, or flag.[13] The postmaster gen-eral, Albert S. Burleson, was granted broad latitude to ban publications from the mails he determined to be seditious, a constraint that was usually enough to put them out of business, and a new office of alien property custodian was created to seize and operate enemy-owned property—the position handed to A. Mitchell Palmer, a Pennsylvania Democrat and a key Wilson ally.

While the loyalty codes, as they might be called, were generally directed at and occasionally used to prosecute foreign operatives, the range of possible offenses went beyond any reasonable definition of foreign agency, and vague drafting and a frenetic sensibility on the part of judges, Justice Department officials, and the staff of the Immigration Bureau saw the scope of their application extend beyond their already expansive limits.[14] The loose usage of terminology was clearly revealed in the debate over the Espionage Act of 1917, which despite its name never solely targeted foreign spies. Indeed, one prowar senator told his peers that there were one hundred thousand German spies already at work in the United States, a claim that could be true only if "spies" was taken to mean anti-interventionists.[15]

Probably the most visible targets of the loyalty codes were left-wing radical groups that led resistance to the war and most obviously blurred the lines between dissent, sedition, and conspiracy. Although most European socialist parties had supported their national governments in the parting of the ways that destroyed the Second International, the majority of American Socialists opposed the war, and the party grew by more than ten thousand members in the first months of the conflict because of its stance.[16] The influential anarchosyndicalist organiza-tion the Industrial Workers of the World (IWW) never formally came out against the war, but the overwhelming majority of its members were also deeply hostile to American intervention. Left-wing anti-interventionists generally believed the war was a continuation of the imperialistic conflicts of the previous generation, driven by plutocrats, munitions makers, and the other capitalist interests who controlled the American state. Rejecting the high-minded language of the Wilson administration, left-wing socialist leaders like Louis C. Fraina argued that it was "a dastardly lie" to say Wilson's war was fought for democracy.[17] "I know what war means," wrote radical journalist John Reed, who had been to Europe to report on conditions in the trenches. "I have been with the armies of all the belligerents except one, and I have seen men die, and go mad, and lie in hospitals suffering hell; but there is a worse thing than that. War means an ugly mob madness, crucifying the truth tellers, choking the artists, sidetracking reforms, revolutions and the working of social forces."[18] Kate Richards O'Hare declared herself as "a Socialist, a labor unionist and a believer in the Prince of Peace first, and an American second," saying she would never give her life "to add to the profits and protect the stolen wealth of the bankers, food speculators and ammunition makers."[19]

While such language skirted the line of revolutionary advocacy, most radicals argued that they were defending a higher national interest, one that would see the American people align with the suffering workers of the world rather than the great European empires, and that as such their protests were not seditious. Opponents, however, argued that by opposing the war, radicals had shown their disloyalty to the country that sheltered them and, by raising the probability of defeat, were aiding the enemy. Prosecutions quickly followed. In June 1917, the Secret Service coordinated a raid in New York and arrested well-known anarchists Emma Goldman and Alexander Berkman for conspiracy to violate the draft. A week later, a grand jury in Freeport, Illinois, ordered the arrest of 134 socialists and members of the IWW for refusing to register. In the fall, dozens more IWW offices were raided, with hundreds indicted, the majority in Chicago. Meanwhile, the attorney general, Thomas Watt Gregory, began proceedings against the publishers of the socialist press.[20]

In a sense, this last effort was superfluous: as with the German-language newspapers, the postmaster general had already banned the major left-wing publications from the mails. Restrictions on IWW mailing rights were so severe that even blank donation-request forms were banned from the post. (Burleson's willingness to clamp down on the smallest sign of dissent led to his banning writings by Thorstein Veblen that the government elsewhere was recommending as valuable propaganda against Germany.) By the end of the war, most of the administration's press targets had been driven out of business.[21]

Probably between a thousand and two thousand individuals, the vast majority left-wingers, were ultimately prosecuted under the loyalty codes.[22] Despite their organization never having officially taken a stance against the war, the IWW suffered the most. Wobbly leader "Big Bill" Haywood was sentenced to twenty years in prison, along with fourteen other IWW leaders, and sixty-eight other members received sentences of between five and ten years each, while a total of $2.5 million in fines were issued.[23] Goldman and Berkman were given two-year sentences, and socialists across the country received exorbitant punishments for speaking out against the war and accusing the government of profiteering. An individual received a twenty-year sentence for circulating a leaflet opposing a congressman who supported conscription. A moviemaker was even tried because a film he made—about the War of Independence, which included scenes of dastardly redcoats bayoneting innocent women and children—was considered to promote disloyalty toward the British wartime ally. The film was seized, the production company forced into bankruptcy, and the producer given a ten-year jail sentence.[24]

As arguably the nation's most famous socialist, a former candidate for the presidency, and a well-known opponent of war, Eugene Debs was the perhaps biggest prize sought by the loyalty campaigners, but he had taken a back seat during the anticonscription fight in 1917. In the end, however, the loyalty campaigns themselves forced Debs into taking a public stand in defense of friends and allies who had been prosecuted by the government. At the Ohio State Socialist Convention of June 1918, he launched a blistering attack on the war, the culture of patriotism, and the elites of Wall Street and was arrested two weeks later. He was tried in September and received ten years. How much had changed. As Beverly Gage notes, "Just six years earlier, Debs had been a viable, if not triumphant, candidate for the presidency. Now he was poised to go to prison—and, with a ten-year sentence, potentially to die there—for what was essentially an unchanged position."[25]

Wilson's loyalty campaigns represented as profound a challenge to American traditions as did his first-term progressive reforms to manage the economy. They blurred the distinction between criminal disloyalty and political dissent in a way that the Constitution had been specifically designed to prevent. Yet, paradoxically, they were sold to Congress and the public as measures to defend the precious heritage of American liberty. From his election in 1912, the president's "New Freedom" agenda had been presented as a liberal response to the supposedly authoritarian inclinations of Roosevelt's brand of big-state progressivism.[26] Wilsonians sincerely believed that the goal of the war was to eliminate the threat of militarized regimes in Europe, not create another one at home. And given the finite resources available to the government, its informal influence over the media, its loose hold on state and local politics, and the strength of popular suspicion of concentrations of power, large federal bureaucracies for accelerating the war mobilization effort would have been difficult to create, would have generated widespread opposition, and would have endangered Wilson's precarious majority in the House of Representatives.

As a result, the largest expansion of state policing power since the Civil War remained circumscribed by a persistent, countervailing desire among its highest officers and its legislative overseers for restraint. Instead of dictators, Wilsonians became ringleaders. When straightforward legal action (or, in some occasions, military action under martial law) was insufficient to achieve administration goals, then public-private partnerships based on local-level, voluntary organizations of concerned Americans would be used to police loyalty instead. These, it was felt, could preserve the best traditions of American citizen government and keep the cost of managing the home front down.[27] Voluntarist campaigns compared to bureaucratic political surveillance in the way militias did to standing armies: they would keep the people at the center of civic life and reduce the possibility that government elites could use their powers to override the people's will.

To push the public into action, the administration launched propaganda campaigns to stir up patriotic feeling, drawing on ideas taken from the new world of public relations. In April 1917, Wilson established the Committee on Public Information (CPI) under the aegis of the progressive newspaper editor George Creel, which rapidly took over from private civic-preparedness organizations in generating propaganda for war. During the course of the conflict, the committee issued more than six thousand press releases, established a government newspaper, and printed more than a hundred million books, posters, and pamphlets.[28] The CPI enlisted more than seventy-five thousand "four minute men," unpaid volunteers, to give hundreds of thousands of public talks, boosting the war effort at schools, colleges, theaters, and churches. Such efforts were not considered to be "propaganda" in the way that pro-German or antiwar speech was; advocates defended their campaigns as simply educating Americans about the "facts" at stake in the world crisis. Nevertheless, advertisements stressed German atrocities through what was then considered to be horribly graphic imagery that played upon contemporary racial and gendered prejudices. Underneath a picture of Leuven burning, a German soldier bayoneting a fallen enemy and a menacing officer dragging away a woman for presumably nefarious purposes, one poster read, "The Hohenzollern fang strikes at every element of decency and culture and taste. . . . It leaves a track so terrible that only whispered fragments may be recounted. It has ripped all the world-old romance out of war, and reduced it to the dead, black depths of muck, and hate, and bitterness."[29]

Given the limited scope and scale of the U.S. government at the time, the demands of total war could probably not have been met in any other way than by relying on the public. Nevertheless, the tendency to distribute semiofficial responsibilities to concerned local citizens and to whip up popular anger without giving it a clear direction held risks, since it offered the power and authority of the nation-state to citizens without mechanisms of accountability or judicial oversight. The clearest example was the American Protective League (APL), a secretive paragovernmental organization sponsored by the Department of Justice that took on the role of policing and investigation in areas the tiny Bureau of Investigation could not reach. Whereas the bureau's field office did not exceed four hundred staff members by war's end, the APL amassed more than a quarter of a million people on its books. APL representatives were able to buy a Secret Service–type badge for seventy-five cents, and many duly presented themselves as government agents, conducting unauthorized raids and arrests in the name of the government but without official sanction.[30] In this sense, ironically, it was the administration's very reluctance to take on an overtly authoritarian role that opened the door for self-selected private citizens to assume the mantle of patriotism and accelerate the processes of wartime repression. And since APL agents were often members of local elites—bankers, businessmen, merchants, and so on—these efforts quickly took on class-based and racial overtones that clouded the national interest with the more limited concerns of America's commercial classes.[31]

The scale of the enterprise was breathtaking, especially in terms of the campaigns against draft dodgers, which were comparable to the activities of modern police states in size, although perhaps not in brutality.[32] In Bisbee, Arizona, APL agents rounded up twelve hundred people they suspected of radical tendencies and sent them off in dozens of boxcars into the New Mexico desert. On a single operation in Chicago in July 1918, the league stopped more than ten thousand individuals to check their draft cards and held more than a thousand overnight when they were unable to produce identification, though most had done nothing wrong.[33] The nation witnessed the largest wave of vigilante violence since Reconstruction—indeed, arguably the largest directed at white people since the American Revolution.[34] This is not to say that political leaders made a conscious decision to encourage extrajudicial violence; however, they were ambiguous about the responsibilities of the patriotic citizen in a time of crisis, unconcerned with restraining popular violence when it took place, and content to benefit from its positive impact on the war mobilization program.

Mob activism grew in the autumn of 1917 and became a frequent item of reportage in early 1918 following the case of Maximilian C. von Hagen, who was abducted and badly beaten by a band of masked men in New Haven, Connecticut, after writing "Deutschland Über Alles" on the top of his naturalization papers. This "crime" had been relayed to the public by distressed government workers who had been offended by the action but of course had no formal right to act.[35] As press coverage of vigilantism grew after the incident, the number of cases rose rapidly, peaking in the spring and summer of 1918. At its apogee, more than thirty or forty cases were documented each month, and presumably the shame of victims meant that more went unreported.

Wartime targets were typically accused of committing violations that the state was unable or too slow to respond to. The overwhelming majority fitted within four broad categories: people who had prosecutions pending against them for frustrating the war effort but were yet to be punished, individuals holding membership in radical organizations that had been identified as disloyal by official spokesmen, those who had German ethnic roots, and people who were caught making inappropriate remarks about the war or the government or otherwise refusing to conform to the patriotic mood of the time. Typically, they were kidnapped by gangs of people—rarely fewer than four or five assailants, occasionally as many as five hundred or a thousand, but normally between ten and thirty—sometimes armed and in vehicles, often but not always masked. Sometimes, individuals were driven to secluded locations and assaulted and threatened, but more often they were taken to highly public locations to be ritually shamed. As with traditional vigilantism, individuals were beaten, stripped, and horsewhipped. Often, signs were hung around their necks identifying their supposed misdemeanors. They were chained up, handcuffed, or tied to lampposts or telegraph poles in prominent public places to face the abuse of passersby or forced to walk long distances along roads without shelter so as to maximize their exposure.

Such vigilantism drew upon a shared set of unwritten social practices of mob violence handed down by oral tradition. Extrajudicial punishment formed a patriotic rite of violence: suffused with elaborate rituals intended to highlight the mob's affinity with national heritage and to imitate or reenact the sanctified past. Some victims were ridden on rails through town, but undoubtedly the most common punishment was tarring and feathering, closely associated in public memory with the heroic mythology of the revolutionary era. While tarring and feathering had persisted sporadically as a southern and frontier phenomenon, it was assumed to be more or less dead elsewhere by the late nineteenth century. During the war, though, "tar parties" spread across the North and East as well as South and West.[36] On some occasions, carbolic acid and other adulterations were added to the boiling tar to increase the victim's pain, but otherwise the practice was identical to actions taken nearly a century and a half earlier.

Richard Maxwell Brown's description of vigilantism as "lawful lawlessness" captures the contradiction lying at the heart of this kind of collective violence. Extralegal punishments were premised upon a radically destabilizing distinction between law and justice: the most extreme end of a tendency toward popular self-rule. Typically, they were encouraged by environments in which there was a widespread doubt over the capacity or will of authorities to enforce local moral codes, especially in zones of revolution or occupation or at the frontiers of the nation-state. At the same time, though, to legitimate claims to a higher justice, ideologies of vigilantism typically clustered around notions of duty, tradition, honor, and republican virtue—values that referenced social responsibilities of sufficient power to override an individual's aversion to interpersonal violence. Despite its radical implications, these values thus tended to direct mob action toward comparatively conservative goals of social ordering and stabilization. In the colonial era and early United States—during the time of the South Carolina Regulators, for instance, or the Whiskey Rebellion—vigilantism could be seen as "a rudimentary exercise of the 'right of revolution' asserted in the Declaration of Independence." By the mid– to late nineteenth century, however, vigilantism increasingly served to maintain existing social hierarchies through the punishment of members of subordinate groups who had stepped out of line. In Richard Slotkin's words, vigilante ideology "transformed from a natural and democratic right-to-violence to an assertion of class and racial privilege."[37] This, by extension, allowed for ambiguous, even complementary, relationships between the state and vigilante groups who notionally appeared to be violating and challenging its prerogatives. Of course, in the South and parts of the West, vigilantism and mob violence had become so enmeshed with regional and racial identity during slavery and Reconstruction that they functioned as a normative extension of legal process rather than a state of exception. But even outside these regions, many authorities, especially in industrial areas, effectively conceded rights of judicial enforcement to local elites and their private agents, creating areas of corporate lawlessness that were nevertheless broadly tolerated by the state since they served more effectively to maintain "order" than did the notionally blind justice of the courts.[38] In this sense, even while it seemed to be operating in revolutionary tension with the reservations of government, vigilantism could often find itself supporting the priorities of institutional groups who had related objectives.

The most distinctive elements of vigilante movements in popular consciousness—secrecy and disguise—were in fact second-order products of the peculiar position vigilantes occupied in the liminal zone between state and society. Secrecy could serve several useful purposes: giving a sense of election to the members of the hidden order, protecting enactors from retribution, and magnifying the symbolic power of punitive action by inculcating fear. Nevertheless, at root vigilante justice remained emphatically public in orientation. Punishment was often widely publicized, while disguises were far from ubiquitous and secrecy was often more procedural than actual—sufficient to ensure that legal action could not be taken against the perpetrators but otherwise skin-deep, with members of a community often knowing exactly who among them had donned the mask.

So while wartime patriotic violence appeared to reflect a collapse of social order, participants believed they were aiding and abetting the government and the war effort. During their punishments, victims were forced to kiss the American flag, swear allegiance to the government, curse the kaiser, or praise Wilson. In one case, a gang even forced a German American resident of Boise, Idaho, to paint his derrick red, white, and blue. A significant number, especially richer individuals and businessmen, were not released until they had bought Liberty Bonds or joined the Red Cross. And in an orgy of violence in Staunton, Illinois, members of the American Protective League stormed dozens of homes in the middle of the night, dragging scores of people from their beds in order to force them to sign printed pledges of loyalty to the government.[39]

At the end of their ordeal, many victims were told to leave town, and often hanging was offered as the alternative; sometimes nooses were slung around the victims' necks to illustrate the point. But ritualized violence toward whites was typically directed toward the inflicting of pain and humiliation and tended not to be murderous. Mob practices enshrined and perpetuated traditional notions of white "honor" that were considered irrelevant to policing black misconduct.[40] Indeed, racial humiliation sometimes played a part in the punishment: before Claude Watson, a farmer from Wynnewood, Oklahoma, was tarred and feathered, the mob forced an African American man to whip him repeatedly, presumably in order to magnify Watson's disgrace.

In a small number of cases, "white capping" was used against black people as an alternative to lynching. However, this was almost always in the case of African American middle-class professionals who posed an economic threat to white supremacy, such as Dr. George W. Lacey, who was driven out of Waverly, Virginia, with threats of tarring and feathering after taking black customers away from white doctors.[41] Ordinarily, African Americans targeted during the war were lynched, just as they were in "normal" times. The denial of constitutional rights was a daily experience for many black people; only for whites was it a state of exception. Deaths during white-on-white rioting came about only when plans were frustrated, because a victim resisted, or because attacks were so bad that the recipient of the attack later died of their injuries. Reports of perhaps the most famous white lynching that took place during the war—of twenty-nine-year-old German Socialist Robert Prager, from Collinsville, Illinois, who was taken from a jail cell by a group of miners in April 1918 and hanged from a large tree for supposed disloyalty—suggest that the mob originally intended to conduct a tar and feathering, but plans changed when no materials could be found and someone in a passing car offered up a rope instead.[42]

The ritualized, performative, and communal elements of these attacks clearly served exemplary as well as punitive purposes. Unlike the moral sanctions enforced by earlier "white capping" movements, though, when the objective was generally to expose private vice to public judgment, these were responses to public "crimes" against the national war effort—although, of course, personal agendas and private grievances and rivalries often lurked behind the veil of outraged citizenship.[43] Indeed, although many IWW members and socialist radicals were disproportionately targeted, not all actions were directed by wealthy citizens toward the poor. Businessmen and planters also occasionally found themselves victims of attacks, and hostility to conspicuous privilege in times of restriction may have formed part of the context to such actions.[44]

Generally speaking, the press offered indulgent interpretations, implicitly recognizing the patriotic symbolism and accepting the credentials of participants as loyal republicans and allies of the government. Northern and eastern newspapers took little exception to historical or extraregional practices entering their communities. Reports routinely identified the mobs as groups of "citizens" or "committees of citizens" that had formed "volunteer vigilance committees," "loyalty leagues," "loyalty meetings," or "loyalty demonstrations"—all phrases implying they were legitimate associations operating under a voluntarist model of distributed governance. German Americans usually became "Germans," and guilt was in almost all cases presumed.[45] The *Hartford Courant* argued that "tarring and feathering a man and riding him on a rail, an old-fashioned punishment, would not be too severe a penalty" were it legal. Since it was not, the newspaper was forced to recommend against its use, but "could not find it in its heart to grieve if by chance his neighbor decided to inflict it." Some journalists even found the events funny: a reporter covering the attack on fifty-three-year-old Frederick William Gustave Ehlen, from Minneapolis, was amused by Ehlen's efforts to appeal to his tormentors for mercy, noting under the headline "Tar and Feathers Make Fred a Good Yankee" that upon his release Ehlen "shook hands with everybody in sight so fiercely that he almost broke the fingers of the shakers."[46]

Unsurprisingly, local official involvement was common, and tolerance even more so. A town marshal led a mob in Lander, Wyoming, in January 1918. Police refused to arrest a Los Angeles woman who shot her wealthy German husband for refusing to buy Liberty Bonds, saying it was a case of "self-defense." And following the rioting in Staunton, Illinois, Benjamin Vollantine, the local chief of police, told journalists that no official complaints had been made and so no investigation would take place. "The only report I have received," he said, "is that there are a lot more Americans in Staunton today than there were yesterday."[47]

Finally, in the rare instance that vigilantes were brought to trial, participants could usually rely on their peers to acquit. The eleven men charged with the murder of Robert Prager were declared innocent in forty-five minutes. Despite instructions by the judge to disregard both the wartime context and Prager's ethnic and political background, it seems the jury agreed with defense attorney Thomas Williamson, who in closing argued that "the present war situation had developed a new 'unwritten law,' which had been invoked by the men who hanged Prager because of his alleged disloyalty."[48]

The widespread acceptance of the idea of an "unwritten law"—a measure that did not exist on the statute books yet in its enforcement did not challenge their authority—was vital for many people to judge sympathetically practices that had previously been condemned as barbaric, historic, peculiarly southern, or frontier-like. The climate of emergency seemingly demanded that citizens support the state by subjecting its supposed enemies to a recreation of revolutionary justice. Significantly, many commentators who disapproved of mob action blamed the government for failing to act decisively enough in advance. The *New York Sun* argued that the "resentfulness of the patriotic citizens of one town is stirred to violent action by news of such action in another; and as long as the causes of these outbursts are not removed the danger of greater violence will increase." The *New York Tribune* attributed the Prager lynching to "inertia at Washington," arguing that it was "as clear as day that if the government doesn't intern enemy aliens many of them will, sooner or later, fall victims to mob violence."[49] Indeed, this may help to explain the decline in vigilantism in the last months of the war. Although a speech by Wilson on July 26 in which the president finally condemned mob action may have contributed, the main reason was probably the passage of the Sedition Act in May 1918, which criminalized many of the antiwar activities that had formerly been policed by informal gangs. The formerly "unwritten" law was written down. If mob violence had originated in elite encouragement of public action, then by the later months of the war it seemed the lines of agency had reversed.

What emerged during the war was a hybrid countersubversive system for the management of political dissent, characterized by the centralization of political power in some areas and the radical delegation of authority in others. By the end of the conflict, the government's middle way between federalism and authoritarianism had produced a sweeping new set of laws to prosecute dissenters, a massive, hundreds-of-thousands-strong informant system, and an army of tens of thousands of prowar enforcers in cities and towns across the nation. Roughly fifteen hundred of five thousand socialist locals were destroyed, while thousands of individuals were harassed and abused in their communities.[50] Radicals and German Americans would remember the attacks they received for generations to come, but individuals at all levels of society excused these repressive practices as natural products of the American people's exceptional commitment to liberty. One concerned citizen of Lincoln, Montana, summed up the spirit, telling senators at a public hearing that he and friends and allies had driven the local IWW organizer out of town using all means at their disposal. "We probably violated all the constitutional provisions of State and Nation," he admitted. "You did credit to the name of Lincoln," one of the senators replied.[51]

*   *   *

Just as opponents of the war had predicted, intervening in Europe led to intolerance at home, culminating in the first major federally sponsored countersubversive campaign for more than a hundred years and a national wave of patriotic violence: a complex public-private partnership that linked government actions to police politics with voluntary networks of local activists.

Whatever their sins may have been, the vast majority of targets were clearly not German agents. They were targeted because they were obstructing the war effort, not because they were working for the enemy. Nevertheless, recognizing that most Americans were deeply committed—at least in theory—to the right to dissent, prowar advocates went to great lengths to obscure this fact. Anarchists Goldman and Berkman, for instance, had clearly violated the selective-service law by denouncing conscription, but this was not enough for the administration. Attorney General Gregory told the press, falsely, that material seized during their arrest proved they were part of an international network of "German spies in foreign countries."[52] Officials regularly declared that German money was behind IWW activism, and when evidence was too flimsy to merit even circumstantial insinuations the administration relied on loose, anonymous briefings to make their case.[53] In particular, the fact that antiwar activism and pro-German espionage shared a goal—keeping America out of the war—was misleadingly used to suggest that they were part of the same conspiracy.

With such a loose concern for the principles of evidence and causation, it was almost inevitable that over time countersubversive politicians would begin to wave the bloody shirt for increasingly tangential purposes: especially to push ahead with long-standing policy goals or for partisan benefit. Alien property custodian A. Mitchell Palmer offered one of the most egregious examples of this. Controlling an estimated seven hundred million dollars' worth of assets by the end of the war, his office was a seat of immense power: in the words of the *New York Times,* "at once the biggest trust institution in the world, director of a vast business enterprise of varied nature, a detective agency, and a court of equity." Palmer had for years been engaged in a series of vicious political battles with the "special interests" in his home state of Pennsylvania that had favored his Republican opponent, Penrose, especially the state's brewing industry (which opposed Palmer's Prohibitionist stance), and had been defeated at every turn. Palmer was so bloodied from these conflicts, he had considered retiring from politics altogether. However, from his new position of wartime authority, he began to exact revenge by accusing the liquor business of being unpatriotic and pro-German and calling for the seizure of their assets. "It is around the saengerfests and the saengerbunds," Palmer claimed, "financed by the rich brewers, that the young Germans who come to America are taught to remember first the Fatherland and second America."[54] The enemy seemed to be trying to sink the American war machine in an ocean of booze: lagers, pilsners, *dunkels,* and *doppelbocks* streaming forth from German-owned factories, getting the average American joe too drunk to tighten bayonet holders onto army-issue rifles properly. The only solution was executive action, loyalty prosecutions, Prohibition, and the expropriation of pro-Republican businesses in Pennsylvania.

Nationalism, party loyalty, ideology, and self-interest thus tended to reinforce each other. Mormon senator William Henry King, a strong supporter of expanded police powers, took Palmer's accusations to Congress, and a legislative subcommittee was swiftly established to investigate. Another staunch Wilson loyalist, Lee Slater Overman, who had been instrumental in getting the loyalty laws passed through Congress, took the chair, and Palmer arranged for military intelligence (MI) to provide a senior officer to act as chief counsel.[55] Between late September 1918 and early 1919, the committee heard from carefully selected witnesses how German immigrants "perpetuated a system of social-segregation in the US." By diluting people's loyalty to the state, the retention of European roots, it was claimed, directly supported the kaiser's efforts to disrupt America's mobilization campaign. Legislative recommendations included a corrupt-practices act to stop interests from manipulating elections, tests of patriotism for all potential American citizens, action to control alcohol use, and legislation to regulate the non-English-language press. The Eighteenth Amendment was ratified in January 1919, just after the first phase of hearings had been completed, and the publicity surrounding Overman's hearings undoubtedly contributed to the final push for Prohibition. In this way, hostility to the German enemy was used to encourage hostility to people of German origin, while opposition to German-owned businesses was used to justify opposition to "German" drinking practices. Subtly, and not so subtly, elements of the long-standing progressive agenda were passed off as a vital parts of the war effort.

Once the Constitution's restrictions on the policing of political activity were broken, opportunities arose for others to accuse their enemies of subversive activities. If, as Palmer and Overman argued, the retention of local culture was itself sufficient to cast one's loyalties in doubt, then virtually anyone outside the mainstream could be accused of acting subversively. After years of failure, nativists within Congress had passed an immigration law just before the declaration of war, which permitted the deportation of noncitizens who advocated the destruction of property or the government. In October 1918, a second immigration act followed, allowing for the deportation of noncitizens if they were shown to be members of a revolutionary organization, regardless of whether they had acted in any way to threaten the state. Robert Goldstein notes that 687 people had been arrested and 60 of them deported under these new immigration laws by the Armistice. As virtually the only countersubversive law passed during the war that would still apply in peacetime, they would become the central repressive tools used during the postwar Red Scare. They also marked a major step toward the implementation of restrictions of immigration for all peoples, whether they were considered politically undesirable or not.[56]

This kind of expansion of state control over individual political freedoms was by no means unique to the United States. Many modernizing nations felt the need to limit the scope of dissent in response to the first modern total war. However, the pseudolibertarian language that underpinned countersubversion in the United States gave political American restrictions a distinctive, exaggerated flavor. Subversion—treasonous conspiracy short of treason—had emerged as the operating concept that overcame antistatist concerns about expanding the federal police apparatus, and to manage the mobilization for war dissenters were shoveled into this category with little concern for their true motives and allegiances. The loyalty laws allowed the federal government to prosecute radicals and antiwar activists, but only if they were assumed to be part of a seditious internal conspiracy directed by a foreign power. In other countries, where the passage of laws against political extremism did not have to meet such rigorous constitutional standards, countersubversives could simply label their enemies as menaces or disorderly influences and be done with them. In the United States, they had to be conspirators. As perverse as it seems to claim that tens of thousands of American radicals were agents of Germany, then, such allegations were necessitated by otherwise strict constitutional limits on political repression.

This shift in language in turn contributed to a broader change in the popular understanding of dissent that was taking place at the time. Radical philosophies—socialism, Marxism, and anarchism particularly—had long been seen as "foreign" in a way that other imported political concepts, such as republicanism or democracy, were not. Now, however, radicals began to be explicitly associated with specific, organized action on behalf of foreign states. The fact that many radicals, including a number of well-known public figures, came from the ranks of an internationalized class of migrant labor added to the idea that the amorphous opposition to the war could be explained in terms of a generalized sense of foreignness.

It was perhaps unsurprising that the panic of war almost entirely eliminated popular distinctions between foreign ethnicities and enemy states. But it was a basic misunderstanding of statistics to assume that because some radicals were immigrants, most immigrants were radicals. Such claims led people to label entire classes as unworthy of constitutional protection simply because of their culture, habits, or place of birth and opened up space for policies that were profoundly alien to the American traditions of limited government.

* * *

Support for the wartime loyalty campaigns was at first overwhelming. However, as time went on, Americans began to polarize over which was the greater threat: the presence of "subversives" on American soil or the campaigns to eliminate them. It was hard not to notice that mob violence and political prosecutions starkly contrasted with claims of the United States as the homeland of liberty.

For obvious reasons, Republicans were more willing to criticize wartime excesses than Democrats, especially when they felt government power grabs were driven by partisan calculations. Republicans led the efforts to water down the censorship clauses of the Espionage Act.[57] Theodore Roosevelt led opposition to elements of the Selective Service Act, criticized postmaster general Burleson for heavy-handedness, and spoke out against the Sedition Act when he thought it might limit his own freedom to criticize the president.[58] Meanwhile, Senator Henry Cabot Lodge voiced concerns about the extent to which federal power was being accumulated. Voting against the Sedition Act, he argued it would do little or nothing to combat genuine German operatives. "The spies or agents do not go around uttering, publishing, and writing," he said. "The dangerous men keep quiet."[59]

Roosevelt and Lodge came from the East Coast, but it was the Midwest and West that emerged as particular centers of Republican civil liberties activism during the war. Three Republican senators, Robert La Follette, George Norris, and Asle Jorgenson Gronna (of Wisconsin, Nebraska, and North Dakota, respectively), had opposed the war from the outset and, joined by William E. Borah of Idaho, spoke out for the right to dissent throughout 1917 and 1918. A further addition was California's governor-turned-senator Hiram Johnson, who emerged as one of the most consistent opponents of the loyalty codes. He complained that the Sedition Act threatened "to throttle honest and legitimate discussion or criticism" and "even purports to prevent one from thinking as he wishes to think." "It is war," he accepted. "But, good God, Mr. President, when did it become war upon the American people?"[60]

Few Republicans with civil liberties reservations expressed sympathy for the radicals, pacifists, and German Americans who were the government's chief targets.[61] Borah called socialist Victor Berger a traitor for advocating the withdrawal of American troops from France. "I cannot think of a more disreputable creature under the protection of the American flag," he declared.[62] Indeed, while La Follette and others were accused of un-Americanism for seeking to protect the personal liberties of dissenters, the truth was the opposite. They precisely identified themselves as defenders of American democracy and argued the Wilson administration was the one abandoning national traditions. At the height of the debate over the Espionage Age, Borah argued that liberty of opinion had come down to Americans as "a blessed inheritance," yet the doctrine was now being "advanced that every citizen, his property, his rights, his liberty, his life are after the declaration of war the playthings of Congress and the Executive." This was "a foreign doctrine, it is the creed of foreign courts, it is the faith of Czars and Emperors," he said. "It is not only unnecessary for carrying on the war, not only un-American, but it is a doctrine fraught with evils the consequence of which no man can foresee or foretell."[63]

Nevertheless, for every Republican expressing concern about the expansion of federal power, there were others who supported the president, realizing that their party was well placed to exploit patriotic zeal. Unsurprisingly, then, the GOP did little to alter the administration's course.

Among Democrats, concern over the politics of patriotism also began to swell, especially in the cities of the North. Dissent within party ranks was potentially far more damaging to Wilson's ability to govern, but partisan imperatives and the power of wartime patriotism ensured its impact would not be felt until after the war ended. Most civil liberties Democrats had supported the president's prewar reform agenda and were generally persuaded of the enlightened ideals behind the war itself. Intellectually, ideologically, and politically, they had much to lose by abandoning Wilson, and this perhaps explains why they found it so difficult to engage honestly with the administration's policies. After all, if one took the claims made by government at face value—that this was a war being waged against German espionage, not American dissent—the only logical conclusion was that the administration had lost all sense of reality. The confusion was intensified by the fact that Wilsonians condemned the mob violence they had helped to stir up, attributing vigilantism to a lack of government involvement and even going so far as to use it to make the case for new laws. "Senators can do as they please about delaying this bill," Senator Overman warned during the debate over the Sedition Act. "The people of this country are taking the law into their own hands on the grounds that Congress is not doing its duty."[64] Creel even advanced a convoluted theory that German agents were behind both IWW antiwar agitation *and* the mobs seeking "to tar and feather the victims of the German propaganda of social unrest."[65] To progressives in later years who looked back at the excesses of the war with alarm but remained committed to the Wilsonian tradition, the lesson was that only bureaucratic countersubversion could render the unaccountable activities of ultrapatriotic groups unnecessary.

For his part, Wilson expressed distaste for the extreme nationalism that came to characterize the war effort. Yet he consistently refused to entertain the notion that his administration bore any culpability for it and was hostile to those who demanded any kind of meaningful action to restrain patriotic crusading. Believing that such sacrifices were the price of global liberation, and aware that civil liberties opposition was weak and disorganized, Wilson disarmed his critics with polite letters of acknowledgment that expressed his agreement with the spirit of their complaints without conceding their substance.[66] He did just enough to preserve his reputation as a guardian of American freedoms without acting in any meaningful way to uphold them. Wilson would raise the occasional query when influential parties complained about overexuberance on the part of the postmaster general, attorney general, or alien property custodian. But he would write only once, telling Burleson, "I am willing to trust your judgment after I have once called your attention to a suggestion."[67] In this way, the president could put his concern for civil liberties on record, yet abdicate responsibility for his appointees' actions, all the while benefiting from the prowar militancy that was the result.

Less blinkered by partisan imperatives, political outsiders often tended to be clearer in their opposition to the wartime repression and more willing to blame the administration for it. As the war dragged on, Wilson began to receive a trickle and then a steady flow of mail from concerned liberals and left-wingers who had noticed the dissonance between the coercions of total war and the president's rhetoric of liberation.[68] If the country was so united, they asked, why was it necessary to combat so aggressively the occasional instance of "impotent disloyalty," as the president himself had described it in his State of the Union address? Why did a war to promote democracy require undermining it at home? And how could the government seriously believe that members of the IWW were German agents? Liberals argued not only that freedom of expression was a right worth defending, but also that it served a broader public good, reducing the chances that the state would make poor decisions in its conduct of the war.[69] "Nothing more discouraging has come out of the war than these revelations of the shallowness of our democracy and our absolute lack of that tenacious English holding to the glorious tenets of personal liberty," bemoaned the *Nation*.[70]

But even outside the bonds of party discipline, many progressives excused the loyalty campaigns as sacrifices made for a higher principle. Some argued repression in a democratic society was fundamentally different from repression in an autocratic society, others dismissed the disturbing events as a temporary aberration, and some even thrilled in the "organic wholeness" generated by the wartime purges.[71] Above all, many assumed that Wilson was innocent, finding it impossible to believe that the beloved scholar-president could have permitted such extensive violations of freedom of expression and assembly. Wilson had lost control; the nation had gone mad; a wave of ultrapatriotism had burst forth from some dank part of the American soul. Wilson's enemies were exploiting citizens who were subject to "group loyalty," the "herd instinct," or "animosity to rival nations or pugnacity."[72] One commentator looked on aghast at "mental epidemics" of war hysteria that, he believed, threatened to undermine the war effort. "President Wilson has earnestly tried to appeal to the German people against their rulers," he wrote, "but these appeals will come to naught if the German people only see us in our unreasoning fury as a mad bull, against whom they must fight to the uttermost."[73] In this way, the language of unreason and hysteria served to explain events without having to focus on progressives' implication in them. It was not the Wilsonian project or the national myth of unity that was behind the war fever; the wrath of the masses was to blame.

Opposition to the loyalty laws could thus easily filter into a broader suspicion of democracy. "The American people, as a people, acquiesced docilely in all these tyrannies," wrote H. L. Mencken and George Jean Nathan in 1920. "Worse, they not only acquiesced docilely; they approved actively; they were quite as hotly against the few protestants as they were against the original victims, and gave their hearty approbation to every proposal that the former be punished too. The really startling phenomenon of the war, indeed, was not the grotesque abolition of liberty in the name of liberty, but the failure of that usurpation to arouse anything approaching public indignation."[74]

This left a confused image of Wilson-era countersubversion in the historical record. It was easy to see wartime nationalism as a perversion of the progressive impulse, a departure from enlightened ideals forced upon the government by a wave of nationalistic "hysteria" emanating from businessmen, nativists, the ignorant masses, downwardly mobile conservatives, or the *geist* of war. But Wilson, his cabinet, and his allies had not only considered their repressive efforts to be in line with their agenda, but even used the wartime national emergency to extend their progressive program, as in the case of Prohibition. Voluntarism, the limits of early-twentieth-century bureaucratic government, and the appropriation of wartime nationalism by other groups extended events beyond the administration's control, but countersubversion was still at a profound level driven by progressive ideals and progressive method. Wilsonians conjured a fictive image of a united, democratic national consensus, and then used this quintessentially progressive fantasy to summarily exclude dissenters from the American community of liberty.

For progressives to understand the mechanics of wartime "hysteria," then, would have required soul-searching. By contrast, radicals and socialists—who had the advantageous perspective of distance as well as the experience of collective victimhood—tended to be more ready to locate the origins of repression in government, and many led the complaints against the administration for violating American liberties. Most notably, Roger Baldwin established a new National Civil Liberties Bureau (NCLB) to defend conscientious objectors from attack. During the war, the bureau attained almost perfect failure in efforts to defend the principle of legitimate dissent. However, it would, as the renamed American Civil Liberties Union (ACLU), remain at the forefront of Bill of Rights activism for the rest of the century.[75]

The wartime loyalty campaigns had begun as exigencies of war. Unions affiliated with the comparatively conservative American Federation of Labor (AFL) were involved in thousands more strikes during the war than the IWW, but because their leadership adopted a prowar position the government responded to their industrial action as industrial action, not as a prelude to revolution.[76] Nevertheless, the need for local allies had quickly seen political policing taking on class-based and racial overtones. Many radicals, especially on the far left of the old socialist movement, saw how countersubversion tended to strengthen the hand of elites and attributed the repressive impulse not to military belligerency but to a generalized sympathy for business and a hatred of workers. To some of them, the NCLB's campaigns for civil liberties within a broadly capitalist system seemed like little more than a bandage on a cancer. Only a far broader transformation of the American Republic, they argued, would break the alliance of businessmen and warriors.

Increasingly, then, the experience of wartime repression encouraged radicals to look elsewhere for hope and inspiration, especially to Russia, where romantic stories were emerging of a small band of idealists overthrowing a bloodthirsty regime in the name of peace, land, bread, and freedom. As he faced prosecution for his antiwar views at home and read news of Moscow and Petrograd, Max Eastman imagined the Soviet experiment as something like an AFL convention led by an IWW majority. Meanwhile, at the Ohio State Socialist Convention in June 1918, Eugene Debs told a rapt audience, "All our hearts now throb as one great heart responsive to the battle-cry of the social revolution. . . . Here, in this alert and inspiring assemblage our hearts are with the Bolsheviki of Russia."[77] By contributing to their alienation, the U.S. government arguably helped form exactly the kind of enemy on the Left that they claimed to be fighting. In this sense at least, then, the loyalty campaigns were deeply counterproductive.

2

War and Peace
Anti-Bolshevism at Home and Abroad

Six months after the Armistice, around midafternoon on the second Thursday in June 1919, New York state troopers and private detectives from the Adams-Grunewald detective agency, maybe twenty in all, swept through Ludwig Martens's office door. Martens was a mechanical engineer by trade, but since January he had been head of the Bolshevik government's new and rather hastily assembled "Information Bureau," an embryonic embassy operating out of the World's Tower building on West Fortieth Street, Manhattan. A revolutionary activist since his youth in Germany, Martens had known Leon Trotsky when they both lived in New York. He had returned to Russia after the February Revolution and then traveled to America again following the October seizure of power on the instructions of the Bolshevik leadership, seeking business deals and friendly ties with the United States as a prelude to recognition.[1] Thanks to this diplomatic assignment, he had been singled out as an apostle of revolution in America.

Martens and four of his colleagues were subpoenaed and bundled out of the building under heavy guard. In private session before the New York State Legislative Committee Investigating Seditious Activities—known as the Lusk Committee, after its chairman, Clayton Lusk—Martens and Santeri Nuorteva, a leader of Finnish Socialist immigrants and one of Martens' coworkers, were interrogated over their backgrounds, the Bolshevik government they swore allegiance to, and the purpose of their offices before being released.[2] The press was on hand to report the events, and it was no surprise in the tense postwar atmosphere, when America was reeling from a barrage of bombs and riots and strikes, that the story swept the headlines the next day.

At least according to press accounts, the raid was conducted with military precision, beginning on the stroke of three o'clock. Once Martens (described as an "ambassador," but never without truculent quotation marks) and the rest of his people had been escorted away, detectives and troopers set about emptying the offices of all potentially incriminating evidence. "Every desk, every index file, every box in the place was opened and all papers in them removed," a correspondent reported. Shelves were swept onto the floor, drawers turned out, a snowdrift of papers shoveled and piled into trucks to be taken away for examination. A red flag was found that the conspirators had apparently planned to raise above their putative embassy, along with several pamphlets by Lenin addressed to the American worker. Reporters were assured that the evidence would be analyzed by Archibald E. Stevenson, indefatigable counsel to the Lusk Committee, for signs of subversion.

Martens branded the events an outrage: "another attempt on the part of reactionary forces to prevent friendly relations between the United States and Russia." The Information Bureau sought only to correct misapprehensions about the Bolshevik government, he explained, and to encourage positive commercial relations with American companies. There was no nefarious agenda; there was no plot against America. But despite these protestations of innocence, one suspects that many readers in 1919 would have agreed with Stevenson, who told journalists, "I have heard all about the raid, and it seems to have been a rather neat job."[3]

Countersubversion may have been invigorated by the war, but it did not end with the Armistice. Like many other actions of 1919, the raid on the Information Bureau showed how loyalty enforcement persisted after the conflict ended, with international Bolshevism coming to replace the former German enemy in the public imagination. However, in deference to America's conception of itself as a nation of reason, subject to the rule of law, postwar anti-Bolshevik crusading was defended by its authors as a rigorous, objective, and empirical investigation of radical influence in America. Bolshevism was criticized because of its "un-American" limits on freedoms of speech, liberty, property, and religion and its contempt for law and order. Raids were explained as operations designed to gather information, not to terrorize. Seeking the moral high ground, seeking to present their innovations as traditions, countersubversives fetishized the symbolism of evidential rigor even while they distorted it to substantiate prior beliefs and simplistic conclusions. And because they based their arguments on evidence gathered from radicals and the testimony of self-designated "experts," they explicitly denied that they were involved in propagandizing—which, after all, was what the enemy did. Their work was instead an unveiling in which the natural common sense of the American people would come to the fore once the facts were laid before them. As Mitchell Palmer put it in a piece written in *Forum* in 1920, "It has always been plain to me that when American citizens unite upon any national issue they are generally right, but it is sometimes difficult to make the issue clear to them."

In truth, it was not even so difficult. With so many accustomed to thinking of radicals as threats to national security after two years of war propaganda, it did not take much to engineer hostility toward Bolshevism's defenders in the United States. The economic dislocations of the war and subsequent demobilization combined with uncertain news from Europe to convince many that America itself could be swept up in a wave of global revolution. In such a context, the presence of Bolshevik agents on American shores took on a particular urgency. "Just the word," a friend had told Lincoln Steffens when they discussed Russian politics in the heady summer of 1917. "Bolsheviki! It sounds like all that the world fears. Bolsheviki! . . . Can't you see it in the headlines? It will stick. It will crackle in everybody's mouth, ear, and brain. Bolsheviki!"[4]

* * *

The government's response to the Russian Revolution, which quickly developed into what David Foglesong has called a "secret war against Bolshevism," followed the characteristic lines of Wilsonian progressive thought. Conservatives were of course uncomplicatedly anti-Bolshevik from the outset. But, as Christopher Lasch and others have noted, the Russian Revolution posed a particular problem for American liberals. Holding to a Whiggish vision of historical progress, most had committed to intervention in Europe only on the assurance that America was fighting to promote democracy. But the October seizure of power suggested that democracy was less easily promoted by war than had been implied, and perhaps called into question the basic belief in a universal, democratic future altogether. For some liberals, the solution to this apparent problem was to deny that it existed—by presenting Bolshevism as the first troubled stirrings of a new democracy. For others, though, a safer option was to treat Bolshevism in Russia in the same way antiwar dissenters had been treated at home: linking them to the wartime enemy and denying the independent legitimacy of their politics. Thus, just as domestic radicals were presented as part of an international subversive network supported by agents of Prussian tyranny in order to discredit the view that a loyal American might nevertheless oppose the war, Bolshevism in Russia was presented as another outgrowth of German conspiracy in order to deny the possibility that free Russians might wish to close the eastern front. After all, had not the Germans been the ones to transport Lenin back into Russia, injecting the revolutionary bacillus into a fragile young democracy? As the president told Congress, "The Russian people have been poisoned by the very same falsehoods that have kept the German people in the dark, and the poison has been administered by the very same hand."[5]

Wilson at first resisted pressure to reopen the eastern front by force of arms and unseat the new rulers of Russia. Perhaps recollecting his earlier troubled efforts to influence the path of the Mexican Revolution, the president argued that aggressive intervention would allow the Bolsheviks to paint themselves as anti-imperialists and Russian nationalists. Instead, the United States would focus on food aid to undermine the causes of revolutionary dissatisfaction and propaganda campaigns to sell the American vision of the war to Russian citizens.[6] The Committee on Public Information (CPI), which had been so successful in engineering patriotic sentiment at home, was charged with the latter task. Its Moscow representative, Edgar Sisson, a former editor of the *Chicago Tribune,* arrived just days after the Bolshevik coup, and American newsreels were soon running in virtually every cinema in Moscow and Petrograd. Fifty thousand billboards carried American posters. Airplanes rained thousands of handbills down on the soldiers at the front.[7] The president appealed to the patriotic spirit of the Russian people and studiously ignored the Bolsheviks. In his Fourteen Points address, Wilson declared the Allies' treatment of Russia to be the acid test of their goodwill. In March 1918, he went so far as to send a message of friendship to the Fourth Congress of Soviets, though even behind gritted teeth a sympathetic reference to the ongoing "process of revolution" in the first draft proved too much for the president. It was replaced with a more palatably American alternative: the "struggle for freedom."[8]

After the separate Russo-German peace treaty was signed at Brest-Litovsk in March 1918 and hopes shrank of a rapid Bolshevik collapse, Wilson toughened his policy, permitting two limited incursions into Russia. To strengthen the case for action, Sisson was recalled to Washington with a series of documents that purported to prove that the Bolsheviks were German agents. As George Kennan later noted, the documents appeared to show "the Bolshevik leaders as taking orders, most abjectly and at that very time, from secret officers of the German General Staff situated in Russia." Though they had little impact on policy in Russia, the sensational coverage that followed their publication significantly shaped American perceptions of Bolshevism. Calling them an "amazing series of official documents," Sisson's former newspaper declared that the material proved beyond any doubt that the Germans had a long-standing plan to exploit revolutionaries and anarchists throughout the world to further their ambitions for world conquest. Calling the Bolshevik leadership "Monarchs of Disaster" who drew "their weekly salary from the Wilhelmstrasse," the *New York Tribune* concluded that "Judas and Benedict Arnold have just been put out of the running as traitors by Leon Trotzky and Nicolai Lenine [sic]." Privately, the president admitted that releasing the Sisson Documents amounted to a "virtual declaration of war upon the Bolsheviki Government."[9] In public, though, no such declaration was sought. Indeed, much of the confusion of 1919 stemmed from the fact that some Americans believed the United States was at war with Bolshevik Russia, while others did not.

The Sisson Documents were forgeries.[10] However, the anti-interventionist *New York Evening Post* was the only major newspaper to challenge their veracity, for which it received a barrage of criticism. The *New York World* condemned its rival and claimed to be pained to discover there were Americans who could question documents circulated by the government. "I do not make the charge that *The New York Evening Post* is German or that it has taken German money," George Creel told reporters, "but I do say that the service it has rendered to the enemies of the United States would have been purchased gladly by those enemies, and in terms of unrest and industrial instability this supposed American paper has struck a blow at America more powerful than could possibly have been dealt by German hands."[11] When Santeri Nuorteva, the Finnish socialist, told the press that Sisson got hold of the documents from anti-Bolshevik activists in Russia and that the material had been disregarded by other Americans officials, Creel declared the information to be a lie, stressing that the Sisson Documents' "authority is backed by the government." Nuorteva subsequently was arrested by military intelligence and briefly held incommunicado.[12] Raymond Robins, a former head of the Red Cross in Russia who had been offered the documents but had doubts about their accuracy, was ordered by the State Department to refuse to respond to press questions.[13] Meanwhile, Creel asked two senior academics, J. Franklin Jameson, editor of the *American Historical Review,* and Samuel Harper, a professor of Russian languages and institutions at the University of Chicago (and, in Christopher Lasch's words, an "avowed apologist for the administration's Russian policy"), to endorse the documents.[14] In this way, the Wilson administration drew upon reserves of both national and scholarly authority to silence doubts and perpetuate an inaccurate view of the anti-Bolshevik material they were circulating. Given the widespread tendency to defer to experts, and given the chorus of agreement among carefully selected scholars, the press, and the government over the apparent facts of the case, it was understandable that many ordinary Americans credited the claims with the truth. Historians have often linked countersubversive instincts to antiintellectualism and hostility to expertise; in this case, however, the problem was that the public proved too willing to defer to figures and institutions of authority who were misleading them.

By the time of the Armistice, then, it was already a matter of widespread belief that Bolshevism was a conspiracy supported and controlled by Germany. Indeed, while conservatives opposed Bolshevism sui generis, for many Wilsonians the real danger of revolutions and revolutionaries was in offering an opportunity for militarists and imperialists to gain a foothold. As long as the war with Germany persisted, then, both prowar liberals and conservatives shared an agenda, but this would not necessarily endure.

Indeed, Wilson's concern over Russia markedly declined with the defeat of Germany, and only months after their dispatch to Russia, the president began quiet preparations for the return of American troops. For tactical and logistical reasons, though, the last troops would not leave until April 1920. Unaware that the president had already fixed his course, the early months of 1919 witnessed an intense effort to shape public views over Russian policy by arguing that if America did not fight the Bolsheviks in Europe, they would eventually have to fight them at home. National security fears during world war had blurred the boundaries between the home front and abroad, as issues of domestic ethnicity and protest had, through the language of loyalty, become tied to geopolitics. After the war, anti-Bolsheviks used similar arguments to suggest that the situation in Russia was a clear and present danger to Americans at home.

Peace did not come easily following the defeat of Germany. During the first months of 1919, as American socialist Morris Hillquit recalled, "practically the whole of Central Europe was politically reorganized under Socialist auspices."[15] The conflict had led to the collapse of three great empires, whose roots, in the case of the Ottoman Empire, stretched back to the thirteenth century. Alongside revolutionary Russia, defeated Germany seemed to be on the verge of social revolution. Bolshevik forces were massing on the borders of newly independent Poland and Finland, and Hungary was about to fall to the forces of the Bolshevik Béla Kun. Rumors of red plots spread from Finland to Romania. Arguably as late as the battle of Warsaw in August 1920, when Polish independence fighters decisively turned back the Red Army, it was not unreasonable to speculate that revolutionary instability in Western Europe might interact with the revolution of military arms being projected by Bolshevik forces in the East. Even if this did not produce a single proletarian dictatorship stretching across continental Europe and large parts of Asia, already it counted as the greatest wave of revolutionary instability since 1848. In this sense, popular anti-Bolshevism was not a product of American exceptionalism: it was fueled by the fear that the United States might be subject to the same forces that were battering nations in Europe.

Events moved at a frightening pace. No one knew how far socialist ideas would reach, or how radical they might become. Bolshevism—or Communism, as it had begun to rebrand itself—had already defied complacent predictions of its destruction. The Communist leadership offered a vision for the end of capitalism through the action of disciplined revolutionary cadres that differed starkly from moderate socialism, and there was strong evidence to suggest its ambitions were global. In response to the Allied invasion, Lenin had called for demonstrations of solidarity from the working classes around the world. In August 1918, he wrote an address to "the American worker," which was circulated in the United States a few months later. The text excoriated Wilson as "the head of the American multimillionaires and the servant of the capitalist sharks" and urged workers to fight their leaders and help defend the Soviet regime. Lenin predicted that the "more fierce and brutal they are, the nearer the day of the victorious proletarian revolution." A second letter was published abroad in April 1919. It predicted that the "workers are slowly but surely coming round to communist and Bolshevik tactics," that "the maturing of the world proletarian revolution has proceeded very rapidly," and identified the imprisoned American Socialist Party leader Eugene Debs, among others, as having specifically taken the "communist path."

Meanwhile, March 1919 saw the creation of the Third International to coordinate revolutionary activities around the world. Lenin's efforts to build international revolutionary alliances might charitably be understood as defensive measures, and his predictions of capitalist collapse in America were clearly optimistic. However, there was no mistaking the calls for revolution. As such, the letters had precisely the opposite effect from that which was intended: instead of weakening support for the intervention in Russia, they strengthened popular fears over Bolshevik influence in America. To anti-Bolsheviks, Lenin's letters and the creation of the Communist International (Comintern) offered indisputable evidence that, as the *New York Times* put it, "Whether or not we are at war with the Bolsheviki, the Bolsheviki are at war with us." "Bolshevism is actively endeavoring to destroy nationalism and nations," editorialists in the *Washington Post* concluded. "It is propagandizing in nearly all countries, including the United States. There is no doubt that its paid agents have actually visited Washington and attempted to start a movement to destroy the present form of government."[16]

Nevertheless, with a public tired of foreign engagement and eager to see its troops return, the end of the war also gave impetus to anti-interventionists, who argued that the United States had no right to interfere in the domestic affairs of another state. Overthrowing an independent government in Russia seemed to affront the very principles for which the United States had claimed to be fighting. "Under existing circumstances," the *New Republic* argued, "a campaign conducted from other countries against the Bolsheviki is practically an attack on the right of the Russian people to national self-determination." In a bitter congressional debate in early January, Senator Robert La Follette read out descriptions of American troops engaged in brutal fighting knee-deep in snow and questioned why there had been no congressional debate prior to launching a war against the Bolsheviks. In typically colorful language, he pointed out that there was no proof of ties to Germany, save the "Sisson papers, over which is the slime of foxification, with fraud and forgery plainly manifest." Whatever claims were being circulated by the "censored channels of the press," he argued, "ought to be subjected to careful study and reflection before being taken as stating the whole truth."[17]

American radicals also spoke out for withdrawal, though unlike La Follette their case mixed attacks on Wilson's policy with more open admiration of the Bolshevik experiment. Little was known about the revolution at the time, yet the appeal of the world's only workers' government was, for many, irresistible. The small numbers of radicals who witnessed events in revolutionary Russia firsthand were feted as prophets. Lincoln Steffens, one of the first to visit Russia after the February Revolution, was ignorant of and frankly uninterested in Russian history, politics, language, or culture, but he saw in Bolshevism a new kind of twentieth-century phenomenon, leaders with a global vision who combined intellect and will, mixing the idealism of the Left with the hardheaded realism of the Right. He concluded they would not be maneuvered into the weak and ineffective positions that had destroyed the old Socialist International. Even while he was complaining about Wilson's loyalty campaigns at home, Steffens concluded that liberalism itself was outdated, destined to collapse in the face of men of action. "I have always been fighting the opponents of liberty," he wrote Senator La Follette. "Hereafter (after Russia) I am going to work on the practitioners of liberty." All the things that repelled moderates seemed to Steffens to be evidence of the Bolsheviks' higher realism: their "scientific" analysis of events and relentless self-criticism, their application of violence and terror as political tactics, and their separation of politics from ethics. Wilson, he argued, was a sailor, "the most perfect example we have produced of the culture which has failed and is dying out." Lenin, by contrast, was a navigator. As Steffens famously told reporters on his return from a second trip in the spring of 1919, "I have seen the future and it works."[18]

Steffens left Russia just weeks before the Bolsheviks stormed the Winter Palace, so it was left to his old friend Jack Reed to occupy the role of chief American radical witness to the October days. Reed, however, was not content simply to observe events that shook the world; he wanted to participate in them. Addressing thousands of Russian workers at the Third Congress of Soviets, he offered the solidarity of the American proletariat to the workers and soldiers in attendance. He and another American radical, Albert Rhys Williams, briefly worked for the Bolsheviks, writing copy that was later distributed in Germany in the hope of aiding the revolution there. The two of them, and Reed's wife, Louise Bryant, all spent time with the Bolshevik leadership and were able to hear their theories firsthand. By the time he returned to America in January 1918 to face prosecution for his role in publishing the *Masses,* Reed had become if not quite an official representative of the Bolshevik government, then certainly something not far from it.

American radicals usually denied that they were calling for revolution in America. Their campaigns, they argued, were simply intended to protect the fragile Russian Revolution. It was certainly true that throughout 1919, pro-Soviet radicals did little to engineer a new American revolution beyond organizing protests and writing newspapers and pamphlets for each other to read. However, quiescence was often due to fear of arrest or harassment, and many declarations in private or to sympathetic audiences extolled the virtues of an American brand of Bolshevism in far more explicit terms.[19] John Reed argued that the chances for revolution in America in the short term were minimal. He described the American working class as the most politically ignorant in the world. But he also said that "hard times and repression" would teach workers to think differently. He predicted, if the labor activist "Tom Mooney stays in jail, if wages go down, if Socialists are arrested and the red flag suppressed, there will be a revolutionary movement in this country in five years."[20] Even when they denied any role in bringing an American revolution about, many left-wing socialists welcomed the prospect and imagined roles for themselves as martyrs to the cause or leaders on the barricades. Speaking in Brooklyn in January 1919, Reed told a crowd that "a new war is begun, and this time it is a war between two ideas for the first time in history. . . . [O]n one side is private property and nationalism, and on the other side is property for the people and internationalism."[21]

As the revolution in Russia endured, a segment of American radicals came to accept the new formulations that distinguished Marxism-Leninism from traditional Marxism, especially the idea that a revolutionary vanguard could use propaganda, organization, and protest to raise the consciousness of the masses and lead them against the bourgeoisie. Ironically, these embryonic communists seemingly agreed with their opponents in stressing the role that could be played by a small, disciplined cohort positioned strategically within the national labor movement. To socialists and liberals who rejected the idea that a tiny group of radicals could shake the earth, the idea was ridiculous. Nevertheless, strong anti-Bolsheviks and pro-Bolsheviks increasingly tended to agree that a new American revolution was a possibility, albeit with one side welcoming the prospect and the other fearing it. This meant, among other things, that the best justifications for anti-Bolshevik politics were often to be found in the overblown propaganda of the Bolsheviks themselves.

At least in public, though, most radicals argued that violence was driven by the capitalist classes seeking to maintain their unjust hold on power and not by revolutionaries. Certainly, the loyalty campaigns supported the argument that the state and its supporters were more willing to use violence than the revolutionaries, but anti-Bolsheviks denounced this position as hairsplitting and cowardly. "When JOHN BROWN was arraigned on the charge of inciting a slave insurrection he did not explain that he was merely taking a few colored folk on a Sunday school picnic," one *New York Times* editorial concluded. "NATHAN HALE did not tell the British court-martial that his wanderings over Manhattan Island were those of a botanical student."[22] In this sense, like Lenin's letters to the American worker, radical attempts to defend Bolshevism proved to be a double-edged sword. By highlighting affinities between Bolshevism in Russia and radicalism in America, they exacerbated the sense of threat and heightened tensions rather than weakening them.

Coming to realize the dangers of relying on unpopular radicals to fight their cause, the Bolshevik regime thus began promoting an alternative image of itself as a friendly state trying to live in peace with its neighbors. Despite being contradictory, these two efforts ran more or less concurrently. Even while the Communist International was being created in Switzerland to coordinate a global network of revolutionary groups, the Bolsheviks set up an Information Bureau in New York to offer a more positive vision of the new regime. As well as challenging the false claims being circulated by anti-Bolsheviks, it was hoped that the bureau would appeal to capitalist hearts in the most direct way that revolutionaries imagined they could be reached: through their wallets. As a side benefit, the bureau could facilitate the exchange of vital commodities that were in desperate shortage in Russia. Ludwig C. A. K. Martens was put in charge of the effort, and the Finnish Socialist Nuorteva was made secretary. Martens was told to seek out contracts for orders of up to two hundred million dollars of industrial supplies, clothing, and basic commodities. A former CPI employee, Kenneth Durant, was brought in to advise on press and public relations, and several dozen other employees were detailed to departments of economics and statistics, legal work, educational activities, and commerce. Effort was made to silo the organization from the activities of American radicals in order to undercut claims it was pushing for revolution in America. As the appointment of Durant suggested, the office was closer to a public relations firm than a revolutionary cell. Other staff included Harvard graduates, economics professors, and a former chief statistician from the Department of Labor. Bureau representatives took pains to deny that their work was "secret, sinister or opprobrious" and appealed for understanding on progressive and probusiness grounds. Nuorteva was even criticized on the Left for being too moderate and willing to cooperate with bourgeois elements.[23]

As the debate over Russia intensified, then, communism in America—as much as such a thing existed—presented a Janus face: one part diplomatic and moderate, focused on securing the withdrawal of American troops from the East and new trade deals in the West; another part undiplomatic and radical, anticipating a revolution in America to echo Russia's. Despite the fact that Lincoln Steffens considered the Bolsheviks to be visionaries, the Russian leadership struggled to reconcile these conflicting constituencies. It was an irony that would persist for much of its history that the domestic amateurs were generally more revolutionary minded than the foreign agents, who tended to put the national interests of the Soviet state ahead of the Marxist ideal of global revolution. In this sense, the failure to adequately distinguish between domestic protesters and international agents was not only a product of countersubversive propaganda, but also a result of ambiguities that lay at the heart of communism itself.

∗   ∗   ∗

The debate over Bolshevism was characterized by misrepresentations and confusion on all sides. The administration invaded Russia in the hope of ousting the Soviet regime, but denied this was what it was doing. CPI press releases declared, falsely, that "Bolsheviki peace and socialistic propaganda against the United States" was launched "at the direction of the German intelligence service."[24] Lenin wrote letters to American workers calling for worldwide communist revolution at the same time as Bolshevik agents in New York stressed Russia's pacific intent. Domestic radicals claimed to have no desire to see the liberal Republic collapse, but privately predicted revolution was coming and welcomed the prospect. In such a maelstrom of opinion, it could hardly be surprising that ordinary Americans struggled to understand Bolshevism or its role and influence in America.

The public craved a clarity that was simply not present, and this created opportunities for powerful groups to shape the narrative to suit their priorities. With its hearings into the brewing industry and pro-German propaganda coming to an end, the Overman Committee took the lead in this process, reinventing itself as the primary congressional platform for crusading anti-Bolshevism. In the process, it became the first countersubversive investigative committee in American history: the original ancestor of the McCarthy-era House Committee on Un-American Activities (HUAC).

Given that it was charged with looking specifically at German covert operations, the shift to Bolshevism was contingent upon making the now-familiar case that Bolshevism was a result of a coordinated international movement inspired by Germany. To do so, Overman relied upon elements of the countersubversive machinery that had been built up during the war, and in particular a witness from military intelligence, Archibald E. Stevenson. During the war, Stevenson had been a member of Wilson's voluntarist army: a civilian attached to the military in New York as a propaganda analyst. A well-connected individual, especially in the state legislature and the powerful Union League Club, Stevenson had cooperated with the Bureau of Investigation, but preferred the trappings of military intelligence, "carrying a card with the seal of the War Department and the signature of General Churchill identifying him as special agent 650." In November 1918, aware that the army was moving away from domestic countersubversion now that the war was over and that his privileged position was therefore in jeopardy, Stevenson submitted a report to Washington describing an alarming spread of Bolshevism and proposed that military files be turned over to the attorney general. Although his superiors decided such action would be "impolitic"—military intelligence was not supposed to be spying on American citizens—they nonetheless praised his dedication and accepted the report. It was perhaps through the Overman Committee's chief counsel, Major Humes, also a member of military intelligence, that the document reached the Senate.[25]

Stevenson was called before the Overman Committee at the tail end of the German propaganda hearings in January and spoke about the alleged links between Germany and American radicalism. His testimony revealed a thorough knowledge of the landscape of radical politics, vital to his credibility as an expert witness, but in the absence of hard evidence linking Germany to the antiwar movement, Stevenson was forced to turn to implication, insinuation, and loaded interpretations to link domestic radicals with the wartime enemy. Like Palmer and Wilson, Stevenson suggested that the shared ends of Germans and radicals were circumstantial proof of a hidden conspiracy, noting that radical antiwar activism "aided and assisted the Germans, unintentionally, and gave force and effect to their propaganda campaign." When asked to expand on the crucial "unintentionally" in his sentence, he admitted that "we do not say what the motives of the people are; we do not know. But we believe that an analysis of the situation would convince anyone that it was the result of German propaganda."[26] Since this pertained directly to the committee's mandate to investigate domestic radicalism, not to mention the bigger question of whether dissenters were genuinely seditious, Senator William Henry King asked for clarification, and again Stevenson resorted to the bait and switch:

> SENATOR KING. Your contention is that this [radicalism] is the result of German propaganda, had its origins in Germany, and therefore would be properly investigated under the resolution of this committee?
> MR. STEVENSON. Yes. The Bolsheviki movement is a branch of the revolutionary socialism of Germany. It had its origins in the philosophy of Marx and its leaders were Germans.[27]

These carefully constructed but ultimately tenuous arguments showed that Overman and Stevenson, both lawyers by trade, knew exactly how far the evidence could take them and were being careful not to make claims that could be explicitly disproved. In this, the participants revealed themselves to be comparatively scrupulous in their legalism even as they sought to shape the evidence to suit a narrowly defined set of prior conclusions. Stevenson even argued that the very lack of clarity about Bolshevism demonstrated the need for further congressional investigations, which could not only get at the truth but also initiate a campaign of publicity to awaken America to the dangers it faced. Stevenson argued that public ignorance had allowed radicals to unify behind calls to defend the revolution, when previously they had been hopelessly divided. In time, the rise of Bolshevism would split the old Left irreparably. But in 1919, the enthusiasm for the experiment did indeed seem to be universal and unifying.[28] Stevenson argued that the comparative meaninglessness of the word *Bolshevik* had allowed it to be employed as a catchall utopia. A lack of evidence about conditions in Russia had seen Bolshevism "degenerate into appeals to the prejudices and animosities that are inherent in the selfish natures of most peoples and little or no appeal has been made to the intelligence of the people." The only solution was a vigorous campaign of investigation followed by public education. In Stevenson's words, "You must employ the same weapons that they employ." Exposing Bolshevism before the searchlight of the committee would cause its seditious character to be recognized by all upright citizens.[29] The people themselves would then be able to act on their own. As with the CPI, the language of enlightenment and education thus offered a way of presenting elite propaganda as simply guiding popular democratic instincts for liberty. The popularity of using congressional hearings as a vehicle for countersubversive propaganda was undoubtedly tied to the presumption—increasingly untrue—that Congress was "investigating" an issue rather than taking an active executive role. This kind of language would become a perpetual refrain in subsequent decades, and metaphors of lights, searchlights, and exposure would abound. Two decades later, Martin Dies's first annual report for the House Un-American Activities Committee stated, "The committee has felt that it is its sworn duty and solemn obligation to the people of this country to focus the spotlight of publicity upon every individual and organization engaged in subversive activities."[30]

Stevenson's testimony would not have been good enough for a rigorous court of law, but it did win an extension for the committee. His efforts were aided at the last minute by two public meetings held in Washington in early February at which Albert Rhys Williams, Louise Bryant, and a number of other pro-Bolsheviks spoke. The combined audience of several thousand ranged from enthusiastic self-proclaimed Bolsheviks to anti-interventionists and vaguely interested passersby; indeed, three congressmen attended the first meeting, and Representative William Ernest Mason of Illinois spoke at one point of the need to get American troops home.[31] Reprising his role in the creation of the Overman Committee, when he had taken Palmer's claims about the brewing industry to Congress, Senator King drew congressional attention to the meetings and declared that it was clear that "the purpose of the advertised speakers . . . was to extol bolshevism and to condemn the Constitution and institutions of our government and to encourage revolution at home."[32]

It seems the Senate took the physical proximity of these meetings to the Capitol as a personal affront and deliberate provocation, and in their wounded outrage lost all interest in the distinction between anti-interventionism and pro-Bolshevism. It is difficult to see why these particular meetings produced such a wave of anger, except that by coming to the District of Columbia the radicals seemed to show a lack of respect for the august institutions of state. The *Washington Post* noted that, "Senators were shocked that the soviet doctrines could be so openly advocated in the National Capital." Senator Henry Lee Myers of Montana asked, rhetorically, "Are we to remain silent and see the dignity and sovereignty of the American government insulted?" Over two stormy hours, senators competed to outdo each other in righteous indignation; even many anti-interventionists expressed their fury at the provocation. Senator Thomas J. Walsh of Montana introduced a resolution expanding the Overman Committee's mandate; it passed unanimously.[33]

The resolution gained support from interventionists and anti-interventionist senators alike because it specifically permitted Overman to investigate Bolshevik activities in the United States, not Russia, and because it appeared to be a neutral investigation rather than a preplanned propaganda operation. However, the hearings that followed in February and March almost immediately departed from this brief. In large part, the switch was due to the paucity of evidence about domestic radicals' links to Bolshevism, especially as Secretary of War Newton Baker abruptly withdrew his support and closed off senatorial access to MI files and staff. Baker had fallen out with Overman, was angered by Stevenson's grandstanding, and was worried that the army might come under scrutiny if the extent of its wartime countersubversive operations became clear. He publicly disassociated himself from Stevenson and placed a blanket ban on his agents appearing before Congress. Overman was reportedly infuriated, but there was little that could be done.[34] To get around the problem, he argued that any examination of Bolshevism in America would first require a thorough study of conditions in Russia in order to understand what kind of a future America faced if it did not act.

Overman and his fellow senators took testimony from a wide range of witnesses. Most were army or State Department employees recently back from Russia who spoke about their frustrations dealing with the Bolsheviks. Others included newspapermen, Russian exiles, and religious missionaries. Even if there was an exaggerated tendency to assume that the Bolsheviks were responsible for everything that was wrong in Russia, many of the accounts of revolutionary chaos were broadly accurate. Others, though, were distorted to the point of absurdity, meaning that reasonable criticisms of Bolshevism were interspersed with extreme statements that undermined the entire investigation. Some witnesses painted a picture of revolutionary Russia as a charnel house, with Red Guards operating as orchestrated gangs of pickpockets, people jailed for having above average intelligence, and "delicate women" compelled to work in the streets simply for coming from prosperous backgrounds. As well as setting about the destruction of organized religion and private property, ending freedoms of speech and assembly, and eliminating electoral democracy, it was claimed that the Bolsheviks had "nationalized" women under the orders of a Bureau of Free Love. Roger Simmons, a representative of the Department of Commerce who had been briefly imprisoned during his time in Russia, produced circulars that, like the Sisson Documents, had originally been concocted by Russian anti-Bolsheviks—this time by anarchist groups parodying Bolshevik authoritarianism. The material stated that the city of Saratov had declared women "the property of the whole nation," with male citizens having the "right to use one woman not oftener than three times a week, for three hours."[35] The sarcasm was apparently lost on the senators. Other witnesses told the committee the Soviet government had made it easy to get married and divorced and as a result Russians had as many wives as they wanted, "in rotation," while brutish Red Guards "rape and ravish and despoil at will."[36]

Overman was raised in a southern milieu in which gender was routinely politicized in order to defend conservative policies in the name of protecting femininity. The Nineteenth Amendment was currently in the process of ratification, and Overman was a vocal opponent of female suffrage. Just as he and Palmer had done with Prohibition, then, the chairman began to use his examination of conditions in Russia as a way of promoting his opposition to giving women the vote.[37] In this way, the anxieties of propertied elites about the revolutionary ambitions of the Bolshevik leadership intermingled with more extreme and sometimes even ridiculous visions of Bolshevism as the inversion of all social norms. In the senators' words, Bolshevism represented a "reign of terror unparalleled in the history of modern civilization, in many of its aspects rivaling even the inhuman savagery of the Turk and the terrors of the French Revolution."[38] Every inch ceded to the Bolsheviks by foreign armies, Simmons claimed, "has been followed by the murder of every man, woman, and child in the evacuated territory."[39] These horrors were used to promote not only a hostile stance toward Russia, but also distinct policy objectives for the United States—not least because many senators struggled to understand Russian politics in terms beyond their personal experience. At one point, when discussing Bolshevik attitudes toward divorce, Overman asked a witness, "They do not have to go to Reno? They have no Reno?" "No," the witness replied.[40]

Other than pushing for a peacetime extension of the Sedition Act, Overman's main priority was immigration restriction. The investigation of American radicalism offered an opportunity to continue the xenophobic lines of questioning he had pursued during his earlier hearings into the brewing industry. To keep radicals out, "Would it do to pass a law that no person should enter this country unless he is a white man—an Anglo-Saxon—for the next 10 years?" he asked Stevenson. Stevenson replied that he thought it would be a good thing. "So do I," Overman concurred. "It would affect the brown man and the yellow man and the black man."[41]

Because socialism in New York was rooted in the Jewish districts, anti-Bolshevism also often folded into casual anti-Semitism. A Reverend Simons, after protesting that some of his best friends were Jews, expressed the views of several witnesses when he told the committee that the Bolsheviks were "Hebrews, apostate Jews," speakers of the "part-German" Yiddish who had abandoned their true faith. He had uncovered a special book that Jews were using to organize a secret anti-Christian conspiracy and a conquest of the world. "I do not want to say anything against the Jews, as such," he continued. "I am not in sympathy with the anti-Semitic movement, never have been, and do not ever expect to be. I am against it. I abhor all pogroms of whatever kind. But I have a firm conviction that this thing is Yiddish, and that one of its bases is found in the East side of New York." Overman remarked that it would be "a very remarkable thing if the Bolshevik movement started in this country, financed by Germans, would it not?" Simons replied, "I do not think that the Bolshevik movement in Russia would have been a success if it had not been for the support it got from certain elements in New York, the so-called East Side."[42]

As well as provoking a storm of protest in America's Jewish community, at least one other witness went out of his way to object to this characterization, and the senators downplayed the anti-Semitic theorizing in their final report. Despite such extreme testimony, the committee looked across the spectrum for anti-Bolshevik allies, and not all witnesses offered simplistic calls for repression. Roger Simmons, for instance, argued that suppressing Bolshevik sympathizers in America would only make martyrs of them. Herman Bernstein, a journalist from the *New York Herald,* articulated the dominant sentiment of the committee when he argued, "I believe the only way of disarming Bolshevism is to tell the truth about what it is doing."[43]

One of the most interesting witnesses in this context was Yekaterina Constantinovna Breshko-Breshkovskaya, "the grandmother of the revolution." A leading Left Socialist Revolutionary originally from a reformist aristocratic family, Breshkovskaya had grown up fighting czarist absolutism, had been imprisoned for thirty-two years, and had worked for the Provisional Government after the February Revolution. Following the Bolshevik coup, she was briefly jailed again and after eight months in hiding fled the country.[44] Breshkovskaya told the committee that the rate of death in Russia was skyrocketing, that the country was plagued by hunger, and that Lenin and Trotsky were working for the enemy. "Do you really believe that Trotzky and Lenine are the tools of Germany?" one senator asked her. "I don't believe it, I know it," she replied, banging her hand on the table.[45]

Witnesses like Breshkovskaya were particularly important because they defied radical claims that the enemies of Bolshevism were simply monarchists, capitalists, and right-wingers. Following an invitation from Jane Addams, Breshkovskaya gave a speech at Hull House where she warned that if the Allies came to Russia with the aim of restoring the monarchy or sought "to make the capitalists the masters of the country," then the Russian people would not want their assistance. "At the start the Bolsheviki had the people with them," she argued. "They promised peace, bread, clothes, education," but now things had descended into chaos. "The farmers will not sell to the Bolsheviki, consequently many of the people of Russia are starving. We have no schools, no communication, no transportation, no bread, no peace, no industry. Russia is destroyed. Not even paper have we to print our alphabet." The only solution was a constituent assembly, democratic liberty, distribution of land to the people, and compulsory universal education. "Bolshevism is not a theory," she said. "It is a behavior. If the American socialists admire the Bolsheviki they do not understand their performances. Perhaps they believe Russia is happy now. It is not."[46]

Recognizing the growing attention accorded the investigations, anti-interventionists also came before the committee to present their views. Raymond Robins, the former head of the Red Cross in Russia and an anti-interventionist, had remained silent over the Sisson Documents on the orders of the Wilson administration. After the Armistice, however, he emerged as one of the foremost figures in the effort to bring the troops home and was accompanied by Senator Hiram Johnson during his testimony, with whom he had become increasingly closely associated. Robins emphasized the argument that Wilson himself had privately conceded in 1918: that foreign invasions helped the Bolsheviks claim the mantle of Russian nationalism. But when asked if the United States should keep "hands off" were it to be shown that "there are murder and rape and starvation in Russia under the Bolsheviki," Robins prevaricated.[47] He agreed when senators suggested that Bolshevism was "the greatest menace now facing the world." Robins felt the Soviet program was "economically impossible and morally wrong" and represented a "fundamental menace" to America. Nevertheless, the only meaningful solution lay in offering a "better alternative," while smears, false accusations, and forged documents offered no hope for a constructive solution to the crisis.[48]

Although many critics of Wilson's expansionist policy were quite clear that their anti-interventionism did not mean enthusiasm for Bolshevism, they sometimes found themselves caught up in complicated circumlocutions, suggesting

Bolshevism was more liberal or democratic than was actually the case in order to preserve the moral framework that notionally underpinned their foreign policy recommendations.[49] In this sense, the argument against intervention was sometimes easier to make for radicals willing to defend Bolshevism outright than it was for anti-interventionists who sought to distinguish their personal anti-Bolshevism from the requirements of American foreign policy.

This became clear when John Reed, Louise Bryant, and Albert Rhys Williams were called to testify. During her time in Petrograd, Bryant claimed to have witnessed none of the things that previous witnesses had described: no stealing of jewelry, no killings, no starvation, no Bolshevik support for Germany, no more beggars than in an average city in America, no press censorship, and no criminals dressed up as Red Guardsmen. The Bolsheviks offered equality for women, not their "nationalization." There was no state-sponsored separation of children from mothers, and the Bolsheviks proposed to end child labor, something that southern senators, including Chairman Overman, had fought tooth and nail to retain.[50] Violence committed by the Bolsheviks was no different from what American revolutionaries did to Tory loyalists. "These people are social democrats," she claimed.[51] To Bryant, her husband, and their allies, Bolshevism represented a hope for the universal liberation of mankind.

Nevertheless, Bryant's dispute with the haughty committee members was about more than just Russia. It was fueled by her identity as both a radical and a woman. In an exchange charged with electricity, she got into a fight about religion before she was even allowed to swear in and technically begin her testimony, since—as Senator King put it—"a person who has no conception of God does not have any idea of the sanctity of an oath, and an oath would be meaningless." Bryant complained that it seemed as if she "were being tried for witchcraft" and that she had not heard of any other witnesses being put through a similar ordeal. Supporters in the public audience made so much noise in response that Overman temporarily cleared the room. As the questioning unfolded, she objected to having her character dissected, to being asked only about her husband's activities rather than her own experiences (a practice, it has to be said, that was common to many radicals as well), and to being patronized because of her sex. "You are a woman and you do not know anything about the conduct of an examination such as we have in hand here. We are going to treat you fairly and treat you as a lady," Overman told her at one point. Bryant retorted that she wished to be treated not as a lady, but "as a human being."[52]

This deeply gendered hostility produced an almost total impasse between witness and senators. At one point, Bryant tried to introduce some of Reed's writings into the record, to challenge the claim that they were calling for revolution in the United States. The committee had already examined an example of Reed's writing, describing it as "an extremely well-written document, and extremely insidious." In theory, they should have been pleased to receive further material in the same vein, but when she tried to put it forward, Senator Nelson told her they had no interest. "You do not care about it?" Bryant queried. "About these papers," Nelson replied. "We want the facts." "These are the facts," Bryant pointed out.[53] It seemed the person who introduced the evidence altered its meaning, shifting its status from "fact" to "propaganda." Of course, this hardly supported the senators' claims to be engaged in an evenhanded investigation.

Reed, Bryant, and Williams all sparred with the committee during their testimony, but the difficulties Bryant experienced were the most severe. Ideological differences were compounded by both her gender and her combative temperament. Both Reed, who should have been a more contentious witness given his increasing eminence in the radical world, and Williams were given far greater latitude. Both denied calling for violent revolution for America and argued that social revolution could take place by peaceful means. Williams seemed even to have a fairly cordial relationship with the senators at times, expressing an awareness of the difficulties of judging the Russian Revolution without historical distance. He made little attempt to challenge previous statements about violence and terror in Russia. Revolutionary society was a disordered, chaotic place, he admitted. He simply argued that the Bolsheviki were Russia's best chance for the future.[54]

The committee's final report downplayed several of the more extreme claims that had been made by witnesses. The nationalization of women had not taken place "on a national level," the senators concluded, even if flexible divorce laws had "practically established a state of free love" in Russia. More important, the senators acknowledged there was no fundamental threat to the American state, although they considered radicals a menace to domestic stability. They even accepted that no radical they examined had called for a Bolshevik revolution in the United States. Although they felt that Bolshevism's "messengers and their friends" had "afflicted this country," they concluded that "only a portion of the so-called radical revolutionary groups and organizations accept in its entirety the doctrine of the Bolsheviki." Bolsheviki and American radicals had a "common cause," which was the "destruction of life, property, and personal security" and the "establishment of a government founded upon the violence of the minority." But many radicals had misunderstood the essentially repressive character of Russian Bolshevism, seeing it as a workers' government when it was in fact an autocracy and believing that power resided within elected Soviets rather than the party apparatus.[55]

Nevertheless, newspaper reporters tended to cherry-pick the most extreme claims made before the committee to maximize attention, and as tensions rose conflict over America's Russian policy began spilling into the streets. Gangs of anti-Bolsheviks attacked Reed and Bryant when they gave public lectures about their experiences in Russia, while Bolshevik sympathizers disrupted Breshkovs-kaya during her own tour of the country, meeting her speeches with catcalls, boos, and hissing. A "near riot" broke out at one meeting in Providence—calmed, journalists reported, only by "a liberal application of nightsticks." At a meeting in Boston, a radical named Yanisky accused Breshkovskaya of being an agent of capitalism. Breshkovskaya responded by asking why Yanisky didn't return to Russia if she was so supportive of its current rulers. "I have suffered all my life for Russia," Breshkovskaya said. "Have any of you suffered for Russia? I am willing to suffer for the rest of my life. Are you?"[56]

*   *   *

As the debate over Bolshevism intensified, the feeling that some kind of reckoning had come was as palpable for those who hoped for revolution as for those who feared it. After years of conflict, many American radicals had come to see attacks upon them as badges of honor. As Harry Winitsky, a radical from New York, told a meeting at the end of the year, "Times have changed." It made no sense to complain about prosecutions and indictments, because any move-ment that claimed to be revolutionary yet met with the approval of the capitalist authorities was "a disgrace to the name."[57] Establishment criticism was taken as a sign that they were on the right track: why would senators be so preoccupied with radicalism if they were not threatened by it?

The debate thus helped to institutionalize the split between moderate and radical socialists that had first come to light in labor disputes earlier in the cen-tury and intensified during World War I. Not one but two American communist parties, directly inspired by the Russian experiment, were created in the sum-mer of 1919 from the left wing of the Socialist Party. The first, the Communist Labor Party, was formed at the end of August after a group of pro-Bolshevik radicals, including John Reed, tried to take control of the Socialist Party and were defeated and ejected. The second was led by Charles Ruthenberg and Louis C. Fraina and constituted primarily from the foreign-language federations that made up much of the socialist base. These activists had rejected Reed's original proposal to co-opt the Socialist Party, considering the old organization to be polluted beyond salvage, and instead established an independent Communist Party of America. Ironically, though opposing its imitation in America, many of those who remained in the Socialist Party also continued to defend the Bolshe-vik Revolution from external attack, despite the fact that the new Communists persistently denounced them as reactionaries.[58]

In this way, the distinction between constitutional socialism and revolution-ary communism began to resolve itself. With few exceptions, the new Ameri-can Communists had no contact with Russia: as Theodore Draper put it, they welcomed Bolshevism "because they imagined that it vindicated the ideas most native to them." They amounted to probably no more than twenty-five to forty thousand people, mostly poor immigrant workers with little power or influence. Despite this, though, the formation of the new Communist Parties marked a watershed. Intellectual, cultural, and emotional rejection of the constitutional order had transformed into a loose but nonetheless very real association with the ruling regime of a foreign state. As Doug Rossinow notes, "This change occurred, it seems, with some not fully understanding what was happening. It stemmed from the combination of Russian assertiveness, immigrant enthusiasm, and the reaction of the left to harsh repression in the United States." "If it wasn't for the 1917 revolution," leading Communist Party member Jay Lovestone once remarked, "I would have become a lawyer."[59] From this point on, countersubversives could point to the American Communist movement as evidence of their claims that foreign ethnicities, revolutionary ideologies, and foreign countries were indeed inextricably related.

Having completed its work, it seemed that the Overman Committee had come to a dead end. Without evidence of a serious domestic threat, the Senate seemed disinclined to support further countersubversive investigations, let alone peacetime sedition laws. Archibald Stevenson thus began to look elsewhere to keep his personal countersubversive campaign going, eventually turning to his home state for support. New York City had been a zone of controversy throughout the war, with upstate New Yorkers and city businessmen looking on the "disloyal" tendencies of the capital with horror. The particularly furious mayoral election of 1917 had raised the question of the city's attitude toward the war to fever pitch. In a four-way race, the prowar Democratic incumbent, John Purroy Mitchel, ran against an outlier Republican; an antiwar Socialist, Morris Hillquit; and John F. Hylan, who was supported jointly by Tammany Democrats and William Randolph Hearst, well-known anti-interventionists. Mitchel declared he was fighting "Hearst, Hylan, and Hohenzollern" and distributed posters of himself dressed as a doughboy skewering the Tammany Tiger. Theodore Roosevelt and other leading politicians queued up to attack Hillquit as an enemy of the state. The *New York World* declared the election would decide "whether New York is a traitor town, or a quasi-Copperhead town or an American town devoted to American ideals and pledged without reservation to the war policies of the United States government." But despite the smears, New Yorkers cast their votes overwhelmingly for the anti-interventionist candidates. Hylan won the greatest plurality in the city's history. Even Hillquit and the Socialists ran within ten points of the incumbent.[60]

With the war over, conservatives looked to reassert the power of the state against the metropolis. In a report to the Union League Club in mid-March, Stevenson laid out the indictment he had been unable to offer to Overman. By looking into conditions in Russia, the Overman Committee had revealed what might happen if Bolshevism was established in America, he argued, but "the study of the problem should be pushed further" in order to establish exactly what plans were already afoot in the United States. Stevenson argued that although American Bolshevik sympathizers were small in number, they were seeking to leverage far-broader popular unrest by working through labor unions and among ethnic and racial minorities. Repeating the theories he had previously told to Overman, Stevenson claimed that radicals were using the symbolic appeal of the Russian Revolution to unite formerly disparate groups into a powerful revolutionary movement. Radicals, he argued, planned to oust AFL president Samuel Gompers and then orchestrate a wave of industrial disturbances across the country as a prelude to seizing power.[61]

Unanimously endorsing the report's recommendations, the club called upon the state congress to set up its own legislative committee to investigate radicalism in imitation of the national Senate.[62] A few weeks later, at a dinner presided over by Charles Evans Hughes, a second resolution expressed resentment over the presence in Manhattan of the Soviet Information Bureau. It was a travesty, they argued, that such a body could be lobbying for recognition even while American troops were "engaged in conflict with the armed forces of the Russian Soviet republic."[63]

Not only did the state senate support the petition, but the committee that was subsequently created under the chairmanship of Senator Clayton Lusk of Cortland County was given extensive funding, broad latitude to subpoena witnesses, and the authority to conduct roving hearings. Unlike Overman, the Lusk Committee was charged with looking into all forms of radical politics in America, not just Bolshevism. And Stevenson was hired as chief counsel.

In the weeks leading up to the commencement of the Lusk hearings, elements within the revolutionary Left once again added fuel to the anti-Bolshevik fire. On April 28, a small parcel was mailed to Seattle's antiradical mayor, Ole Hanson, wrapped neatly in brown paper and postmarked from the Novelty Department of the Gimbel Brothers store in New York. Inside was a wooden tube about eight inches long with a top that, when unscrewed, was designed to break a vial of sulfuric acid over a number of mercury percussion caps and a stick of dynamite, thereby igniting them. The device did not go off only because Hanson's clerk had turned the tube upside down when he opened it.[64]

A similar package arrived the next day at the home of Georgia's former senator Thomas W. Hardwick, a cosponsor of the 1918 Immigration Act. In the midst of a torrential hailstorm, Hardwick's daughter heard a tremendous explosion from the other end of the house and ran to see what had happened. She found her mother standing dazed and stunned, with burns on her face and her clothes shredded. The kitchen windows were shattered, furniture was destroyed, plaster had been ripped from the ceiling, and blood was spattered across the walls. As neighbors rushed in to help, it gradually became clear what had occurred. Hardwick's wife had taken the delivery but, believing that it contained lead pencils, handed the package to the family's African American maid, Ethel Williams, to unpack and store in a kitchen cabinet. As the maid untied the strings holding the parcel together, the device exploded. Both Williams's hands were blown off.[65]

The parcels were early arrivals, intended to be delivered on May Day. Over the following forty-eight hours, nearly three dozen others, each carefully constructed from wooden boxes, were seized in post office branches in New York, North Carolina, Salt Lake City, and elsewhere across the country, most of them located before reaching their destination because of insufficient postage. Sixteen were intercepted in one go after a quick-witted postmaster in Harlem noticed the similarity of descriptions in the press to a pile of packages sitting in his office.[66]

The addressees were a roll call of nationally known countersubversives, including postmaster general Albert Burleson, former alien property custodian A. Mitchell Palmer, Supreme Court justice Oliver Wendell Holmes, and capitalists like John D. Rockefeller and J. P. Morgan.[67] Judges who had presided over the prosecution of IWW members during the war were targeted, as were advocates of immigration restriction and lawyers who had prosecuted radical activists. The North Carolina package was addressed to Senator Overman and was nearly opened by one of his daughters in the belief it was a wedding gift; the Salt Lake City package was sent to Overman's fellow committee member William Henry King.[68]

Agencies of law enforcement at state and federal level were put on high alert, and investigations were opened in several cities to identify the perpetrators. Radicals blamed the devices on agents provocateurs, saying they were intended to stigmatize the labor movement. Countersubversives, by contrast, argued that the bombs were "of dual origin, that is that the I.W.W. and the Bolsheviki participated."[69] Both claims were in all likelihood wrong: the Department of Justice later traced ink and paper used in their construction to Roberto Elia and Andrea Salsedo, two anarchists who followed the teachings of the Italian American anarchist Luigi Galleani. (Galleani was deported soon after, for activities unconnected to the bombings. Elia was found dead outside Justice Department offices in May 1920, apparently defenestrated.) A month later, just days before the Lusk hearings were due to begin, a second series of bombs exploded at locations in eight different cities. Radicals again blamed government provocation. John Reed said that the campaigns were planned "by some one who was interested in terrifying the ruling class into destroying the radical labor movement in this country."[70] But the anarchist delivering the bomb that exploded outside the house of attorney general Palmer, shattering its windows, was blown up in the blast—and his corpse seemed to suggest otherwise.

The attacks raised popular fears of revolutionary terror to a new level, especially in New York, from which most of the bombs had been mailed. Press reports declared the Lower East Side, prior home of Leon Trotsky and permanent home of "scores of Jews," to be "the breeding place of revolt in the New World."[71] A state law banned the display of the red flag at public meetings.[72] The leader of the state senate declared that radicals had received a half-million dollars from Russia. There was, he claimed, "a thoroughly organized plan worked out by the Russian Bolsheviki to seize the reins of government in this country. And the heart and brains of the Red Terror is right here in New York City."[73]

The feverish atmosphere in New York explains much of the difference in tone, method, and argument between the Overman hearings and Lusk's later investigations.[74] Even while it exaggerated facts to suit prior prejudices, the Overman Committee had shown a sensitivity to the limits of the evidence before them and was determined to preserve the dignity of the Senate by conducting its investigations in a lawyerly way. Witnesses had often claimed that radicals, IWWs, socialists, and labor activists were secretly Bolsheviks in disguise, but the committee, conforming to the image of austere congressional statesmanship, generally resisted making too sweeping claims about radicalism generally. Virtually none of this restraint was shown by Lusk. His committee shifted into a new gear: stepping beyond campaigning and publicity into active political repression and abandoning the specific concern about a potential Bolshevik conspiracy led from abroad in favor of a more indiscriminate antiradicalism. Under Stevenson's guidance, with little regard for the separation of powers, committee staff, private investigators, and police raided dozens of leftist offices during the summer and fall of 1919, usually on the dubious grounds that groups were breaching the peace. The *New Republic* likened its arbitrary usage of search warrants to the behavior of George III's representatives in the colonies. Since many radical groups tended to do little more than print pamphlets and newspapers, these raids produced great piles of radical boilerplate but little else. Nevertheless, details of the seizures were reported salaciously in the press, the sheer volume of printed matter conveying the impression of a large and well-organized conspiracy.[75] Even when seized evidence was lacking in subversive content, bookending interpretations could give it a sinister guise. Deputy attorney general Roscoe Conkling admitted that one set of papers were "so carefully and cleverly phrased" that he could not find a single sentence in violation of the law. Yet, he assured the public, "taken as a whole the documents are seditious."[76] In such a way, a small fire could be made to yield a great deal of smoke.

Perhaps the culminating triumph of the committee came on January 7, 1920, when Lusk activists encouraged the state assembly to suspend from office five

Socialist congressmen who had been elected from districts in Lower Manhattan. All but one of the 141 other members of the assembly supported the decision, and in March they were expelled.[77] However, by this time, the scare was fading. By contrast, at the moment the Lusk Committee commenced its hearings, in the summer of 1919, the United States was gripped by fears of radical insurrection and calls for decisive action to uncover the source of terroristic violence. "You may be willing to take the trouble to deport these traitors," Seattle's Mayor Hanson had declared, "but I am ready to hang them to the first convenient light pole."[78] Indeed, on its very first day, Stevenson targeted the most visible Bolshevik institution in America. At the pinpoint of three o'clock in the afternoon, private detectives acting on his orders crashed into the offices of bureau representatives Ludwig Martens and Santeri Nuorteva and carted them off to face a grilling before the committee.[79] In the afterglow of the raid, a reporter quizzed Lusk on whether he thought the Soviet Information Bureau was seeking to defend the Soviet form of government in Russia or advocating it for America. "It is pretty hard to draw a distinction," Lusk replied. "But we are less concerned with the purpose of the propaganda than its effect."[80] Bolshevism was crackling in American ears, mouths, and brains, just as Lincoln Steffens had been told it would.

3

Red Scare
The Triumph of Countersubversion

Hindsight encourages us to see 1919 as an auspicious moment for countersubversive politics, with the war's legacy of intolerance and the global climate of insecurity leading to a yearlong campaign of domestic repression. But despite the disorder emanating from Europe and the controversy over the presence of pro-Bolshevik radicals in America, the coming of peace also raised serious problems for countersubversives. The Wilson administration had sponsored domestic countersubversion in 1917 and 1918 on the grounds that antiwar dissenters were aiding Germany by undermining the war effort. For many supporters of the war, only the clear and present dangers of great-power conflict justified the imposition of sweeping federal restrictions on civil liberties.

Far from charging toward a Red Scare, the government actually began 1919 by beating a retreat from political policing. The Sedition Act had been passed as a measure of war and was no longer legislatively applicable. Attorney general Gregory resigned in February to attend the Paris peace talks and before departing told the American Protective League to wind up its operations and sharply reduced the number of bureau agents investigating radicalism.[1] A judge dismissed legal proceedings against John Reed and a number of other radicals in April, raising hopes of a more general amnesty.[2] The new attorney general, former alien property custodian A. Mitchell Palmer, warned that, absent the swift passage of a peacetime sedition law, hundreds of "dangerous aliens" would soon have to be turned loose onto American streets.[3] But Congress showed little interest, especially after Overman completed his hearings in the spring. Some states began to take matters into their own hands: unrestricted by questions of federalism, state sedition laws could take up the slack where the national government fell short. Nevertheless, optimistic liberals tentatively began to voice the hope that the excesses of the war years were coming to an end and that the United States was returning to a more tolerant position on political dissent.

Nevertheless, much of the private-sector machinery of countersubversion still remained in place. Voluntarist groups were less concerned with constitutional restrictions on political policing than Congress or the White House and, having benefited directly from the wartime campaign, sought to continue their activities. In so doing, they tended to drift away from the basic question of national security that had, at least in theory, shaped wartime policy and toward matters of personal interest. Having already demonstrated their efficacy, national security justifications for countersubversive activism persisted, but they became increasingly tenuous, as individual groups sought to denounce their rivals as disloyal, treasonous, and a danger to the general good.

The radicalization of countersubversive politics over the course of 1919, then, was linked to the continuing shift of political initiative away from the state and toward groups within the private sector, a process that had already begun during the wartime loyalty campaigns. Indeed, federal countersubversion during the Great Red Scare took place toward the end of the year, effectively following in the wake of local and nonstate politics.

Taken at face value, the idea that radicals represented an existential threat to national institutions—institutions that had persisted across more than a century of political discord, survived a civil war, and endured military conflicts with several of the world's great empires—was absurd. To support their arguments, then, private-sector countersubversives pointed to the wave of industrial instability that followed the end of the war, blaming social discontent on radical activism and suggesting it was the first step on the path to revolution. Rather than seeing revolutionary politics as a symptom of a broader socioeconomic crisis, Bolshevism was depicted as the source. Confusing correlation with causation, countersubversives argued that radical machinations were creating the unstable conditions necessary for the seizure of power by coup and that only their repression would return America to normality.

In his classic account of the history of political repression, Murray Levin characterizes the Red Scare as the result of an "almost universal belief in the imminent destruction of American civilization by a highly organized, brilliantly directed, and well financed Bolshevik conspiracy in America, which, in fact, did not exist. . . . This national panic without real cause was political hysteria." It was certainly true that there was no powerful Bolshevik conspiracy in America: there was only Ludwig Martens and his Information Bureau and the disorganized membership of the Communist and Communist Labor Parties. But the suggestion that the fears of 1919 were without real cause and therefore hysterical runs the risk of imposing what E. P. Thompson famously called "the condescension of posterity" on the millions of Americans who supported countersubversive action in 1919 and early 1920. If the war years had decisively weakened independent radical organizations like the IWW, broader social and economic changes had strengthened the union movement and made its members far more militant. "Seen in this light," writes Robert Goldstein, "the red scare of 1919 was a very rational response on the part of government and business elites who accurately perceived that extremely serious threats to the status quo were developing."[4] So although it was wrong to lay social instability at the door of an international Bolshevik conspiracy, it was not absurd to believe that America was heading toward an unknown and uncertain future; it was a fact.

The war years had been a boom time for the American economy. Fueled by orders from wartime allies and the government's own military expenditure, economic output grew rapidly. From a mild depression in 1913–14, the gross national product rose 15 percent. In sectors directly affected by war production, the expansion was remarkable. Iron ore, copper, and zinc production nearly doubled. The nation exported around six million dollars of explosives in 1914; by 1917 it exported more than eight hundred millions worth.[5] Cotton fetched four times more on the open market in 1920 than it had in 1915, wheat three times more. Farmers mortgaged themselves to the hilt to increase the volume of land under cultivation.

Financing for this extraordinary economic explosion came from Allied war payments and loans and bonds arranged by the government. Gold flooded across the Atlantic, while the national debt of the United States shot up from around a billion dollars to more than twenty-six billion. With the combination of large deficits, rising demand, and a rapid expansion of the money supply, inflation began to spike. Whereas the annual rate was roughly 1 percent in 1914 and 1915, it rose to nearly 8 percent in 1916 and between 1917 and 1920 never fell below 15 percent. At its peak in November and December 1918, annualized rates were running at more than 20 percent. At no point in its subsequent history has inflation in the United States ever been as high as it was in the final months of World War I.

At the same time as manufacturing went into overdrive to fuel the insatiable demands of destruction, the government raised and trained an army of more than 4 million troops and sent half of them to Europe, removing them from productive occupations. Moreover, due to the disruption of war, immigration— the primary source of new workers, as the birthrate had been declining for decades—fell off rapidly.[6] So while inflationary pressures created the conditions for a classic wage-price spiral, the supply of labor was tighter than at any point in a half century. Even the decisive entry of 1 million new female workers into the economy could not alter the basic shift in relative power from capital to labor. Union membership grew from about 2.7 million in 1917 to more than

4 million by the end of the war. Feeling the pinch of rising prices, these new unionists were militant and assertive, determined to use their collective power to keep wages in parity with prices and to secure permanent rights to bargain collectively.

Ironically, this placed the national leadership of the AFL in a difficult position. After a decade of stagnation, union bosses were eager to use their growing influence to demonstrate the material benefits of solidarity. During the war, many union leaders had accepted weak pay settlements as a patriotic obligation. But many of their leaders had grown concerned over rank-and-file militancy and, having witnessed the assault on the IWW, feared that they might be smeared by employers' groups if they appeared too belligerent.[7] Equally, if they were not activist enough, then left-wing groups offering more radical proposals might steal their members away. Arguably, one of the central features of union policy making was an unstated fear among the leadership of the radical potential of their own rank and file.

AFL president Samuel Gompers, an implacable foe of what he called "socialist impossibilism," concluded that the best way both to achieve real benefits for his workers and to avoid accusations of disloyalty was by placing the federation at the forefront of the countersubversive movement.[8] Between founding the AFL in 1886 and dying in 1924, Gompers's strategy was nothing if not consistent: to whatever problem America faced, the solution was always unionism. During the Progressive Era, he had claimed that unions were "the only power capable of coping with and (if necessary) smashing the trusts." In the war years, the AFL became the surest guarantor that "the spirit and methods of democracy are maintained."[9] Now, in 1919, the best defense against radical insurgency was to be found in the American Federation of Labor. On the eve of departing for Europe to participate in an international labor conference that ran alongside the peace talks, Gompers announced that radicalism was "as great an attempt to disrupt the trade unions as it is to overturn the Government of the United States" and that only the loyalty and patriotism of American workers would ensure the threat was contained.[10]

Labor was on the march, but business was no less aggressive in its postwar ambitions. To organize the economic miracles of the war, the state had relied upon a series of planning boards and agencies to control output, distribution, and prices and to manage consumption of food and fuels: voluntaristic associations that paralleled the loyalty apparatus that had been set up in the Departments of Justice and War and through the CPI. The bankers, industrialists, and merchants who took leading roles in these agencies came to believe that business had won the war. When orders began to be cut back in 1919 and production was curtailed, employers were in no mood to listen to labor's complaints, believing that griping about pocketbooks showed an absence of national spirit. Owners of capital, from those in the upper middle class to the captains of industry, instead looked to roll back the union movement and reassert the authority of property in American life.

In short, the war polarized industrial relations. In 1919 there would be more than thirty-six hundred strikes involving 4 million workers, more than twice the number of 1917, which had itself been a bumper year. Although scholars have been quick to note that this created the conditions for widespread red-baiting against the union movement, it is important to note that moderate union leaders also used fears of radicalism for their own ends. Indeed, in a detailed recent study of the topic, Jennifer Luff comments that antiradicalism was "bred in the bones of the AFL." Rather than a straightforward case of antiradical employers fighting union activists standing up for civil liberties, strikes often became contests over competing prescriptions for managing the supposed subversive threat.[11]

For much of the twentieth century, Washington State, like New York City, was considered a notoriously "unreliable" place to live. Franklin Roosevelt's postmaster general James A. Farley once raised a toast at a dinner to "the American Union—47 States and the Soviet of Washington." In early 1919, the *New York Tribune* argued that "so far as there is any approval in the labor movement for Bolshevism, this demand is confined to the territory about New York City and to the territory between Butte, Mont., and Seattle in the Northwest." Seattle in particular was well known for its labor militancy. Some 60,000 of its 250,000 workers were organized. Most were class conscious, the IWW and socialists were a strong presence, and workers had decades of experience of labor conflict. Through this, strong horizontal ties of solidarity had developed between union locals—often transcending loyalties to the national AFL.[12] It was fitting, therefore, that the first battles of the Red Scare erupted here.

During the war, wage improvements ordered by the Shipbuilding Labor Adjustment Board for the 30,000 workers that manned Seattle's port were three times lower than the rate of inflation. After it became clear that the Metal Trades Association (the employers' organization) had no intention of readjusting wages to parity following the end of the war, a shipping strike was ordered, and in a spirit of solidarity delegates from a range of other locals joined the action.[13] Builders, teamsters, printers, service workers, cooks, painters, and many other groups stood with the stevedores. A General Strike Committee was hastily convened and on January 22, 1919, announced that from early February, the city of Seattle would shut down.

Links between the strikers and the Bolshevik movement were virtually nonexistent. However, many undoubtedly sympathized with the workers of Russia. Some, no doubt, had an unrealistic and romanticized image of Bolshevism, sought the withdrawal of American troops from Soviet territory, and had opposed the wartime loyalty campaigns. Raymond Robins, Louise Bryant, and Albert Rhys Williams were all invited by the city's Central Labor Council to speak on Russian politics, and port workers had attempted to interrupt arms shipments on their way to the White Army in Vladivostock.[14] No doubt, either, that some workers sought a revolution in America, and radical literature was certainly disseminated.[15] One radical activist, for instance, produced a pamphlet calling for the seizure of the shipyards entitled *Russia Did It,* and many locals believed the material was officially sanctioned by the strike committee.[16] None of this added up to a genuine danger, but it sufficed to raise fears among conservatives of what might develop if the strike was left unchallenged. As Corey Robin notes, even when reformers seek goals that are "minimal and discrete—better safety guards on factory machines, an end to marital rape—. . . they raise the specter of a more fundamental change in power."[17] So even without simmering Bolshevism, the risk to the establishment was real.

Countersubversive instincts were thus inflamed by the amorphous challenge to existing authorities rather than any demonstrable ties between Seattle's workers and Russian Bolshevism. In particular, the mayor, Ole Hanson, found himself facing a personal crisis as he began to lose control of the city. Arguably, the biggest challenge came when the labor committee announced it was planning to operate the utilities on its own. Turning on the strikers, Hanson declared that "anarchists in this community shall not rule its affairs" and threatened summary execution for anyone caught trying to assume municipal functions.[18] Employers and state officials began to label the strike as a planned first step on the road to revolution. Fearful residents started hoarding food supplies, gun shops sold out, and rumors started that the strikers were going to detonate the city's water-supply dam and shut off the electricity. Two battalions of soldiers and a company of machine gunners were summoned, and sandbag emplacements were set up on street corners. "As near as we are able to judge from this cismontane distance," the conservative *Chicago Daily Tribune* argued, "it is only a middling step from Petrograd to Seattle."[19]

In fact, far from bringing anarchy to the streets, the strike turned out to be surprisingly orderly. On the first day, the city ground to a halt. Streetcars were stopped, and restaurants, schools, newspaper presses, and theaters all closed. But between the troops and ad hoc "labor guards" set up by the General Strike Committee, civic order was preserved. This was primarily because both sides had a vested interest in avoiding violence and demonstrating their capacity to run the city. Some accounts claim that crime actually fell during the week or so the strike lasted.[20]

Lacking a clear sense of purpose and unwilling to embrace the politics of rebellion, the workers' front began to fall to pieces as soon as it became clear that no concessions were forthcoming and public opinion was turning against them. Hanson made it clear that soldiers would stay on the streets for as long as was necessary, and if needed ships would be diverted to San Francisco for unloading. The strikers, who had organized soup kitchens to feed their workers while the restaurants were closed, found it hard to get food supplies, as the effects of the shutdown began to turn back upon them.[21] Meanwhile, the AFL leadership, who were worried they would be attacked as Bolshevik if they showed any signs of support, threatened to withdraw affiliate status from unions who participated in the strike. The city administration got the streetcars running again, and the press and conservative civic groups began wildly praising the mayor for his tough line.

Symbolic attacks on foreign subversion were a central part of the effort to present the contest over political authority as a question of national security. Local congressman Royal Johnson pointed to "a grand array of Slovinskys and Ivan Kerenskys and names of that sort" among the participants in recent riots.[22] On February 11, several dozen immigrants were rounded up and sent to Ellis Island for deportation. These individuals appear to have had no links to the strike committee, but the press nevertheless described the "fifty-four Bolsheviki who are soon to be exposed to seasickness and their own reflections" as "collateral" in the war for Seattle.[23]

For all the glory of the days when the city rang quiet, the strike repeated the patterns shown elsewhere: in the campaign to defend Bolshevik Russia, for instance. In a nation with a powerful middle class, radical politics served to mobilize countersubversives far more effectively than it did the workers. The big winner in Seattle was Mayor Hanson, who emerged as the first of a series of celebrity antiradicals; for standing firm against the protest, he was soon touted as a potential presidential candidate. "A man of known, long and generous sympathy with all legitimate aims of labor," one reporter wrote, Hanson "was strong enough and brave enough to stand up against the insolent alien efforts to reproduce here the horrible disorders that have ruined Russia." Another reported, "On Mayor Hanson's desk at the City Hall stand great bouquets of flowers, gifts of Seattle citizens who are courageously behind his brand of Americanism."[24]

The wave of strikes in 1919 reflected a systemic confrontation between workers concerned about wages, conditions, respect, and union rights; employers determined to reassert their dominance over the production process; and politicians worried above all about their credibility. Ironically, they typically involved workers notionally affiliated with the supposedly "patriotic" AFL—not the "disloyal" IWW, which had been severely weakened by wartime prosecutions and whose leadership was still largely incarcerated. Nevertheless, accusations of radicalism and Bolshevism were used to divert public attention from questions of economics and industrial policy, while worker militancy made visions of dangerous instability seem plausible. Even when employers resisted the temptation to accuse workers of Bolshevism directly, many still called for efforts to resist "Bolshevistic" behavior. This kind of vague phraseology neatly sidestepped the question of whether militants actually had any relationship to Russia in favor of an implied affinity. In a kind of domestic domino theory, caving in to strikers came to be seen as the first step toward handing industry over to forces of disorder, destroying all forms of political authority, and giving the national economy up to foreign powers.

Indeed, questions of political authority *were* at stake in these conflicts, though it was by no means clear that an uncompromising stance was the best way to solve them. And distinguishing between widespread industrial violence and the opening stages of a revolution was easier said than done. Mexico, China, Iran, Germany, and much of Eastern Europe had experienced revolutions in the previous generation. The British Empire was struggling to contain an armed insurgency in Ireland. The *New Republic* presciently noted that even if the "basis of revolution" did not exist in America, there was certainly "the possibility of great disorder . . . Revolution there will not be, but a great deal of rioting there may be."[25] Misjudgments, exaggerations, and calculating misrepresentation, not hysteria, were therefore the discursive currency of the time. The fears that many people felt were, if misplaced, nevertheless very real.

By high summer, industrial unrest had reached the steel industry, one of the most consolidated and significant sectors of the economy. In the last year of the war, conditions for steelworkers had deteriorated badly. While they worked twelve-hour days, inflation forced upon them massive real-term pay cuts. AFL representatives had attempted to intercede, but Judge Elbert H. Gary, the intransigent chair of the board at U.S. Steel, refused even to meet with union representatives. Between August 1918 and the summer of 1919, AFL organizers led by John Fitzpatrick, head of the Chicago Federation of Labor, and William Z. Foster, a charismatic union leader who was a socialist and a former member of the IWW, signed up tens of thousands of disaffected workers in the steel towns of the North.[26] Caught up in the militant spirit, and aware that the momentum would be lost if the AFL could not deliver for its new members, Foster and Fitzpatrick ignored the instructions of the national leadership to resist striking and announced that workers would down tools on September 22. That day, 275,000 steelworkers walked out; within a week, another 90,000 had joined them. In just seven days, roughly 4 percent of the entire industrial workforce simply stopped working. If they had not been aware already, middle-class Americans now came to realize the scale of their dependence on people they had spent their lives trying to ignore.

As with Seattle, the relationship between worker militancy and the specter of Bolshevism proved critical to the outcome of the strike. Though the large numbers of foreign workers in the steel plants strengthened public fears of radical instability, the reputation of William Z. Foster quickly emerged as the central factor in the public debate, reducing a complex industrial conflict to a debate over a single man's loyalty. Foster's radical past was used as evidence that subversives were trying to capture the AFL—to "bore from within," as it was known at the time. Not only did this accusation help the corporations present themselves as patriotic bastions, but it also placed great pressure on the AFL leadership, who appeared to be unable to control their own members. U.S. Steel denounced the strike as inspired by Moscow, called Foster a Bolshevik, and declared that the workers were unassimilated, unpatriotic immigrants, unwilling to work as hard as honest American citizens. Soon, sporadic violence began to break out between strikers and company agents. Guards with firearms were stationed at plants, and thousands of local citizens were sworn in as temporary deputies. Union meetings were broken up by vigilante gangs and infiltrated by private detectives. One hired hand explained how his preferred method of deterring protest was to "grab a man's right arm" and then "bring down the blackjack across the hand bones or wrist." He boasted of thirty-five people in the local hospital "with broken wrists and hands" thanks to his efforts. Rabbi Stephen Wise, who attempted unsuccessfully to mediate the conflict in Duquesne, Pennsylvania, was informed by a town burgess that even "Jesus Christ couldn't hold a meeting in Duquesne." Meanwhile, unemployed African Americans were brought in as strikebreakers, and tensions quickly rose with the largely white strikers, adding an ugly racial element to an already simmering class conflict. When black workers were brought into a plant in Gary, Indiana, in front of picketing whites, rioting broke out. Indiana's governor, James P. Goodrich, sent in eleven companies of the National Guard to restore order, supported by three hundred deputies and five hundred special policemen. The next day, the strikers stormed the plants, and several were killed.[27]

In a sign of how militarized American life had become, it took a declaration of martial law to restore peace. General Leonard Wood—an old friend of Theodore Roosevelt, a former military governor of Cuba and governor-general of the Philippines, and in 1919 the commander of the armed forces in the central region—took strikers roughly in hand, emerging in the process as a second countersubversive hero alongside Seattle's Mayor Hanson. The army worked with employers to present the steel strike as part of a revolutionary conspiracy. Soldiers seized radical literature and released it to the press, suggesting that the violence had been preplanned by Bolshevik agents.[28] Wood's experience projecting power within the new American empire had accustomed him to repressing dissent in the name of civilization and order and had conditioned him to see subversion as a natural product of the emotional character of inferior races. In this sense, the industrial repression of 1919 represented the fruit of the American empire coming home.

At first, President Wilson tried to force the steel companies and union leaders into mediation. But as violence spread, the mood turned decisively against the unions, and the government—the only force capable of forcing the corporations to the table—retreated. Gompers was caught between his need to maintain solidarity with the locals and his knowledge that the steel-plant strikers were tainting the reputation of the entire federation. Following weeks of steel owners' obstructionism, Gompers finally walked out of national talks, keeping solidarity with the workers on the picket lines. But despite this, the strike failed. In early January 1920, more than three months after it began, with more than one hundred thousand still not returned to work, and more than twenty people killed in pitched battles, the strike was called off without a single concession won.[29]

The Great Steel Strike marked a decisive moment in the history of American industrial politics. The AFL's cause was set back a generation, with disastrous consequences for American workers and, ironically, weakening American efforts to fight radicalism. "In a cloud of feverish talk about Bolshevism," the *New Republic* pointed out, "a group of leading citizens professing to represent the practical, conservative, farsighted American business man, had aimed what was intended as a fatal blow at the one labor organization which throughout the world stands as the symbol of anti-Bolshevist labor."[30] In at least one case, the conflict helped turn the useful fiction of Bolshevik conspiracy into a reality. Although the AFL had stood by him, Foster abandoned his fragile faith in moderate unionism in the wake of the steel debacle and gravitated toward the pro-Bolshevik radicals emerging from the left wing of the Socialist Party, eventually becoming one of the two most important figures in the American communist movement. Gompers and his successors would never forgive what they saw as Foster's betrayal. For the next thirty years, each time countersubversives conducted investigations into the danger of revolution in America, the AFL would stand ready to provide evidence against the Bolsheviks, and Foster in particular.[31] For both Gompers and Foster, and for the labor movement more generally, the steel strike permanently sealed the division between reformists and revolutionaries that had opened up over the previous decade. Deeply divided, the Left effectively ceded political power to the Right for a generation.

Often, radicalism proved most shocking when it came not from expected sources like immigrants and steelworkers, but when it materialized among groups that symbolized nationalism and civic respectability. The idea that disorder could reach into even the most conservative parts of society seemed to reveal the scale of Bolshevism's corruptive force. This element of shock perhaps explains the reaction to the events in the state of Massachusetts in September, just as the Red Scare began to peak.

Police forces had been experiencing the effects of inflation as much as anyone during the war years. But as emergency workers tied to a no-strike rule, they had little power to negotiate for pay improvements. Since 1913 the standard wage for a first-year patrolman in Boston had risen by less than 20 percent, while the cost of living had risen more than 90 percent. Spending on the service was deteriorating, station houses were falling to pieces, police were expected to buy their own uniforms, junior staff were treated like errand boys, and many worked seventy-five-hour weeks. Many felt that the government was exploiting their loyalty in order to deny them the benefits that ordinary workers were able to obtain through industrial action. Seeing no other alternative, in August 1919 the Boston Police Department's officers organized themselves into a collective body and applied for affiliation with the AFL.

Police commissioner Edwin U. Curtis—a stern disciplinarian, unflinching conservative, and staunch believer in the chain of command—responded by amending the general orders, banning policemen from external affiliations, and placing the organizers on suspension. When, later in the month, the force threatened to walk out unless proceedings against their leaders were dismissed, Curtis called for public volunteers to be temporarily sworn in and threatened to sack everyone who struck. As Mayor Hanson had done at the beginning of the year, Curtis immediately depicted the dispute as a fundamental question of authority on which no compromise could be broached. Whereas Boston's mayor, Andrew J. Peters, spent the last weeks of August desperately trying to find a way through the impasse, Curtis seemingly relished the confrontation. But from the moment he decided to pursue an uncompromising line, patrolmen—conditioned to work in extremely dangerous situations by relying implicitly on their partners—had no honorable option but to follow through with their pledges to each other. The strike deadline came without concession from either side, and on Monday, September 8, Curtis convicted twenty-nine of his own men for violating orders and suspended them from duty. The overwhelming majority of the rest of the force walked out.

Whether the public sympathized with the striking officers or not, few were prepared to see their city unprotected. Amid overblown stories that criminals from across the country were descending upon Boston for a frenzy of looting and pillage, hundreds of members of the public signed up to join Curtis's temporary force, the first volunteer supposedly being a Harvard professor of physics. But the temporary replacements were scheduled to come on duty only the day after the strike began, so when a rock thrown through a window late on the first night set off a riot, no one was around to respond, and it swelled terrifyingly. Reports suggested that sailors from docked ships were involved in the violence, robberies, and destruction of property that followed, though it seems likely that much of the criminality was opportunistic. The next morning, the mayor surveyed the damage, called in the National Guard, and appealed to the state governor, Calvin Coolidge, for support. By late afternoon, the two had arranged for seven thousand federal troops to patrol the streets, the last of which would still be pulling shifts three months later. Coolidge assumed direct control of the police force and issued statements fully supporting Curtis. "There is no right to strike against the public safety," he told the press, "by anybody, anywhere, anytime."[32] Every single striking policeman was fired.

President Wilson offered his full-throated support to the governor. "When the police of a great city walk out and leave that city to be looted they have committed an intolerable crime against civilization," he declared in a public address, to "long and loud" applause.[33] Coolidge was swiftly elevated to the countersubversive pantheon alongside Hanson and Wood. His emphatic response dissuaded police forces in the rest of the country from attempting to follow Boston's lead. But in the effort to hire nearly a thousand new officers, the city government was forced to concede improvements in pay and conditions that went far beyond those originally called for. By treating the industrial dispute as a matter on which no compromise could be permitted, the price paid by the state ended up being far greater than a more moderate response based on understanding and negotiation would have been.

Combined with reports of collapsing European countries and the protracted dispute over the return of American troops, the wave of strikes convinced many Americans that a revolutionary moment was indeed shaking the world. In virtually every case, strikes had revealed little organized radical influence, whether from anarchists, communists, or members of the IWW.[34] Nevertheless, the national mood shifted. Violence began to generate violence, and the climate of fear and intimidation itself became evidence of crisis. No region of the country was free from unrest, as labor conflicts developed in the major cities of the East, the industrial zones of the Midwest, the mills of the South, on the loosely policed borderlands with Mexico, in the Pacific ports, and in the timberlands of the upper West. Groups on both sides of the political divide began to set themselves up as shock troops of social warfare, as the temporary divisions of the era began to be institutionalized in new associations, organizations, alliances, and corporate bodies.

Employers' groups began to systematize their previously ad hoc efforts to associate "Americanism" with antiunionism. After Seattle, West Coast employers' associations had begun collaborating in antiunion drives. Attempts to roll back wartime unionization in Texas saw a propaganda cartel emerge there as well. In the fall, the manufacturing corporations of the Midwest weighed in, as Judge Gary encouraged fellow employers to follow the steel companies' uncompromising approach toward worker militancy. The National Council for Industrial Defense solicited dozens of members to support U.S. Steel. Soon, hundreds of corporate associations, led by the powerful National Association of Manufacturers, began printing leaflets and magazines and lobbying their representatives to promote the "open shop" as the only alternative to revolutionary radicalism.[35] The open shop, it was argued in a neat piece of branding, was the "American plan."

Alongside the new business networks, the countersubversive movement was substantially strengthened by returning veterans. The American Legion was set up in 1919 in Paris by disgruntled officers fed up with being stuck in Europe while they read newspaper reports of Bolshevism running rampant in America. Within a year of its founding, the organization boasted more than a million members.[36] As a veterans' body, its chief concern in theory was the management of demobilization, especially obtaining jobs for returning soldiers. However, in its first national convention in St. Louis in May 1919, countersubversive politics immediately came to the fore. A radical soldiers and sailors council from Seattle was refused accreditation by the legion's coordinating committee, and a series of resolutions were quickly adopted calling for the deportation of radicals and slackers, the enforcement of "100 percent Americanism" (a phrase adopted as the legion's official motto in Minneapolis in November), and public campaigns to teach patriotism to America's children through a regimented deployment of baseball Little Leagues.[37]

The defining moment in the organization's early history came on the first anniversary of the end of the war, in the town of Centralia, Washington. Like much of the region, Centralia had experienced tensions between the IWW and local business groups for more than a generation, which had burst into violence on several previous occasions. In the weeks leading up to the Armistice Day celebrations, rumors spread that legionnaires were planning to use the occasion to drive the Wobblies out of town: a reprise of wartime "slacker raids." The organizers provocatively declared they would march straight past the local headquarters of the IWW.

According to veterans' testimony, on the day itself the head of the parade came to a halt in front of the IWW hall, marking time while the tail caught up. Moments after the procession halted, shots were fired at the marchers by marksmen stationed in four directions around the area. Most of the parade scattered, though some veterans charged the building, smashing the windows and battering down the doors. IWW accounts claimed the opposite, saying the parade halted as part of a predetermined plan to assault the IWW building, and shots were fired only afterward, in self-defense. Either way, four former servicemen—one having recently returned from the anti-Bolshevik expedition in Archangel—were left dead at the scene, shot by IWW gunmen.[38]

The local judicial system tried to respond to the perceived outrage: eleven Wobblies were put on trial, and in the spring of 1920 eight were convicted, each receiving sentences of at least twenty-five years. But this was not swift enough for many locals. On the night of the violence, the city's power was mysteriously switched off, and a lynch mob took one of the arrestees, Wesley Everest, from the local jail. Everest was beaten, castrated, and thrown from a bridge with a noose around his neck, three times, until the last throw finally killed him.

Legionnaires echoed the rhetoric of wartime vigilantism, presenting the lynching as the assertion of law and order rather than its abandonment. A telegram sent to the legion's second national convention, which was under way in Minneapolis at the time, read: "Civil authorities have situation well in hand. One man has been hanged. Sixteen in jail but no positive evidence of killing on their part. Government has ordered out Tacoma guard"—as if the lynching had simply been part of the judicial process. Meanwhile, surrounding cities began identifying radicals and driving them out of town. As far away as Oakland, legionnaires broke into radical meeting halls, wrecked property, and burned literature, while in Centralia itself a vigilante mob rounded up IWW members and ferried them to the city limits. For days afterward, reports were heard of bands of armed men roaming the countryside, hunting for fugitives.[39]

Despite coming to symbolize the distinctive chaos of 1919, the violence of the Centralia affair showed how countersubversive violence, however rage fueled, built upon long-standing fault lines in the localities, some of which had been developing for decades. So even while countersubversion had by the end of 1919 moved far beyond the systematic organizing influence of government, acts of even the most furious anger often contained within them a certain kind of ruthless social logic.

* * *

American Bolsheviks may have been small in number, but to countersubversives they could always be found at the center of trouble. Used interchangeably with "radicalism," "anarchism" and "IWWism," Bolshevism seemed to link the instability in Europe, the conflicts over U.S. foreign policy, the industrial warfare of the "red summer" of 1919, and the local violence of incidents such as the Centralia massacre. According to many countersubversives such as Archibald Stevenson, support for the Bolshevik Revolution was the thing that united these disparate affairs, and that support was considered prima facie evidence of conspiracy. The simple but utterly deceptive question of "cui bono?" allowed countersubversives to imply that Bolsheviks had planned everything. In fact, as Arthur Koestler later noted, both radicals and countersubversives were responding to the same unstable conditions. It was the sense of living through a moment of moral and social crisis that pushed countersubversives into action as much as it pressed communists into the party.[40]

Although historians usually argue that it was the bombing of his home in early June that convinced attorney general Palmer of the need for the federal government to return to the countersubversive fray, the palpable public hunger for action was a crucial precursor to his decision to act. Someone as personally ambitious as Palmer could hardly fail to note how countersubversive leaders were being feted as potential presidential candidates after taking uncompromising stands for law and order. Meanwhile, the nation's chief law enforcement officer was being attacked for doing nothing.

Thus, after six months of relative quiescence, the attorney general announced a major administrative reorganization in the summer of 1919 that signified the dramatic return of the federal government to countersubversive activism. He successfully appealed to Congress for a half-million-dollar emergency appropriation, raised the number of field officers to more than a thousand, and established a new General Intelligence Division within the bureau.[41] Commonly known as the Anti-Radical Division, the unit was put in the hands of a young, talented, and aggressive bureaucrat named J. Edgar Hoover, who—adopting practices that had developed in the context of industrial labor management—began assembling an enormous card index of suspected radicals. (Both the card index and the related "spiderweb chart," which was designed to map out interlocking relationships among radical groups, were tools used for organizational and labor management and reapplied to track radical politics more generally.)

The path chosen by the Justice Department was shaped by the contours of American law. The most significant federal legislative tool available for peacetime countersubversive action was the 1918 Immigration Act, which allowed for the deportation of members of revolutionary organizations if they were noncitizens. As a secondary benefit, it was believed that placing the action under the notional authority of the immigration authorities in the Department of Labor would allow the bureau to sidestep the slow and troubling practices of legal due process, since these would technically be deportation procedures, not arrests. The legal mechanism even influenced the selection of targets, since the immigration law made it pointless to arrest radicals who were citizens and therefore could not be deported. The Union of Russian Workers (URW)—which, as its name suggests, was largely populated by immigrants—and the new communist parties were identified as the best places to find revolutionary-minded individuals who were also aliens. In this sense, the implementation of laws that selectively targeted foreigners helped to cement the xenophobic presumptions that had underpinned their creation in the first place.

The Anti-Radical Division proceeded carefully at first, beginning with several months of preparatory investigations. Indeed, Hoover's microscopic gathering of evidence became a source of frustration. By October Palmer was being attacked in Congress and the press for vacillation.[42] Nevertheless, the planning was necessary to assemble a list of targets matching Palmer's and Hoover's ambitions. A nationwide plan was constructed, to be put into action on November 7, 1919—to coincide with the second anniversary of the Bolshevik Revolution.

Justice Department agents who had infiltrated the target organizations were instructed to get local groups to put on celebratory events so as to maximize the number of people at meeting halls. URW locations were then raided in at least a dozen cities, with hundreds arrested.

The raids were intended as dragnets rather than precision efforts to "decapitate" the URW's leadership. Palmer explained that "the individual agitators were so migratory in their habits and so cautious in their oral utterances that it was quite difficult, if not impossible, to pick them off one by one."[43] The implicit goal was to demonstrate the awesome power of the state and deter others from challenging it. But while the URW was indeed led by radicals, many of its members were struggling migrant workers more concerned with the daily challenge of survival in America than with engineering a revolution. Moreover, the bureau relied upon state and municipal forces and even private citizens to provide the manpower for the raids, and patrol officers, private detectives, and strikebreakers were used to using nightsticks first and asking questions later.[44] The raiders typically arrested everyone in sight. During raids in New York, several people were allegedly arrested and beaten up simply for passing along the street at the wrong time.[45]

The Russian People's House on New York's East Fifteenth Street was essentially a community center, built around several classrooms in which immigrants were taught English, math, auto repair, and other skills. When raiders broke into the building, teachers and pupils were arrested indiscriminately and many of them beaten savagely. According to accounts gathered by radicals after the fact, a fifty-year-old teacher, Mitchel Lavrowsky, was interrupted in the middle of an algebra class by agents who pointed a gun at his head, ordered him to remove his glasses, and then, when he did so, struck him over the head. Arrestees were forced to walk down a corridor lined with police, each hitting them with a club or a blackjack as they struggled to pass. Lavrowsky said he was attacked by three agents, thrown down a staircase as policemen beat him with wood from the banister as he fell past, and then ordered to clean up his own blood so that reporters waiting outside would not see what had happened.[46] The building was then taken to pieces—doors pulled off their hinges, desks ripped open, carpets pulled up, and furniture shredded—in a search for incriminating evidence.[47]

Of the hundreds of people seized in the raids, just under 250 were eventually processed for deportation—though debate immediately began as to whether this proved that they consciously endorsed a revolutionary agenda simply by being members of an organization with revolutionary clauses in its constitution. The rest walked free without charge. A cursory examination would have revealed that even many of the "hard core" were far from professional revolutionaries. But, in a canny piece of political spin, Hoover also ordered the rearrest of anarchists Emma Goldman and Alexander Berkman, whose opposition to the war effort and advocacy of revolutionary violence were known nationally. Goldman's and Berkman's names dominated the headlines as the government announced the mass deportation of arrested aliens, coloring the image of the other detainees. On December 21, to widespread public acclaim, the U.S.S. *Buford,* nicknamed the *Soviet Ark,* set sail from Ellis Island with the detainees aboard, destined for Europe.

During a second phase of raids in early January 1920 that targeted the two communist parties, between 3,000 and 5,000 people were arrested in an indiscriminate frenzy of violence in thirty-three cities spanning twenty-three states.[48] Raiders in New York cavorted before detainees wearing masks of Eugene Debs and Karl Marx. In a town in New Jersey, a group of immigrants was arrested after soliciting funds for the burial of a Polish friend. In Hartford, Connecticut, sixty-four workers were arrested for joining a cooperative designed to purchase an automobile. In Lynn, Massachusetts, thirty-four were arrested for trying to set up a bakery. Detroit's House of the Masses was having a ball on the night of January 2. The band was arrested, along with dancers and diners—as well as students attending a geography lesson elsewhere in the building.[49]

Federal investigators continued to rely on locals for implementation, and this produced great varieties in practice by region. Agents of the Lusk Committee, for instance, were heavily involved in operations in New York, coordinating 500 officers on raids of seventy-one locations associated with the Communist Party. But almost everywhere, police authorities and their volunteer allies assumed almost total impunity to act without due process of law. Because the prosecutions were considered immigration investigations, not judicial trials, people were arrested without evidence, held incommunicado, refused access to lawyers, and ordered to be deported without trial, that is, without—in the words of former Ellis Island immigration commissioner Frederick Howe—"as much of a trial as we accord to a common drunk in the police court."[50] One URW member arrested in Bridgeport, Connecticut—who insisted that he was not interested in politics—was held for twelve weeks without trial, regularly beaten, and kept in solitary confinement in a room next to a desperately hot boiler.[51] (Unfounded rumors quickly spread that this was a matter of design rather than neglect, and even that the police were periodically blasting steam into rooms as a method of torture.) When one immigrant came to a police station to visit one of the Hartford "automobile conspirators," he too was arrested and held secretly for a fortnight. He later claimed that Department of Justice officers had tied a rope around his neck and threatened to hang him if he did not sign a confession.[52] When the wife of one arrested immigrant, Alexander Bukowetsky, went with her two children to see her husband in jail and talked back to a jailer, she was knocked to the ground. When her husband tried to intervene to protect her, he was pistol-whipped.[53] Some of the accounts gathered by investigators after the fact may have been exaggerated by the victims; it is, however, almost impossible to believe that all of them were, and all revealed consistent patterns of brutality and disregard for the Constitution.

The police quickly discovered that one of the most immediate problems they faced was finding somewhere to house the detainees. Around half of those arrested in New England were sent to Deer Island, in Boston Harbor, where they were left without heating, blankets, or food. One inmate committed suicide, another went insane, and several contracted pneumonia.[54] In Detroit around 800 people were taken to a small federal building. Many were held in a windowless and airless corridor with no toilet facilities or food. More than 500 were held for more than a week, with 100 others transferred to a cellar in a second building measuring twenty-four by thirty feet. Those not supplied by relatives were given coffee and biscuits to live on.[55] Eventually, Detroit's mayor, James Couzens, intervened, calling the conditions a menace to public health. Four hundred and fifty detainees were then taken to a disused army fort, 120 were deported, and the rest were released for lack of evidence. Three months later, 384 were still awaiting decisions on their immigration status (of which around 240 were on bail and the rest still in the fort). Even a delegation from the Board of Commerce criticized the length of time the detainees were held without trial. Conditions were so miserable—poor food, cold cells, brutal treatment from guards—that, according to inmates, one person died and two others lost their minds. The arrestees banded together to write an open letter that was subsequently published in the press. "We stand ready to leave this country where we have met with nothing but terrorism," it read, "especially now when we expect to be sent to free Soviet Russia."[56]

Despite such defiance, though, the Palmer Raids were highly effective both in destroying the targeted organizations and in deterring others from challenging the authority of the state. As the bureau's director, William J. Flynn, declared to the press, the raids broke the "backbone of the radical movement in America."[57] The residue of the Communist Party was forced underground. Dues-paying membership fell below 3,000, and both it and the Communist Labor Party were riddled with government spies and informers. Riven, the American communist movement seemed to be dying in its infancy.

*   *   *

In much the way the clashes over Bolshevik Russia, the postwar industrial crisis, and the anarchist bombings reinvigorated the Department of Justice after its postwar inertia, they encouraged greater federal activism across the board, producing an interlocking set of countersubversive policies that would persist for a decade. At its center were three key components: refusal to recognize Soviet Russia, prohibition of alcohol, and strict quotas for immigration, all of which were sold to the public as measures to safeguard the nation from radical instability. Building on deeper trends stretching back into the Progressive Era, they reflected the tendency of politicians to respond to crisis by recommending policies they already supported. But in each case, countersubversive rhetoric provided the final push, helping turn preferences and traditions into law. As they had during the war, countersubversive fears offered a way of overcoming resistance to the expansion of federal power, whether that meant regulating social habits, strengthening the nation's borders, or sustaining an assertive and idealistic foreign policy.

Arguably, the most important element of this countersubversive settlement was the official nonrecognition policy adopted toward Bolshevik Russia, an embryonic containment doctrine suited to a prenatal Cold War. There were many reasons for America's enduring postwar hostility toward Russia: including geopolitical tensions, a lingering sense of betrayal following the Russians' early exit from the war, the absence of Anglo-Saxon-style electoral democracy, the nationalization of private property formerly owned by American investors, and Bolshevik attacks on organized religion.[58] At the policy level, however, nonrecognition was justified almost exclusively on countersubversive grounds, specifically in reference to the Bolsheviks' rhetorical commitment to world revolution and alleged sponsorship of radical groups in the United States.

This position was formally enshrined in the Colby Note of August 1920, named for Wilson's third and final secretary of state, Bainbridge Colby, but in part authored by the prowar socialist John Spargo. The "note," actually an open letter to the Italian ambassador in Washington, stated that the refusal to recognize the Bolshevik regime had "nothing to do with any political or social structure which the Russian people themselves may see fit to embrace." It was solely a product of the Bolshevik's revolutionary expansionism, a commitment that made them "determined and bound to conspire against our institutions."[59]

In making this case to the public, the Soviet Information Bureau proved to be crucial. Ludwig Martens had spent the early months of 1919 encouraging business groups to promote normalization, dropping hints that supporters might secure valuable concessions when trade resumed. Corporations that responded positively included all-American names such as General Electric, General Motors, Proctor & Gamble, and Ford. Even red-baiting U.S. Steel expressed an interest in doing business with Russia.[60] However, following the June raid on the bureau's headquarters, the Lusk Committee ordered Martens to hand over dispatches and cipher codes he used to communicate with Russia. Martens refused, claiming diplomatic privilege—which, without State Department accreditation, he did not have. This noncooperation was then cited as evidence of conspiracy and used as a pretext for a resolution of condemnation in the

Senate, put forward by New Hampshire senator George Higgins Moses. Sensing the direction events were traveling in, several American firms engaged in export negotiations began to distance themselves, denying they had anything to do with the bureau.[61]

An investigation into the bureau was launched by the Senate Foreign Relations Committee in early 1920. An attempt by Moses to parachute Archibald Stevenson in as counsel was halted when Senator William E. Borah threatened to resign the hearings if, as he put it, the Lusk Committee was transferred to the Senate, but little else went right for Martens.[62] Insisting that the Information Bureau had no subversive political agenda, he admitted having addressed revolutionary meetings but denied any aspirations for a Bolshevik regime in America. Although much of the case against him was tendentious, senators were able to point to the two letters sent by Lenin to American workers to suggest that the Bolsheviks had promoted revolutionary politics in the United States. They also quoted the American radical Gregory Weinstein, who addressed a meeting that Martens had attended in March, stating, "We come here to tell Comrade Martens that we intend to prepare to take over this great country, just as the working class has taken over Russia." Martens claimed, incorrectly, that Lenin's letters were both written before he had been appointed and added that he had no responsibility for what American communists said or did, even if they were addressing him. He also disavowed revolutionary statements written by Bukharin and disassociated himself from the Third International. "Revolution is going on everywhere without Russia and without any propaganda from Soviet Russia," he told the skeptical committee.[63]

The substance of Martens's defense was the same as John Reed's and Louise Bryant's: that Bolshevik calls for revolution were responses to an undeclared war waged against them by the Allied powers. Even if true, though, this was hardly helpful to Martens's cause, since it placed him in the position of unofficial ambassador to an enemy state. After issuing a negative report, the Senate turned him over to the Department of Labor for an immigration hearing, and as long-winded procedures for his deportation unfurled, Martens was ordered home by his superiors and the bureau was closed.

Thenceforth, the basis of nonrecognition did not substantively change under Warren Harding, Calvin Coolidge, or Herbert Hoover, preserved in large part by progressive-minded and legalistic Republicans who had supported Wilson's anti-Bolshevik agenda, such as Charles Evans Hughes, Frank B. Kellogg, and Hoover himself.[64] Thanks to their efforts, the United States would be the last major international power to recognize the Soviet state, holding out for sixteen years before establishing diplomatic relations.

Peter Filene has argued that nonrecognition was a policy that suited a decade characterized by parochial desires for "security, prosperity, and fun."[65] But in truth, it was an activist policy out of keeping with the deregulatory spirit of the twenties, a legacy of the triumphant countersubversive politics of 1919, and constantly challenged by the introspective tendencies of the twenties.

Nevertheless, this was far from an unqualified victory for Wilsonian crusading. The president believed that social revolution could be contained only if new multilateral institutions were created to promote global order and in late 1919 and early 1920 had spent much of his political capital and, in the face of severe illness, rapidly diminishing physical energy trying to link fears of subversion to his campaign for ratification of the League of Nations treaty. Time and again during his famous tour in the fall of 1919, Wilson argued that social unrest in the United States was the result of an unstable international environment. After comparing the Boston police strikers to soldiers who had deserted their posts before a battle, he suggested that there were "disciples of Lenin in our own midst," followers of "chaos, night and disorder," and he stressed the vulnerability of the United States to Bolshevism if it did not support the league.[66] "Do you honestly think, my fellow citizens, that none of that poison has got in the veins of this free people?" he asked. "Do you not know that the world is all now one single whispering gallery? Those antenna of the wireless telegraph are the symbols of our age. All the impulses of mankind are thrown out upon the air and reach to the ends of the earth." Technology had opened America to the dangers of the world. "And quietly upon steamships, silently under the cover of the postal service, with the tongue of the wireless and the tongue of the telegraph, all the suggestions of disorder are spread through the world." Wilson warned, "So long as the world is kept waiting for the answer to the question of the kind of peace we are going to have and what kind of guarantees are to be behind that peace, that poison will steadily spread, more and more rapidly, spread until it may be that even this beloved land of ours will be distracted and distorted by it."[67]

Wilson's behavior here paralleled Harry Truman's later decision to follow Senator Arthur Vandenberg's advice and "scare hell out of the American people" when lobbying Congress to support the Marshall Plan in 1947. The great difference, though, was that Truman's strategy worked. In Wilson's case, the president was squeezed between two powerful and conflicting alternatives, just as liberalism itself struggled to maintain its coherence in an atmosphere of growing political polarization.

The first, from a consolidating anti-interventionist movement, contended that an unstable Europe was not America's problem and that an unstable America was caused, not prevented, by Wilson's global crusading. California's Hiram Johnson argued that postwar strikes and domestic instability were a product of inflationary pressures stemming from Wilson's expansive foreign policy commitments.[68] Indeed, to Johnson it sometimes seemed that the president himself was a subversive influence. "Mr. Wilson intends, with his league of nations, to adopt a new government for the United States of America," he warned. "The choice is between Mr. Wilson's internationalism and Americanism."[69] The second alternative, coming from the conservative wing of the Republican Party under Senator Henry Cabot Lodge, also rejected Wilson's attempt to present the League of Nations as a countersubversive policy. Conservatives argued that the rise of Russian Bolshevism showed exactly why the United States should not be constrained by entangling multilateral alliances.

In the end, Wilsonians found it was easier to raise concerns about subversion than to control how people responded to them. Most people who feared Bolshevism in 1919 preferred either to retreat from the world or to enter it untrammeled by institutional constraints. America's countersubversive inclinations would not be enough to persuade its people to cede sovereignty to a supranational power. The argument that fighting Bolshevism required a commitment to liberal internationalism would have to wait more than two decades before receiving a second hearing.

Following in the wake of Palmer's wartime allegations against the Pennsylvania brewing industry and the xenophobic investigations of the Overman Committee, Prohibitionists also found success by denouncing their opponents as dangerous radicals. Temperance advocates argued that alcohol was drunk primarily by workers and immigrants, that anarchists tended to meet in German beer halls, and that inebriation promoted disorder, the fertile ground in which radical ideas grew. Speaking before the Nineteenth Convention of the Anti-Saloon League in early July 1919, Congressman Alben Barkley told assembled delegates, "I know nothing in the world that contributes more to ignorance and want than the liquor business. And I know of no institution in this country that will contribute so much to Bolshevism as the doctrines that are now being promulgated by those interested in the maintenance of the liquor business in the United States."[70]

Following the ratification of the Eighteenth Amendment in early 1919 and the passage of the Volstead Act in October, Prohibitionists were quick to claim their policies would inaugurate a new climate of order in America. The bishop of Harrisburg announced that because "anarchism and Bolshevism thrive where the discontented and evil-minded throng the liquor saloon, this amendment has been passed just in time to protect the nation." The bishop even suggested that had the czar done the same thing, "the great peril which stalks Russia would never have gone to such maddened successes, and a constitutional democracy of sober men would be in control."[71] Prohibitionists implied that their opponents were subversives for not respecting the law once it passed. Senator Wesley Livsey Jones of Washington called opponents of the Prohibition statutes "defiers of law; breeders of revolution; teachers of Bolshevism, un-Americanism and unpatriotism."[72] Echoing wartime complaints over the dangers of radical propaganda, in 1924 the Prohibition commissioner, Roy A. Haynes, argued that efforts to enforce the law were undermined by a cynical campaign that was "at once the most extensive and the most intensive the United States has ever known. . . . [Even t]he stage and the motion picture screen are turned to account. . . . Those who carry on extensive propaganda must have money," he said. "Many believe that a considerable part of it comes from foreign countries."[73]

These claims echoed accusations made against radicals elsewhere—that they were stirring up trouble among otherwise contented laborers and using subtle propaganda techniques to distract the American public from the truth—but were directed toward a novel end. As with the antiunion drive, scaremongering was based on the implicit conclusion that dissent was inherently subversive. As late as 1936, William D. Upshaw, the 1932 Prohibition Party candidate for president, was still arguing that it was his "honest conviction that if this nation falls in this generation or the next, or even the next, it will be ground to powder between the 'upper and nether millstones' of Communism and the Liquor Traffic." Not that there was any real connection between the two, he admitted. But "the seeds of poison—the seeds of destruction for humanity and civilization—are in both."[74]

The outstanding historian of American nativism John Higham called the immigration restriction bills that passed through Congress in the early 1920s "both the climax and the conclusion of an era of nationalistic legislation."[75] They were also the final triumph of the countersubversive politics that had emerged since World War I. They marked an abandonment of America's traditional commitment to open borders and a fulfillment of trends dating back at least to the 1880s. Establishing blanket racial quotas for immigration, the bills went beyond even the restrictive acts of the war years, which, at least in theory, had been aimed only at immigrants with proven revolutionary affiliations. As opponents had predicted, the association of immigrants and radicalism had within a matter of years strengthened opposition to immigration altogether. By 1920 even many reformist Americans were conceding that some form of control over America's borders was inevitable.

The Emergency Quota Act of 1921 originated in early 1919 as a bill to keep communists out of the country. In making the case for its passage, Madison Grant, eugenicist and author of *The Passing of the Great Race* (1916), argued, "When the Bolshevists in Russia are overthrown, which is only a question of time, there will be a great massacre of Jews and I suppose we will get the overflow unless we can stop it." The bill was defeated, but the Palmer Raids provided a fillip to the cause, and it was reintroduced in 1920. The chief sponsor was Congressman Albert Johnson, a violently anti-Semitic, intemperate nativist from Washington State who argued that European instability and violence were bringing to America a flood of "abnormally twisted," "unassimilable," "filthy," "un-American" Jewish refugees.[76] Johnson proposed a complete restriction on immigration that, under pressure from business-minded senators, was modified into a quota system that set immigration rates in proportion to the existing racial composition of the nation. Wilson, who had been fruitlessly fighting efforts to restrict immigration since his first term, vetoed the measure. But his successor quickly approved the law when it was sent through Congress for a second time in 1921. In 1924 its proscriptions were intensified in the National Origins Act, which limited the number of migrants to 164,000 annually. The principle of welcoming the tired, huddled masses of the world permanently ceased to be the foundation of American immigration policy.

In at least one way, the new restrictions on immigration were actually quite damaging to the countersubversive cause. Since the majority of people leaving postrevolutionary Russia were fleeing Bolshevism, not bringing it with them, many refugees would have been valuable assets to countersubversives had they been welcomed in the way Eastern Europeans and Cubans were during the Cold War. More than 1 million Russians left their homeland between November 1917 and March 1921, establishing anti-Bolshevik relief organizations, Orthodox churches in exile, and political action groups in more than fifty countries around the world.[77] The impact Breshkovskaya had during her tour, or the reception given to Alexander Kerensky, the prime minister of the Russian Provisional Government ousted by the Bolsheviks, during his visit in 1927—crowds coming to see him speak at New York's Century Theater were so large that in the crush to get through the door, a bronze candelabrum weighing five tons was torn from its stand—shows how a firsthand account of Bolshevik terror could dramatically influence public debate.[78] But immigration restriction (combined with the more prosaic issue of distance) helped ensure that only a few thousand refugees reached America in the 1920s, compared to more than 500,000 who went to Germany.[79] Only as extremism passed through Europe in the later 1930s and refugees were forced to travel ever farther in the search for sanctuary did the number of anti-Bolshevik exiles in America begin to reach significant levels.

In this sense, countersubversive policies were often internally contradictory. Countersubversive rhetoric was never straightforwardly owned by any one group, or directed toward any single clear or coherent end. Those who sought to exploit fears of radicalism to push the state in one direction would often find their rivals using similar arguments to opposite effect. John Spargo, who coauthored the Colby Note and was a virulent critic of the Communist Party, was also deeply opposed to many of the wartime restrictions imposed under the Espionage and Sedition Acts, while the midwestern senator George Norris supported immigration restriction despite speaking out against the wartime loyalty campaigns and the Palmer Raids.[80]

Despite this, both critics and supporters were inclined to see countersubversives as a singular army of "100 percent American" patriots marching in unison, not a series of querulous factions with divergent policy concerns, material interests, and personal objectives. The scale of the loyalty campaigns during the war, the violence of the Palmer Raids, and the crushing of the labor unions in 1919 had all helped consolidate this perception of triumphant unity. Black-and-white rhetoric tended to make people think there were only two sides of the political debate. As Congressman Jasper Napoleon Tincher of Kansas explained, "On the one side is beer, bolshevism, unassimilating settlements and perhaps many flags—on the other side is constitutional government; one flag, stars and stripes."[81] Subsequent years, however, would defy such assumption, as the concerted ranks of voters did not materialize. Instead, the kind of countersubversive politics that had achieved such success during the war and its immediate aftermath began a process of slow decomposition.

PART II

Professional Patriots

4

Divided Loyalties

Countersubversion in the 1920s

"Like a prairie-fire," attorney general A. Mitchell Palmer wrote in 1920, "the blaze of revolution" had swept across America. It had eaten "its way into the homes of the American workman, its sharp tongues of revolutionary heat were licking the alters of the churches, leaping into the belfry of the school bell, crawling into the sacred corners of American homes, seeking to replace marriage vows with libertine laws, burning up the foundations of society." The only solution had been to "tear out the radical seed" and sweep "the nation clean of such alien filth."[1]

The Palmer Raids of the winter of 1919–20 were the most draconian single instance of federal repression in the United States' peacetime history. Nothing in the McCarthy era can compare to the mass arrests and beatings, arbitrary incarcerations, and summary deportations that took place in dozens of cities across the nation. Capping off a year of industrial crisis, foreign insecurity, and political conflict, they helped solidify the divisions of the war years, institutionalizing them in an underground communist movement on one side and new patriotic organizations on the other. In the aftermath, it seemed as if a pall of conservatism had fallen across the nation. Over the next decade, America would witness a roughly 30 percent fall in union membership, a series of regressive tax cuts for the wealthy, conflict over the teaching of Darwin, the rise of the Ku Klux Klan to a national organization of some four or five million, widespread local harassment of radicals and civil rights activists, state-level laws against criminal syndicalism, and the executions of Italian anarchists Nicola Sacco and Bartolomeo Vanzetti on falsified charges of armed robbery and murder.[2] *Bolshevism* became a term of such widely used opprobrium that it was rendered almost meaningless. Catholics blamed divorce, birth control, and anticlericalism on Bolshevistic thinking. Protestant fundamentalists complained that communists had infiltrated the mainstream churches in order to press for social reform. Nativists and anti-Semites associated radicalism with unassimilated immigrants crowding into the Lower East Side of Manhattan. The Real Estate Owners' Association accused the New York state legislature's Lockwood Committee of being "Bolshevik all through" for advocating rent-reduction measures. During divorce proceedings, the wife of James A. Stillman, a former president of the National City Bank, said her husband was "abnormal" and "worse than a Bolshevik" in his "mania for making money." In a dispute among the organization's leadership, the founder of the Ku Klux Klan, William Simmonds, was accused of being "a leader of Bolshevik Klansmen betraying the movement." And, commenting upon an alarming rise in the consultation of psychics and mysticism, a reporter for the *New York Times* declared the Ouija board to be "the Bolshevik of the spirit realm, and her Soviet of Ghosts threatens to . . . lay in ashes the little Swiss republics of our certainties."[3]

Given the power of the repressive politics that took root between 1917 and 1920, it is therefore a surprising and problematic fact that, with the exception of the immigration laws of 1921 and 1924, the national Republican administrations of the 1920s saw no new countersubversive policies developed, while in many areas the state power accrued during Wilson's second term was rolled back. With hindsight, the Palmer Raids represented a high-water mark in federal countersubversion, not to be equaled for decades to come. Meanwhile, ambitious politicians who had established strong countersubversive records, figures such as Palmer and General Wood, had sought to ride the wave of popular countersubversive sentiment into power in 1920.[4] But quite against expectations, their reputations ended up condemning them to defeat.

Why the seeming power of countersubversion in 1919 and its apparent weakness only a year later? Was this a reflection of the "hysterical" or "paranoid" character of countersubversives, a demonstration of their fundamentally erratic and irrational natures? More likely, it revealed the degree to which the countersubversive impulse had, despite appearances, always been promoted by a multitude of different groupings with subtly diverging interests, which became increasingly clear. The slow collapse of countersubversion in the 1920s was a straightforwardly political phenomenon and principally a product of the peculiar structure of American party politics in the years before New Deal realignment. Rather than attitudes toward countersubversion dividing the two major parties, both Republicans and Democrats developed deep internal splits that sharply reduced the value of countersubversion as a political tool, moved the government away from activist positions, and sidelined countersubversive celebrities. As with the politics of slavery prior to Kansas-Nebraska, countersubversion turned out to operate in tension with the requirements of party loyalty.

For this reason, federal countersubversive politics was more or less stopped in its tracks.

Resistance to the politics of countersubversion was initiated by a small number of liberal-minded politicians, bureaucrats, and lawyers who for various reasons were well placed to challenge the actions of the Justice Department, beginning with assistant secretary of labor Louis F. Post, who because of his position was required to sign off on all the deportation cases resulting from the Palmer Raids. Suspicious of the tendency to wrap politics in the American flag, Post had long believed that loyalty to country if separated from a higher commitment to justice was "a despicable sentiment," one that translated only into loyalty to officeholders and a meaningless idolatry of the flag. "The patriotic pagan banishes principle from his patriotism," Post had declared as far back as 1903, "and substitutes brilliant bunting."[5] Examining the cases as they came before him, he personally vetoed around two thousand orders for deportation, releasing the vast majority of detainees without charge.[6] Anyone who denied understanding the revolutionary implications of Communist Party membership or who recanted and quit was immediately freed. Attacked by Palmer's defenders for making decisions endangering national security, Post released a book detailing the violations of the raids and condemning what he called the "deportations delirium."[7]

Meanwhile, reversing the trends of the Overman and Lusk hearings, both the House and the Senate launched investigations into the alleged "illegal practices" of the Department of Justice. Called to testify, the attorney general sought to neuter criticisms by presenting accusations of police brutality as unreliable complaints made by radical conspirators. "So far as I am concerned," Palmer told the subcommittee of the Senate Judiciary Committee, when a defendant "swears that he has been beaten up and brutally treated and manhandled . . . and the agent named comes here and files a sworn affidavit to the effect that he did not touch this man . . . I believe the agent. I have no difficulty about it whatever." However, in a virtuoso piece of cross-examination, Senator Thomas J. Walsh, an Irish Catholic from Montana, swept Palmer's arguments away, in the process making the attorney general himself look dangerously un-American. No doubt to Palmer's surprise, Walsh began by entirely conceding the argument about the untrustworthiness of the alien, thereby firmly placing himself on the side of law and order. "Anyone who has had experience with the criminal law realizes that nearly every fellow that is put in jail has some complaint to make about it," Walsh agreed. "That does not concern me at all." He would always believe a policeman over an unassimilated immigrant. Everyone could agree that communism was noxious and that aliens who preached revolution were unwelcome on America's shores, Walsh continued. The only real issue at stake in the Palmer Raids was of constitutionality. There were a series of clear violations of lawful practice by the bureau. The Department of Justice had assumed functions delegated to the Department of Labor. It had held both citizens and noncitizens incommunicado and denied them counsel. And it had conducted a series of searches and seizures of property in a manner expressly banned in the Bill of Rights. The Espionage Act permitted the Department of Justice to conduct search and seizure, but only when investigating crimes. The Palmer Raids were deportation cases in which no crime had been alleged, and therefore there was no justification for going through people's private property. Palmer had no real response to this, as he had explicitly instructed his agents to search for evidence of Communist Party membership during the raids and not signs of broader criminality. Ironically, then, the fact that these were immigration matters—a fact that had at first seemed to offer up such broad opportunities for rapid policing—ended up specifically limiting their rights to gather evidence.[8]

Walsh made great play of the fact that Justice was violating conservative statutes written by the founders to preserve the sanctity of the home and the supremacy of private property. In taking the stand after Palmer, prominent civil liberties lawyer and Harvard professor Zechariah Chafee pressed the point even more explicitly. Palmer had defended extended detentions as a necessary measure to avoid suspects absconding, but Chafee pointed out that any constitutional system was likely to restrict the easy functioning of justice. "It is simply a choice of whether you want the German or French system, the complete state scheme, or whether you want our system, which gives considerable leeway," he said. "To say that because you have a desirable purpose, you have the right to disregard the law, is a revolutionary attitude."[9] The insinuation that Palmer's actions had been revolutionary must have stung intensely. "There are signs of an overthrow of our Government as a free government," wrote assistant secretary Post. "It is going on under cover of a vigorous 'drive' against anarchists, an 'anarchist' being almost anybody who objects to government of the people by tories and for financial interests."[10]

Unlike Walsh, who offered no criticism of the laws that he had, as a member of the Judiciary Committee, had a hand in drafting, Chafee repeatedly criticized Supreme Court decisions upholding various prosecutions under the Espionage and Sedition Acts. In an influential article in the *Harvard Law Review,* he argued that even in times of war Congress was obliged to comply with both the letter and the spirit of the Constitution. One of the most damaging elements of the wartime laws, he said, was their tendency to enshrine the principle of "indirect causation"—the idea that because certain kinds of dissent may conceivably lead to problems down the line, it was better to deal with them preventatively—

"better to kill the serpent in the egg," as he put it—as this allowed the government to apply disproportionate aggression without evidence.[11]

For speaking out, Chafee quickly became a target of bureau surveillance. Anonymous claims were circulated that he was linked to the Communist Party, and conservatives tried to have him ousted from the Harvard Law School. A heated "trial at the Harvard Club," however, failed to provide any evidence to support claims that Chafee was a "Red." Jurisprudential integrity narrowly won the day—by a single vote—and Chafee retained his office.[12]

Beverly Gage rightly notes that Palmer's critics made a conscious effort to co-opt the language of Americanism for their own ends. Roger Baldwin of the ACLU noted, "We want to get a good lot of flags, talk a good deal about the Constitution and what our forefathers wanted to make of this country, and to show that we are really the folks that stand for the spirit of our institutions."[13] But the reversal of Americanism was not just a cynical strategy; it reflected the feelings of a broad mass of the public who remained committed to a vision of America free from the repressive political regimes characteristic of old Europe. While figures such as Post, Walsh, and Chafee had disproportionate influence because of their roles in national political life, similar arguments were rehearsed across the land during the spring and summer of 1920. Not solely the preserve of left-wingers and victims of attack, moderate businessmen, politicians, church leaders, and other members of "respectable" society expressed concerns about state heavy-handedness and popular vigilantism. Conservative satirist H. L. Mencken declared, "Between Wilson and his brigades of informers, spies, volunteer detectives, perjurers and complaisant judges, and the Prohibitionists and their messianic delusion, the liberty of the citizen has pretty well vanished in America. In two or three years, if the thing goes on, every third American will be a spy upon his fellow citizens."[14]

Liberals and conservatives alike argued that, with hindsight, radicalism was a menace to public order but not a threat to American democracy and that things had been blown out of proportion by politicians and demagogues seeking personal advancement. As an editorial in the New York World concluded, "In spite of the poses of the professional politicians and platform orators," there was no revolutionary challenge in the United States that "an ordinary capable police force cannot deal with." Any more than that, and the United States ran the risk of losing the freedoms that made the Republic exceptional. Bolsheviks and IWWs may be peculiar and unscrupulous, but "the American people are not fools and they have not gone crazy. They do not need a nurse to take them to work in the morning and bring them home at night lest they be corrupted by the seditious doctrines of soap box orators. They have a great deal more sense than the politicians who are worrying about the quality of their Americanism, and whenever they are put to the test they prove it."[15]

Despite such statements, many civil liberties critiques of Red Scare "hysteria" contained elitist themes, especially a belief that the repression of recent years had been driven by a Faustian alliance between unscrupulous demagogues and the irrational, narrow-minded middlebrow masses, neither having a proper understanding either of communism or of the American Constitution. Depictions of Palmer as radical, unstable, and irrational in his disregard for American traditions thus often betrayed a barely concealed intellectual contempt. In this, the civil liberties backlash traded on many feelings of respectability and civility that had in 1919 been used to fuel hostility to radical revolutionaries. In a book attacking business spies paid to infiltrate and disrupt union work, for instance, investigative journalist Sidney Howard declared, "This sort of thing is not quite credible in a country where the Anglo-Saxon tradition of fair-play and sportsmanship is supposed to cut at least some ice." A member of the Commission for Industrial Relations was quoted saying that covert countersubversive operations inevitably led to violence. "The union spy is not in the business to protect the community," he argued. "He has little respect for law, civil or moral." Explicitly linking businessmen to vigilantes and extremists, Howard remarked, "An extralegal force is a dangerous thing to have around. Mollie Maguires, Vigilantes, Ku Klux Klanners—we don't like them. We don't like detectives and it's a pity we've got used to them." Even the American Legion's Teddy Roosevelt Jr., the son of the former president, concluded that the expulsions of Socialist delegates from the New York assembly violated his sense of fair play.[16]

The backlash to the Palmer Raids thus solidified an image of an administration contemptuous of the law, which was ironic, considering that Palmer and his supporters had believed that their actions had precisely been designed to reestablish law and order after it had become degraded by radical insurgents. For generations to come, the Palmer Raids would stand as a symbol of the brutality and barbarism of American countersubversion, understood as a product of brute anger and a departure from normal, reasonable conduct. If Mitchell Palmer won his battle with radicals during the Great Red Scare, he decisively lost the war over historical memory.

The basic problem for any politician like Palmer who was seeking to red-bait his way into national office was that opposition was as likely to come from within one's party as without. Though reluctant to break with the leadership and consign themselves to an era of opposition, many northern, urban Democrats had opposed the intolerant drift of their party's leadership during Wilson's second term of office, and demographic shifts ensured that during the 1920s these forces gained increasing influence over party policy. Working-class Democrats supported Wilson for his reform record and endorsed immigration restriction measures that promised to reduce competition for jobs, but they saw how countersubversive smears had been used to attack even conservative unions. Catholics and recently naturalized voters often opposed Bolshevism instinctively, not least for its anticlericalism, but they strongly objected to being accused of disloyalty simply for not being Anglo-Saxon or Protestant. With some justice, they considered Prohibition to be an attack not on radicalism but on their own way of life. Many—especially German Americans—had been burned by the wartime loyalty campaigns and were determined to ensure that their party no longer had a hand in such illiberal measures.

These groups gathered around New York's Democratic governor, Al Smith, who emerged as perhaps the most vocal opponent of government authoritarianism in the state. Smith overruled the Lusk-influenced state legislature and returned to office the five expelled Socialist delegates.[17] As a descendant of Irish, Italian, and German immigrants, Smith instinctively objected to the blanket characterization of immigrants as disloyal and was deeply suspicious of efforts to determine who immigrants should or should not choose to represent them. Despite being "unutterably opposed to the fundamental principles of the Socialist Party," Smith found it "inconceivable that a minority party, duly constituted and legally organized, should be deprived of its right to expression." When Lusk affiliates successfully pushed through state laws establishing teacher loyalty oaths, student patriotic education programs, and measures to "Americanize" immigrants, the governor vetoed them all, calling them "repugnant to the fundamentals of American democracy."[18] Smith was defeated by conservatives in 1920, and his replacement signed the Lusk bills into law, but he was reelected two years later only to revoke them once more. More or less single-handedly, Al Smith ensured that the Lusk Committee would leave no legacy in the pages of American law. (Meanwhile, a story emerged that Lusk had accepted silverware from law enforcement officials, and—choosing not to run for reelection—the former chairman of the New York Committee on Seditious Activities departed ignominiously from public life.)

As the primary campaigns heated up, Smith made it clear that his supporters in the North would under no circumstances tolerate attorney general Palmer's candidacy for the presidency. Indeed, the *New York Times* concluded as early as mid-January 1920 that Palmer had "offended permanently a large element of the labor class."[19] The attorney general's national reputation kept the possibility alive that he might overcome such resistance, and the Pennsylvanian found to his surprise that he was welcomed as a hero in the South. However, he was written off soon after the Michigan primary in April, where a combination of anti-Prohibition and prolabor opposition propelled him into last place on the ballot.[20] Abandoning Palmer, the party selected instead an unimpressive candidate for the presidency, James M. Cox, who offered a limp middle position on the League of Nations, a prolabor record, and no direct links to either Prohibition or countersubversive activism. The fact that he was pretty much unelectable seemed only a minor consideration when compared to his lack of offensiveness to both northern and southern Democrats.

Basically, the same political dynamic would isolate countersubversives in the Democratic Party for the rest of the decade. In 1924 William Gibbs McAdoo, Wilson's anointed successor, was blocked by the Smith wing of the party following corruption allegations and because of his reputation as a supporter of the Ku Klux Klan.[21] A compromise candidate, John W. Davis, was chosen after a record-breaking 103 ballots at the 1924 convention, satisfying virtually no one. The disastrous running of Davis helped Al Smith earn the party nomination in 1928, becoming the first Catholic ever to do so, but he was promptly defeated in a wave of antiwet, anti-Catholic hostility.

On each occasion, countersubversive politics divided Democrats from each other and aided their political rivals. Thus, when Franklin Roosevelt contested the election of 1932, he cast himself as a Democratic reformer in the Wilson tradition but carefully straddled the party, appealing to Smith Democrats yet making sure he was still palatable to southern voters. Northerners were able to see him as part of the historic shift of the Democracy northward, yet southerners were able to vote for a Protestant blue blood of unimpeachable loyalty. Northerners voted for the governor of New York, southerners for an "adopted son of Georgia."[22] As he set about securing the nomination, then, virtually the only unambiguous thing about Roosevelt was that he said nothing about the politics of countersubversion—a topic that could be guaranteed only to cause problems.

If the Democrats were hopelessly split in the twenties, Republican countersubversives also struggled to align their political priorities with party interest. Several candidates for the Republican nomination in 1920 sought credit for attacking Bolshevism, though General Wood excelled his rivals in pugnacity, suggesting that one should deal with the red flag "as you would a rattlesnake, and smash those who follow it, speak for it or support it."[23] Courting nativists, Wood assailed "the alien vote" in the big cities for voting for "the agitator and faker."[24] Although "good Americans are glad that America has been . . . the refuge of the oppressed of all lands," he argued, the nation must not become "the dumping ground for the degenerates of other lands."[25] To cement his reputation as a battling countersubversive, he even ostentatiously suspended his campaign to return to his regional military command and put down a wave of strikes. Yet Wood's approach inflamed a powerful minority of Republican progressives, especially in the Midwest and West: often anti-immigrant and often antiurban, but also deeply hostile to federal power and the kind of military adventurism represented by Wood, the hero of the Spanish-American War. Reprising his dissenting role during the loyalty campaigns, Red Scare, and League of Nations fight, Hiram Johnson emerged as the principal leader of this anti-Wood faction, attracting independent and Democrat voters as well as disaffected Republicans during the primaries on a carefully crafted platform of "Americanism, freedom of speech, and justice with law and order."[26] Johnson declared that the "recent exercise of autocratic power must be made forever impossible" and expressed his contempt for "the patrioteer who wraps himself in the American flag and hides a mass of ugly sores behind that banner." Turning the language of liberty against the rhetoric of loyalty, he said he believed in law and order as much as the next man, but "the trouble with some people for law and order is that they want a law of their own making and then will order us to obey it." Ultimately, he said, "Americanism means the Constitution of the United States, preservation of the Republic, a government by all the people, and not by a few selected gentlemen living or doing business in a narrow street in New York City."[27]

For many Republicans, hostility to socialism and communism was part of a broader objection to the centralization of power away from local communities and the individual. The Wilson administration's efforts to create a secret police force, the deceptive campaigns to drag the nation into war in Europe, their willingness to nationalize utilities and regulate the free market, and postwar efforts to bind the United States into a permanent supranational League of Nations were, in this view, all an abandonment of American traditions in favor of the statist politics of Europe. George Lockwood, editor of the *National Republican,* declared that the people were "weary of government by fear. . . . They are tired of being called 'pro-Germans' and 'disloyalists' if they fail to accept without shadow of question whatever is handed down from high places as the law and the gospel . . . tired of being bullied and threatened into doing things their judgment does not approve." To Lockwood, the chaos of revolutionary Russia and the authoritarianism of the Wilson administration both reflected a tendency to set group against group and to place the state above the individual, a view that left him ironically more comfortable with the vigilante than the bureaucrat. "Patriots must meet the challenge of lawlessness," Lockwood declared, both on the streets and in government. "Americanism means a classless, casteless republic," in which "all the variant strains of European race and tongue" were brought together in "loyalty to one nation and one flag." However, it also meant the restoration "of the three independent and coordinate branches of government established in the American Constitution. It means an end to executive dictatorship, real or attempted," and "the abandonment of all the schemes of politicalized industry, of state socialism, of either the Prussianized or Russianized scheme of the exaggerated state, under which citizenship is only a form of slavery to government."[28]

These small-town views contrasted in many ways with the metropolitan values that drove people like Smith or Chafee. Both sides, however, rejected the foundational equation of nationalism and countersubversion that underpinned the Palmer Raids. Like Johnson, Lockwood argued that loyalty politics had ceased to be about the national interest and was being put forth instead by "private groups and classes and elements engaged in swishing clubs around the ears of the people." Neither elite civil liberties activism nor populist antiauthoritarianism precluded xenophobia, chauvinism, nativism, or even hostility to radicals. Indeed, the success of the effort to roll back the Red Scare in part resulted from the fact that they were able to turn the language and symbolism of Americanism to their own ends. But what activists in both parties did share was a profound commitment to what they understood to be the real meaning of American liberty.

This antiauthoritarian mood was strong in a party built upon free-labor ideology, independent smallholding farmers, and self-reliant communities suspicious of a distant federal government, and sometimes extended to foreign as well as domestic affairs. Johnson allied himself with former head of the Red Cross in Russia Raymond Robins to challenge Wilson's Russian policy, while other anti-interventionist Republicans rallied around him. Borah, who believed that isolating Russia was the surest way to push it into an alliance with Germany, declared that Russians had as much right to a Soviet government as Americans had to a republican one, while Norris complained that American troops had been sent to die on the Russian steppes for no better reason than "because our Government says that the Russians have not set up a government there according to our liking."[29]

In the race for the party nomination in 1920, Johnson and Wood effectively found themselves contesting the memory of Theodore Roosevelt, who had at times been both reform minded and jingoistic. Commentators noted that if General Wood's campaign could "hold the main part of the Progressive wing of the party, the old Roosevelt men, against the efforts of Johnson," then he could overpower his conservative opponents and "his nomination would become almost a foregone conclusion."[30] But Johnson showed strongly in the Midwest, and Wood turned to smear tactics in frustration, complaining that "radical elements" were "trying to get into the Republican Party . . . trying to bore from within, so to speak, to break the organization up, to make it the vehicle of radicalism."[31]

As with the Democrats, then, countersubversive rhetoric divided the Republican Party internally rather than establishing a clear distinction between them and their opponents. In the lead-up to the Republican National Convention in Chicago in the summer, one senior senator announced that the dispute over the nomination had soured the entire party's image. "Let us wipe the slate clean of declared candidates for the nomination and pick somebody else who will measure up to the Presidential standard," he said in frustration.[32]

Between them, Johnson and Wood divided the Roosevelt legacy: Johnson speaking softly, as it were, and Wood wielding the big stick. After four ballots at the Chicago convention, the Californian's support began to collapse, but he had taken enough delegates to ensure that Wood lacked the strength to eliminate the third-place candidate, Frank Lowden. Without a knockout blow, the nomination was effectively handed to the party's establishment. After much wrangling behind the scenes, the reliable but undistinguished senator Warren G. Harding was awarded the nomination, despite having run a terrible primary campaign and having said virtually nothing about radicalism. "It was agreed," the press reported, "that he had few enemies, that he was entirely acceptable to the conservative element in the Senate and the party, and that he was liked by the Progressives."[33] Johnson, "sorer than a boiled owl," flirted with running a breakaway movement, but in the end party loyalty trumped ideology and he campaigned, albeit in curmudgeonly fashion, for Harding.[34]

To those who expected the countersubversive mood of 1919 to inaugurate a new era of state-sponsored reaction, the elimination of virtually all the major countersubversives during the 1920 primaries was nothing short of remarkable. Conservatism was in the ascendancy, but countersubversion was nowhere. At the end of a fiery campaign full of clear policy differences emerging from three highly eventful years, both parties had ended up with bland candidates from the second tier of national life, while the political careers of the major countersubversive celebrities were effectively over. After the election, Wood became governor-general of the Philippines, a role he occupied until his death in 1927. And although Palmer struggled on through a series of heart attacks until 1936, the first in 1922 already postdated his political demise.

During the election proper, Massachusetts' governor, Calvin Coolidge, was selected as Harding's running mate, and the pair denounced radicalism in speeches during the campaign. But their rhetoric was starkly muted in comparison to Palmer's or Wood's. The lesson had been learned: countersubversive campaigning would expose fissures in the major parties that could potentially lead to defeat. Harding downplayed the threat of revolution in America, was quoted saying that too much had been said about Bolshevism, and campaigned instead for a return to "normalcy"—an idea that was widely credited for his landslide victory but hardly presaged Palmer-style campaigns to come. Combined with a temporary calming in the industrial and economic climate, this change in tone led to a rapid moderation of the public debate in the later months of 1920.

The rapidity of countersubversion's disappearance from federal politics seemed to justify liberal arguments that the whole thing had been a product of national hysteria in the first place. In truth, though, it was the divided loyalties of ideology and party affiliation that made countersubversive politics a poor issue on which to contest the presidential election and the distractions of the democratic process that helped the country move on from its postwar fearfulness.

* * *

The balance of political forces that had sidelined countersubversives during the election campaign only accelerated during Harding's incomplete term of office, setting in train a series of events that would over the next decade ultimately lead to the dismantling of the antiradical settlement itself. At the center of this process were the midwestern and western politicians who had supported Hiram Johnson in 1920 in his fight against Leonard Wood. This loose grouping comprised longtime senatorial mavericks such as Idaho's William E. Borah, Nebraska's George Norris, and Wisconsin's Robert "Fighting Bob" La Follette, alongside more recent arrivals such as Iowa's Smith Wildman Brookhart and, following La Follette's death in 1925, his son and successor, Robert "Young Bob" La Follette Jr. Mocked by Senator Moses as "sons of the wild jackass," they generally expressed a rural, Protestant reformism quite distinctive to the urban liberalism of northern Democrats. Drawing support from farms and small towns far from the great conurbations of the East, they supported immigration restriction and denounced life in the cities as hopelessly corrupted, but supported social reforms they felt accorded with republican ideals of fair play and individual autonomy.[35] That this was a product of regional culture as much as political affiliation—in the words of one contemporary, "the neighborly, nationalistic, agricultural and bumptious feeling of the West against the cliff-dwelling, international, industrial and city-slicker complex of the East"—was reflected in the fact that the Republican insurgents often cooperated with the two Democratic senators from Montana, Thomas J. Walsh and Burton K. Wheeler.[36] Walsh had shown his civil liberties credentials in his attacks on Palmer in the Senate. Never afraid to defy the party line, Wheeler had been state attorney general in Montana during the war and had attained both national prominence and his Senate seat by refusing to prosecute a single IWW member under the loyalty codes.[37]

Considering themselves the true inheritors of the progressive mantle, this group saw the greatness of the United States as lying outside the international system: a shining city upon a hill uncorrupted by tyrannical European-style government. They argued that reform at home depended on the demilitarization of American life, and that meant the United States should stop sending its troops to sort out other people's problems. Republican insurgents thus combined campaigns to normalize relations with Russia with fights against corruption and regressive taxation at home. To their critics, this was indistinguishable from Bolshevism, and as a result they emerged as a primary target of red-baiting in the 1920s.

The progressive insurgents were a minority in the Republican Party, but their ability to frustrate the leadership's agenda became clear when they led campaigns on Capitol Hill to investigate corrupt practices under the Harding administration. La Follette, Borah, and Walsh were instrumental in uncovering the huge bribes that secretary of the interior Albert Fall had accepted in exchange for opening the naval oil reserves at Teapot Dome and Elk Hills to private corporations, a revelation that effectively paralyzed the Harding administration in the year before the president's death in 1923. During the investigations, the progressives also uncovered evidence that Harding's attorney general, Harry M. Daugherty, had instructed the Bureau of Investigation to run cover for the administration, even sending plainclothes detectives to raid senatorial offices in a search for incriminating evidence.[38] (As with the Watergate scandal a half century later, the underhand effort to fight accusations against the administration proved to be as damaging as the crimes themselves.) This seemed to confirm their prior belief that the federal investigatory apparatus had been turned to corrupt purposes.

New Senate hearings into secret bureau activities were duly launched, chaired by Brookhart and largely driven by Wheeler.[39] Never a stickler for precision, Wheeler's revelations were largely based on the dubious testimony of individuals formerly affiliated with the Harding administration, including Gaston Bullock Means, a senior agent at the bureau, and Roxie Stinson, the divorced wife of one of the members of Harding's inner circle. Means's testimony was particularly problematic: on trial at the time for various Prohibition violations, he clearly hoped that acting as a friendly witness might delay his indictment.[40] He held forth with abandon, lifting the lid on the seamy politics of the bureau and the blurred borders between the public and private sectors, interspersing scandalous revelations with even more scandalous falsehoods.[41] By mid-March 1924, however, Wheeler had thrown sufficient mud at the bureau's reputation that the new president, Calvin Coolidge, was forced to sack Daugherty. With the now discredited Bureau of Investigation under intense scrutiny, Daugherty's replacement, Harlan Fiske Stone, swiftly began dismantling the machinery of domestic surveillance that had been built up during the war.

Daugherty was outraged, aware of the exaggerations and lies in the case against him. Convinced that progressive attacks stemmed from his hard-line views on Russia and his willingness to use federal force to put down strikes, he concluded he had been the victim of a Bolshevik conspiracy.[42] When Gaston Means failed to escape prison, he disavowed his previous statements and told

Daugherty that in fact he and Wheeler had conspired to smear Daugherty. This, he explained, was part of a larger plan to bring down the Harding administration in order to strengthen the case for the normalization of relations with Russia.[43] Daugherty attacked Wheeler as part of "the plans, purposes, and hellish design of the Communist International" and "the chief representative of Soviet Russia on the floor of the Senate." "Wheeler is no more a Democrat than Stalin, his comrade, in Moscow," he said.[44]

Insurgent activism under Harding and Coolidge thus contributed to a curtailment of Justice Department powers, as well as a growing sense among counter-subversives that they were under attack. After a period of remarkable growth between 1917 and 1920, between 1920 and 1923 the number of bureau employees halved, to around six hundred, and following the dismissal of Daugherty the number continued to fall, while its budget was fixed at two million dollars annually. The bureau was increasingly seen as a shadowy bureaucracy populated with unscrupulous criminals and private-sector detectives on the make rather than an institution protecting American liberty; it was not the Department of Justice but the Department of Easy Virtue.[45] When questioned during the Daugherty investigation, J. Edgar Hoover was asked directly if he was going to "get rid of those professional double-crossing detectives" employed by the bureau. "Most positively," he was forced to reply.[46]

The resulting retrenchment effectively halted ongoing investigations into the Communist Party and other revolutionary groups. The last federal raid on the Communist Party came in 1922, at a national party convention in Bridgman, Michigan. It was not an inspiring experience. Operating once more under strict constitutional restraints, the bureau relied on local forces for the legwork and used state laws to prosecute arrested radicals. This then generated a protracted battle over who was to bear the cost of the operation, the state or federal government. Attempts to prosecute Communist leaders, among them the disaffected steel strike leader William Z. Foster, dragged on for the rest of the decade without a single delegate imprisoned and were eventually called off for lack of money. By August 1924, there was not a single member of the bureau formally investigating radical activities in the United States.[47]

In 1924, with a hopelessly divided Democratic Party and a Republican Party dominated by Coolidge conservatives, the progressive insurgents opted to launch a third-party campaign for the presidency: the first breakaway movement since Roosevelt's Bull Moosers. The aged lion of the Senate, Robert La Follette, was nominated as the candidate of the new Progressive Party, and, following his prominent role in the Harding scandals, Democrat Burton K. Wheeler was offered the vice presidential candidacy. This, the organizers hoped, would attract reformers from both parties and help to realign national politics on more strictly ideological lines.

When accepting the nomination, La Follette drew a direct line from the Palmer Raids to the Teapot Dome scandals, claiming that they were both a product of the baleful influence of businesses and trusts on American political life.[48] He explicitly disavowed the support of the Communist Party or any organization with which it was associated and pointed to stalwart countersubversive supporters such as Sam Gompers to prove the point.[49] But conservatives, bitter over his defection from the Republican Party, accused him of flirting with Bolshevism anyway, likening his political maneuver to a coup d'état and declaring La Follette's stated anti-Bolshevism to be "as funny as the celebrated pot remarking about the complexion of the equally celebrated kettle."[50] The intemperate vice presidential candidate on Coolidge's ticket, Charles C. Dawes, assailed La Follette as a "leader of a mob of extreme radicals of which the largest part, the Socialists, fly the red flag."[51] Drawing insinuations by inference, a typical editorial in the *Los Angeles Times* claimed that since "La Follette and Wheeler stand for the immediate recognition of the bloody dictatorship of the Bolsheviki," a vote for them amounted to "a vote of commendation for communism."[52] Republican editorialists claimed that La Follette had instructed his subversive minions in the GOP to "bore from within," with the goal of "revolutionizing the principles of these parties while retaining their names," and alleged that the "Soviet lovers" in America were quitting William Z. Foster to "Boost 'Bob.'"[53] Meanwhile, the Republican National Committee released documents drawing attention to Senator Wheeler's "unpatriotic" war record, claiming that his refusal to prosecute radicals had turned Montana into a "hotbed of sedition and treason," mitigated only by "decent patriotic Americans" in Butte who took the law into their own hands by whitecapping a local radical and driving the rest out of town.[54]

President Coolidge was not much of a booster. "One of the most important accomplishments of my administration," he remarked in 1929, "has been minding my own business." His natural tendency for gloomy understatement can be seen by his quite astonishingly muted reaction to the death of Lenin in January 1924. "I don't think I have anything especially to say, other than what would occur to anybody," he told a press conference. Lenin "cast a good deal of influence over the destinies of Russia for a considerable length of time and it would be very unbecoming of anyone in the Government of the United States to undertake to make any criticism of a man in his position having passed away."[55] But even the resolutely gray-toned "Silent Cal" was unable to resist the temptation to smear the progressives with Bolshevism, and he now made it clear that the question for voters to consider was "whether America will allow itself to be degraded into a communistic or socialistic state or whether it will remain American."[56]

In part because of such maneuvers, most progressive Republicans stayed loyal to their party, and the breakaway movement took as much support from Democrats as the incumbents. Coolidge was reelected by a landslide, and the insurgents returned to the Republican fold.[57] In this sense, red-baiting worked. Nevertheless, Republican countersubversive energies had again been directed toward disciplining members of their own party rather than attacking the Democrats. The first instance of explicitly anticommunist political campaigning during a national election thus set an unappealing precedent.

Looking back on the 1924 election, many Republican loyalists came to believe that the third-party campaign had been the hidden motive behind the progressives' investigations into the Harding administration from the beginning. Stories began to circulate of a contorted plot inspired by Moscow: first to break the Harding administration, second to disable the Bureau of Investigation, and then finally bring to power reform progressives who would swiftly recognize Moscow. Among conservatives and party loyalists, resentment toward the party's progressives thus persisted despite Coolidge's reelection. Even a decade later, one prominent countersubversive claimed that "the investigating force for subversive activities [had been] abandoned through Communist machinations in 1924."[58] Another, writing in the *Army and Navy Journal*, attacked the entire Teapot Dome affair as a Red plot. "There was no scandal. No one sought to rob the government. . . . What these elements seek is to so intimidate government officials that such officials dare not move to check the purposes of Communism."[59]

Daugherty, meanwhile, continued to paint himself as a martyr, "the first public official that was thrown to the wolves by orders of the Red borers of America."[60] This suited not only his carefully nursed sense of victimhood, but fitted into a wider conservative tendency to assume that anyone who favored political reform and the normalization of relations with Russia must secretly be a Russian agent.

This Manichaean assumption was so widespread in the twenties and beyond that it is worth dwelling on briefly. It was variously expressed in biblical terms, as in Revelations 3:16: "So, because you are lukewarm—neither hot nor cold—I am about to spit you out of my mouth"; philosophically, in the contention that a compromise between a true statement and a false statement was logically false; but most often through countersubversive vernacular. Noncommunists who sought similar goals to Bolsheviks but denounced Bolshevism, or people who defended radicals' right to participate in politics, were dismissed as "dupes," doing the Communist Party's bidding without knowing it, or agents, secretly "boring from within" to co-opt established institutions and turn them to communist purposes. As one countersubversive, R. M. Whitney, put it, such figures were "conscious or unconscious tools of the Communist party, helping in the cause of world revolution, brushing aside the question as to the willingness with which the tools might accept such a designation."[61]

In this way, the language of countersubversion consistently obscured meaningful differences between groups who believed the recognition of Soviet Russia was in the best interest of the United States and those who were seeking it in order to promote Soviet interests. This meant that there could be no compromise with communism, that cooperation was indistinguishable from surrender, and that there was no real difference between a communist and someone who associated or worked with communists.

*   *   *

A nation dominated by conservative ideas, recently having passed through an unprecedented Red Scare, and run by a party of business: one might consider these circumstances to be perfect material for a continuing politics of countersubversion. Yet the 1920s saw only occasional examples of red-baiting at the federal level and the emergence of no figures comparable to A. Mitchell Palmer or Joseph McCarthy. While both parties had substantial constituencies who enthusiastically supported measures to combat radical influence, there was no clear political motor for federally sponsored countersubversion when ideological differences clashed so intensely with partisan allegiance. With a cautious political leadership and a constrained Justice Department, efforts in the rest of the decade to defend or advance the countersubversive agenda would thus be left to private-sector activists. And without federal support, they proved to be troubling defenders of the nation.

In May 1920, Harry Chase Brearley, a leading member of the National Board of Fire Underwriters—"for fifty years a civilizing force"—addressed a carefully selected group of influential public figures attending a lunchtime meeting sponsored by the New York–based National Civic Federation. As his principal host, Ralph Montgomery Easley, had just explained to his audience, Brearley was the man who had organized 125,000 fire insurance agents to support the loyalty campaigns during the war. His subject today was to be what he humbly called "the Brearley Plan."

Ruefully aware that countersubversive politics was on the wane, Brearley lamented the passing of "the national spirit of the public good which was so conspicuous and inspiring a feature of war-time patriotism." By mid-1918, he said, "we had pretty well passed through the flag-waving and band-playing stage of our patriotism and had settled down to such definite systematic and closely organized work" that America had come to fight as "a single, vast, unified organism of almost unmeasurable strength." The key to fighting today's enemies lay in regenerating this wartime unity. If Americans could be pulled together as they were during the war, "Presto! There is an organized nation."

"Most antiradical efforts," Brearley explained, "have started out with the thought that new organizations are needed. This is not the case. The organizations already in existence are ample and efficient. They possess all the necessary machinery, all the necessary brains, and all the necessary patriotism; they need only to be awakened and set to work, when they will operate with an efficiency not to be expected of any new organization." A national federation would enable local groups to act as agents both of lateral "communication," sharing information and influencing policies in Washington, and of local "application," using specific local expertise to combat the Red Menace in the areas they knew intimately. "Thus," he concluded, "no committee would be dependent upon the success of any other but all would contribute directly to the general result and collaterally to each others' morale."[62]

In short, like most other countersubversives in the 1920s, Brearley considered the voluntarist model of political action that had been adopted by the Wilson administration during the war to be the truly American way of keeping society secure: balancing the nation's historic commitment to limited government with the security needs of a modern society. Rather than strictly representing a "Brearley Plan," his intuitive logic was widely shared, and many countersubversive groups sought to construct exactly these kinds of networks of communication and application in the 1920s, through civic meetings, publicity campaigns, and correspondence with like-minded individuals across the nation. They also tended to overlook the degree to which the state had been the central part of these alliances during the war and overstated their ability to conduct effective intelligence operations on their own.

One of the most significant examples was the organization hosting Brearley's lunchtime meeting, the National Civic Federation (NCF). The NCF had been created in Chicago as an industrial relations arbitration body at the turn of the century, then extended to a national scale under Easley's energetic and somewhat manic leadership. At first, it was dedicated to the principle that capital's and labor's interests could be reconciled through negotiation rather than confrontation. Samuel Gompers held a vice presidential position, and John Mitchell of the United Mine Workers of America (UMWA) had been head of the Trade Department, while leading Republican senator Mark Hanna took an active role in promoting its causes among businessmen and industrialists.[63]

The NCF, then, was a thoroughly progressive organ. At its peak of influence, it helped arbitrate disputes in coal, steel, iron, and many other industries. Easley claimed to have helped settle more than a hundred strikes.[64] Things started changing during the later years of Theodore Roosevelt's presidency, as radical critiques of progressivism emerged from the left wing of the labor movement, on the one hand, and as the state began to take a more interventionist role in the politics of labor, on the other, rendering the federation comparatively redundant. While Gompers and other conservative members of the AFL remained loyal to Easley, the more radical-minded UMWA insisted that Mitchell resign his post, accusing the NCF of being an employers' body hiding behind a thin coat of paternalism.

During the First World War, the federation followed other business-minded, prowar progressives in a nationalistic direction, becoming increasingly consumed with questions of loyalty and subversion. Easley and Gompers co-organized a prowar "American Alliance for Labor and Democracy" that was supported by the Committee on Public Information and worked closely with the National Security League.[65] The NCF cooperated with government agents seeking to uncover German espionage activities and developed close ties with William J. Burns of the notoriously unscrupulous Burns detective agency (Burns was later director of the Bureau of Investigation and J. Edgar Hoover's direct boss under Harding).[66] After the war, the federation established itself as a preeminent countersubversive organization, working with both the Overman and the Lusk Committees. Easley set up a Department for the Study of Revolutionary Movements to lobby for nonrecognition of Soviet Russia. By the mid-1920s, he was calling for peacetime restrictions of the mails, the outlawing of communism, and "the use of machine guns if necessary" to put down revolutionary threats.[67]

At the center of the NCF's administrative apparatus lay Easley and his intemperate wife, Gertrude Beeks Easley. The two had fallen in love as Easley's enormous handlebar mustache tickled the pages of shared municipal reform projects in the Progressive Era; they were married in the midst of the Red Scare and worked closely together on countersubversive schemes in the twenties. Providing them with legal advice was the former counsel to the Lusk Committee and perennial red-hunter Archibald E. Stevenson.[68] And despite continuing accusations from liberals and socialists that it was nothing but a vehicle for big businessmen, leaders from the AFL—Gompers until his death in 1924, then AFL vice president Matthew Woll, who became acting president of the NCF and a member of its executive committee—continued to be involved in the organization's operations.

As the Brearley Plan implied, the NCF worked laterally with similar institutions elsewhere in America, sharing information and contacts with dozens of local groups ranging from employers' bodies, veterans' organizations, and fraternal and civic societies to individual countersubversives, most of them focusing their attentions on a specific region where their influence was concentrated.[69] Easley even contributed to the costs of funding the prosecution of radicals following the troubled Bridgman Raid.[70]

Among Easley's regular correspondents was Father Edmund A. Walsh, S.J., vice president of Georgetown University and founder of its School of Foreign Service. Steve Rosswurm suggests that the Jesuit order was a particularly fecund location for the growth of countersubversive thinking because of its intensely gender-segregated and competitive organizational structures that tended to reinforce already strong Catholic commitments to established social norms on the family, authority, and social discipline and led them to distinguish emphatically between ordered liberty and "license."[71] Walsh established himself as arguably the foremost expert on revolutionary Russia in the American branch of the Catholic Church, after spending much of 1922 and 1923 as a papal envoy on a Vatican mission to famine-wracked Russia.[72] Although the mission was ostensibly to aid starving Russians, Walsh became caught up in efforts to defend church property from Bolshevik expropriations and protect Petrograd archbishop Jan Cieplak and his clergy from attack. Both efforts failed: the churches were taken, and Cieplak was arrested for sedition and executed. As his biographer notes, Walsh returned to the United States with "ample experience to supply him with material for writing and lecturing for the rest of his life."[73]

Also in Washington was Walter S. Steele, editor of the *National Republic* and head of the influential American Coalition of Patriotic Societies. Steele was, for decades, routinely one of the first countersubversives called to testify before congressional investigations into subversion. Meanwhile, in California, Easley communicated with the Better America Federation (BAF), an organization set up by Eli P. Clark, a real estate millionaire, and Harry E. Haldeman, head of the Pacific Pipe and Supply Company, using residual networks of wartime Liberty Bond salesmen as union informants. More reactionary than Easley, the BAF argued that the founding fathers had created a republic, not a democracy; that there should be strict limits on the right to vote; that Mussolini was the best thing to happen to Europe; and that Easley went too far in working with the AFL. In a 1920 membership drive reminiscent of the wartime CPI campaigns, the BAF paid for advertisements at cinemas and sent committees to give speeches in every precinct of the city highlighting the supposed dangers of radicalism.[74] Later in the decade, they fought efforts to unionize city teachers and pressed the Los Angeles Police Department into creating an countersubversive Red Squad that would attain national notoriety for its brutality and corruption.[75]

A similar organization, the American Vigilant Intelligence Association, ran out of Chicago under the leadership of a dedicated countersubversive named Harry A. Jung. Jung had also begun in antiunion work, conducted by his National Clay Products Industries Association. He offered small stipends to around six hundred individuals to inform on fellow workers, paid for in turn by the thousands of fearful business owners who took out subscriptions to Jung's newsletter to find out more about the threats supposedly coursing through their workforce.[76]

Easley also tapped into countersubversive women's groups, particularly the Daughters of the American Revolution (DAR). Following the passage of the

Nineteenth Amendment, the women's movement had fragmented: on the Left, "social feminists" argued that newly attained voting power should be used to promote what they considered to be a specifically feminine set of policy reforms, such as child labor laws; and on the Right, groups argued that women should vote along the same (meaning conservative) patterns as men. This faction increasingly came to attack their erstwhile allies on the left as Bolsheviks, and the DAR became their home.

This network was numerically comparatively small, but, just as Brearley claimed, its influence reached widely: into the media, the churches, federal and state politics, labor unions, and the remains of the countersubversive apparatus in the State Department, Treasury, and Department of Justice. More problematic than their limited size, though, was their lack of coordination and their clear political bias. To an outsider, it was hard not to conclude that such groups were more concerned with protecting the class interests of businessmen, employers, and conservative union members than with preserving the nation's security. Instead of building their arguments and actions on material gathered and condensed for them by the Department of Justice or military intelligence, they fell back upon their own, limited, investigative capacities and their local concerns and priorities.

Certainly, those looking to discredit countersubversives in the 1920s did not have far to look. Reformists ridiculed figures like Fred R. Marvin, the self-styled "senator from Alaska" who published a countersubversive newsletter, *Searchlight*, as well as writing for the *Los Angeles Times*.[77] Marvin claimed Bolshevism was a "world-wide conspiracy to overthrow governments, confiscate property, abolish Christianity and wreck civilization" that had inherited its mission from the Order of the Illuminati. Communist transmission belts in America, Marvin claimed, included socialist and labor organizations, the ACLU, the *Nation*, and the *New Republic*. Such was Bolshevism's influence, Marvin argued, that it had even infiltrated the Ku Klux Klan. Many of the crimes committed by Klansmen, he explained, come "from Communists within the movement."[78] The flip side to Harry Brearley's optimistic belief that a decentralized associational network would build upon each other's successes now became clear. As any one group was exposed to public ridicule, the whole network was tarnished.

In fact, the Klan was arguably one of only two organizations in the 1920s that seemed, in the absence of meaningful state sponsorship, genuinely capable of building an effective national countersubversive politics from below. The other was the American Legion. Both were large grassroots bodies that appeared at first glance to be perfect vehicles for crusading countersubversion, but in the end both ended up alternatively condemned for extremism and ridiculed for hysteria. Despite their extensive differences—and in many regions an intense mutual hostility—both organizations provided shock troops to throw unionists and radicals out of town. In some places, the Klan recruited former members of the wartime American Protective League for precisely this purpose.[79] But Klan militancy was typically focused on enforcing social conformity, beating up adulterous husbands, or wrecking bootleggers' stills, while virulent racism in the South and anti-Catholicism in the North made it repellent to counter-subversives who were wedded more closely to the nation's liberal tradition. In short, the Klan had none of the coherence, discipline, or intellectual capital that could be provided by a modern state bureaucracy or political party. Even more important, the organization's finances were fissiparous, dependent on high-volume but low-value financial donations, functioning more like a vicious pyramid scheme than the fascistic mass movement it has often been described as. Despite its influence in the mid-1920s, it almost ceased to exist by the end of the decade when American budgets became strained.[80] Thus, despite its often brutal impact in various regions, above all in the South, the Klan had little real impact on countersubversive policies at the national level.

The American Legion was a more disciplined operation, developing a professional, centralized structure of information sharing with local offices relaying information on suspicious radicals to a nationwide clearinghouse and a well-connected national lobby with strong contacts among national politicians. Its leadership was also less singularly focused on monetary reward and its membership more diverse than the Klan. Cemented by the unity forged in conflict, the American Legion carved for itself an identity of broadly Anglo-Saxon, conservative, probusiness values: a commitment to democracy but not necessarily the Bill of Rights, a desire to sustain the racial status quo, and militarism tempered by memories of the destruction of war.[81] Whereas many politicians quickly gave up on red-baiting as it began to lose its political value, legionnaires sustained their criticism of figures such as secretary of labor Louis F. Post and campaigned to keep Eugene Debs and other prominent radicals in prison. Long after the Red Scare disappeared from the national headlines, legionnaires faithfully manned their posts and sent reports to their superiors on suspicious activities across the country.

The enthusiasm with which they went about this task varied from place to place. In some areas, countersubversive activity was more or less absent; in others, the American Legion operated as a virtual vigilante organization. Following the Centralia affair, legionnaires formed a military wing in California that patrolled radical locations, assaulted protesters, and harassed union organizers.[82] Moderating over time, many legionnaires found ways of combating radical activities that did not require directly infringing the law: particularly by using their influence to close off access to public venues. The arrival of designated subversive elements in unsuspecting communities would be publicized through the American Legion News Service so that impromptu groups of veterans could assemble and disrupt meetings and gatherings or persuade owners to rescind their invitations to speak. In such a way, it became extremely hard for left-wingers and socialists to gain hearings for their arguments.

While the resources that funded many other countersubversive organizations dried up under the economic squeeze at the end of the decade, the American Legion's campaign for jobs for a million veterans actually saw its numbers grow in the early Depression years.[83] This kind of resilience would guarantee the legion a central role in the countersubversive matrix for a half century: the best exemplar of the power of the voluntarist model of antiradical countersubversion. But even the organization struggled to sustain a coherent countersubversive agenda. While American Legion leaders could get their members to engage in demonstrative Fourth of July celebrations and other patriotic rituals asserting members' "100 percent Americanism," by the end of the decade the bonus and the repeal of Prohibition were arguably higher on the average legionnaire's list of political priorities than new laws for fighting Reds.

Together these were the "professional patriots": a national network of antiradicals that, in the absence of government, was the most significant force sustaining countersubversive politics in the 1920s, yet became the single biggest reason for its discredit by the end of the decade. They were a perfect demonstration of the traditional American belief that local people were the most adept at ordering their society. But over time, their activities increasingly came to resemble a class-based pastiche of true nationalism.

Liberals and leftists responded to them with hostility and ridicule. The *New Republic* concluded that the war's legacy had made it "possible to make a fat living by frightening rich old women." According to investigative journalist Sidney Howard, who wrote a series of exposés of the professional patriots in the mid-1920s, the forces of what he called the "American Fascisti" fell into three camps: "The bulk of them are merely fools. Some of them remain common and hopeful opportunists who trust to fate that something will always turn up to make them seem valuable. But the kernel of organized patriotism has very definite fish to fry for very recognizable appetites." Ralph Easley and his kind, he argued, were driven by "prejudice and class interest," serving "individual powerful business interests and policies." The *New Republic* agreed that countersubversives *had* to be either selfish or paranoid, since there was so little radicalism left to repress. "Militancy in the labor movement has declined; the radical political movements do not arouse fear. Insurgency of any sort is at a minimum." State criminal syndicalism laws and the Espionage Act remained in force. Fifteen hundred people were still in prison for loyalty violations. "The professional patriot," in short, "continues his activities primarily because he gets a fat living out of them. His credulous victims pay him handsomely for his tales of red bugaboos; he can lecture at large fees to audiences which would not hear him at any price on any other subject."[84]

Socialist Norman Thomas called them the "lunatic fringe of Rotarian America," some "honest neurasthenics," others selfish entrepreneurs who "get an easy living by preying on the fears of moneyed morons." As a whole, Thomas felt, "these professional patriots from the almost forgotten Archie Stevenson down to Fred Marvin are more exasperating than successful." Still, their existence was evidence "of an underlying movement toward imperialism." "Fortunately, these gentry are going to such lengths that they are likely to defeat themselves," Thomas concluded. "Their accepted technique would prove that the Pope is a heretic because he has shaken hands with Protestants."[85] Thomas was right: through their failures, antiradicals would ultimately come to expose the limits of the traditional ideal of self-governing liberty to which they claimed such close affiliation.

5

Red Herrings

Anti-Bolshevism, Smearing, and Forgery

In the immediate aftermath of the October Revolution, expansion abroad had seemed to be both a rhetorical commitment and a strategic priority for the Bolshevik movement. The seizure of power in Russia was the first stage in a global revolution that would witness the end of warring nationalities and a global peace forged through an interconnected series of proletarian revolutions. To this end, in March 1919 the Bolsheviks established the Third, or Communist, International, as a tool for coordinating the activities of vanguard revolutionary parties throughout the world.

This seemed to be a practical necessity as much as an ideological commitment, for Russia had only a tiny urban proletariat and relatively small manufacturing base and was vulnerable to capitalist invasion. As Eric Hobsbawm notes, Lenin knew well that "the conditions for a socialist revolution were simply not present in Russia. For Marxist revolutionaries in Russia, their revolution had to spread elsewhere."[1] With several neighboring states witnessing widespread social insurrection, it seemed for a while that revolution might indeed spread. Once the initial period of euphoria had ended, though, it became clear that the Bolsheviks would have to compromise their ambitions or risk losing power altogether. Not only did the capitalist nations of Western Europe recover from the destruction of the war, but they were augmented by new reactionary movements whose anti-Bolshevism was more visceral than traditional conservatism. Hopes that the Bolsheviks might promote revolution by the sword receded after the Red Army became bogged down during conflict with Poland, while the immensely destructive civil war and subsequent famine of 1921 confirmed that Russia was at most a languishing giant. Facing almost complete economic collapse, Lenin announced a New Economic Policy (NEP), retreating from the fundamentalist war communism promoted by Trotsky and allowing small businesses and farmers to conduct a degree of private business. Efforts were accelerated to foster trade with capitalist nations on straightforward, commercial terms.

Until Lenin's death in 1924, then, the Communist commitment to worldwide revolution coexisted uneasily with the need to solidify power in Russia. In these years, American communism became tightly entwined with the Comintern apparatus but paradoxically more moderate and participatory in outlook.[2] The Comintern pressed the Communist and Communist Labor Parties to unite and to legalize their operations as the Red Scare faded.[3] Officials denounced radical hopes of revolution in America as "infantile leftism" and instead stressed the need to build public support for Soviet Russia and develop influence in the labor movement. Efforts were made to renew economic diplomacy following the enforced departure of Ludwig Martens and closure of the Bolshevik Information Bureau.[4] In 1923 some trading and informal diplomatic links were reestablished through the American branch of the All-Russia Co-operative Society, or Arcos: a Soviet trade bureau based in Britain. The following year, a more coordinated effort began with the creation of the American Trading Organization, known as Amtorg. Amtorg, effectively the successor to the Martens bureau, would become the single most visible target of countersubversive attacks in the twenties.

After Lenin's demise, Russian politics took further precedence over global revolution. Trotsky, the most internationally minded of the Bolshevik leadership, was sidelined, as Nikolai Bukharin and Josef Stalin combined to defend the NEP and promote "socialism in one country." This approach, inaugurating the so-called second period in the history of the Communist International, culminated in 1928 with the defeat and exile of Trotsky and the purging of his supporters from both the Russian Communist Party and the Comintern apparatus around the world. In the United States, Trotskyites affiliated with leaders James P. Cannon, Max Shachtman, and Martin Abern were expelled from the party and went on to form the breakaway Communist League of America (Left Opposition).[5] But after 1928, the situation reversed again, as Stalin turned on his former ally, Bukharin, and assumed absolute control over the party. Stalin declared that a new "third period" had arisen. With the final collapse of capitalism on the horizon, the movement needed to return to the purist revolutionary principles of traditional Bolshevism: absolute state ownership in Russia, revolutionary struggle in the rest of the world, and no compromise with progressives. As Stalin assumed near-total control over the party apparatus, Russia inaugurated a Five-Year Plan of accelerated industrialization and forced agricultural collectivization that would eventually lead to famine in the Ukraine and the death of millions. The American party embarked upon a radical phase of nonparticipation that would last until 1935, in which putative allies on the Left were denounced as "social fascists." Individuals affiliated with Bukharin—

most significantly the party secretary, Jay Lovestone, and former Communist vice presidential candidate Benjamin Gitlow—were expelled, as the Trotsky-ites had been before them. They and a few hundred others combined to form the Communist Party (Majority Group), while Stalinists consolidated around William Z. Foster, who rose in the party ranks in no small part because of his loyalty to Stalin.[6] Stalinists viciously attacked Lovestone's supporters as traitors to the cause, "renegades," "defeatists," and "opportunists."[7] By threatening the integrity of the party, they argued, "splittists" represented a greater menace to the revolution than enemies without. In this way, once close friends and com-rades were transformed into specters of fascism. In its intolerance for dissent, the party matched, mirrored, and sometimes even exceeded the worst habits of its persecutors.[8]

The Comintern had comparatively little difficulty in persuading locals to bend to its will. Many critics have concluded from this that the Communist Party of America was simply a "foreign" organization, even though many of the key players in the 1920s and 1930s were born-and-bred Americans, such as the Massachusetts-born Foster, or Earl Browder, a Kansan who would emerge as the dominant force in the party in the New Deal era. In truth, utopian vi-sions of Russia as the homeland of revolution combined with radical domestic traditions in ways that were impossible to unpick. Nevertheless, each successful purge effectively strengthened the bond with Russia, since those with dissenting minds were expelled while loyalists and careerists were promoted. Meanwhile, the international apparatus provided crucial intellectual and practical support to American Communists. It operated as a court of arbitration, a venue of last resort in the case of irreconcilable differences between factions. And until 1929 at least, the persistence of dissent within the Soviet hierarchy preserved at least the illusion of free and open debate. Divisions in the United States could be superimposed on Russian politics to give the impression that American Com-munists participated actively in defining their own destiny.

American Communists became habituated to the idea that unity was a vital source of strength, that discipline did not limit individual freedom but was in fact essential to it.[9] Critics have often noted that the Leninist model of "demo-cratic centralism" turned out to be long on centralism and short on democracy, but many Communists were willing to overlook this because they recognized the reductive limits of bourgeois individualism and believed the Comintern was privy to a deeper understanding of the process of revolution. A single person bobbed aimlessly on the tide of history, subject to personal whims and foibles; the Comintern represented the combined knowledge of revolutionary scholars from across the world, reading and interpreting the words of Marx: a grand Marxian ulama. As Italian Communist Antonio Gramsci put it, "By subjecting oneself voluntarily to discipline, one becomes independent and free. Water is pure, free and itself when it is running between the two banks of a stream or a river, not when it is messily spread on the ground, or when it is released, rarefied, into the atmosphere."[10]

Indeed, there was an element of truth in this. In a climate of continuous persecution, discipline was the only alternative to destruction. To this end, the American branch of the party embarked upon a sweeping Bolshevization campaign, setting in place a party hierarchy structured on Leninist lines.[11] A Central Executive Committee provided a locus of power, and local groups were reorganized by factory and neighborhood to break down residual community loyalties.[12] After coming out of the underground, the party maintained an "illegal" wing that liaised directly with the Russian secret service, the Ob'edinennoe Gosudarstvennoe Politeschkoe Upravlenie (OGPU), and many American radicals traveled to Russia, informally and formally, to build links with the international apparatus.[13] An "Anglo-American Commission" of around eight to ten Comintern staff carefully followed events in the United States, providing a "constant stream of letters by courier with advice, observations, criticisms [and] exhortations" on a myriad of issues.[14] Gradually, internationalism ceased to signify equal membership in a global revolutionary community; instead, it meant defending the revolutionary heartland at all costs. The core of the Communist Party in America gradually changed from a motley assemblage of revolutionary dissenters into a small but nevertheless meaningful extension of Russian power.

In the short term, the most visible result of these changes was a shrinking from the mid-1920s of the party's already microscopic membership base: fewer than ten thousand people by the end of the decade.[15] Even as the case for seeing Communism as a genuinely subversive movement became stronger, then, it became harder and harder to take it seriously as a threat. In 1930 the New York Police Department found itself in the curious position of defending a Lovestoneite meeting from Stalinist raiders sporting bricks and sawed-off billiard cues.[16] John J. Bennett Jr., New York's state commander of the American Legion, said the Communists were nothing more than "a bunch of misguided schoolboys. I don't regard them as a bit of a menace. The less attention is paid to them the better."[17]

Of course, this should have been welcomed by countersubversives. But the parlous condition of American communism softened tempers at home and thus undermined the domestic basis for the policy of nonrecognition toward Russia, which remained the centerpiece of the countersubversive settlement.[18] Countersubversion had been most effectively stoked during World War I by fears of an expanding German empire, not an ailing Russian one. As with the fight to restrain the Department of Justice, then, efforts by progressives and reformers began over time to crack the edifice of nonrecognition. In 1922 Senator Borah helped remove the old Russian ambassador to the United States, Boris Bakhmatev, from his formal relationship with the State Department.[19] A year later, Senator Brookhart traveled to Russia to investigate its cooperative farms and returned praising them as a model for reform in his home state.[20] In a separate journey, Senator La Follette even persuaded Overman Committee member Senator King of Utah to join him. Senator Wheeler traveled to Moscow in 1923 and returned arguing that it was crazy that France and Britain were trading with Russia while America was not.[21] The conservative *Chicago Daily Tribune* concluded that "senatorial visits in the darkness of Russian anarchy and intrigue give cause for disquieting suspicions."[22] Nevertheless, they contributed to a warming of relations between the two countries. More important still, in 1924 Borah replaced the strongly anti-Bolshevik Henry Cabot Lodge as chair of the powerful Senate Foreign Relations Committee, creating new opportunities to press the case for normalization.[23]

Soviet economic diplomacy also made real progress. The volume of trade between Russia and America steadily grew, so that by 1930 America led all nations in exports to the Soviet state.[24] Corporate calls to forgive and forget past offenses naturally accompanied this burgeoning commercial alliance, with larger export-oriented producers in particular arguing that American consumers could not fail "to benefit richly by the exploitation of Russia's great economic resources."[25] The business-minded Council of Foreign Relations concluded that reconciliation with Bolshevism might be exchanged for a commitment to paying past debts.[26] By November 1930, even the strongly anticommunist Matthew Woll was forced to admit that Russia was less a world menace than "a world nuisance."[27] As one historian summarizes, "If the Communists were not an immediate threat, perhaps the West could do business with them."[28]

Whether one welcomed the prospect or detested it, U.S.-Russian relations were clearly thawing as fears of American radicalism dissipated. Ironically, however, this contributed to an increasingly shrill tone from antiradical countersubversives, not only in recognition that public opinion was moving against them but also because pragmatic antiradicals tended to be the first to fall silent, leaving the stage to the more dogmatic or unprincipled. Countersubversive politics thus became progressively more associated with hard-liners or self-interested groups seeking to use fears of subversion for their own ends. Perhaps nowhere was this clearer than in the decadelong effort to red-bait revolutionary Mexico.

Since the turn of the century, Mexico had emerged as a central part of the U.S. oil economy, a commercial world that had already been implicated in the corruption of the Department of Justice during the Harding scandals. Following the Mexican revolution, American oil magnates had been angered by Mexican nationalists, who looked to reassert domestic control over the country's natural resources. Powerful businessmen came to believe that conflict between the two nations might produce a business-friendly protectorate akin to the ones set up in Cuba and other Caribbean nations during the previous generation.[29] On repeated occasions between World War I and the Great Depression, oilmen pushed for war with Mexico by claiming it was an outpost of Bolshevism in the Americas. In 1919 a lobby group called the National Association for the Protection of American Rights in Mexico accused the Carranza regime of being pro-German and Bolshevistic and of acting as a conduit for revolutionary propaganda to the United States.[30] In 1921 lobbyists tried to encourage Harding's secretary of state, Charles Evans Hughes, to forcibly seize Baja California; a former Justice Department employee of dubious ethics, Jacob Nosovitsky, was hired to find evidence of Bolshevik influence in Mexico.[31] In the midst of the 1924 Progressive Party campaign, claims began to circulate that Mexico had been acting as a conduit for money sent from Russia to Senator La Follette.[32] In December 1926, when marines were sent to Nicaragua, both Nicaraguan and American conservatives claimed that violence was being provoked by a Mexican government seeking to "drive a Bolshevist wedge between continental United States and the Panama Canal."[33] Early the next year, Frank B. Kellogg, secretary of state, presented a paper on Bolshevik aims in Mexico to the Senate Foreign Relations Committee in which he argued that Latin America and Mexico were a forward base for Bolshevik revolutionary activity against the United States.[34] And in December 1927, newspaper magnate William Randolph Hearst syndicated accusations that Mexico, in collusion with Soviet Russia, was funding and promoting Nicaraguan rebel activities and planning to build a canal to challenge the American position in Panama. More explosive still, his papers claimed that Mexican president Plutarco Elías Calles had paid $1.2 million in bribes to progressive politicians including Senators Borah, Norris, and Robert La Follette Jr. Beyond these major incidents, on numerous other occasions in the later 1920s senior politicians, public figures, and newspaper editors were quietly handed documents that purported to show that Mexico City was promoting Bolshevik interests in the United States.[35]

On virtually every occasion, the smears were exposed as false almost immediately.[36] The most widely publicized example, the Hearst documents, had been purchased without verification from a notorious con man and onetime employee of American military intelligence now working out of Mexico City, while another set of forgeries was traced back to Germany, where local police raided an apartment occupied by a former czarist official who quickly confessed to his part in a European anti-Soviet propaganda network.[37] "The truth is," Senator Borah told reporters, "effort is being made to get this country into a shameless, cowardly, little war with Mexico."[38] Indeed, events in Mexico revealed the absurdity of the claims. In the later 1920s, relations between Russia and Mexico had soured, and diplomatic relations might well have broken down entirely had the United States not taken such a hostile attitude toward its neighbor.[39] In 1927, after the antiradical ambassador to Mexico, James R. Sheffield, was replaced by Dwight Morrow, a former vice president of J. P. Morgan and an advocate of reconciliation, relations between Mexico and Russia fell apart in almost direct correlation with the improvement in relations between Mexico and the United States. The Mexican Communist Party was swiftly outlawed and by mid-1929 had been driven underground, and in January 1930 Mexico broke off all diplomatic relations with the Soviet Union, not to be restored until 1943.

One might think that conspirators in such schemes would take care to cover their tracks. Yet most attempts to conjure fears of a Bolshevik threat in Mexico turned out to be surprisingly inept, not least because they were opportunistic affairs. Once it had become clear that wealthy individuals were willing to pay large amounts of money for evidence of Bolshevik spookery, forgers throughout the world set about producing material to meet the demand. Thanks to the individuals who exposed these false accusations, the Senate repeatedly rejected the case for war with Mexico. They also provided opportunities to denounce the politics of countersubversion. Senator La Follette Jr. declared himself a victim of "an infamous and dastardly fraud," assuring his fellow senators that he would not "deviate so much as a hairsbreadth from the course which I have marked out . . . towards Mexico or any other power."[40] In an open letter to Hearst, Senator Norris accused the newspaper magnate of being unfair, dishonest, and entirely without honor. He wrote, "The record which you have made in this matter is sufficient to place your publications in disrepute in the minds of all honest men, and it demonstrates that the Hearst system of newspapers, spreading like a venomous web to all parts of the country, constitutes the sewer system of American journalism."[41]

If it worked, smearing offered the opportunity to influence government policy decisively. But when exposed, it damaged countersubversive politics in general. The *Nation* declared that American attitudes toward Bolshevik Russia had passed beyond the realm of sense. Nonrecognition was no longer a question of law or logic, but a product "of the hysteria of bureaucrats and politicians, who require red herrings to distract public attention from their own ineptitude."[42] As Borah remarked, "No living man, nothing less than omniscience, can separate the truth from falsehood, the genuine from the forged documents, in this mass of lying and crimination and recrimination."[43]

* * *

In May 1929, Matthew Woll, vice president of the American Federation of Labor and acting president of the National Civic Federation, wrote the newly elected president, Herbert Hoover, with news of "the astounding discovery of the existence here of an active and venomous underground Communist organization, bountifully supplied with money and operating under the direction of the notorious and criminal O.G.P.U."[44] The letter was the culmination of several months of cloak-and-dagger work by the NCF's guiding light, Ralph Easley, and marked the beginning of a three-year sojourn for the organization into the dark heart of Soviet espionage in America.

Easley had been approached by former Department of Justice agent Gaston B. Means, the man who had testified against attorney general Daugherty during the Harding scandals and had subsequently been imprisoned for Prohibition violations. Means explained that after gaining his freedom, he had been working for the head of the U.S. branch of the OGPU, a Scandinavian-Russian polyglot by the name of Nels Jorgenson. Jorgenson had entrusted Means with sixteen trunks and cases full of detailed documentation on Soviet espionage activities in the Americas, which were currently residing in a rented house in Bethesda, Maryland. Means, growing disenchanted with the job, offered to turn the trunks over to Easley.[45] He explained that Jorgenson was in dispute with the Bolshevik leadership in Amtorg over party policy and that the federation might exploit this internal split to get hold of the trunks and deliver them to the government. Sensing a major opportunity, Easley raised the matter with his most influential contacts, and, following Woll's May letter, NCF representatives were invited to the White House to unravel the conspiracy before an astonished President Hoover.

As the nearest equivalent to an embassy, Amtorg was the first place one would expect to find Soviet agents in the United States. The British equivalent to Amtorg, Arcos, had been caught conducting espionage activities in the United Kingdom in 1927, leading to a temporary breakdown of diplomatic relations between Britain and Russia. Exposing Amtorg operatives as undercover OGPU agents thus offered the chance both to strengthen the case for nonrecognition and to damage, perhaps fatally, the primary Soviet vehicle of economic rapprochement.

A week after their first meeting, Means led Easley into the reading room of the Library of Congress and surreptitiously identified Jorgenson—working innocently at a desk as if he were just another journalist conducting background research for an article. In further interviews, Means revealed extensive details of Soviet espionage activities. Payments, he confirmed, had indeed been made to progressive senators in exchange for their efforts to get the United States to recognize Russia and avert war in Mexico.[46] Amtorg had amassed an arsenal of weaponry big enough, in Easley's words, "to blow up this entire country from one end to the other," some of which had found its way into the Chicago underworld.[47] Means even briefly sneaked Easley and his wife into the safe house in Maryland to view the boxes and trunks. Means informed Easley that some of Amtorg's financial assets—a half-million dollars in unregistered Liberty Bonds—were also being stored inside.

However, Easley's efforts to get hold of the trunks kept going awry. First, they were moved from the safe house. Then, after Means managed to persuade Jorgenson to exchange the documents for a cash bribe, Easley's details were accidentally leaked to Amtorg agents, placing him in considerable personal danger. In the fall of 1929, Jorgenson left for San Francisco. Easley gave Means a thousand dollars to follow the OGPU head and put him in touch with the Better America Federation in case he required further assistance on the West Coast. Through September, Means continued to report back on his activities (which mostly consisted of following Jorgenson up and down the coast and into Mexico and back), while the two devised a new plan for getting the trunks. They decided that Means would seize them, buy off Jorgenson with a bribe of twenty-five thousand dollars, and deliver them to Easley's brother-in-law, who would hire a Pullman car and bring them in person to Washington. But at the critical moment when the plan was due to go into action, Means disappeared. Easley, used to receiving regular reports either by telephone or by telegraph, had no idea what had happened and began to panic, fearing his agent might be in serious trouble.

Eventually, Easley was contacted by a Los Angeles–based private investigator formerly attached to the Bureau of Investigation named Lucien C. Wheeler, who informed him that Means was being held captive by Bolshevik agents in an arid homestead in the middle of the Arizona desert.[48] Wheeler offered to try to get both Means and the trunks back for twenty-five thousand dollars.[49] Easley told him to assist in any way he could.

More silence followed. Finally, in the new year, Wheeler reported that after a daring raid on the homestead, he had recovered the documents and helped Means to escape. Operating under the alias "Morrison," Means had been spirited over the border, and because the material included information on Mexican as well as American communism it was agreed that he would take the documents to the Mexican government before bringing them back to Easley.[50] When the Mexican Communist Party was outlawed by President Calles shortly afterward, Easley could hardly contain himself—informing Edmund Walsh that "the action of Mexico breaking with the Soviet Government is entirely due to our work."[51] The only thing that remained was to repatriate the material and pass it on to the American press and the government.

At roughly the same time, Easley was contacted by another potential asset, a man named James F. La Salle. La Salle told Easley that he had worked in the copy room of Amtorg and offered, for six thousand dollars, to obtain duplicates of documents identifying OGPU agents who were pretending to be legitimate Amtorg workers.[52] Easley agreed, arranged for the documents to be translated, and then passed the photostats to two close associates in the New York countersubversive community: Republican congressman Hamilton Fish and the city's police commissioner, Grover Whalen.

A wealthy municipal politico with a not entirely spotless political reputation, Whalen was at that time under severe political pressure following his role in a heavy-handed response to an unemployment demonstration in Union Square, during which hundreds of protesters had been badly beaten by the police.[53] The League for Industrial Democracy had called upon Mayor James J. Walker to investigate police malpractice, and the ACLU had announced plans to file for Whalen's dismissal.[54] Whalen responded by claiming that the demonstrations had been organized by Soviet Russia and that more were planned in the future as a prelude to revolution. As the complaints against him persisted, he decided to release the documents he had received from Easley to the press to substantiate his claims of Soviet conspiracy. However, significantly, he implied that the material had been obtained through undercover police work rather than from a private source. (As a result, the materials became known as the "Whalen Documents.")[55]

Fish, the other recipient of Easley's material, had placed a resolution before the House calling for an investigation into Bolshevik activities in America. At first the proposal was killed by the Rules Committee, which was unconvinced there was a prima facie case for investigation.[56] But after Whalen released the documents to the press, Fish reintroduced his resolution, and not only was it passed by Rules, but the suggested appropriation was raised fivefold. With incendiary headlines of Bolshevik conspiracy in the background, congressional approval swiftly followed, with only eighteen dissenters. "Let's have this investigation," Fish declared during the floor debate, "and find out who our enemies are."[57]

Hamilton Fish, son of Hamilton Fish, grandson of Hamilton Fish (and, since 1926, father of Hamilton Fish), had served as a major in the U.S. Army during World War I and had an exemplary record, decorated with the Croix de Guerre and Silver Star. He led Company K of the Fifteenth New York National Guard, the "Harlem Hellfighters": the first African American regiment to serve in World War I. When the war ended, Fish helped form the American Legion, chairing a committee that wrote the preamble to its constitution. His family was as aristocratic as their unimaginative naming strategy implied and passed on to him a traditionalist vision of Anglo-Saxon America and a strong spirit of public service. His grandfather was Grant's secretary of state and his father a prolific, if fairly unremarkable, Republican congressmen under Taft. "William Foster may have drawn his strength from a sense of history moving implacably towards the destruction of Hamilton Fish and all his sisters and his cousins and his aunts," one journalist later wrote, "but Hamilton Fish had a no less powerful sense of history as name, family, and Harvard."[58]

Fish entered the House as a Republican congressman during the conservative sweep in 1920. He considered himself a Roosevelt progressive and claimed he had never been a reactionary in his life. In later years, he supported the anti-lynching law and as late as 1944 called for "capitalism shorn of its abuses and ugly greed to exploit labor and mankind for the almighty dollar." Had he not fallen down on the other side of the debate over countersubversion, it is tempting to imagine that Fish might have made himself an ally of the Republican insurgents, not least because of his strong anti-interventionist tendencies. A Zionist, high school football star, war hero, aristocrat-politician, and friend of Fulgencio Batista, Fish was a man of many contradictions and inordinate energy. In the summer of 1929 alone, he appeared in the press denouncing Jim Crow laws in the South and praising the African American war record, defending the Kellogg-Briand Pact as a glorious bloodless revolution for peace, attacking Franklin Roosevelt and Tammany Hall, calling for intervention to defend Jewish settlers against Arab violence in Palestine, and involving himself in a complicated debate with various political opponents, the State Banking Department, a judge, and J. P. Morgan over the proposed construction of a canal connecting the Great Lakes to St. Lawrence. Later in the year, he launched another ball into the air, correcting several misstatements made in an ongoing debate over "who was the tallest American President?"[59] Yet underlying this inordinate, apparently directionless enthusiasm was a more straightforward and familiar political agenda: a passionate desire for power.

If the newly created Fish Committee was to be a springboard to national fame, though, things did not begin auspiciously. The first item on the agenda was the Whalen Documents, and it became clear before the committee had even convened that they were another set of forgeries.[60] Enterprising opponents of the committee discovered that the documents had been made using letterheads provided by a printer named Max Wagner. Wagner had come forward almost immediately, but Whalen had declined to question him. Desperate to prove a point that he, Easley, and Fish instinctively believed to be true, the commissioner avoided applying even the simplest principles of criminal investigation to the evidence.

Fish's biographer claims that the three conspirators knew the material was forged before Fish's resolution had even been approved, but decided to say nothing.[61] If so, the committee found itself in an awkward position entirely of its own making. Looking into the documents' origins would show that Whalen had been dishonest in claiming they were obtained through police undercover work, yet avoiding them altogether would be an admission that they were a fabrication. At first, Fish brought Whalen and others before the committee in the hope he could defend the integrity of the documents. But as it became increasingly hard to deny that they were forgeries, he distanced the committee from the material, stressing that its mission was in no way dependent upon any single piece of evidence.

To fill the gap, he called antiradicals before the committee to speak against Amtorg and the Communist Party and even interrogated senior Communists, including William Z. Foster.[62] Easley helped arranged for representatives of the Daughters of the American Revolution, the American Federation of Labor, and the American Coalition of Patriotic Societies to testify.[63] Fish brought in representatives from the American Legion. A former vice president of Amtorg, Basil W. Delgass, who had fallen out of favor and was afraid to return to Russia, testified that Amtorg indeed had been hosting Soviet agents.[64] And although strictly speaking it fell beyond the committee's domestic remit, investigations of Soviet trading activities uncovered some of the earliest reports of the hundreds of thousands of people being sent to the Gulag. Nevertheless, in the context of a burgeoning depression and the doubtful provenance of the Whalen Documents, the press, the public, and fellow congressmen seemed uninterested, even hostile. Congressman Fiorello La Guardia attacked the Fish Committee for doing the dirty work of big business; even *Pravda* reportedly began mocking the committee as a sideshow.[65]

In July 1930, Easley circulated to the press a letter from the veteran countersubversive and NCF president, Elihu Root, calling for an expansion of the Bureau of Investigation. The *New Republic* responded sarcastically. Apparently, America needs "an American Cheka to hunt down wicked Communists, just as wicked capitalists are hunted down by the Russian Cheka." This was news "to the old-fashioned people who believe that secret police organizations are a tool of autocratic governments" and "that they can be dispensed with by democratic republics like the United States."[66] The *New York Times* concluded that the police were perfectly capable of dealing with Communists. The paper reasoned, "It will take something diabolically horrendous before 'the American people' will shake in their shoes at the proceedings of those ingenious and thrasonical Muscovites."[67] It seemed the exposure of the Whalen Documents as forgeries threatened to render the Fish Committee impotent. Easley briefly met with President Hoover in mid-August to update him on the OGPU investigations and appeal for support.[68] But the president told Easley to continue working through Fish, ensuring the committee would remain the lynchpin of any attempt to push forward the anti-Bolshevik agenda in Washington. With the cards almost played out, Nels Jorgenson's stolen trunks seemed to offer the only hope of redemption.

In the months since the Fish Committee began its hearings, Means had continued to provide Easley with information about OGPU espionage.[69] The convoluted effort to retrieve the trunks extended to include Jorgenson's boss, C. N. Weltz, and both now needed to be managed. Fortunately, the pair were eminently corruptible and willing to turn a blind eye to the theft of the trunks for twenty-five thousand dollars each. Easley was therefore able to reassure Fish that whatever the problems with the documents provided by La Salle, all would be well once Means's OGPU material was recovered. Indeed, Easley declared Means to be an unofficial investigating agent for the Fish Committee at five hundred dollars a week.[70] A short while later, Means announced that he had shifted the trunks to a warehouse in Baltimore, where he, Easley, and Fish could go and get them. Easley and Fish began planning a sensational raid, replete with press and photographers, to seize the material and transport it in triumphant, validating procession to the committee.

On November 18, 1930, Easley, Means, and Fish, along with Easley's attorney and another lawyer, traveled to Baltimore. Members of the press were a few minutes behind. Arriving at the warehouse, the conspirators were exhilarated. Fish tightly gripped a subpoena, to hand to Means once the documents were received so that the agent's personal account could also be delivered into the *Congressional Record*. Easley's attorney, the marvelously named Wheeler P. Bloodgood, looked around excitedly at the local police officers who were brought in to assist.[71] But none could have been more nervous or expectant than Ralph Montgomery Easley, who had by this time invested more than a year and a half of his life and tens of thousands of dollars in the pursuit of the OGPU papers.

The group was met at the doors of the storage company by a bemused owner, who replied to all questions about secret Russian documents with quizzical confusion. "At response to our expressions of astonishment," Easley explained in a later letter to President Hoover, "he told us to go ahead and search which we did without any results."[72] While Easley attempted to discover how, why, and where the documents had disappeared to, the light began to dawn on Fish that the story had been just another fabrication, and he realized that a rapidly arriving press corps could quickly be photographing the end rather than the bright beginning of his political career. Easley demanded Fish "grab everybody here at the warehouse." Means suggested that they get the U.S. marshal to arrest everyone. But Fish informed the others that he wanted nothing more to do with the operation and rushed for the door.[73] Easley and Means disappeared soon after. By the time the reporters arrived, all that was left was an empty sidewalk "strewn with broken vegetable crates and loose heads of lettuce."[74]

*   *   *

Alongside public ridicule, one of the more significant consequences of the debacle that exposed Gaston B. Means as an incorrigible liar and Easley as a gull of the first order was an unraveling of ties within the antiradical community. When news got out of the eighteen-month-long OGPU wild-goose chase funded by the National Civic Federation, Easley's reputation became mud. No longer could he gain access to the White House or obtain interviews with the president. Contact with Fish became frosty, as the congressman—who had been planning to launch a national organization, the American Alliance, on the back of his congressional hearings—distanced himself from the federation in the hope of saving his reputation.

At first Easley expressed his regret over the mess to Fish, "which was all the more humiliating to me because I knew I had been largely responsible for getting you into it."[75] But as time progressed, Easley reacted to public ridicule by standing more staunchly in Means's defense. Fish told journalists that Woll and Easley had cynically profited from the investigations; in retaliation Woll questioned Fish's sincerity, and Easley wrote that Fish was acting "like a big overgrown school boy."[76] He was not crooked, Easley decided, but he was "a fool and a jackass."[77] By June 1931, Easley was writing bitter and personal tirades in response to rumors that Fish was badmouthing him in the capital. "Your concern about my standing in Washington recalls to my mind that you did not have a very high standing there yourself at the time you were pulling the strings in the effort to bring about the adoption of your resolution," Easley wrote to his former friend. "You told me that 'the Powers that be' had said that you were a 'four-flusher,' a 'hot air artist,' 'an unreliable' and a lot of other things. I found that your information on that score was straight because, when speaking of you to me, they used the same epithets and a few others which stick in my mind, such as 'brainless nincompoop,' 'a schemer for notoriety on any and all occasions' and so forth and so forth." The most aggravating thing was Fish's attempt to blame the federation for his failures. "As a matter of fact," Easley argued, "had it not been for the work of the 'ineffective' National Civic Federation and myself in obtaining, from representative men and women, throughout the country, letters endorsing your resolution, it is doubtful if that resolution would ever have been reported out" and "doubtful you would ever have been made Chairman."[78]

With this final embarrassment, the Fish Committee quietly descended into oblivion, leaving behind it a report reflecting the divided conclusions of the participating congressmen. Such was the unrelentingly negative publicity, Hamilton Fish admitted, that it was difficult to keep his enemies "from writing in to the report a definite attack on what they termed 'Professional Profiteers.'"[79]

As a capstone upon a decade of disappointment, countersubversives had once again become associated with ingenuous and unconvincing misrepresentations of reality. One later commentator summed up Fish's efforts as an "utter failure to get the legislation he demanded for eradicating communism from American soil."[80] The *New Republic* said that the committee's report did "not merit serious consideration, though even as a piece of humor it leaves much to be desired," and called Hamilton Fish a "heavy-witted young man whose lack of sense of the ridiculous turns out to be a fatal defect." Indeed, "even the most conservative of the daily newspapers" had brushed him aside "as not deserving serious consideration."[81] As Walter Goodman later noted, "Years after the Fish committee concluded its work, critics were still pointing out that it took testimony from 225 witnesses in fourteen cities, produced a voluminous report, and passed at once into obscurity."[82]

It is not clear exactly how much money passed through Easley's hands to Means and his associates during the long OGPU con, but the amount was at least $286,982 (the total Easley later gave as a comprehensive account to the NCF board), and quite possibly more.[83] The first payments in 1929 had been organized by a group of supportive donors via a close associate of Easley's, General Samuel McRoberts. The moneys were primarily provided by rich individual donors, including the mining plutocrat John Hays Hammond; Cyrus H. McCormick, the son of the founder of the International Harvester Company; Samuel Insull, a Chicago electrical and railroad magnate; George Cortelyou, the former secretary of commerce and labor, secretary of the Treasury, and postmaster general under Theodore Roosevelt and Taft; and an assortment of other wealthy and influential figures.[84] Gertrude Beeks Easley obtained the bulk of the money from Helen Shepard, the heiress to the fortune left by the Gilded Age speculator Jay Gould. (Independently, Helen Shepard and her husband had met with Means and—convinced that they were threatened by Soviet agents—paid him $32,000 for protection.)[85] Aside from this impressive list of high-society donors, Easley spent $40,000 of his own money funding Means's travels.[86] In today's terms, this would mean that somewhere between $3.5 and $4 million was invested in the fictional OGPU investigations. All that the federation had to show in return were a few forged documents, some concocted affidavits, and seven hundred thousand words of carefully typed-up notes of their folly.[87]

It is hard to believe that anyone with even the most superficial knowledge of Gaston Bullock Means's past could have credited anything he said with the truth. As Easley himself put it, "I think that after having worked for 15 months as closely as I have worked with M., I ought to know if he were making a fool of me!"[88] Aside from well-known prewar work he had conducted on behalf of the German government, his collaboration with the notoriously dishonest detective William J. Burns, and the Prohibition violations and other frauds for which he was sent to prison earlier in the twenties, Means had been involved in a string of public scandals that had been well covered in the press. In September 1917, he had narrowly escaped imprisonment for his involvement in the death of a rich, credulous widow from Concord, North Carolina, from whom he stole tens of thousands of dollars.[89] Shortly afterward, Means became involved in an expansive deception that also nearly landed him in prison when he tried to sell "secret German espionage papers" to the Hearst press. Military intelligence got involved. Means showed a set of unopened boxes supposedly containing the documents to an MI operative, but before the exchange was made they mysteriously vanished.[90] When questioned, Means explained these scandals away as either events in a past life for which he sought now to make amends or lies circulated by his enemies. But when one looks at the record, it is hard to disagree with Means's biographer, who called the man "the most spectacular rogue who ever lived in America."[91]

Despite this, the secrets of Means's success as a fraudster were disarmingly simple and reveal much about why antiradical countersubversives in the 1920s were so vulnerable to smearing, forgery, and con artistry. First was his incredible gift of gab. This allowed him to talk his way out of absurd situations with fantastical stories, recognizing that when it came to true believers the key to credibility was not reasonableness but a persistent and belligerent refusal to accept the truth. When Means was arrested in November 1931 for beating his wife, he told Easley that actually he had been beaten by the police and that the charge he faced was designed to divert attention from their brutality.[92] For Easley, heavily invested in Means's claims, "the darker his record the greater would be his overwhelming desire to rehabilitate himself for the sake of his wife and his son."[93]

This was a testament to Means's impressive capacity for invention: the innocent-looking man at the Library of Congress whom he had identified to Easley early on as Nels Jorgenson was in fact Walter Liggett, "an amiable Washington newspaper correspondent."[94] But it also reflected the way in which an exploitable cult of victimhood had already come to form a central part of antiradical identity by the late 1920s. Despite operating in a milieu of conspicuous and unusual privilege, many antiradicals saw themselves as an embattled minority fighting against a complacent liberal majority who had overseen the dismantling of the nation's countersubversive apparatus and were pushing for normalized relations with the Soviets. Individuals who, like them, appeared to be victimized by the system earned their sympathy.

Means also took care to set up his next sting while the first was still ongoing, piggybacking on the good names of his targets. By continually moving, he could navigate circles of reputable society accompanied by glowing letters of introduction. Ironically, this made countersubversives particularly susceptible to fraud not because they were part of the irrational masses that some later historians isolated as the source of antiradical paranoia, but because they formed part of a closed elite. Before meeting him, Easley had received favorable reports on Means from Senator George Higgins Moses, the Republican congressman who orchestrated the deportation of Ludwig Martens in 1920, and from Senator James Watson of Indiana. When Means traveled to the West Coast, Easley had in turn written a letter recommending the con artist to the Better America Federation and repeatedly vouched for him to Fish and other Washington politicians.[95] The ease with which Means was able to recover from exposure testifies to the power of a good reference and the degree that credibility in the corridors of power was a product of who, not what, you knew. Lacking the personnel, professional skills, resources, and good fortune that would be needed to gain access to the real Amtorg and the real Communist Party, countersubversives were forced to rely on mutual trust as the currency of their operations. Their faith in each other, however, opened them up to exploitation from an unscrupulous gamer who was able to trade on their solidarity.

Alongside old-fashioned blarney, Means relied upon subtle evidential techniques to give his fabrications the illusion of truth. False information would be tightly bound up with carefully recorded and verifiable public evidence. For instance, the fictitious story about being spirited from Arizona to Mexico was opportunistically integrated into the real events of deteriorating Russo-Mexican relations. This created an information short circuit, whereby those attempting to check the accuracy of Means's claims would find material in the press accurately substantiating the truthful elements of the cover story. They would, in effect, be testing information against itself. Means also relied upon associates, like Los Angeles detective Lucien C. Wheeler, who appeared at first to be unrelated to Means but in fact had been working with him from the beginning. Such individuals created an echo effect by "accidentally" endorsing fabrications relayed elsewhere by Means.[96] Revealingly, at one point, Easley defended himself from accusations of gullibility on the basis that "Means furnished me a lot of stuff that I know is all right because we have other people who know all about it. When stuff is corroborated, you know it is all right."[97] In fact, such simple corroboration was next to useless.

Easley should have known better, as he employed the same technique when he used Fish and Whalen as ciphers to release the anti-Bolshevik forgeries provided by James La Salle in 1930. Apparently separate claims from the New York police, Washington politicians, and private sources all appeared to substantiate each other but in fact originated with the same man. The antiradical community as a whole was engaged in much the same exercise when it orchestrated its testimony before the Fish Committee but represented its findings publicly as coming from a series of unconnected, independent organizations. A basic strategy in propaganda work, this was the reason antiradical countersubversives were absolutely wrong to base the credibility of an argument on the volume, rather than the verifiable substance, of any particular evidence.

History shows that the Bureau of Investigation and military intelligence were perfectly capable of making spectacular blunders. But both groups had familiarity with these tactics—all basic problems in intelligence work—and would have speedily uncovered the holes in Means's web of dissimulation. At the very least, they would have examined Means's horrendous record with a degree of skepticism. By contrast, amateur countersubversives like Easley tended to have so much invested in their claims that they refused to question their beliefs even when evidence mounted beyond all reasonable doubt. Police commissioner Whalen undoubtedly had people working for him who would have been capable of looking into the provenance of the documents he received from Easley, but he conspicuously avoiding asking them. In this sense, it was deeply ironic that this slapdash community was so regularly attacked at the time for being "professional patriots," as *professional* was one of the least-accurate words that could have been chosen to describe them.

Easley was never able to admit that there had never been any documents, no Jorgenson, that Borah and Wheeler were not Soviet agents—that the labyrinthine stories he had been fed existed only in the impressive imagination of Gaston B. Means. Over two years, he had spent hundreds of thousands of dollars of donations, used up his personal savings, sold his Liberty Bonds, and mortgaged his farm, all for nothing. Even as the Baltimore episode ran its course and the Fish Committee crunched to an ignominious halt, he still refused to accept the blackness of events at face value. He had invested too much in his project, like a poker player who has bet his car, his best friend's house, and his pet dog and keeps desperately searching for collateral to stay in the game. In November 1930, a well-connected friend wrote to say that J. Edgar Hoover had personally told him not a word Means said was to be trusted. But Easley continued to search for explanations that would redeem his agent and leave the possibility open that the money he had lost could be recovered. In the end, he decided that the trunks had been stolen at the last minute before the Baltimore raid by Amtorg agents via a secret tunnel hidden under the warehouse. Through extended tales and convoluted plotlines, Means continued to extract money from the federation for several years after the collapse of the Fish investigation, until he was finally arrested for stealing more than one hundred thousand dollars from a friend of the Lindbergh family after promising he could recover their child (who had disappeared in one of the most famous public crimes of the early 1930s and was later found dead).[98] As late as 1938, Easley was still describing the nonexistent Nels Jorgenson as "the most dangerous man who ever trod our shores."[99] It would have been too much for his pride to take to abandon the affair.

Means was prosecuted in September 1934 for his Lindbergh plot and sentenced to fifteen years in prison.[100] He fell ill two years later, suffering from bladder and kidney pains that turned out to be gallstones, but struggled on until December 1938, when he died.[101] J. Edgar Hoover reported that throughout his final years, Means continued "sending me offers to solve whatever mystery confronts the Federal Bureau of Investigation—if only we can get him out for a while."[102]

Doubts over the responsibility for the death of the Lindbergh baby remain to this day. What was clear, though, was that the American public expected the government to intervene in such tragic cases, not least in order to separate genuine leads from hucksters and hoaxers like Means who sought to make a quick buck from people in the depths of their suffering. In response, Congress passed what became known as the Lindbergh Law, making it a federal offense to kidnap individuals across state lines. This was the first significant enlargement of bureau power in a decade. In a perverse way, Means had helped to expand the Bureau of Investigation, but hardly in the manner Easley had hoped.

J. Edgar Hoover attended Means's trial and sentencing in 1934. "Gaston," he said, as he walked past the defendant at the end of the hearings, "it was a pack of lies." "Well," Means replied, "you've got to admit it made a whale of a good story!"[103]

* * *

Whatever the truth about Soviet covert operations in the United States, and available evidence suggests that in the 1920s it was minimal, countersubversive attempts to argue that the United States was genuinely under threat had been deeply compromised by the smears and forged evidence that played such a major role in the political debate over subversion between 1920 and 1933. These were not unfortunate side effects but endemic problems in a period when countersubversive politics was dominated by a decentralized, unaccountable, and informal network of enthusiastic and prejudiced amateurs with little clarity in their understanding of international communism, little evidence to justify their allegations, and little sense of what it took to get to the heart of a disciplined revolutionary organization. On the one hand, the repression of Communist Party activities, the conservatism of the age, and the almost total exclusion of Soviet diplomatic institutions from American territory made the likelihood of uncovering Bolshevik espionage activity remote. Since nonrecognition largely halted meaningful foreign policy engagement with Russia, anti-Bolshevism tended to transform into red-baiting and business imperialism. On the other hand, the success of the progressive insurgents in challenging federal countersubversive efforts ensured that agencies capable of conducting counterintelligence work with even a modicum of sophistication were banned from doing so. Antiradical countersubversion became a realm of money, chimerical enemies, and amateur sleuths. When this was revealed in moments of scandal or embarrassment, the public impression created was of cynicism, self-interest, or idiocy. When more accurate claims about Soviet activities were made in the 1930s and beyond, many reasonable people saw them as crying wolf.

Having largely failed to make their case to the American people, countersubversives witnessed a new Democratic president abandon wholesale the policies of the Republican administrations of the twenties, beginning with the longstanding nonrecognition policy toward Russia. FDR realized that the general public was largely indifferent to foreign politics at a time of domestic crisis and that many of the chief opponents of recognition had been discredited. The November 1933 agreement between the Soviets and the United States was one that any willing administration government could have secured at any point since 1921, as it required no meaningful concessions from Russia, yet its passage was contingent upon the weakness of the countersubversive cause.[104] The Soviets agreed to enter negotiations over outstanding debts, but made no promise to their outcome. They promised to respect religious liberty, which the Bolshevik regime had always claimed it had done, anyway. And they offered what became known as the Litvinov Pledge: assurances that the Soviets would not interfere "with life and affairs within the jurisdiction of the United States" and would "restrain all persons and organizations directly or indirectly under its control ... from agitation or propaganda within the United States or its territories."[105] Flush from his success, Roosevelt claimed he had even gotten Litvinov to doubt his atheism.[106] But commitments born of persuasion rather than self-interest are rarely honored, and Litvinov had not been born again. The Soviets realized that Roosevelt was determined to normalize relations and knew they could agree to what Roosevelt demanded without meaningful change. In fact, even the Litvinov Pledge represented no fundamental concession on the Soviet side, because the Bolshevik government continued to maintain that the Comintern was not under its control.[107] The Russian government thus made no effort to dissolve the CPUSA or distance itself from its operations. And just as antiradicals had predicted—just as most powers do—the Soviets began to use their new diplomatic apparatus to coordinate covert espionage in their rival's territory.

At the time, Roosevelt's turn was widely seen as a triumph of good sense over prejudice.[108] It was certainly true that Wilsonian nonrecognition had wrought little meaningful or positive. By contrast, antiradicals could point to only one thing that could give them any cause for hope for the future: President Roosevelt's willingness to expand the scope of Bureau of Investigation activities during the Lindbergh affair suggested that it might again be allowed to recommence countersubversive investigations. But even this was not something that followed from their actions so much as the crime wave that followed a decade of Prohibition. The efforts of the professional patriots during the 1920s had proven to be an unmitigated disaster.

6

Subversive Capitalism
Fordism, Business, and Antiradicalism

Detroit had become a center of American manufacturing in the early twentieth century in large part because of its reputation for amenable, docile, mostly immigrant labor. It was known as the open shop capital of the country, brought about through the assiduous efforts of the local Employers Association, city police, and government in breaking strikes and undermining union membership, all the time using countersubversive rhetoric to justify their actions. Because workplace controls were more or less absent, employers needed to pay little attention to safety; adolescent and child labor was common, and piecework was typical.[1] But Henry Ford was never a man to abide by convention. As he rose to national prominence, he steered away from his rivals' approaches to factory management in counterintuitive but effective ways: moving to an eight-hour day instead of the ten or eleven typical at the time, announcing an unprecedented five-dollar-a-day basic salary, and making sure that factory and machine design kept safety paramount.[2] He used his company's profits to have a hospital built, which opened in autumn 1915, and insisted on employing former convicts, the disabled, and the handicapped alongside able-bodied workers to demonstrate the power of rehabilitation through labor.

Ford argued that such social innovations were not charity—a concept he frankly despised as archaic and likely to induce dependence and idleness—but a matter of good business sense: he called it "profit sharing and efficiency engineering."[3] Not only would well-paid and happy workers be proud and hardworking, but they would also be loyal, trustworthy, and more productive.[4] The saved costs generated through employee retention almost immediately covered large parts of the wage increases; absenteeism also declined. Cynics pointed out that high wages brought in a wave of workers to Detroit from across the country, ensuring a larger pool of the unemployed to use as strikebreakers.[5]

But enthusiasts, such as the editors of the *Michigan Manufacturer and Financial Record,* declared Ford's actions to be "the most generous stroke of policy between captain of industry and worker that the country has ever seen."[6] John D. Rockefeller called Ford's empire "the industrial miracle of the age."[7]

Ford's publicists responded evangelically to suggestions that the system offered a more general model for national development. They began conflating the automobile, Ford Motor Company, and the American way. Company advertising presented the freedom offered by the automobile as a new, modern version of traditional American liberty, expressed not through autonomy, individuality, or localism, but through consumption and mobility.[8] Highland Park, Ford's gleaming new factory built on the outskirts of Detroit, was depicted as a microcosm of a well-run America. Fordism was the future path for American society and Henry Ford the ideal American man. Despite being essentially corporate propaganda, it seems that many Americans agreed with this assessment: one survey of college students placed Ford third as the greatest man of all time, behind Napoleon and Jesus.[9]

It was notable but less commonly mentioned, however, that Ford's reforms involved no concessions of authority. Profits could be shared and efficiency engineered, but the system as a whole was organized on a strictly hierarchical basis. Indeed, enthused by his success, Ford began reaching deeply into his employees' private lives. Policies that were originally intended to sustain the virtuous combination of productivity growth and individual rewards gradually became more intrusive and even demeaning. The company established an on-site English school so that immigrant workers could learn to better understand workplace instructions and more strongly identify with the corporation.[10] They created a Sociological Department, with armies of assessors sent to workers' homes, investigating every employee whose wages were lower than two hundred dollars per month, appraising their lives and families under all manner of categories: marital status, dependents, nationality, religion, finances, health, hobbies, habits, and diet.[11] Workers were encouraged to improve their personal conduct, move into better housing, straighten out their lives. Ford withheld the five-dollar wage from workers who drank excessively, had bad personal habits, gambled or fornicated, were dirty, or sent too much of their earned cash to relatives living abroad.[12] Dean Marquis, who was in charge of the department, explained, "There are two ways of spending money—constructive, and destructive of self, family and community. A Ford man must be a builder. If he is not, he is called to the office and his destructive habits are pointed out to him. His profits are taken away until he reforms." Marquis admitted that some felt such efforts "interfered with their personal liberty and independence. So far as my experience went I found such complaints came from men whose individual liberties had been interfered with, but they were such liberties as getting drunk and beating up one's wife, abusing one's family, and wasting one's money."[13]

In the Fordist system, national concerns over the relationship between loyalty and liberty were translated anew in relationships between employees and management. Much as the wartime loyalty campaigns were presented as a harmonious, popular national project of liberation, Ford Motor's reforms were sold as an expression of mutual interests of employer and employee, a demonstration of the natural harmony between labor and capital. Whereas an employer could impose upon the employee because he better perceived the worker's interests, other organizations that purported to act for the worker were denounced as alien. Ford declared emphatically that there was "nothing that a union membership could do for our people."[14] He attributed expressions of employee dissatisfaction to the subversive influence of outsiders, and as war fever began to grip the United States this equation became increasingly explicit. Stephen Meyer III notes that, like many other business leaders during the war, "Ford officials turned high rates of efficiency and productivity into the patriotic duty of Ford workers. Thus, they interpreted their workers' tendencies towards soldiering and output restrictions as examples of treasonous behavior."[15]

Between 1917 and 1920, the mood at Ford began to change. The company found itself ailing under increasing competitive pressure. Rivals adopted many of the innovative tools and techniques Ford's men had dreamed up. An attempt to regain control of corporate stock left Ford with a personal debt of thirty-three million dollars. Wartime inflation decreased the pulling power of the once-radical wage structure and reacquainted Ford workers with the long-term benefits of unionization as opposed to the temporary palliatives of good pay. The deskilling, repetitive practices, and constant invasions of privacy that epitomized Fordist rationalization began to generate a groundswell of dissatisfaction. One Ford worker told William A. Logan, president of the Auto Workers Union (AWU), "If I keep putting on Nut No. 86 for about 86 more days, I will be Nut No. 86 in the Pontiac bughouse."[16] Reports circulated that union leaders had secured thousands of new members, few of whom were actually getting the much-vaunted minimum wage. By late 1919, the AWU had organized forty-five thousand workers in the region and was pushing for more influence over factory conditions. One AWU representative declared that soon, "we will get what we think is just, and not what The Ford Motor Co. thinks."[17]

Following the Great Steel Strike, the AWU struck the Wadsworth Body Company, one of Ford's chief suppliers, and Ford was forced to intervene when Wadsworth failed to break the action.[18] He recalled that "the costs of manufacturing everywhere were out of control. Labor gave less and less in return for high wages."[19] Finally, the postwar slump saw sales begin to decline. To maintain output, the company cut prices below the cost of manufacture.

Ford responded to the mounting challenges with an aggressive wave of business rationalization and productivity improvement at all levels of the system, essential for lowering costs to a point where sales would again mean profit.

In December 1919, as the nation was digesting the first wave of Palmer Raids, Highland Park was shut down for housecleaning, for two weeks that stretched to six. Unnecessary plant workers and office staff were removed, production plans accelerated. The Sociological Department's educative programs were scaled down, then eliminated, while direct monitoring of worker behavior increased.[20] The strategy seemed to work: while industry volume fell by a quarter over the period of the depression, Ford at least held market share.[21]

The Ford plants formed part of a more general tendency in postwar American capitalism to rely on the stick over the carrot, to squeeze workers more tightly into the holes between the machines. This policy was driven by the cold exigencies of competition but enforced with all too human brutality. As early as 1916, Ford hired a pugnacious bully named Harry Bennett to work for him after he had been spotted brawling in the street: "a small and wiry [man], with sharp blue eyes and thinning brown hair which is slicked down carefully to cover an incipient bald spot."[22] Bennett became a general fixer for Ford and hatchet man, discreet enough to take on unpleasant disciplinary duties without compromising the grandfatherly image of the industrialist.[23] His job was to head up the quite inaccurately named Service Department: a network of spies, informants, observers, and hard men distributed around the Ford plants who monitored employees for signs of dissent, disobedience, or attempts to unionize. Bennett took advantage of Ford's eagerness to hire former criminals to fill the rank and file of the department with people willing to get their hands dirty. He recollected that "Mr. Ford gave the public to understanding that he hired these people for the purpose of rehabilitating them. But I didn't see much of that sort of thing happen."[24] Bennett also developed links with the criminal underworld, who were occasionally given kickbacks or franchises to do favors for the company on the side.[25] After taking over the Personnel Department in 1927, Bennett began dispensing patronage on an ad hoc basis to influential criminal outsiders.[26] (Bennett was not afraid to exploit rumors of his underworld connections to enhance his terroristic image. According to Irving R. Bacon, Ford's official artist, Bennett warned people "never to make derogatory remarks regarding him in the hearing of his Italian guards or workmen, for you might disappear as others had, who had attempted to take his life and were never heard from again.")[27] But the Service Department was also populated with "ex-police inspectors and men of that caliber," and Bennett reportedly organized his staff like a police force, "with regular beats for the Servicemen and compelled them to report to headquarters at brief intervals throughout the day."[28] Friendly links to the national intelligence establishment were diligently maintained. Meanwhile, the official Highland Park and Detroit police forces were filled with former company employees, some still receiving generous benefits from the company, while others upon retiring were reemployed by the company to maintain close relations, ensuring that the lines between state authorities and corporation became blurred. Bennett assisted police investigations, boasting to journalists that he had helped solve crimes all over northern Michigan.[29] In one particularly famous Prohibition-era case, Solly Levine reportedly holed out on a Ford boat after testifying against three members of the famous Detroit mobsters the Purple Gang.[30]

Fact and myth inevitably intersect in such an anarchic environment. Bennett, whose accounts of his career came in retirement, had good reason to exaggerate his influence and exploits. It is hard to tell exactly how many "Service Men" were employed by Ford, but some estimates range as high as fifteen overseers for every hundred employees, if one counts foremen, Service Department officers, spies, and informants.[31] Reports from undercover operatives were routinely sent to Bennett's office, but after Ford's death all the records were destroyed and so the level of activity is now unclear. Nevertheless, notes taken by historian Allan Nevins during his research into the company in the 1950s give some indication of the scale of the operations. A single unidentified "Operative 15," for instance, sent in around a hundred reports during 1919 and 1920 on IWW, AWU, and Socialist and Communist Party activity in the Detroit region. He reported on membership drives and the arrival of professional organizers from out of state, identified key figures for observation, and put forward divisive proposals in workers' meetings in the hope of fomenting discord.[32] In the workplace itself, operatives kept tabs on radical tendencies among workers, especially immigrants.[33] Through such activities, managers came to know not only who were the suspicious individuals in the plants, but also their tactics—such as distributing literature early on Sundays so as to avoid police harassment.[34]

This was an antiradical operation whose ruthless professionalism contrasted with the amateurish efforts of many other patriotic groups at the time. Well before Ford began his cost-reduction drive in late 1920, the Service Department and Ford's other agents had driven local unionists to the point of paranoia. Following the Centralia affair, Operative 15 reported that IWW members were hunkering down and avoiding new recruitment efforts.[35] Membership in the AWU fell drastically, while other radical groups were destroyed almost completely. The way was cleared for capitalism to continue its relentless modernization of American life.

*   *   *

Ford's industrial empire oriented around two great factories, both built by his favorite architect, Albert Kahn. A German immigrant and rabbi's son, Kahn was a pioneer in the use of new types of reinforced concrete that allowed industrialists to create large industrial spaces without interior walls: perfect for rational and unimpeded assembly lines. The first, Highland Park, lay a few miles north of metropolitan Detroit along Woodward Avenue. Driving into the site, a visitor would see five huge chimneys rising over the main entrance to the power plant, dominating the center of the view, then the administrative offices in a block immediately to the right with "Ford Motor Company" emblazoned in great letters above. Behind the power plant was the main structure, running lengthwise along Woodward, "rising on the plain, uncompromisingly utilitarian in its rectangular lines, but giving an impression of lightness and airiness in its immense window spaces."[36] Christened the Crystal Palace, the four-story building included more than fifty thousand square feet of glass in steel framed windows imported from England and was nearly nine hundred feet long.

For such an enormous building, there was little adornment. The occasional curlicue—a "delicate pediment" roofing the building, "a compositional design in the support bricks of the vertical facility towers"—insinuated the traces of art into the building, but otherwise it stood as a proud rejection of purposelessness.[37] All form followed function. Inside, the plant "resembled nothing so much as a beehive," a buzzing network of "clangorous noise and bewildering movement; machines whirring, grimy laborers in caps and overalls piling materials, groups standing at benches putting strange contrivances together, leather gauntleted mechanics handling dangerous-looking levers; live steam springing in one area, men with oxygen torches brazing metal in another; belts whirling, presses clanging, chutes rumbling, and trains of low-wheeled trucks filled with metal parts moving across the floor."[38] It was a symbol and highest expression of Henry Ford's industrial philosophy. "This is an age of utilitarianism, of the practical, and today's architecture is a manifestation thereof," Albert Kahn argued. "We do not lack appreciation of the beautiful and there [exists] the desire to encourage art—but only to the degree that it will not interfere with the chief object, namely—the serving of a particular purpose."[39] The purpose was scientific method in business: in particular experimentation, standardization, and repetition.[40]

Ford's second plant, the River Rouge Complex in nearby Dearborn, dwarfed even Highland Park: at the point of completion, it was the largest factory in the world. However, it came to be seen less as a crystal palace and more of an industrial monster. Walter Reuther, who would in the 1940s become president of the United Auto Workers (UAW), declared, "Highland Park was civilized, but the Rouge was a jungle. The humanitarianism that Henry Ford had shown so dramatically in his early days just didn't exist anymore."[41] Independent accounts of the Rouge repeatedly stressed not light and air but darkness, fire, dirt, grime, and violence.

Of course, this was a projection. Both plants were built by Kahn, both responded to the same social and economic forces, both had their share of industrial problems and supply of Service Department agents. The two factories simply came to symbolize the change that had taken place in the Ford Motor

Company between the Progressive Era and the 1920s, and, through that, something of the contrary sides to Ford's own character. One plant represented Ford's dedication to the principle of trial and error: a belief that what worked was right, and that no standard should be held if it ceased to benefit the company. The other suggested that what was right should work, that one needed only to respond to the owner's will and everything else would follow.

From the Red Scare onward, Americans began to be exposed to the ambiguities of Ford's effort to subsume all ethical considerations to his definition of practical necessity. Although Fordism was in many ways the epitome of high rationalism, like the pediment that ran along the factory rooftop at Highland Park it was never possible entirely to remove the functionless from the design of the system, to entirely replace the prejudicial with the rational. Indeed, as Ford accelerated his efforts to purge his plants of dissent, he also took steps to impose his own moral framework on society, beginning with a systematic effort to discredit the union movement by associating it with Bolshevism. "There is in this country," Ford wrote, "a sinister element that desires to creep in between the men who work with their hands and the men who think and plan for the men who work with their hands. The same influence that drove the brains, experience and ability out of Russia is busily engaged in raising prejudice here. We must not suffer the stranger, the destroyer, the hater of happy humanity, to divide our people." Naturally given to their station, Ford argued, even the lowliest workers would accept a subordinate position as long as mischievous elements that sought to disseminate naive and destructive ideas were kept at bay. "The average worker," Ford concluded, "I am sorry to say, wants a job in which he does not have to think. The vast majority of men want to stay put. They want to be led. They want to have everything done for them and to have no responsibility." Of course, he admitted, "radical agitators have tried to stir up trouble now and again," but his workers "regarded them simply as human oddities and their interest in them has been the same sort of interest that they would have in a four-legged man."[42] In casting unionists as carpetbaggers, Ford resembled the antebellum planters who asserted the contentedness of their slaves while hiring ever more brutal overseers to police them. And like the racism of the old South, his antiradical rhetoric served to obscure the glaring disjuncture between his assertions of natural loyalty and his accelerating efforts to root out dissent.

Ford also went to great lengths to depict himself as an exemplar of an authentic, traditional Americanism. Publicists were set the task of spreading details of the Ford myth: his local Michigan roots and abiding adherence to the life and values of a simple American farmer, his quaint agrarianism and naturalism (including keen ornithology and collection of early Americana), his unsophisticated pleasures—he loved to dance the quadrille—and a dedication to hard work that led him from childhood fascination with clockwork watches to a personal workshop in his family home in Dearborn where he spent his free evenings. Like his products, Ford was simple and straightforward—and all the more universal and valuable for it. The *Detroit Saturday Night* reported that Ford "had not worn a dress suit more than half a dozen times in his life."[43] He did not smoke and refused to curse. Ford's reluctance to give personal interviews was considered just another sign of his naturally modest and retiring homeliness, rather than a suggestion that the man of the headlines was as much corporate caricature as reality. A biographer later stated, "Throughout his manhood he has cherished one wife. Jewelry to him has meant a watch. Food and drink are means of health, not of gratification. In exercise, as in diet, he is moderate."[44] Much was made of his youthful enthusiasm for the *McGuffey Readers* and his down-home "American" (meaning suspicious) approach to intellectuality, and in terms of personal faith he was commonly identified with the kind of practical, rugged, undoctrinaire Christianity seen by many as the bedrock of American society.

Ford aligned himself with the uncomplicated instincts of midwestern Protestantism, especially when it came to alcohol. Temperate by inclination, Ford was disgusted by the boozing behavior of his workers: because of the image of the company they sent out, because of the damage alcoholism did to home lives, but most of all because of its impact on production. He was the most vocal supporter of Prohibition in Michigan before it was banned in 1918 (before the Eighteenth Amendment was passed nationally) and vigorously promoted the virtues of sobriety thereafter, often explicitly linking alcohol consumption to radicalism. The industrialist lavishly funded the Detroit Anti-Saloon League and was touted on several occasions as a potential presidential candidate for the Prohibition Party.[45] In response to growing evidence of illegal trafficking from Canada, Ford urged the government to call out the army to patrol the border.[46] He met with President Coolidge in early 1927 to make the case for Prohibition, and again with President Hoover in mid-1929, arguing the only response to infringement was "absolute enforcement."[47] "Business and booze are enemies," he declared.[48]

Among the observers of this was Antonio Gramsci, who wrote about the logic of Prohibition from his prison cell in Italy. Making clear reference to Ford, he commented, "In America, rationalization and prohibition are undoubtedly related: inquiries by industrialists into the private lives of workers and the inspection services created by some industrialists to control the 'morality' of workers are necessities of the new method of work."[49] But since such behavior aligned with old religious values, it was possible to pass novelty off as tradition. Gramsci noted how ideas were "inserting themselves naturally into traditional Puritanism, that is, presenting themselves as a revival of the morality of the pioneers, or of the 'true American spirit,' etc."[50] Innovative and transformative elements of industrial society were therefore disguised as a harking back to an older, purer America.

Ford drew upon other local "traditions" as well. Most notoriously, he dedicated ninety-one consecutive issues of Ford's personal newspaper, the *Dearborn Independent,* to publicizing theories of a secret conspiracy of Jews attempting to subvert the nation.[51] In this, Ford authorized the first American printing of *The Protocols of the Elders of Zion,* which posited the existence of a secret world Jewish council that sought to undermine all independent state power. Originally forged in Russia at the turn of the century, the documents had found their way into Ford's hands through a Russian émigré and former member of the aristocratic anti-Semitic organization the Black Hundred, named Boris Brasol.[52] Brasol, who had been originally introduced to Ford by members of U.S. military intelligence, ensured that Ford's anti-Semitism would be more than just a continuation of indigenous traditions; his brand of xenophobia was augmented by theories from turn-of-the-century pogrom-ridden Russia.[53].

It is hard to overestimate the scale of the operation. The industrialist embarked upon it with the absolute commitment he gave to any of his corporate projects. William Cameron, editor of the *Dearborn Independent;* Ernest Liebold, the company's general manager; Brasol; and, to a smaller extent, Bennett all collaborated on the campaign, although Bennett later denied involvement. Agents were ordered to investigate employees, rivals, and public figures (including Presidents Taft, Wilson, and Hoover) for suspected Semitic affiliations. Nearly five million dollars over eight years was sunk into printing and distributing the *Dearborn Independent,* and car dealers were forced to sell it on their forecourts. Circulation hit a half-million copies weekly. The anti-Semitic articles were collected together as a book and sold as *The International Jew* under Ford's name. More than ten million copies were distributed in the United States, nearly one for every tenth person in the country. It was translated into sixteen languages, making its way onto the shelves, among many others, of many Nazis. Albert Lee notes that Ford has the dubious honor of being the only American to be mentioned in the pages of *Mein Kampf.* And "next to Adolf Hitler's desk at Nazi Party Headquarters in Munich hung a life-sized likeness of Henry Ford."[54]

Ford's anti-Semitism was intimately linked to his uncompromising authoritarianism and belief that the "natural" order of Ford Motor Company could be upset only by outside conspirators. Ford believed he was assaulted on two fronts, above and below: by rivals funded by Wall Street, which he deeply mistrusted, and by unionists. Yet he saw one enemy behind both schemes, variously described as Bolshevism, Judaism, or international moneymen. "The professional financiers wrecked Germany," Ford wrote in 1926. "The professional reformers wrecked Russia. You can take your choice as to who made the better job of it."[55] Jews were to blame for the general debauchery of public life. Ford decried a "general letting down of standards . . . felt everywhere."[56] As Leo Ribuffo notes, "Jews were accused of spreading religious modernism, fixing the 1919 World Series, and founding farm cooperatives to corrupt the heartland."[57] In *U.S.A.*, John Dos Passos mockingly wrote that Ford believed the "Jews were why the world wasn't like Wayne Country, Michigan, in the old horse-and-buggy days; the Jews had started the war, Bolshevism, Darwinism, Marxism, Nietzsche, short skirts and lipstick. They were behind Wall Street and the international bankers, and the whiteslave traffic and the movies and the Supreme Court and ragtime and the illegal liquor business."[58] All the problems of the world—the corruption of politics in Europe and the continent's apparent abandonment of liberty, venality in big business and decadence in popular life, the ceaseless desire of government to bring in unnecessary and destructive legislation, Ford's inability to retain market share—followed from a conspiracy of the Jews, "a nasty Orientalism [that] has insidiously affected every channel of expression."[59]

In this way, Ford took documents originally created in czarist Russia, tied them to a homegrown anti-Semitic tradition, and used them to disassociate himself and his corporation from modernity, to identify himself with the traditional values of an older Christian America and deny the fact that many of these changes were in truth being driven by the onrush of Fordist capitalism.[60] Tellingly, Ford's editor, Cameron, claimed in 1952 that when he began the initial anti-Semitic campaign, he had not even read *The Protocols*. He knew only one book on the subject, Werner Sombart's sociological treatise, *Jews and Modern Capitalism*, which—in the manner of Max Weber's work on the Protestant ethic—explicitly linked Jewish culture with modernity.[61]

To Ford, the Russian Revolution was the clearest example of the worldwide Jewish conspiracy in action. Bolshevism was "the international program of the Protocols, which might be 'put over' by a minority in any country," Ford argued. "Only Jewish pens are trusted with Bolshevist propaganda."[62] In the United States, only "Jewish, alien, Communist and Negro" people knocked the country, and the "professional Communist is often a Jew, and nearly always an alien."[63] Even conservative Jewish critics of Ford, like Louis Marshall of the American Jewish Committee, were dismissed as Bolsheviks.[64]

Ford's ideas may have served a certain utility, reinforcing popular antiradical instincts by appealing to prejudices in the public psyche, but it is hard to believe that they were implemented entirely cynically. Indeed, Ford clung to his fantasies about Jewish-Communist conspiracies long after any corporate advantage had evaporated. In 1927 he was sued after making libelous statements about a Jewish attorney from Chicago and was forced into a humiliating retraction. Ford unconvincingly claimed that he had been exploited by anti-Semites within his company.[65] From this time on, the corporation increasingly talked of the dangers of communism without putting the word *Jewish* beforehand. This was something the industrialist knew he could do without fear of reprisal, yet would still be understood by other anti-Semites as a code word for Jew.[66]

Ford had given in to a hyperrationality that transformed all attacks on him into a vast singular conspiracy. Just as his company was a single system with him at the head, all problems, all enemies, all rivals were part of a single network, a single interlocking causality. And because spying, Prohibition, corruption, and heavy-handedness did not ultimately stop the decline of Ford Motor Company in relative terms, the threat had to be of a terrifying scale. Ford was a superstitious man. But Bennett, who had observed him more closely than most, noted that "he had ways of rationalizing these things. He'd say 'If a black cat crosses the road and you're superstitious, then you'll drive more carefully and that's a good thing. Anyone who will walk under a ladder deserves to get a paint pot on his head.'"[67] Perhaps this is the crucial point about Fordist antiradicalism. Industrial rationalization transformed existing processes, broke them down into parts, and modified them, making use of the material available. It began from a priori assumptions like anything else did, even if those assumptions were illogical. Prejudicial ideas were used if they might benefit the company, but departing from these ideas altogether, when they had become a liability, was difficult. They were built into the framework of Fordism as much as Albert Kahn's concessions to art were hidden in the brickwork at Highland Park.

* * *

If his efforts to revolutionize the economy of Michigan were not enough, the absurdity of Ford presenting himself as a traditionalist was amply demonstrated by his curious relationship with revolutionary Russia. At the same time his staff were attacking the Bolshevik Revolution as a practical manifestation of a Jewish campaign for world domination, representatives of the Ford Motor Company were secretly negotiating with the Bolsheviks to secure business deals. As early as 1919, Ford had covertly discussed vehicle export agreements with the revolutionary regime, despite the fact that trading with the Soviet regime was, at this point, technically still illegal. He met with Ludwig Martens of the Soviet Information Bureau, and negotiations were proceeding well until the bureau was shut down by the Lusk Committee. Ford subsequently secured a small export agreement with the Bolsheviks via a front organization.[68] Bolshevik booster Armand Hammer, who had worked for the Soviet bureau, claimed he met with Ford in early 1922 to discuss expanding trade; both Hammer and his father, Julius—the pair were active Communists—floated the idea of setting up a Ford plant in Russia.[69]

The complex interrelationship between company interests and personal prejudices thus led to a quixotic attitude toward communism, a tendency to disparage its "foreign" presence in the United States but a conciliatory approach toward it in Russia. Articles in the *Dearborn Independent* in 1919 defended Russia's conduct in the war, arguing that it did not "quit" the war but was forced to withdraw because of the bankruptcy of the czarist system. They even contended that America no longer held the monopoly on liberty, that there was "now a whole progressive world with which to keep step," noting that when Trotsky lived in the United States, "in this 'land of equal opportunity' the future leader of Russia found that each separate meal of victuals and each clean collar was a problem and an uncertainty."[70] The *Independent* concluded that, "Nothing but a revolution would have cleared away that black condition [of czarism]," and not even "the American Revolution was achieved without violence."[71] Ford's editor, William Cameron, later said that they felt that the American Revolution was "completing its circuit of the world" and "manifesting through less well-prepared minds than it did with our forefathers, coming out in curious forms with the same spirit. Mr. Ford probably had the feeling in the beginning that this was another as it looked then."[72]

The contradictory attitude of the *Dearborn Independent* toward Bolshevism should not be seen simply as an incoherent editorial policy, although it un-doubtedly showed signs of that. Despite exploiting fears of Bolshevism to attack unions at home, Ford also used the pages of his newspaper to lay the ground-work for business forays abroad. This latter effort stalled when the Soviets placed a temporary ban on American vehicles. But in the middle of 1925, relations again warmed. The *Dearborn Independent* ran a report from a correspondent who had recently returned from a trade fair in Nizhny Novgorod. The reporter found Russia transformed. "Communism is very fine," he said, "but money is what's needed right now."[73] An article in October 1926 argued that Jewish groups were being thrown out of Russia.[74] A month later, a piece was published called "Red Russia Turns Pink." "Under Stalin," it claimed, Russia "is leaving behind the doctrines of world revolution and pure Marxism." Stalin had "thrust aside at least temporarily the Jewish ideal of world revolution" and instead was con-centrating on "building up Russia." "The defeat [of the Jews] augurs well for Russia," it concluded.[75] In the best Kremlin style, the newspaper was by way of careful nudges and winks paving the way for a rapprochement.

Later that year, the Ford Trade School accepted around fifty Russian students, and the company began to export a small number of vehicles to the Soviet state, adding up to perhaps about twenty-five thousand by the end of the decade.[76] Ford had already become a folk hero for Russian farmers whose lives had been transformed by the arrival of the tractor; *Fordizatsia* came to mean modern, progressive methods even in parts of the country that the combustion engine had not yet reached.[77] But his engagement accelerated dramatically under Stalin. In 1928 the first Five-Year Plan was launched, which included a call for a new automobile plant in Nizhny Novgorod with a capacity to produce one hundred thousand vehicles annually. Ford was offered the concession. At the end of May 1929, the industrialist signed a contract with Amtorg to build a plant capable of manufacturing automobiles similar to the Model A automobile and Model AA truck. The Russians also committed to buying more than seventy thousand American-manufactured vehicles over the next four years. In exchange at least fifty Russian engineers a year would be brought to Highland Park to learn about car manufacturing firsthand. Ford director Charles Sorensen traveled to Russia for a "wildly exciting week during which he and Perry [a colleague] were treated like emperors."[78] Then Albert Kahn was summoned over to design a four-million-dollar plant in Stalingrad and was feted as a hero of the revolution.[79]

In the first year of the contract, the Soviets bought more units than originally agreed.[80] In December 1930, Albert Kahn told the Cleveland Engineering Society, "As to Russia meeting its financial obligations, we have neither complaint nor misgivings. From what we know, we believe it safe to say that the present form of Government is stable and here to stay, though many modifications undoubtedly will be necessary." Kahn said he was not interested in their politics: "We feel as Mr. Ford so well expressed it, that that which makes for the upbuilding of Russia is bound to prove of benefit to all nations, America included."[81]

Despite Kahn's optimism, relations deteriorated from late 1931, and the business agreements fizzled out in the mid-1930s, after Stalin had assured himself that Russian engineers had gained the technical capability to produce vehicles by themselves. Nevertheless, for a brief period, Ford was instrumental in aiding the first Five-Year Plan, supporting the Amtorg Corporation and helping to normalize relations with Russia. In this, like so many other things, where Ford led others followed. By the late 1920s, several of the more ambitious and risk-taking corporations in the United States had begun to take an interest in Soviet Russia as an emerging market. Although reports continued to suggest that the regime had been destroying churches and persecuting religious leaders, business elites seemed largely unconcerned, inclined instead to recognize in Russia a resurgent nationalism and buoyant, youthful, energetic society. By the end of 1930, Radio Corporation of America, Du Pont, General Electric, and Westinghouse were all doing big business with the Bolsheviks.[82] Unimpressed, the New York Evening Post commented, "While American industry is responding to this call for assistance from revolutionized Russia, the people of the United States continue to feel utter antipathy for the Communist principles of the Soviet regime."[83]

Ford's bipolar attitudes reflected a broader ambivalence within the business world. On the one hand, many business representatives were leading antiradicals. The New York City Chamber of Commerce had set up a committee to "defend the American government" and launch a "militant fight" against Bolshevism. Other groups alleged that the Soviet government was employing unfair dumping tactics to offload Soviet produce in America and destabilize the country, pointing out that Russia was using forced labor to produce exports more cheaply than American businesses. Darkly noting the importance of raw materials in wartime, they implied that this was not just a trade disagreement but the first step in a broader Soviet plan to bring America to its knees.[84] Supporting the claims, Father Edmund Walsh argued that Soviet dumping was "part of a program that was being executed simultaneously throughout the world," an evolution into the economic sphere of the traditional Bolshevik desire for world domination.[85] For a short while, the government even approved an embargo of certain Soviet products. Arthur M. Hyde, the secretary of agriculture, accused the Russians of selling wheat short to depress international prices and push American wheat out of the market. Three farmers' associations supported the claims, accusing Russia of "communistic activities in the United States threatening the welfare of the American farmer."[86]

But on the other hand, as powerful as these arguments seemed, they meant little to many American businessmen looking for new market opportunities in the midst of the Depression. As a result, when Hamilton Fish turned to the business world for support during his committee hearings, he found a divided community. By the start of the 1930s, the United States was earning as much as $150 million in trade with Russia annually. Alongside other big businesses opening concessions in Russia, Ford managers appeared before the Fish Committee to declare that their economic relationships with the Bolsheviks had been entirely favorable and conducted with integrity. Brooklyn businessmen who had worked with Amtorg vouched for the reliability of Red traders; meanwhile, representatives of the Chicago Board of Trade took issue with Secretary Hyde and the Grangers on the wheat issue, stating that the short selling would not have significantly depressed prices.[87] Taken as a whole, then, business offered nothing like the consistently anticommunist vision they would present to Americans in later decades.

*   *   *

The tremendous growth of the automobile industry in Michigan between the turn of the century and the Second World War was for inhabitants of the state the experience that linked all others. The employment generated by the industry and its suppliers was the chief reason for the astronomical growth of the city. As it moved from a world of coach and buggies to honking horns and traffic cops, Detroit swallowed surrounding communities as if it were some kind of macroscopic phagocyte. Sewage pipes, electricity grids, paved roads, and housing followed the signposts of the city outward, and when the distances involved became sufficiently large it boiled upward as well. Skyscrapers stretched into the air, mimicking and modifying the styles of Chicago and New York, while the Ambassador Bridge and Detroit-Windsor Tunnel rolled across the straits to Ontario. From this unprecedented expansion came the many social tensions common to modern city life: cultural, linguistic and ethnic clashes, conflict over public spaces, housing shortages, political corruption, and labor politics. Amid this disorder and chaos, Detroit came to resemble a frontier town writ large.

Naturally, the fears as well as the aspirations of Detroit citizens were stimulated by this transformation, yet the sheer power and wealth generated by industrialization ensured that the negative consequences of capitalism were rarely associated with the industrialists principally responsible for them. Instead, anxieties were displaced upon the communist enemy, the industrial activist, the foreigner, the subversive, or the Jew.

Nevertheless, over time it became harder to buy public affection. Reformers began to point out that the uncompromising policies adopted by industrial elites had created conditions that actually strengthened the hand of extremists. The destruction of the Auto Workers Union in 1919 by Ford and his peers had done nothing to reduce workers' alienation, but it had helped Communists seize control of the wreckage of the organization. Faith in the AFL was low. One activist, Frank Marquart, recalled that "we all knew that 'the AF of Hell' was not in the least interested in organizing a strong industrial union because such an organization would threaten the entrenched jobs of many craft union leaders."[88] Only those accustomed to repression and committed ideologically to organizing industrial workers were able to function in the climate of physical intimidation, arrests, beatings, arbitrary dismissals, and strikebreaking that characterized interwar Detroit. Communists were willing to run such risks and, importantly, able to deploy external lawyers, organizers, financiers, and publicists to defend their members. Moreover, through their foreign-language associations, the party could appeal to non-English-speaking autoworkers. Over the decade, party membership slowly climbed to around five hundred people in a dozen or so shops scattered about Detroit, a tiny number among a laboring class of hundreds of thousands, but nevertheless an active and influential group with real roots in the community and the industry, and a growing body of organizational expertise.[89]

Communists naturally targeted Ford, both as Detroit's largest industrial conglomeration and as the nation's most visible symbol of free-market fundamentalism.[90] In April 1926, they began printing the *Ford Worker* to provide a voice for grievances about pay and conditions. Letters written to the editor made it clear how far conditions differed from the sparkling crystal palaces found in company press releases. One contributor wrote, "The dirt and filth is awful! In some places it is an inch thick on the floor," and there was no ventilation. "During the hot weather we go home covered with cotton dust, grease and sweat." With no breeze, the dust "settles over everything. We breathe it into our lungs and we eat it during lunch period. We are not allowed to sit on the stock to eat, so like pigs and dogs we eat on the floor."[91]

Meanwhile, since the introduction of Prohibition, Detroit had seen not only the rapid rise of organized crime, but also a massive increase in the public consumption of alcohol. The *New York Times* estimated that there were thirty thousand speakeasies in the city by the end of the twenties, twenty times the number a decade earlier. Eighty-five percent of the illegal alcohol brought into the United States came over the Detroit River.[92] The reported murder rate at the end of the decade was lower than the peak year of 1926, but it was still nearly three times the 1922 level and would not rise as high again until the 1960s. Things got worse as times got tougher: between 1929 and 1933, reported crime in Detroit rose by 30 percent.[93] The police were so comprehensively on the take—whether from Capones or corporations—that faith in the criminal justice system was virtually nonexistent. The city was overcrowded and squalid. Growth had led to a drastic housing shortage, public health systems in desperate need of reform, and simmering class and ethnic tensions. Some 575,000 people had come to live in the city in the 1920s, taking the population to 1.5 million.[94] Detroit had engorged even Highland Park, although Ford's influence ensured that in municipal terms it remained an indigestible administrative oasis within the city limits. Factory owners could still expect employees to speak dozens of languages; a quarter of all Detroit residents were foreign born and probably a majority of Ford's employees. Wealthier white residents moved away from the city; the African American population rose to nearly 10 percent of the city, squeezed into the unsanitary, dangerous, and overcrowded area ironically called Paradise Valley that extended from the city center up toward Highland Park along Woodward Avenue. And whereas average wages had stayed roughly the same over the decade, the cost of living had marched on so that real earnings for many workers had fallen.

Even if the crash of 1929 was the product of an apparently abstract and dissociated financial crash, then, the alienated and disaffected of Detroit were not short of evidence of deeper malaise. One need only to hop to Belle Isle on a Sunday and look at the beautiful dresses and sharply ironed suits of the Grosse Point establishment picnicking together, laughing and joking. Or turn one's eyes from the dirty streets of Paradise Valley to the inspiring silhouettes of the Penobscot or the Albert Kahn–designed Fisher Building, both architectural marvels completed in 1928. For many, such wealth in proximity to such poverty could mean only robbery in concealed form. Increasingly desperate, people began to look to the extreme alternatives American capitalism was supposed to have made redundant: whether radical preachers, radical labor groups, or even radical ethnic associations such as the Nation of Islam, born in the crucible of the city's segregated neighborhoods in the midst of the Depression years.

Virtually every year of the 1920s had seen an increase in the total number of cars sold in the United States. Nelson Lichtenstein estimates that by 1929, the auto industry accounted for almost 13 percent of the value of all manufactured goods and directly or indirectly involved one-sixth of all working Americans.[95] In Michigan alone, Ford, General Motors, and Chrysler employed more than 200,000 people.[96] But with the Depression, this extraordinary period of growth came to a halt. Between 1929 and 1931, the number of cars sold fell from four to two million and halved again in 1932.[97] Responding to falling demand, Ford fired tens of thousands of workers and dropped his minimum wage to four dollars per day, sinking below the five-dollar rate that had been announced to such acclaim more than a decade and a half before.[98] By April 1930, 750,000 workers were unemployed in Michigan.[99] But since Ford's heartland in Highland Park was technically outside the city limits, despite being entirely surrounded by Detroit, the company was not legally obliged to contribute to the city's overstretched relief rolls.[100]

The unfettered liberties enjoyed by the automobile magnates in the 1920s left Detroit with two unwelcome honors: the highest unemployment rates in the country and one of the largest concentrations of Communist activists in the nation. Nevertheless, the inevitably ruthless response to the recession was presented as an inescapable reaction to market forces, a particularly ironic argument given that Ford staff had previously stressed that their high-wage strategy enabled workers to buy cars themselves and thus produced a virtuous circle of consumption and production. When unemployed workers began marching in protest, industrialists responded predictably. A strike at the Fisher Body Plant in July 1930 was denounced as an orchestration of "foreign agitators and Communists." A local police chief declared that "thwarting Communism required him to 'violate the law' and that, if necessary, he would 'continue to do [so].'"[101]

The turning point came with the Hunger March of March 1932, orchestrated by Communists and other labor activists, attended by several thousand unemployed workers, and directed, as usual, at Ford. The plan was to march from the center of Detroit north for four miles along Woodward to Highland Park, but at the city line between Detroit proper and Highland Park the local and municipal police attempted to turn them away. Attempts to use tear gas to disperse the crowd were frustrated by strong winds, and the marchers continued to the gates of the plant.[102] There, the marchers came face-to-face with Ford Service Men and police officers, and the confrontation descended into a pitched battle. Hearing reports of the violence, Harry Bennett sped to the scene in a car and leaped from the vehicle waving either a white flag, tear-gas gun, or revolver (depending on which account one believes). A rock was thrown from the crowd, striking him on the head. The police and Service Men opened fire indiscriminately.[103]

Four were killed and dozens injured in what quickly became known as the "Ford Massacre." Perhaps as many as ten thousand protesters joined the funeral procession a few days later.[104] The Detroit Federation of Labor denounced the behavior of the police as "wanton and disgraceful," and a grand jury was set up to investigate the events.[105] In the weeks following, Ford Motor Company again sought to deploy the tactics of diversionary red-baiting. Wayne County prosecutor Harry S. Toy argued that the whole event was orchestrated by the Communist International—converting the grand jury, in one critic's words, "into an anti-Red carnival"—and the grand jury acquitted all the defendants. Meanwhile, prosecutors used a state criminal syndicalism law to prosecute the march organizers. Some sixty individuals were charged with membership in proscribed organizations. No attention was paid to Bennett's men. Their revolvers were not even taken for comparison with bullets taken from the bodies by police ballistics officers.[106]

Nevertheless, the flagrancy of the attempt to divert attention by claiming Communist conspiracy was not lost on those Detroit citizens aware that Ford's anticommunism seemed curiously weaker when it came to trading with Russia. The populist Catholic priest Charles Coughlin, for one, drew attention to the industrialist's double standards, noting in sermons that it was difficult "for any sane man to comprehend why the communists should take action against the Ford Motor Company in view of the fact that Ford men and Ford money and Ford machinery probably have done more to perfect the Soviet Five-Year-Plan than was contributed by any other single agency in America."[107]

In his sympathetic biography of Ford, William Adams Simonds claims that overlooking the area where the Ford Massacre occurred was "a great room in which were seventy Soviet engineers, learning to take back to Communist Russia what the American Communists were bent on destroying." As the events unfolded, the engineers stared out of the window, "marveling at what they called 'the fools' in the road below."[108] But if Ford's supporters saw this as evidence of the destructive absurdity of the protesters, others took it as a sign of the hypocrisy of Fordist capitalism. Ford's reputation as entrepreneur and folk hero was being called into question, just as the close equation of capitalism and Americanism seemed also to be challenged for the first time in a generation. Residents of Detroit were as likely to associate Ford's empire with the ruthlessness of Harry Bennett's Service Department, the anti-Semitic campaigns of the *Dearborn Independent,* or the deaths of the Ford Massacre as with the innovative industrial methods that had brought such prosperity to the region fifteen years earlier. Likewise, across the country, many ordinary people began vaguely to perceive that perhaps unfettered capitalism had more in common with the nightmares of communism than superficial assumptions might suggest.

A culminating demonstration of this peculiar revelation came in 1933, when Edsel Ford, Henry Ford's son, paid the Mexican Communist Diego Rivera twenty thousand dollars to paint a mural on the walls of the Detroit Institute of Arts.[109] Given that, under Depression pressure, the budget for the institute as a whole had fallen to forty thousand dollars—a tenth of its level four years earlier—the fee was enormous. Given the layoffs that were taking place at the Ford plant because of supposedly inescapable financial pressure the company was under, it was scandalous.

Despite Rivera's communism, he and Ford got along famously when they met. They shared a progressive fascination with technology and a belief in the power of industry to release mankind from poverty that transcended their political differences. Rivera, who called Ford "a true poet and artist, one of the greatest in the world," chose to depict the River Rouge plant in his murals as the essence of Detroit (much to the chagrin of Detroit's high society, who considered industrial activity a subject unfitting for art).[110] Religious leaders took particular offense. Reverend H. Ralph Higgins complained to the *Detroit Free Press* that local citizens had been "violently upset" by the paintings. Meanwhile, a Monsignor Doyle "felt it was an affront to millions of Catholics that a man who was a Communist and an anticlerical should have been given the commission."[111]

According to Rivera's recollections, an attempt to whitewash the murals was halted when eight thousand local workers volunteered to guard the room in shifts morning to night until the scandal died down. It is hard to know how much of this was exaggeration—perhaps a great deal—but the strange arrangement of forces was nevertheless remarkable. Workers were standing at the doors of the city's Institute of Arts in order to defend a cultural icon from assault by Detroit's elites. The artwork had been paid for by capitalist money given to a Mexican Communist, who in turn had chosen to extol the virtues of factories built by an antiradical and anti-Semitic industrialist. It could not have expressed any more clearly how dissolute the countersubversive message had become in the early years of the Depression.[112]

Ford's public relations crisis therefore reflected a broader Depression-era tendency to see unfettered capitalism and revolutionary communism as two halves of the same problem. Southern agrarians, for instance, writing in defense of the long-lost antebellum order, declared that communism would come to America in the wake of "the blind drift of our industrial development," and in the end Americans would end up with "much the same economic system as that imposed by violence upon Russia in 1917."[113] The similarities between extremes of Left and Right were even visible from the other side of the Atlantic. In 1932 a man born in Godalming, near Surrey, published a book that made explicit the curious associations the Great Depression seemed to have exposed. Aldous Huxley had read Ford's *My Life and Work* and was taken with the practical similarities he saw between extreme capitalism and extreme communism. His novel

Brave New World offered a dystopic vision of the future that made a trenchant critique of contemporary society from a centrist, antiauthoritarian perspective. In the book, Fordist and Bolshevik terminology are used interchangeably: characters include Bernard Marx, Lenina Crowne, and Henry Foster. In the future world, Christian imagery has been replaced with industrial terminology: dates are marked AF, "After Ford"; the model of a T comes to replace the cross; and exclamations of surprise see *Lord* transformed to *Ford*. Readers at the time would have understood immediately the political implications of the book.

Ultimately, as David E. Nye writes, Henry Ford "existed for the public as a malleable bundle of contradictions ambiguous enough to admit of many interpretations."[114] His success saw him transformed into a representation of business in human form, and the story of his company in the 1920s and 1930s came to represent the fortunes of free-market politics altogether. In fact, Ford was extreme and idiosyncratic, representative of nothing other than himself. Nevertheless, it was not surprising that people saw the Henry Ford of 1920 as the epitome of capitalist antiradicalism. The man set up a ruthless and repressive system of industrial control, promoted the criminalization of drinking as a measure to reorder society, and launched the largest anti-Semitic campaign in American history as part of a larger project to fight radicalism. He ranked with Morgan and Rockefeller among the triumvirate of great devils for the Communist Party of the United States, more hated even than the Republican presidents of the era. Yet by 1933, a small but growing number of Americans had begun to see Henry Ford as a dangerous radical, someone who was destroying traditional America. The Fordist prescription had brought incredible growth, but it had not brought stability. It had certainly failed to limit the appeal of radicalism. According to his critics, Ford reduced human beings to the role of cogs in vast industrial machines. And, as if to perfectly demonstrate the point, the great industrialist pointed to the future of America by inviting Bolshevik designers to his plants and Communist muralists to "deface" the home of Detroit's limp cultural industry.

The collapse of Ford's reputation was therefore a dramatic illustration of the profound shift in the political landscape of the United States taking place under the force of the Great Depression. For the next few years, it would be liberals and reformers, rather than conservatives, businessmen, and right-wingers, who would drive forward the twin meanings of American loyalty and liberty. For these groups, only reform offered the chance of saving America from an otherwise inevitable revolution.

7

Troubled Spirits

Christianity and Antiradicalism

Somewhat improbably, German American writer and propagandist George Sylvester Viereck found himself interviewing Henry Ford in 1928 for an article in the Rosicrucian journal, the *Mystic Triangle.* After being shown in to the industrialist's office and exchanging the usual pleasantries, Viereck began quizzing Ford on his religious beliefs, which Ford expounded upon with a glazed and distant look in his eyes. "Somewhere there is a Master Mind which sends brain waves or messages to us," he explained calmly and seriously, "the Brain of Mankind, the Brain of the Earth." Ford felt that he had "never done anything by my own volition. I was always pushed by invisible forces within and without me." Although much of the wisdom of the ages could be found in the Bible, reincarnation was "the essence of all knowledge." "Life," Ford argued, "is perpetual and continuous."[1]

Reincarnation provided Ford with a sense of purpose he could find only in an absolute order generated by a coherent structure underpinning the universe. "The discovery of reincarnation put my mind at ease," he explained to his interviewer. "I was settled. I felt that order and progress were present in the mystery of life. I no longer looked elsewhere for a solution to the riddle of life." The eternal animating spirit was something like a "Queen Bee in the complicated hive which constitutes the individual. You may call it the Master Cell or you may call it the Soul."

These beliefs have since become part of the mythology surrounding America's most famous industrial pioneer. In E. L. Doctorow's 1975 novel, *Ragtime,* for instance, Henry Ford appears as an idiot savant. Invited to New York to discuss theology with financier J. P. Morgan, Ford finds himself impressed by the analogies the banker draws between Ford's factories and the Egyptian pyramids, but is too busy making cars to travel to see the wonders of the ancient civilization for himself. Asked by Morgan for his theological views, Ford explains, "Reincarnation is the only belief I hold, Mr. Morgan. I explain my genius this way—some of us have just lived more times than others."[2]

The interview with Viereck was nevertheless a remarkable confession. Ford and his publicists had gone to great lengths to assert the manufacturer's credentials as a mainstream orthodox Christian at a time when to be anything else was a cause of suspicion. The Protestant church was a pillar of the establishment and the alliance between vestry and director's office central to the procapitalist consensus of the decade. Although the marriage of God and mammon was at root a utilitarian relationship, it was enacted through avowals of shared beliefs and values: evangelical affirmations nestling in corporate statements, assurances of industrial piety made over drinks at Chambers of Commerce banquets, free-enterprise rhetoric emanating from the pulpits on Sunday mornings. Speaking at St. Peter and Paul's Cathedral just down the road from Ford's Highland Park factory, Rev. John A. McClorey reassured his parishioners that "*immoderate* love of money is the root of all evil"—a qualification providing ample vindication for the acquisitive instincts of his ambitious corporate parishioners.[3]

A shared hostility to radical politics was a central part of the process by which the alliance of church and industry was cemented. Antiradical ethics expressed a point where religious and corporate conceptions of the good seemingly came together, since Bolsheviks challenged the established norms both of this world and the next. Indeed, Ford had explicitly argued that the reason "Bolshevism did not work, and cannot work, is not economic," but "because it was both unnatural and immoral."[4] In an interview given a year after the one with Viereck, Ford told journalists that he read the Bible every day and kept a copy in every room of the house. Religion was like electricity, he explained. The fact that it was invisible did not mean it did not exist.[5]

As with other elements of the fragile antiradical coalition of the 1920s, though, a friendly relationship between religion and free enterprise was by no means a given. Neither group was homogenous or necessarily conservative, nor did antiradicalism necessarily mean procapitalism. Businessmen objected if religious leaders interpreted the gospel in ways that questioned their right to use private property freely for personal gain, which was to them the essential problem with radicalism in the first place. Churchmen, meanwhile, worried that the apostles of the phenomena they were denouncing—whether divorce, crime, cosmopolitanism, modernity, birth control, doctrinal impurity, or even communism itself—were not radicals but their ostensible allies in the business world.

How might conservatives in the church reconcile their theological priorities with secular allies? After all, the new Ford system was unfamiliar to many religious leaders who looked with romanticized nostalgia at nineteenth- and eighteenth-century America for a vision of the ideal society. While his faith in

Queen Bees and master minds presumably helped Ford justify to himself his role at the head of an enormous hierarchy of individuals, it must have been of concern to Michigan's religious community. Careful avowals of homeliness and Bible study helped mollify religious leaders in the short term, but as the Depression approached evidence grew of the apparently alien nature of what capitalism was doing to American life. This challenged the dominant influence of religious antiradicalism and gave new strength to reformers within the church. After all, should the organizer of the largest network of industrial plants in the country really be allowed to do as he pleased with several hundred thousand souls if his faith was as, well, *strange* as Viereck's interview seemed to suggest?

As with the secular world, tensions had emerged between liberals and conservatives in the Protestant churches in the late nineteenth and early twentieth centuries, particularly in the northern Baptist and Presbyterian denominations that tended to have the most diverse congregations in socioeconomic, ethnic, and political terms. Under the influence of Walter Rauschenbusch and the historicist school, liberal ideas filtered through the church, giving rise to a vigorous social gospel movement focused on deploying the moral force of religion to push for social reform. As the First World War approached, however, opposition to this reformist and pragmatic doctrine strengthened markedly, particularly in the Midwest and Northeast. These reactions were typically evangelical (concerned with the redemption of souls through revivalist preaching and spiritual rebirth rather than good works), fundamentalist (holding to a faith in the inerrant literal truth of the Bible), and increasingly premillennial (believing in the imminent return of Christ following the end days as supposedly detailed in biblical prophecy).

In institutional terms, moderates and reformers largely controlled the interdenominational Protestant umbrella group set up in 1908, the Federal Council of Churches (FCC). Indeed, the very idea of interdenominational cooperation through a national bureaucracy was at root a liberal solution to a set of perceived liberal problems, although liberals typically failed to see it in these terms. With some justice, fundamentalists felt their preference for localized, communitarian, supernaturalistic Protestantism had little place in the *gesellschaft* bureaucracy of the FCC and, unsurprisingly, were hostile to the principle of ecumenical consolidation if it meant the promotion of habits they rejected.[6]

Although conflict manifested itself through institutions like the FCC, at root the division between conservatives and liberals was theological, orienting around the questions of how one should interpret the teachings of the Bible and whether the purpose of the church was to redeem souls or construct a Kingdom of God on earth.[7] Indeed, there was not always a straightforward correlation between reformist and fundamentalist approaches to Protestantism, on the one hand, and left-wing and right-wing politics, on the other. The evangelical tradition that had given birth to the new fundamentalism had been a central part of the American reform movement in the nineteenth century, and Progressive Era campaigns for moral regeneration, most clearly in the case of the prohibition of alcohol, enjoyed support from both modernizers and fundamentalists. Nevertheless, over time fundamentalism increasingly entailed a conservative politics for several reasons. First, focusing on individual redemption encouraged fundamentalists to downplay the importance of collective action as a method for dealing with social ills. This was especially true in the case of state-based activism, which formed a much more central part of reform politics in the twentieth century than it had in the nineteenth and was antithetical to the church-centered order preferred by fundamentalists. Second, presenting the teachings of the Bible as absolute and rejecting any compromise as an acquiescence to falsehood encouraged an intolerant attitude toward alternative beliefs. Third, emphasis on service and obedience to the law provided opportunities to blur the distinction between God's and man's authority, even though this was explicitly condemned by orthodox fundamentalists in principle. Finally, a basically pessimistic attitude toward the idea of historical progress—premillennialists held that the world would descend into a maelstrom of increasing violence and chaos until Christ returned to rescue the faithful—encouraged a defeatist, or at least distant, attitude toward the problems of the world. For many religious conservatives, the belief that man could move earth toward heaven was the height of modernistic hubris, a presumption of godly power on the part of the fallen, who should spend their time instead attending to their redemption.

Even before the World War I, then, fundamentalists revealed conservative inclinations. Nevertheless, the war marked the point when fundamentalism firmly shifted to the right, as attacks upon their loyalty transformed existing tensions with reformers into open warfare. Different fundamentalists responded in different ways to the war in Europe. Some, like fire-and-brimstone preacher Billy Sunday, were unparalleled in their jingoism. Sunday claimed at one point that if you turned hell upside down, you would find a sign saying "Made in Germany" on the bottom. But because of their hostility to state power and skepticism about Wilson's utopian internationalism, more resisted American engagement than reveled in it. William Jennings Bryan, the nation's foremost evangelical politician, resigned as secretary of state because of his opposition to the war. Meanwhile, prowar liberals such as Professor Shirley Jackson Case of the University of Chicago began attacking fundamentalism as subversive: archly claiming that their money came from German sources, that premillennialism lent itself to "the purposes of I.W.W. propaganda," and calling on Congress to investigate them.[8] Alva W. Taylor, writing in the liberal *Christian Century*, even compared fundamentalists with Bolsheviks, because both groups oriented their belief systems around the desire for a revolutionary cataclysm.[9]

Unsurprisingly, fundamentalists rejected this characterization, likening the allegations to the Salem witchcraft trials.[10] After all, at least as far back as the 1860s, fundamentalist preachers had attacked the "seething, surging, rioting masses of the dangerous classes of the ground tier" and the "armies marching and countermarching with banners on which are emblazoned dynamite, anarchism, communism, nihilism."[11] They interpreted attacks upon their war record as part of a broader liberal conspiracy to dominate the church conferences by casting doubt on their patriotism, loyalty, and sanity and shift Protestantism as a whole in a reformist, centralized direction.

As well as defending their Americanism, many fundamentalists responded by turning the smears back upon their rivals. The real subversive influence was not old-time religion, they argued, but the expansive, totalizing modernity that had produced the state war machines. As the influential fundamentalist theologian from Princeton Seminary J. Gresham Machen put it, modernism was "a totally diverse type of religious belief, which is only the more destructive of the Christian faith because it makes use of traditional Christian terminology." Once unmoored from the authority of the Bible as a literal description of the truth, they believed, there was no stopping until one reached a position of absolute relativism: the difference between liberalism, socialism, and communism was therefore only a matter of degree, not kind. All shared a worryingly "Catholic" enthusiasm for singular centralized authority. The denial of individual freedom, Machen wrote, "is most clearly seen in socialism; a socialistic state would mean the reduction to a minimum of the sphere of individual choice." But "the same tendency exhibits itself today in those communities where the name of socialism is most abhorred."[12] Victimized during the war, fundamentalists began to present modernizers as a conspiratorial cabal seeking to override the democratic will. Responding to the attacks on them in kind, fundamentalists declared liberals to be apostates in the house of the Lord.

The First World War, then, sharpened the political implications of ongoing theological disputes in the Protestant world, making coexistence between rival doctrines more difficult and putting the idea of subversion into theological debate on both sides.[13] Almost as soon as the war was over, these tensions came to the fore as liberal clergymen organized the Interchurch World Movement (IWM) to promote progressive religious politics; in response, fundamentalists formed their own interdenominational alternative, the World Christian Fundamentals Association.[14] Institutionalization immediately escalated tensions, as the IWM launched a major funding drive that inevitably drew money away from individual churches, including fundamentalist ones.

The national debate in 1919 over radicalism folded into this dispute, although ironically liberals and fundamentalists now more or less reversed the roles they had adopted during the war. Studies have found no single case where the liberals in the FCC sought to challenge Wilson's war policies.[15] After the war, however, they became heavily associated with the civil liberties backlash to the politics of countersubversion. Alva Taylor, who had maligned fundamentalists in 1918 by likening them to Bolsheviks, declared in the midst of the Great Red Scare that the "Soviet government has as much right to its trial in the court of mankind as monarchy or republicanism." A combine of ministers signed a public letter of protest following the ejection of the five Socialists from the New York State Assembly. Others denounced the Palmer Raids and Lusk laws in sermons, calling for amnesties of radicals imprisoned during the war. Perhaps the most headlines came when the Interchurch World Movement conducted a major investigation into the Great Steel Strike and concluded that the allegations of Bolshevik influence were a "glare of baseless excitement" used to divert attention from demands for collective bargaining rights. Antiradical smears were based on "inaccurate, prejudiced and misspelled reports" filled out by an army of paid corporate spies.[16] William Z. Foster declared the report to be "complete vindication of the workers' contentions in the great strike."[17] Over the next few years, the IWM cooperated with reformers in the National Catholic Welfare Conference (the Catholic version of the FCC) and the National Council of Rabbis to successfully end the twelve-hour day in the steel industry.

Conservatives responded by accusing the IWM of being infested with radicals. Rev. I. M. Haldeman, a Baptist minister from New York, predicted that within five years, it would "produce an ecclesiastical autocracy on the one hand and a church sovietism on the other."[18] In an address to the Boston Ministers' Meeting at Pilgrim Hall, the minister of South Church, Andover, Rev. E. Victor Bigelow, attacked the IWM steel report as "untrustworthy and lop-sided" and concluded, given the radical aspirations of William Z. Foster and his allies, "Does any one doubt the wisdom, justice and necessity of a spy system on the part of the U.S. Steel Corporation in sheer self defense?"[19] Indeed, anger over liberals' defense of radicals often turned out to be greater than hostility toward radicals themselves. Some conservative churchmen had voiced concern about Wilson-era political repression on antistatist grounds. Machen, for instance, considered the Lusk laws (which required patriotism to be taught in the classroom) to be a dangerous violation of the church-state divide. He mocked the tendency to excuse a man guilty of beating his wife by casting him "as the victim of some more of that Bolshevistic propaganda."[20] Yet, by contrast, any sign of liberal churchmen being soft on radicalism was condemned as heresy. Just as was the case for many other American countersubversives, state-based countersubversion may have been a path to tyranny, but a vigorous private crusade to keep the church pure was an entirely different matter.

Fueled by the liberal-conservative schism and the countersubversive spirit of the time, fundamentalists thus came to conclude that the churches themselves were a vehicle of Bolshevik influence in America. From a strictly organizational position, this was of course absurd. Some Protestant clergymen were openly socialists but only a handful among tens of thousands were ever Communist Party members.[21] Nevertheless, to fundamentalists and conservatives, it was "socialistic" thinking, not membership in the CPUSA, that marked out the compromised preacher, and it was precisely their presence inside the church that made them so dangerous. Liberal tolerance toward Soviet Russia or their defense of radical strikers was evidence that wrongheaded thinking had penetrated even among people who considered themselves immune to radical influence.

Because it was increasingly articulated in countersubversive terms, perhaps unsurprisingly fundamentalist anger at the rise of liberal theology swiftly hitched itself onto political and business groups seeking to challenge socialism and unionism for their own reasons. Ralph Easley of the National Civic Federation, for instance, joined attacks on reformist ministers in the IWM.[22] Woodrow Wilson's former secretary of state Robert Lansing (a Presbyterian elder) was asked to head an anti-Bolshevik "National Inter-church Board" to undercut the prolabor activism of the IWM.[23] A headline in the *New York Times* stated that authors of the IWM's steel report were "Pink Tea Socialists and Parlor Reds."[24] The religious establishment strongly supported antiunion campaigns such as the assault on the Auto Workers Union in Detroit. Rev. Ames Maywood, of the city's Cass Avenue (Methodist Episcopal) Church railed against the "destruction of the home" brought about by radical communistic propaganda, arguing that America was imperiled by a "poison which has been working steadily for a generation or more through unrestricted immigration and unchallenged immorality. It is time we restricted one and challenged the other."[25]

The effect was to strengthen the antiradical movement as a whole and to consolidate the links between religious and secular conservatives. Conservatives successfully forced the Northern Baptist and Northern Presbyterian Conventions to disaffiliate themselves from the IWM in 1920. Followed by the controversy over the Steel Strike report, the organization was more or less stopped in its tracks.[26]

Fundamentalists thus offered a powerful strain of antiradicalism to the countersubversive world and from the Great Red Scare onward augmented secular campaigns against radicalism and unionism, and against Soviet Russia and its defenders. In unison with business conservatives, Arno Clemens Gaebelein, Methodist preacher and editor of the fundamentalist journal *Our Hope,* declared that, "The exposure of nationwide plots to establish a Soviet government in our country and to overthrow the government of the United States has been startling. Many of the strikes during the past year, the steel strike, the New York printers strike and the coal miners strike were brought about by radical, anarchistic agitators of foreign birth, aiming at the abolishment of law and order so that an industrial chaos might result."[27]

The scale of the impact of conservative theology during the Great Red Scare is too amorphous to quantify, not least because so many people played dual roles as businessmen and members of a congregation, church board, or lay organization. What is clear, though, is that church groups did not just add quantitatively to antiradical movements in postwar America; they altered them qualitatively. Religious conservatives were able to situate their attacks within a powerful supernatural framework of good and evil lacking in purely secular critiques of radicalism. As Gaebelein later wrote, "There have been blasphemies in the past, unspeakable blasphemies," but none of them compared to the "Satanic Christ-hating, Christ-despising spirit" manifested by the "godless Soviets."[28] Billy Sunday, in his usual effulgent form, denounced the "good-for-nothing, God-forsaken, weasel-eyed, hog-jowled, bull-necked, ragg-shagged, bob-tailed, riff-raff bunch of radical, revolutionary, Red IWW Bolshevik imps" as "a deadly poison to every element of American idealism."[29] Premillennialist preachers claimed that the "King of the North," who according to their interpretation of scripture would participate in the battle with the Antichrist at Armageddon, meant the Soviet regime.[30] A few even linked the biblical "tribulation" to the revolutionary upsurge of the postwar years. Pentecostalist founder Charles Parham warned that Bolshevism, "now sweeping Europe, is as sure to reach this country in its devastating influence, as the plagues of Europe always found their way to this country. You could no more quarantine against this power than you could against a pestilence." J. C. Whalte declared, "Lenine is simply the awful shadow of the great Red king who is surely coming to reign over a great Red world . . . It will be a Red religion that will flaunt the red flag of communism, and drench the world with the red blood of the martyrs. Keep your eyes on the Red religion O man of God. Watch! Its theme is communism, federation, social service and the red light of spirit séances."[31] Some fundamentalists even adopted *The Protocols of the Elders of Zion* to buttress their ideas about the supposed role played by "apostate Jews" in the army of the Antichrist. Such religious anti-Semites used the Bible and the *Protocols* in combination to draw literally apocalyptic conclusions about the presence of Jews at the highest levels in the Bolshevik regime.

Nevertheless, as with so much of the countersubversive politics of the 1920s, a shared antiradical rhetoric tended to obscure the substantial differences between religious conservatives' underlying concerns and those of their corporate allies. Although allergy to liberal theology gave the alliance impetus, fundamentalists' uncompromising hostility to all forms of modernism brought them into conflict with capitalist elites. Believing that they were winning the battle against liberalism, fundamentalists launched campaigns to ban Darwin from American schools, setting them on a collision course with mainstream America. The fundamentalist movement prided itself on its rigorous intellectual and even (in their understanding of the term) scientific thought, and included many highly educated theologians who had emerged from the major American seminaries. But the publicity surrounding the Scopes "Monkey" Trial of 1925, when William Jennings Bryan was ridiculed by Clarence Darrow on behalf of a suit filed by the ACLU, proved transformative and humiliating. Popular (and conservative) critics such as H. L. Mencken lampooned fundamentalism as an essentially anti-intellectual, rural, and backward ideology of boobery with which reasoning Americans could have no truck.

Rather than looking to a movement that feared the future, corporate-minded Americans tended to prefer interpretations of the Bible that gratified their entrepreneurial consciences, and other religious leaders—busy building new churches paid for by the easy capital of the stock market boom—responded in kind. The best-selling nonfiction title of 1926, Bruce Barton's *The Man Nobody Knows,* used Jesus's life as a good practice guide for the modern American businessman in a way that seemed sacrilegious to many fundamentalists.[32] Jesus was presented as an exemplar of leadership success, thanks to his charisma, virility, "wonderful power to pick men . . . the born leader's gift," and recognition of "the basic principle that all advertising is news." "Surely no one will consider us lacking in reverence," Barton wrote (rather optimistically), "if we say that every one of the 'principles of modern salesmanship,' on which we businessmen so much pride ourselves, are brilliantly exemplified in Jesus' talk and work."[33] To fundamentalists, it was not clear whether it was the businessman who was intended to be glorified by the comparison or Jesus. "Unquestionably," historian Robert Moats Miller writes, "ministers who placed God in the company of Henry Ford and Judge Elbert Gary were conferring upon Him their highest accolade."[34]

In the end, fundamentalism in the 1920s proved to be out of step with an America of skyscrapers, automobiles, and corporate ledgers, and it met with a series of practical reversals and a precipitous decline in influence. Efforts to insert rigid conservative clauses into church constitutions were undercut by liberal maneuvering in the national conferences, while the anarchistic streaks of the major fundamentalist leaders made it very hard for them to work together.[35] Fundamentalist cooperation turned out to be as tough as herding cats, especially after the only figure with sufficient prestige to command universal deference, William Jennings Bryan, died in 1925.[36] Other leaders were sidetracked by embarrassing personal crises. William Bell Riley was put out of action for six months after an automobile accident.[37] J. Frank Norris was tried for murder after he shot and killed a man who had come to confront him over allegations he had misappropriated church funds. With the exception of the effort to deny the 1928 election to Al Smith, in which fundamentalists overcame their differences to join the fight against Rome, the movement was already in serious crisis by the mid-1920s. As the decade wore on, more and more liberal commentators began speaking of fundamentalism in the past tense and mocked the antievolution fight as a last failing grasp for relevance. The *New Republic* argued that "if they could not attack the Modernists," fundamentalists would "have nothing to say and could no longer make the sensational tours of the country of which they are so fond."[38] *Christian Century* concluded, "Anybody should be able to see that the whole fundamentalist movement was hollow and artificial" and "wholly lacking in qualities of constructive achievement or survival."[39] In 1927, Sinclair Lewis, whose extraordinarily popular novels had already taken stinging potshots at the pieties of bourgeois culture, published *Elmer Gantry*. The book laid out a stylized version of the fundamentalist preacher, presenting him as a hypocrite and money grabber and promptly swept to the top of the best-seller charts. Between Barton and Lewis, it was no exaggeration to say that antifundamentalist literature dominated the bedside tables of the reading public in the middle years of the decade.

Many of those who had been calling for a fundamentalist takeover of the churches immediately after the war thus found themselves retreating by the end of the 1920s. Their Cave of Adullam turned out to lie in the South, where the challenge of higher-criticism theology to old-time religion was far weaker. Some fundamentalists remained affiliated with mainstream denominations, hoping to continue the fight against liberalism from within, but others concluded that the existing churches and institutions had been hopelessly corrupted and shifted instead toward building a new grassroots movement from the ground up that would suit their desire for autonomy and doctrinal purity. (This difference in strategy quickly became another issue for fundamentalists to fight over.) In the long term, separatism would provide the institutional and congregational foundations with an incredible rise to power in the second half of the century. Even as they were excluded from the mainline churches, fundamentalist congregations continued to grow. But in the 1920s, this served only to intensify their isolation and confirm the liberal tendency to malign fundamentalist instincts as the paranoid attributes of people who had basically failed at the task of living in the modern world. The mood by the end of the 1920s was one of alienation and persecution.

With the fundamentalist collapse, much of the energy of antiradicalism in the churches was sheared away. The dominant tendency in Protestantism remained firmly probusiness, as the popularity of books like *The Man Nobody Knows* revealed. Social activists in the FCC hierarchy complained that during the coal strike of 1927–28, "the rank and file of churches, ministers, and church members seemed to be largely uninformed and lacking in conscience on industrial matters." In a yearlong strike in the Passaic textile mills, only two local ministers were willing to have anything to do with the FCC representatives working with the strikers. The *Nation* concluded that despite "stirring individual exceptions, the Protestant church in America is the ally of the interests which feed it [financially]."[40] Nevertheless, the growing divisions between militant and moderate conservatives allowed reformists space to challenge the assumption that the primary function of the church was to preserve the existing social order. The young Lutheran Reinhold Niebuhr was a case in point. A practicing minister in Detroit from 1914, he witnessed Ford's innovative industrial methods deteriorate into sweat-shop conditions during the 1920s and worried the terrible conditions were providing space for communism to grow.[41] To Niebuhr, the supposedly miraculous methods of industrial production perfected by Ford closely resembled Marx's description of repressive capitalism systematically stealing surplus value from workers and their families. Visiting an automobile plant in 1925, he saw how "the men seemed weary. Here manual labor is a drudgery and toil is slavery. The men cannot possibly find any satisfaction in their work. They simply work to make a living. Their sweat and their dull pain are part of the price paid for the fine cars we all run." On the release of the Model A in 1927, Niebuhr calculated that the car cost Ford workers fifty million dollars in lost wages from workers laid off during retooling. "No one knows how many hundreds lost their homes in the period of unemployment and how many children were taken out of school to help fill the depleted family exchequer, and how many more children lived on short rations during this period," he said; "no one asks about the toll in human lives."[42] The church, meanwhile, had become "a façade for these technically efficient middle class industrialists who were riding high, who were building an industry, who were making Detroit prosperous, but who were not going to have any one of their prerogatives or powers challenged."[43]

When the AFL launched a halfhearted organizing drive in Detroit in response to communist inroads on the shop floor, Niebuhr and leaders from a dozen other churches offered their support. As Niebuhr later recollected, however, "The business community of Detroit, which had always breathed sweetness and light, showed its fangs." The Chamber of Commerce "shrewdly sent committees that would be most influential in each particular church situation to the pastor and to the board members to ask for the withdrawal of these invitations." Rather than resigning over the matter and risk plunging their families into poverty and unemployment, most ministers deferred to their church boards and rescinded the invitations. Apart from Niebuhr and the Unitarians, all of the churches ultimately withdrew their offers in what the unmarried Niebuhr unsympathetically deemed to be "a rather abject way."[44]

Niebuhr tried to point out how damaging this no-compromise policy was for the social fabric.[45] In a series of articles for *Christian Century,* he argued that "the rising tide of resentment among Ford workers has no avenue of expression except through the communistic weekly sheet, the *Ford Worker*," and that if re-spectable labor leaders failed to organize, "the revolutionary radicals who are now the only spokesmen of the discontent of Ford workers will gain in influence out of all proportion to their qualities of leadership." At first, the solid power of industry in Detroit ensured little response. Probusiness politics dominated the vestries, largely through the donation box. Liberal religious newspapers were vocal in their indictments of the business world, but flaccid in their prescrip-tions.[46] As the decade drew to an end, though, a growing number of religious figures began to voice their frustration at the implicit alliance with business and echoed Niebuhr's claims that a failure to act might itself open the door for radicalism. In Detroit in 1929, for instance, Herbert Johnson, dean of St. Paul's Cathedral, made a passionate speech on the obligations of the church to labor and resigned his office. "Our pulpit was closed not only because of the Board of Commerce, but because of the vestry of the cathedral," he complained. Rev. Woodruffe of St. John's Church added, "The pulpit is not free. Try to preach our church's principle of the right of labor to organize in an open shop city and the big stick begins to swing."[47]

The same trickle of reformism took place elsewhere, and as the Depression hit and layoffs began, dissent in the churches grew to a torrent. By the time Roosevelt was elected, liberal angst over a decade's inactivity had begun to manifest itself in bouts of self-flagellation. The *Christian Advocate* declared that Christians must ask "whether or not money is going to tie our lips and prevent us from speaking the message that must be sounded forth from every pulpit if the Church is not to fail society."[48] Most reformers were informed by a hostil-ity to communism that bristled at Marxism's interpretation of religion as an artificial expression of man's material suffering. But a large number, beginning with Niebuhr, also believed that Marx's critiques of capitalism could no longer simply be ignored.

At the height of the Depression in 1932, the FCC revised its Social Creed in a strikingly radical direction, calling for a subordination of the profit motive and a turn to social planning, credit programs for poor farmers, a classless society, and the sharing of wealth. As Paul Carter notes, they used the phrase "cradle to the grave" a full decade before the Beveridge report was issued, and—more astonishing still—spelled out the "frankly Marxist 'from each according to his ability, to each according to his needs.'"[49] Some even began to question the negative depiction of life in Soviet Russia, a nation that seemed to be driving onward and upward while the American system had stalled. Harry F. Ward, a senior faculty member at Union Theological Seminary, spent a year in Russia in 1931 and returned arguing that the Soviet system offered a superior way of managing society, having eliminated the profit motive as the primary incen-tive of economic behavior. The Soviets, he claimed in his 1933 book *In Place of*

Profit, had "banished economic insecurity," focused on "improved technique and higher wages" to raise worker productivity, and delivered "no inconsiderable improvement in their living conditions," which was "the opposite trend for rural life in the United States."[50] Under Ward's influence, the Methodist Federation for Social Service affiliated with a Communist Party front, the American League against War and Fascism—an organization in which Niebuhr also briefly participated (as well as J. B. Matthews, who would go on to earn greater fame as a McCarthy-era red hunter). Even further along the political spectrum, a small Socialist Ministers' Fellowship led by a Chicago Methodist, W. B. Waltmire, declared in 1934 that the New Deal was fascistic and that Communist Party membership was compatible with Christianity, certainly when compared to a capitalism that, "by its brutal denial of the good things of life, either destroys belief in a good God or fosters idea of religion on a superstitious level."[51]

The *Unitarian Christian Register* wildly overstated the case when it concluded, "No one who studies the religious press steadily and carefully can doubt that American Protestantism has gone over in its sympathy to the Russian experiment and the basic idea of the Russian philosophy."[52] Few clergy would have gone as far as Waltmire or Ward in their praise of Russia. Nevertheless, pro-Soviet ideas were treated with polite respect in reformist circles, and it is surprising with hindsight how many Protestant leaders used the Russian example as an implicit rebuke to the acquisitive culture of the United States. When Roosevelt made the decision to recognize the Soviet republic, even many notionally anti-Bolshevik liberals praised the decision in remarkably callous terms. The *Christian Advocate* argued that, after all, "Lenin the Terrible was not more bloody than Ivan the Terrible," with whom Americans had been content to do business.[53] From the sidelines, fundamentalists looked on in horror. Truly, the churches had fallen into the arms of Satan.

*   *   *

Roman Catholicism was pushed by the same reformist and conservative currents as Protestantism in the first half of the twentieth century, but the role played by Catholics in the history of interwar countersubversion was different from Protestants'. Distinctive institutional, theological, and socioeconomic contexts meant that Catholics were often more vehemently antiradical than Protestants and kept loyal to the countersubversive cause long after many Protestant groups had begun to question their views about the dangers of Soviet Russia. Yet Catholics were often also more closely tied to the working class, more sympathetic to the outsider in society, more reform minded, and more likely to contest the dominant intellectual associations of antiradicalism with antiunionism, Prohibition, federal power, and Anglo-Saxon political supremacy. Indeed, as the decade continued and many other groups abandoned the countersubversive movement, the distinctive character of Catholic antiradicalism contributed to a substantial shift in the national terms of debate. In part due to their influence, by the Depression years countersubversive arguments were almost as regularly being used to advocate reform as to defend reaction.

The unitary institutional structure of the Roman church and the unchallenged authority of the pope, whose words were considered as infallible as the Bible was to fundamentalist Protestants, were the basic reasons for the centrality of antiradicalism to modern Catholic politics. Through encyclicals issued by Pope Leo XIII in the late nineteenth century, most notably *Rerum Novarum* (1891) and *Testem Benevolentiae Nostrae* (1899), the Vatican condemned liberal individualism, socialism, and communism as heresies; asserted the goal of an established Catholic church in every Christian nation; and warned the American episcopacy not to compromise with Protestant or secular thinking. Leo's successor, Pope Pius X, followed up with the 1907 decree *Lamentabili Sane Exitu* and encyclical *Pascendi Dominici Gregis,* attacking modernity in general and evolution in particular, ordering all Roman Catholic officials to swear an oath against modernism. Following these instructions, most Catholic clergy opposed left-wing politics in their communities and during the Great Red Scare echoed, indeed sometimes exceeded, the conservative denunciations of right-wing Protestants. The Jesuit Rev. Fr. John A. McClorey of Detroit, for instance, warned his parishioners, "The bolsheviki are fattening now on the carcass of Russia and look greedily toward the rich spoil of this country" and spoke of nefarious propaganda spreading "secretly and by underhand methods."[54] Many Catholics, including editors and writers in the popular Catholic magazine *America,* praised Mussolini as an antiradical hero and depicted criticisms of fascism as Bolshevism by the back gate.[55] (Alongside Bruce Barton and Sinclair Lewis, the third most successful author of books about religion in the 1920s was the Italian Giovanni Papini, whose *Life of Christ* was a top seller in 1923 and 1924. The book marked the middle point of a personal journey from atheistic futurism to born-again Catholicism and, ultimately, pro-Mussolini fascism.) Many saw an insidious Bolshevik influence in the anti-Catholic campaigns launched by the government of postrevolutionary Mexico. When in 1929 the Vatican signed a concordat with fascist Italy, voices of opposition were rare. Even committed reformers like Msgr. John A. Ryan balanced their muted criticisms with complaints that liberal antifascists had failed to speak out equally strongly against Mexican anti-Catholicism.[56]

Catholics thus established themselves as some of the most vocal antiradicals in the interwar period. Episcopal "hero worship" of J. Edgar Hoover was so strong that many believed (incorrectly) that the bureau director was himself a Catholic. As Steve Rosswurm astutely notes, this affinity was cemented in an antimodernism founded upon a particularly strong commitment to the maintenance of patriarchal gender norms and hierarchies of authority.[57] At the same time, however, the doctrine of grace through good works limited the kind of unworldliness that characterized fundamentalist Protestantism. *Rerum Novarum* spoke of the suffering of the working classes around the world and of the Catholic responsibility in addressing such matters, endorsing the principle of workers' rights within a vague but nonetheless powerful assertion of the mutual codependence of capital and labor. "Let the working man and the employer make free agreements, and in particular let them agree freely as to the wages," Leo XIII wrote, but "there underlies a dictate of natural justice more imperious and ancient than any bargain between man and man, namely, that wages ought not to be insufficient to support a frugal and well-behaved wage-earner."

In line with this policy, the Vatican had grudgingly permitted Catholics to join the Knights of Labor and, latterly, the American Federation of Labor. Many of the most important figures in the AFL in the early twentieth century—including leading antiradicals like Matthew Woll—were Catholics whose prounion antiradicalism was heavily influenced, if not driven, by religious belief. Like Protestant fundamentalists, though concerned about the government policing of loyalty, they were deeply committed to voluntarist efforts to purge both the church and the unions of radical influence.

Unlike in most European nations and in the rest of the Americas, Catholics in the United States were largely excluded from the political establishment and disproportionately filled the ranks of the working classes. With a violently anti-Catholic Ku Klux Klan on the march, and regular and unthinking anti-Catholic rhetoric found in many mainstream publications, many felt their community was denied basic citizenship rights, despite genealogies often stretching back generations. After the war ended, the National Catholic War Council—established in 1917 to provide a coordinating voice similar to the Federal Council of Churches and to contest the wartime assumption that Catholics were disloyal—issued a "Bishops' Program of Social Reconstruction," to considerable fanfare. Released in February 1919, before the Red Scare had decisively muted postwar progressive aspirations, the program used the language of *Rerum Novarum* to justify an ambitious plan of public insurance, labor rights, and guaranteed minimum wages.[58] None of this came to fruition until the New Deal, but even during the worst years of the 1920s a hard core of Catholic reformers, led by John A. Ryan, continued to make the case for change, using the pope's words as justification. As director of the Department of Social Action of the National Catholic Welfare Conference (as the National Catholic War Council had been renamed), Ryan traveled to strikes, offered moral support to workers, and pressed local preachers to abandon their traditional alliances with industrial elites.

Political controversies in the Catholic Church tended to manifest in differential interpretations of the pope's words, rather than the institutional schisms endemic to American Protestantism. Whether one stressed the pope's assertion of the freedom of contract or his declaration of the right of all workers to a just and living wage, the shared acceptance of pontifical authority ensured that the church hierarchy was able to maintain a corporate unity that was manifestly lacking in the Protestant world. Tensions thus tended to emerge not laterally, between denominations, but instead vertically, between leaders and congregation. Many bishops and archbishops in industrial regions mistrusted their flocks and worried that church strictures would offer insufficient solace to suffering workers, who might instead turn to radical secular alternatives. This ensured that even the most prounion bishops and clergymen were doubly antiradical, Pope Leo's blandishments combining with the more immediate and self-interested questions of keeping parishioners in the pews to stave off redundancy.

If Catholic instincts were antiradical, then they were also distinctly Catholic. Protestant conservatives tended to equate antiradicalism with antiunionism, whereas Protestant liberals inverted the equation, assuming that prounionism also meant tolerance or even support for radicals. By contrast, Catholic antiradicalism was less intimately tied to hostility to labor unions and couched instead in terms designed to assert Catholics' patriotic credentials and challenge the norms of Protestant America.

Undoubtedly, the most colorful example of this could be found in the heartland of Fordist America. Rev. Charles Edward Coughlin, a naturalized Canadian immigrant of Irish ancestry, was appointed to the Royal Oak parish a few miles north of the Highland Park plant in 1925. He quickly gained fame speaking out via the new technology of wireless radio against the Klan, who had left a burning cross on the lawn of his house when he first moved to the area. Coughlin proved so popular as a broadcaster that by the end of the decade, his weekly sermon was syndicated across the nation by CBS, attracting an audience of millions. In Detroit the sound of the "Radio Priest" was so ubiquitous, it was said that you could walk the streets and not miss a sentence of his sermons as you passed from one open window to the next. "In Brocton, Massachusetts," Alan Brinkley writes, "referees halted schoolboy football games shortly before three o'clock on Sunday afternoons so that parents, coaches and players could get to a radio in time to hear Father Coughlin. When the sermons were over, the games resumed."[59]

By the end of the decade, the flow of donations in response to the radio sermons was so large that Coughlin was able to commission a new Shrine Church of the Little Flower to replace the old run-down building he had formerly been using to preach in. As opposed to the concrete and glass of nearby Highland Park, with its ostentatiously artless rectangles and planes, the Shrine Church was constructed from all-American handcrafted stonework, Massachusetts seam-faced granite, and Bloomington limestone, interspersed with blocks brought from all the states and territories (each carved with the official flower of the respective state) and intricately covered with phrases, images, sculptures, and artifacts. The centerpiece, the Charity Crucifixion Tower, stretched up a hundred feet, supporting a twenty-eight-foot image of Christ on the cross decorated with carved branches of palm, olive and fig trees, and a glass halo that glowed with the light coming from inside the tower.

The church was consciously designed as an expression of Coughlin's religious politics. Unlike the rigid utilitarianism of Highland Park or the River Rouge, the Shrine Church was intended to solicit an emotional response from visitors as much as to fulfill a functional agenda, to present a vision of Catholicism as both an American and a deeply antiradical religion. Most Catholic churches built in greater Detroit in the early 1920s tended to invoke high-medieval styles taken from the European nations from which immigrant Catholic communities originated. Coughlin, by contrast, built a skyscraper in miniature. To demonstrate his nationalistic credentials, quotations from (Protestant) political leaders were engraved around the base of the tower, including George Washington and Abraham Lincoln. At one exit was an Art Deco engraving styled on Manet's *Execution of the Emperor Maximilian* (1867), depicting the execution of Father Miguel Agustin Pro, shot by firing squad on the orders of the Mexican revolutionary leadership during the Cristero rebellion of the late 1920s. Coughlin, devoted to the Cristero cause, claimed to have somehow obtained Pro's bloodstained shirt and would clasp it "fervently" before coming on air.[60] Meanwhile, painted on the oak panels of the chapel of St. Joseph in the southeast corner of the main building were the words of *Rerum Novarum*, "Capital cannot do without labor; labor cannot do without capital," illustrated through the busy antics of characters running alongside the words in vertical panels. Clad in the white- and blue-collar clothing of modern America, the product of one provides raw materials for the next, grain figuratively converted into gold. Across the main doorway, in Art Deco lettering, that most un-Fordian of words, "CHARITY," was written in capitals, framing Coughlin's figure as he raged against poverty, communism, *and* capitalism on an external staggered-stone pulpit replete with five carved images of the archangels designed to allow public sermons in the summer for the overflowing thousands who came to hear him speak.

In aesthetic form, then, the church revealed Coughlin's rejection of the triangular equation of America, Protestantism, and free enterprise. According to the Radio Priest, Communists preached atheism, relativism, and divorce. They called for the destruction of religion, for a single world government, and for "contraception, birth control and abortion," seeking "to socialize all mothers and all infants." But it was the selfish and unthinking behavior of the great capitalists, showing no regard for the little man, who drove conditions to the point of crisis where communists might take over. Coughlin told his listeners, "Communism is a social disease which is bred in the lurid ulcers of unjust poverty." His newspaper, *Social Justice,* claimed that "the maggots of Russian communism" fed on the "rotten carcass of modern capitalism." Capitalists exploited workers. They limited the supply of money, they cared more about international trade than the national good, and they robbed the worker of his small pleasures by banning the consumption of alcohol, "making hypocrites of Americans, criminals of citizens, and potential bandits of the youth of our country."[61] In sum, Coughlin believed the two extremes of the social order were siblings in sin. Only Christian ethics could provide a third way between plutocracy and the proletarian state.

CBS dropped Coughlin in April 1931 when they felt his sermons had become too political. Unperturbed, Coughlin organized his own national network and continued broadcasting. Indeed, if anything, he intensified his rhetoric.

Unlike the rigorously intellectual Niebuhr, Coughlin did not always make his thinking clear. As with the design of his church, his ideas were more mélange than catechism. In his fulminous speeches, the language of a nineteenth-century evangelical Populist intermixed with the ideas of the *Rerum Novarum.* He saw little distinction between communism and socialism; sometimes he claimed that one was the organization and the other the ideology. And he oscillated between the idea that both revolutionaries and international capitalists were contributing to the same disaster and the more extreme theory that they were in fact part of the same conspiracy. When the Fish Committee rolled into Detroit, Coughlin made himself the star attraction, ostentatiously declaring before the assembled national media that there would be a revolution in the United States by 1933, driven by the "international industrialism" of Henry Ford. "There is a movement, an international labor movement in this world," he explained, "and that movement is headed by Mr. Henry Ford."

This kind of incoherence helped his critics present him as superficial and absurd. But since Henry Ford was hosting Bolshevik technicians at Highland Park and his son had put a Mexican revolutionary painter on the payroll, perhaps his ideas did not seem so ridiculous at the time. As Coughlin explained to Fish, "Mr. Ford is now assisting [Russian agents] . . . with money earned by our laborers, in his factories, to establish and give aid to this Amtorg Corporation. I am telling you Mr. Ford is assisting in this international industrialism."[62]

Certainly, listeners responded to the message, believing they understood the spirit of the sermon even when the logic was lacking. Both communism and capitalism undermined the local foundations of community—church and family—and, with an advancing depression, only religion could provide an ethical alternative. "His crusading messages clung to the hearts of men as Dejanira's shirt adhered to her body," swooned one particularly adoring fan.[63]

Despite the profound differences in style, then, both Niebuhr and Coughlin were part of a growing tendency to contest the meaning of Christian antiradicalism away from the procapitalist orthodoxies of the twenties. In the 1932 presidential campaign, Coughlin declared that Franklin D. Roosevelt was the only man who could save the nation from communism. For his part, Niebuhr supported the Socialist candidate and Presbyterian minister, Norman Thomas. Roosevelt, hoping to woo Catholic voters smarting from his defeat of Al Smith in the battle for the Democratic nomination, met with Coughlin several times on the campaign trail, and when FDR was duly elected the Radio Priest claimed credit. This was probably unwarranted, but he was not alone in noting that Roosevelt's first inaugural, in which the new president said that the people had driven the moneychangers from their high seats in the temple, owed much to Coughlin's regular use of the same phrase in his radio sermons.[64]

* * *

One of Coughlin's favorite means of attacking Henry Ford was over his support for Prohibition, one of the central policies that had been promoted during the Wilson years as a necessary measure to fight radical subversives. "Why, we have one mass productionist here in Michigan, a great moral supporter of prohibition, who has gone so far as to threaten that he would not build his automobiles in a place that was given over to the manufacture and sale of intoxicating beverages," he said. "Nevertheless, I believe that he operates his mass productionism in Canada, in England, in France, in Germany, in Italy, and in Ireland from which last place he imports tractors into America duty free! Oh, what a jewel is this thing called consistency!"[65]

Michigan had emerged as a central battleground in the 1920s war on alcohol; historian Larry Engelman calls it the government's "Waterloo for liquor."[66] At first, following the passage of the Prohibition laws, petty crime rates had dropped significantly. Even AWU boss William A. Logan had tentatively supported the measure, saying sober men "talk better and think better. They also pay their union dues much more promptly and regularly than ever before."[67] But soon the benefit was outweighed by a rise in violent crime among liquor traders and importers. Sicilian and mainland Italian underworld families such as the Giannolas and Vitales moved into Detroit, much as they did other major cities. They were joined by enterprising Jewish hoodlums like the Purple Gang, who hired themselves out as rent-a-thugs and, among many other schemes and rackets, supplied Canadian whiskey through Detroit's adjoining city Windsor to Capone's organization in Chicago.[68] The rise in violent criminality reached its peak during the Cleaners and Dyers War of 1928, in which the Purple Gang rampaged across the city, wiping out rivals and legitimate union leaders and being wiped out in turn in a bloodbath that lasted several weeks.

Illegal importation of alcohol across the long river border with Canada grew into Michigan's second largest industry behind automobile manufacturing. Ingenious rumrunners used fast boats and even planes to evade the authorities.

When the river froze over in winter, they sledded, ran, and drove cars loaded down with barrels of liquor across the straits. By 1928 the Canadian government was taking around thirty million dollars a year in taxes from illegal exports alone. Such was the widespread disregard for the law that the Hotel and Restaurant Employees and Beverage Dispensers International Alliance began to unionize cooks and waiters at speakeasies. Only in territories of the Ford empire, at Highland Park and Dearborn, did the authorities get close to drying out the populace. "It was absolutely impossible to get a drink in Detroit," one contemporary journalist recalled, "unless you walked about ten feet and told the busy bartender what you wanted in a voice loud enough to hear you above the uproar."[69]

Since the Prohibition movement had sought to associate wets with radicalism, supporters of repeal—among which Catholics were an influential part—naturally looked to turn hostility to radicalism to their own ends. They argued that the saloon, as an outlet for day-to-day frustrations, in fact reduced the likelihood that dissatisfied workers would turn to revolutionary movements as expressions of their anger against employers. As early as 1919, the Association Opposed to National Prohibitions had claimed that a ban on alcohol was the principal reason for growing support for the IWW. Samuel Gompers argued that Prohibition worsened the industrial situation and allowed radicals to gain influence. "In the year and two months since prohibition went into effect," he claimed in 1919, "the alteration in Detroit conditions has been amazing, not to say sinister and threatening." Pointing to the people attending meetings at Detroit's House of the Masses, he said Prohibitionists were "aiding and abetting Bolshevism by oppressive legislation depriving the workers of their beer." Similarly, in a Senate hearing on repeal in 1932, Matthew Woll "blamed radicalism in the United States on the Eighteenth Amendment."[70]

Michigan's Gilbert A. Currie, a dry congressman, told the press that Gompers's "ridiculous statement insults our intelligence. Reds and radicals stand for crime. Their favorite rendezvous is the saloon."[71] Such responses, though, showed that Prohibitionists were increasingly on the defensive. As arguments for repeal gained purchase, Catholics and reformers were joined by conservatives and Protestants who had come to doubt Prohibition on broadly antistatist grounds. In 1923, Michigan senator and former Ford general manager James Couzens told the press there were parallels between Prohibition and the conditions that prevailed before the Russian Revolution. Quoting an *Atlantic Monthly* article by Woodrow Wilson that argued that the 1917 revolution came about because the czarist government restricted "the things normal men desire and must have if they are to be contented and within reach of happiness," Couzens said that if beer continued to be denied Americans, we would have a revolution here too. "Not that the people are so anxious to have beer for its own sake," he hastily added. But it was a slippery slope; soon they "may take away other rights and privileges—the use of tobacco, for instance."[72]

In an era noted for interdenominational tensions, the campaign to end Prohibition offered a remarkable example of mainstream Catholic-Protestant cooperation on a shared project to roll back state power. Perhaps the strongest pressure for repeal followed publicity campaigns launched by the Association against the Prohibition Amendment (AAPA). The money behind the organization came from the Du Pont family. Leading lights included Protestant politicians ranging from Yale Skull and Bones man and Republican politician James W. Wadsworth Jr. to former Democratic nominee for the presidency John W. Davis and Jouett Shouse, chair of the Democratic National Committee's executive committee. But some of the most influential Catholics in politics were also tied to the organization, including Du Pont senior executive and chair of the Democratic National Committee John J. Raskob and Al Smith. Presenting Prohibition as an un-American infringement on traditional liberties, the AAPA deftly roped repeal to the tradition of antistatist liberty. In so doing, they presaged the kind of interdenominational alliances against big government that would become a central part of anticommunist politics from the mid-1930s onward.

With the intervention of the Du Ponts, the battle over Prohibition took on a decidedly vehicular flavor. The owners of General Motors were joined by fifteen other board members in the AAPA, facing off against the Ford-sponsored Prohibition Party.[73] It was perhaps fitting, then, that the battle to characterize wets as un-American was lost for good in the Motor City in mid-September 1931, when the American Legion came to town for its annual conference. The critical issue for veterans at the time was the bonus, and at the last minute it was announced that President Hoover would address the conference on the issue. But Detroit could not escape its symbolic importance as the main front in the war over the liquor trade, particularly as legion conventions had earned a reputation as particularly sodden occasions. Since the legion could mark itself at the forefront of groups whose membership was opposed to Prohibition but whose patriotism could not be denied—during the conference legionnaires passed resolutions calling for immigration restriction, stronger deportation laws, and "a more vigorous war on communism"—prorepeal attitudes at the convention were a watershed in the history of efforts to paint free alcohol as a patriotic measure.[74]

The legion leadership tried to keep Prohibition off the agenda. National commander Ralph T. O'Neil told the press that the convention must focus on the bonus and unemployment. "Work must be found for those who are ready and willing to work," he said, "to save them from the stigma of pauperism and the dole, and to save our government from the menace of the racketeer and the Communist."[75] But it was unconvincing to many, particularly in Detroit, to argue that "the menace of the racketeer and the Communist" could so easily be separated from the question of illegal booze. After two days of behind-the-scenes wrangling, it was agreed that Prohibition would after all be debated, on the Monday afternoon immediately following the president's speech.

Around one hundred thousand conventioneers descended on the city over the weekend. "With their gay uniforms, holiday spirits and pranks," the *New York Times* reported, they turned a "sober industrial city into a gigantic fairground." The city was painted blue and gold. "Bands paraded up and down the crowded, traffic-clogged streets, and played constantly in the lobbies of hotels." The carousing went on well into the night, no doubt to the annoyance of the more conservative of Detroit's residents. Protestant Prohibitionist Clarence True Wilson, who had come to Detroit so he could be outraged firsthand, observed widespread drinking in the streets. "The delegates," he blustered, "were preparing for an orgy. . . . Everywhere was general evidence, evidence that anyone could interpret, of unpatriotic disregard of the laws of the United States." Customs officials confiscated more than twenty-five hundred bottles of beer, whiskey, champagne, and liquor from legionnaires traveling back across the Ambassador Bridge from Windsor, Ontario, the bottles broken in front of crestfallen revelers and the contents drained away.[76]

President Hoover arrived at the convention at midday on the Monday and spoke for only ten minutes. His efforts to enlist the patriotic spirit of the legionnaires in support of "a peace-time war for world prosperity" were broadly successful, and he was cheered with good grace. Indeed, a later resolution rejecting calls for immediate cash payments on the bonus was, on the heels of his intervention, passed by 902 votes to 507.[77] But, scandalously, the end of his speech was disrupted from the floor by chants from the garrulous assembly, whose shouts grew until they shook the roof, with cries of "We want BEER!"—a policy demand and call for refreshment in one. Hoover pretended not to hear, waved at the California delegation, and fled for the door.

Hoping to avoid further scandal, the leadership pushed through a compromise resolution that stopped short of calling for outright repeal in favor of a referendum. Nevertheless, the resolution concluded that the Eighteenth Amendment "has created a condition endangering respect for law and security of American institutions," firmly placing the patriot on the side of repeal.

Clarence True Wilson expressed little surprise that the American Legion had "taken the wet side." "If you had seen the outfit that gathered in Detroit as I did, you would be surprised that 394 men [the number that voted against the resolution] could be found who would stand up for the Constitution and decency and sobriety." Wilson was appalled that "such numbers of staggering drunks disgraced the uniform and yelled for beer."[78] But Coughlin launched himself into an extended defense of the veterans as true American heroes, dubbing Wilson the "Caesar" of Prohibition, comprehensively assaulting the dry laws in a special radio show dedicated to the subject and returning to the issue repeatedly throughout the next season.[79] The flag of liberty was flying for free alcohol.

At face value, religion and business occupy separate realms. Religion concerns itself with the metaphysics of value; business is rooted in the quotidian profit motive. Yet capitalism has enjoyed an almost spiritual hold on many Americans, whereas Christianity has found it impossible to escape everyday politics. And both have had to come to terms with the state. In the 1920s, modern industrial commerce had become infused with new and innovative approaches to marketing and advertising, manufacturing desires that simultaneously shaped American identity and transformed concepts such as "freedom" and "liberty" from issues of personal autonomy into expressions of mobility, status, and consumption. Religion, meanwhile, had become increasingly caught up in public policy, such that at times, as fundamentalists ruefully noted, Christian groups had seemed more like lobby groups than a theological community.

As pillars of the social order, businessmen and religious leaders often found their interests intersecting. Indeed, the assumption that the concerns of each should be coincident underpinned the politics of the era. Through an affirmation of kindred spirits, religious and secular conservatives were able to unite to resist pressure from those who sought to expand federal power or build a labor movement. More often than not, this was based on a shared belief that to be godly, and to be American, required one also to be loyal, law abiding, and antiradical. Yet the political content of Christianity was never unified, not straightforwardly probusiness. By the Depression years, cracks had appeared in the coalition of church and corporation. Echoing the claims that fundamentalist critics had been laying at the door of liberalism for a half century or more, a tranche of Protestant reformers began to argue that a true commitment to the teachings of Christ could no longer permit an uncritical endorsement of modern capitalism. A few iconoclasts even began experimenting with the idea that God might be reconciled with Marx. Meanwhile, Catholics sought to maintain an uneasy balance between the need to assert their "authentic" credentials as a community of American citizens with a desire to challenge Protestant social and political norms. Christianity was thus unable to speak with one voice on what it meant to be American. And as the 1930s began, the interlinked significance of ideas like liberty, free enterprise, faith, and nationhood—all of which underpinned what it was in turn to be antiradical—seemed once again to be open for meaningful debate.

PART III

The New Anticommunism

8

American Fascism

The New Deal and the Radical Right

In 1932 Franklin Delano Roosevelt won New York, New Jersey, Rhode Island, and Massachusetts—and every state south or west of Pennsylvania. The new president received seven million more votes than the incumbent, Herbert Hoover. Not even Al Smith's home state of New York had voted Democrat in 1928, yet in 1932 Democrats swept to victory from the Hudson to the San Francisco Bay. As usual, returns for the Democrats in the Solid South would have not looked out of place in a dictatorship—91 percent in Georgia, nearly 96 percent in Mississippi, 98 percent in South Carolina—and they were dominant in the cities and industrial zones. The triumph of 1932 was more than just a reconstruction of the Wilson coalition, though. In the staunchly Republican Midwest, Michigan fell for the first time since the Civil War. Wisconsin gave more than 63 percent to the Roosevelt ticket, and in the West Idaho passed into Democratic hands with nearly 59 percent of voters. Even in patrician New England, Hoover's margin of victory in Connecticut and New Hampshire measured in the low thousands. Across the nation, people emphatically signaled their anger over the economic crisis and desire for a new direction in American politics.

Among other things, the election results suggested a widespread rejection of traditional antiradicalism, discredited by more than a decade's political smearing, partisan divisions, and industrial and Prohibition-related violence, and capped off by the most severe depression in living memory. Within a year of taking office, the new president and his supporters in Congress had dismantled large parts of the countersubversive settlement of the 1920s: repealing the Eighteenth Amendment, recognizing the Soviet Union, and renewing the push for union rights. Following the passage of the 1933 National Industrial Recovery Act (NIRA), the president turned the language of patriotism in a new direction, targeting the industrialists who had so successfully branded the open shop as the "American Plan" in the 1920s. A new logo featuring an American eagle was designed; only employers who signed up to codes of conduct that typically included the rights of workers to ballot on unionization were allowed to display the seal. The public was encouraged only to buy with the Blue Eagle.[1] The NIRA was struck down by the Supreme Court in 1935, but the subsequent Wagner Act went even further in guaranteeing workers' rights. By the mid-1930s, only the strict limits on immigration remained from the antiradical policies passed after World War I.

Even Emma Goldman, the most celebrated and hated deportee of the Great Red Scare, was briefly allowed to return to America for a speaking tour following the publication of her autobiography. Goldman's enthusiasm for the Bolshevik Revolution had faded within weeks of her deportation to Russia in 1919, and since departing the country in 1921 she had traveled widely and written about her disillusionment with the Soviet experiment. But throughout the 1920s, she remained barred from the nation that had been her home for thirty-four years. This book tour was her first chance to come back to America, albeit briefly and only on the condition she would resist speaking about politics.

Most Americans responded to her visit phlegmatically. Many former critics were almost affectionate, remembering her as a symbol of a rugged, individualistic America that was fast disappearing under the pressure of corporate standardization. The imminent threat she seemed to pose a generation earlier had been rendered minuscule by an economic crisis that had left at least one in four workers unemployed and the banking system on the verge of total collapse. With nostalgia the *Portland Oregonian* concluded, "The times when we thought Emma meant trouble were truly the halcyon days. We knew not the meaning of trouble."[2]

The election witnessed no mass endorsement of revolutionary or extremist thinking. Compared to the collapsing political orders of Europe and elsewhere in the world, politics in the United States remained almost worryingly conventional. Despite their success in the Hunger Marches and their slow work building party cells in industrial plants, William Z. Foster, who ran as the Communist Party candidate for president in 1932, received just 103,000 votes, five times the level of 1928 but still only a quarter of a percent of the total number cast and less than an eighth of the Socialist vote.[3] Communists probably enjoyed a tenth of this number in paid-up members. The Socialist Party also won fewer votes than Debs had received in 1912, despite the nation's population having grown by a third. By 1936 their tally would fall to below 200,000. Unlike the political crises generated by the Depression in much of the world, the Roosevelt era witnessed the establishment of a strong and surprisingly stable political majority in favor of moderate reform and a regulatory state.

That said, for some on the Left, particularly those for whom the clarity of the revolutionary ideal outshone the complications, ambiguities, and compromises of life in the real world, communism was rendered legitimate as the enemy of the enemy. The long history of spurious and self-interested denunciations from antiradical countersubversives had made it hard to assess communism neutrally, while the apparent invulnerability of the Soviet Union to the global depression seemed to suggest that they had a plan the capitalists lacked. Stalin was praised as an admirably pragmatic dictator, in contrast to the revolution-ary dogmatism of the exiled Trotsky. The *Nation's* correspondent in Moscow, in the words of historian Richard Pells, told his readers that the Soviet Union was "everything America had once been and was no longer."[4] To widespread public interest, Lincoln Steffens had published his autobiography in 1931, chart-ing his own passage from progressivism to revolution, his life story offering a compass for those who had come to reject liberal individualism and capitalism. "Soviet Russia," one historian has written, "became for Steffens a new religion, admitting no doubts, no criticism."[5] Even the skeptical literary critic Edmund Wilson praised William Z. Foster's sterling defense of communism before the Fish Committee and noted that whatever their faults, at least Communists were prepared to die for their faith.[6]

The Communist Party seemed to be heading forward with purpose, and this generated new wellsprings of support among reformers disenchanted with the mainstream parties. Whereas the *Nation* and the *New Republic* endorsed Nor-man Thomas and the Socialists as the best of a bad bunch, fifty-two well-known intellectuals, writers, and artists—including such luminaries as John Dos Pas-sos, Lewis Corey, Waldo Frank, Granville Hicks, Sidney Hook, and Langston Hughes, as well as Steffens and Wilson—signed a public letter supporting the Communists.

The extent to which some were prepared to overlook conditions within the Soviet Union was revealed starkly by Roger Baldwin of the ACLU. Despite spending his career defending civil liberties in the United States, Baldwin argued at this time that it was right and necessary to defend the Soviet regime "by any means whatever," including Stalinist dictatorship. A visit to Russia reassured him that "the fundamentals of liberty" were "firmly fixed in the USSR." Despite meeting several political prisoners, Baldwin admitted, "I just could not bring myself to get excited over the suppression of opposition when I stacked it up against what I saw of fresh, vigorous expressions of free living by workers and peasants all over the land."[7] It is a deep irony that the principal complaint laid against McCarthyite excess in the 1940s and 1950s would be its failure to dis-tinguish between democratic liberalism and Stalinism, yet so many supporters of Russia in the early 1930s seemed to make precisely the same mistake.

Historians have debated at length why so many American reformers, many of whom revealed few other Leninist inclinations, defended Bolshevism in the 1930s.[8] Some have seen in it a flaw in the nature of American liberalism, a "softness" that made liberals ill-fitting custodians of the nation. For a section, undeniably, there was a vicarious thrill to be found in defending a romantic ideal of revolutionary activism in which they dared not directly partake. Even in the 1920s, there had been a powerful substrate of thinking that sought to engage with Bolshevik values pragmatically, even positively, as a site of investigation and even emulation. But the apparent failure of the American system in the face of depression encouraged others simply to turn their hopes toward the most obvious alternative that still held at least rhetorically to Enlightenment ideals of equality and progress and one that could be used to promote a domestic agenda focused on government planning; the fact that many of the worst excesses of the Soviet system were hidden from public view also meant that individuals could imagine their own idea of life in Russia rather than worry about more troubling realities. Moreover, the engagement with communism and Communists in the 1930s went far beyond the emotionally enamored. As the decade wore on, the Soviet regime seemed to be the only power willing to stand up to fascism on the international stage, and for this alone supporting it could be seen as vital to the preservation of democratic hopes in the future.

Ultimately, there were probably as many reasons for misrepresenting the Bolshevik experiment as there were individuals who did so. Nevertheless, it is important to add to existing historical analysis the note that these illusions had been gestating for a decade without any kind of persuasive response from countersubversives. In fact, utopian images of Russia were often reinforced by the constant exposure of antiradical claims as self-interested falsehoods. Few specific accusations made by the antiradical community had stood up to close examination in the 1920s. It was but a small excess of logic to conclude that the other side must therefore have had some access to the truth.

Compared to the relatively small number who actively endorsed the Soviet experiment, many more Americans simply rejected the myths of imminent subversion and the either-or constructions that so many countersubversive arguments were based on. These figures did not necessarily believe that the Soviet Union offered a model for the United States, only that a reformist attitude and commitment to democracy permitted working with Communists at home and engaging with the Soviet Union abroad. They dismissed the idea that communism was a threat to the American system; indeed, the superiority of the American system was precisely a product of the fact that it was willing to defend the civil liberties of people who would not return the favor. In this sense, the 1930s saw a return to a broader conception of the left-of-center world characteristic of the era before Wilson. As Doug Rossinow suggests, New Deal alliances may thus be seen as a resurgence of a deeper tradition of collaboration between liberal reformers and left-wing revolutionaries that had been decisively broken during the political realignments of the Red Scare era. Despite their in many ways contrasting goals and ideologies, both groups shared concerns over the effects of uncontrolled capitalism and "constructed bridges of cooperation" in the attempt to build "a more acceptable society."[9]

In short, the pejorative connotations of radicalism in the 1920s had been so widely abused that they lost persuasive force. As one of John Steinbeck's characters expressed it in *The Grapes of Wrath*, "A red is any son-of-a-bitch that wants thirty cents an hour when we're paying twenty-five!" It was certainly hard to perceive any real threat emanating from the CPUSA, whose activities now oriented almost wholly around union work, unemployment marches, civil liberties activism, antifascism, and campaigns for ethnic and racial equality. Indeed, they seemed more like a moral beacon than a conspiratorial cabal. Although the party had wasted much of its energy during the twenties in self-destructive infighting, the purges had reordered the CPUSA on a more strictly disciplined and hierarchical basis. And even though it remained politically aloof throughout the Third Period (1928–35), denouncing those near it politically as "social fascists," events on the ground served to build sympathy among the noncommunist Left. One of the ironic effects of the constant low-level harassment of CPUSA activists had been to force the Communist Party to develop an independent legal apparatus, consolidated in 1925 as the International Labor Defense (ILD). Though rarely offering much protection against the vagaries of day-to-day abuse, the notionally nonpartisan ILD was effective in publicizing miscarriages of justice at a national and international level and helped to project an image of the party as a legitimate part of a broader worker's movement under assault. The ILD thus helped to normalize the image of communism among rights activists long before official party policy endorsed cooperation with noncommunist groups. In the most famous civil liberties case of the late 1920s, the flawed trial of anarchists Nicola Sacco and Bartolomeo Vanzetti that resulted in their executions in 1927, the ILD joined socialists, anarchists, and liberals in protesting the conviction, while the CPUSA helped organize Sacco-Vanzetti solidarity clubs across the country in which many noncommunists participated. The ILD also kept track of unresolved cases stemming from the Centralia Massacre, Palmer Raids, and other World War I and Red Scare events that liberals as well as radical left-wingers memorialized.

As strikes broke out in southern textile mills, midwestern mines, and manufacturing regions, local authorities responded by clamping down, and the ILD found itself with a growing client list. Arrests of protesters, usually on grounds of disturbing the peace or disorderly conduct, reached endemic proportions. The ILD's annual report for 1929 recorded more than four hundred incidents related to distributing leaflets or giving speeches, more than six hundred arrests at mass meetings and demonstrations, ninety-seven deportation cases, more than thirty-five hundred arrests at strikes and pickets, and thirty-five prosecutions under state criminal syndicalism laws.[10]

When in 1931 nine black men were falsely convicted of raping two white women on a train near Scottsboro, Alabama, the ILD led the appeal. This caused tension with the National Association for the Advancement of Colored People (NAACP), which also wanted to defend the so-called Scottsboro Boys and felt that the Communist Party was more concerned with the political impact of the case than securing the defendants' release. More widely, though, the energy shown by Communists on behalf of noncommunist victims of white aggression was hugely important in challenging assumptions about the party. When the ILD sought to defend the convicted Communist Party activist Angelo Herndon, who had been given a twenty-year prison sentence in 1932 for attempting to organize black workers in Atlanta, they found themselves with many noncommunist allies motivated by a sense of reciprocity and solidarity. After two years' work, they temporarily secured Herndon's release. Six thousand people met him at New York's Penn Station to celebrate.

In union politics, it also became increasingly difficult to ignore the Communists, because of the skills they had learned under extreme conditions during the 1920s, the inroads they had made in certain specific industries, and their advanced attitudes toward questions with which many others were grappling. In the wake of the unemployment demonstrations in Detroit, pressure had grown within the AFL for a renewed drive in the auto plants. But with a working membership of less than 6 percent of the state's 420,000 autoworkers and little knowledge of the terrain, the AFL had little choice but to cooperate with the Communist-dominated Auto Workers Union if it wanted to rapidly mobilize.[11]

Over the next two years, radicals led the charge to unionize American industry, while moderates struggled to keep up. Trotskyites led a successful Teamsters' strike in Minneapolis, the Communist Party mobilized longshoremen in ports along the West Coast in a strike lasting more than eighty days and even coordinated a four-day general strike in San Francisco, and socialists from the American Workers Party led autoworkers in Toledo. Pitched battles between the Ohio National Guard and thousands of strikers, leading to the deaths by shooting of several protesters, forced the federal government to intervene in the Toledo strike, negotiating a settlement that included mass unionization, anticipating a renewed federal engagement in industrial politics.

The AFL responded with organizing drives in the steel, auto, and rubber industries, but conservative unionists continued to be outflanked by radicals because of their basic ambivalence toward comprehensive industrial unionization. Growing increasingly frustrated, a number of unions within the AFL, led by John L. Lewis of the United Mine Workers of America, formed a separate bloc within the federation to push for a more militant approach. Tensions culminated in the 1935 AFL convention in Atlantic City, when the brawny Lewis punched and floored the conservative William Hutcheson on the convention stage in front of a packed crowd who had not expected to be attending a boxing match. Shortly afterward, the bloc departed to form the separate Congress of Industrial Organizations (CIO). Lewis had a long history of fighting Communist influence in the United Mine Workers, but anyone with will and expertise was allowed to join the new organization, including Communists.

Communists earned perhaps the most sympathetic hearings in contexts where even moderates could see little space for progress through the ballot box. Nowhere was this more true than in the rural South, where a one-party state maintained a rigid system of racial segregation that permitted little dissent at any level, from state capitols to street corners, and revolutionary politics seemed as reasonable a response as futile attempts at democratic reform. Since 1928 the Communist Party had pursued African American allies, calling for the establishment of a separate national homeland for blacks in the South and offering one of the few integrated national organizations in America.[12] In Alabama, for instance, Communists made inroads among industrial workers, coal miners, and poor black sharecroppers, often trading on a reputation first put out by segregationists for being a new kind of carpetbagger. Homegrown black revolutionaries rode the rails to attend the Workers' School in New York, and a half-dozen black Alabamans were even sent to Moscow, experiencing, in the words of one historian, "a sense of freedom that was unheard of in the South."[13]

The party made gains among black people in the North as well. Harlem had one of the fastest-growing Communist branches in the country, playing a major part in protests over Scottsboro, housing discrimination, and unemployment.[14] Many black leaders had grown frustrated with the legalistic approach of the existing civil rights struggle. Even the NAACP slowly came to realize the importance of moving out of the courtroom. Following a conference at Howard University, dozens of major civil rights organizations came together to form the National Negro Congress, including the NAACP, the Brotherhood of Sleeping Car Porters, the National Urban League, Howard, and church groups. James Ford, the Communist Party's vice presidential candidate, was an invited delegate, and the party leaped into the organization's campaigns with enthusiasm, growing more influential within the organization every year.

The incorporation of the Communist Party within broader alliances of reform was therefore under way even before the official adoption of the Popular Front line in 1935, although this shifted the effort to a new gear. The drift toward engagement was matched by gradual changes in party leadership. Following his imprisonment after the 1930 Union Square riot repressed by Grover Whalen, a series of party squabbles, and a heart attack, Foster's dominant role within the party became attenuated; in his place rose the Kansas-born Earl Browder. Despite being Foster's protégée, Browder had emerged from the twenties comparatively unsullied, not least because he had spent several years as a Comintern agent in China. This made him doubly valuable as an apparatchik: of proven reliability to the international leadership yet comparatively inoffensive to many local partisans, having had no part in the party's troubling local history. In 1934 he was made party chairman.

Under Browder, the party's drift to the center became policy. Browder's biographer notes that he was the first head of the party who exhibited pride in being American.[15] But, ironically, it was as much the changing international scene as any sense of nationalism that led Browder to push for reform. Like many of those attuned to world politics in the early 1930s, Browder had seen the ease with which an isolated Communist movement in Germany had been destroyed when the Nazis assumed power. To him, this proved beyond doubt that Communists could not expect to go it alone in a head-to-head battle with fascism. Working with the noncommunist Left would ensure that any "reactionary" attempts to uproot communism would end up targeting reformist allies as much as Communists themselves.

As he later recollected, "with more or less enthusiasm," enough party leaders agreed with him that supporters of the Popular Front were able to "liquidate all serious opposition."[16] Although a substantial segment of the cadre believed the Third Period rhetoric that portrayed Roosevelt's election as a step toward a fascist America and many Communists looked down on woolly liberals as naïve or worse, it was clear that building a mass party required a change in direction. Once approved by the Comintern hierarchy, the decision to abandon leftist isolation, then, was welcomed by a substantial segment of the leadership—if not for itself, then at least as a strategic maneuver—and imposed on the rest with a minimum of fuss. And as Roosevelt became more openly antifascist in his international politics in 1937 and 1938, Browder moved the party into "more or less full support of Roosevelt."[17]

The party began participating in New Deal operations directly where they could and elsewhere worked with allies in the American League against War and Fascism, the National Negro Congress, the International Labor Defense, and the CIO—as part of a broader and in many ways successful effort to produce what Michael Denning has called "the laboring of American culture."[18] The party attempted to deflect allegations that it was overly centralized by diverting a greater proportion of its funds to local branches away from the central directorate.[19] They even attempted to draw a distinction between membership in the Comintern and obedience to Stalin. If it ever received orders from Moscow, Browder told a New York state legislative committee in 1938, the party "would throw them in the wastebasket."[20] Gone were the old Fosterite calls to march toward a Soviet America. The new party slogan was "Communism is Twentieth Century Americanism."[21]

Browder believed a "tide in the affairs of men" had turned. Although many critics felt the growing influence of the Communist Party was a sign that America was moving in a dangerously revolutionary direction, Browder recognized the opposite was the case. The party was not gaining influence for its extremism, but because the Communists had learned to keep their revolutionary aspirations quiet and focus instead on the immediate problems Americans faced. The CPUSA was supplanting the Socialist Party as "the party of practical reform," joining the New Deal as "a sort of silent junior partner, not openly accepted but still tolerated because of the services it could render."[22] In this way, though it never gained the mass working-class following it dreamed of, the Communist Party in the 1930s was able, for the first time in its history, to play a meaningful role in American political life.

∗   ∗   ∗

Roosevelt had come across as a relatively conservative candidate during the campaign for the presidency, criticizing the Hoover administration for over-spending as well as failing to get American out of the Depression and winning a fair degree of support in conservative parts of the South and West. His worldview included orthodox concerns with controlling costs and balancing the deficit-laden federal budget; indeed, in 1937 he would plunge the American economy back into recession in an attempt to cut spending. Nevertheless, it soon became clear that America was in the midst of seismic events that would require anything but a conservative response.

At first there was virtual unanimity behind the need to act swiftly in order to prevent the total collapse of the banking system. It is hard to find a political event in American history that commanded such generalized support as Roosevelt's reorganization of the banks in his first weeks in office. Congress signed measures granting sweeping executive authority before they had even been printed or read by legislators. But the scale of the crisis quickly forced the administration into taking unprecedented steps toward activist federal government and the creation of a rudimentary welfare state, and as the economy moved off the critical list a growing number of Americans were first antagonized and then infuriated by the president's agenda. Federal agencies, they believed, undermined the powers of elected politicians and state governments, work relief programs competed directly with private-sector firms, and handouts tied individuals to the largesse of the state rather than depending on personal initiative.

Impressively, the New Deal managed to infuriate both foes and supporters of bigness in American politics. To conservatives, deficit spending and dropping off the gold standard raised fears of inflation; to populists, FDR's fiscal policy was not inflationary enough. Collective-bargaining laws and other new industrial regulations restricted the freedom of employers to manage their businesses as they pleased, and government oversight conjured the possibility of private enterprise subject to rule by bureaucrat; yet at the same time the abandonment of traditional antitrust restrictions in the National Recovery Act raised the possibility of vast corporate monoliths destroying small businesses through anticompetitive practices. And since at least some New Dealers seemed willing to offer benefits to Americans regardless of ethnic origin or color, administration policy also seemed to suggest that the dominant position of whites, Anglo-Saxons, and Protestants might be under assault from a cohort of bespectacled social engineers.

The slow integration of communism into the polity, the growing activism of the government-supported union movement, and FDR's decision to recognize Soviet Russia, then, seemed to enemies of the New Deal to be signs that the occupant of the White House was walking the road to socialism. Of course, there was little desire to establish state ownership over the means of production, whether by reformist or by revolutionary means. Nevertheless, Roosevelt did share with Woodrow Wilson a suspicion of the conservative constraints imposed upon executive power by the Constitution, and the New Deal certainly represented a profound challenge to the idea of an unfettered private sector. To many on the Right, this was enough to pass the "duck test" for communism. As the embodiment of the most profound shift in the nature of the American Republic since the Civil War, Roosevelt became a target of increasingly bitter and personal criticism, condemned as a liar, a philanderer, a syphilitic, an alcoholic, a Machiavellian, and, most commonly, an aspiring dictator. His programs and laws were routinely denounced as communistic. Even the 1935 Potato Control Act was attacked as "a travesty of constitutional liberties."[23]

Many of the efforts of the first two years of Roosevelt's presidency turned out to benefit big businessmen first and others a distant second. However, the reformist course of New Deal politics intensified during 1935 and 1936, and the administration drew closer to unions and urban reformers in the lead-up to the election. Social Security legislation forced employers to fork out benefits to protect their workers and required state governments to expand unemployment relief. A new Revenue Act raised the top rate of taxation from 63 percent to 79 percent. Other new taxes were imposed on corporate profits. After his successful reelection, Roosevelt went further, attempting to "pack" the Supreme Court with compliant judges who would no longer strike down his reform bills and to institute a broad reorganization of the executive branch. As the decade drew to a close, the president sought to push the United States toward the Allied side in the emerging conflict with the fascist regimes of continental Europe and Japan and made the unprecedented decision to run for a third term in 1940. Historians have gone to great lengths to reveal the conservative instincts underlying many of the president's most notable policies. Roosevelt was, and remained, a reluctant Keynesian; his most dramatic fiscal experiments came in the 1940s, products of total war, not the Depression crisis. His policies were designed to resurrect capitalism rather than bury it. Nevertheless, given this record, it should not be surprising that to critics in the 1930s, accustomed to a level of federal activity that had bordered on the comatose, the president's actions appeared to be nothing short of revolutionary.

Opposition grew rapidly and remarkably consistently throughout the New Deal years, and with it came a resurgence of countersubversive smearing. By the middle of Roosevelt's first term, such rhetoric was being wielded as if the embarrassments of the past had never happened. The significant difference from the 1920s, though, was that the people running the country had now become the principal targets for attack, rather than radicals and others on the margins of society. The New Dealer gradually yet perceptibly replaced the Lower East Side Jew or unwashed Eastern European immigrant as the principal caricature of the communist within.

Yet in both policies and language, some of Roosevelt's most vocal critics seemed more radical than the person they were attacking. Indeed, the most extreme came close to forming an American form of fascism. Radical populists combined deep rage about the "uncaring" political elites of Washington and their "unaccountable" new agencies with ambitious reform programs of their own to help "the forgotten man." Fueled by ethical, moral, or institutional imperatives that made it impossible to accept the role of loyal opposition, and antagonized by political exclusion, some turned toward virulent strains of anti-Semitic and profascist countersubversive thinking to explain their misfortunes, until, at the far end of the spectrum, a small number openly called for the replacement of electoral democracy with some usually ill-defined charismatic dictatorship.

In some cases, political extremism was driven by ideologies that explicitly valorized persecution. Many Protestant fundamentalists, for instance, believed that as the millennium approached, true believers would become an embattled minority in a world dominated by godlessness. The humiliations and ridicule heaped upon them in the late 1920s could therefore be seen as a fulfillment of their theological expectations. Besides, what was the Great Depression if not providential judgment wrought upon a land that had embraced a sick modernity and looked to the state rather than the human soul for salvation? Driven by these ideas, several major fundamentalists moved away from the old battles over Prohibition, evolution, and Catholicism and became increasingly obsessed with anti-Semitic and anticommunist conspiracy theories that sought to explain their setbacks in reference to a vast conspiracy against Christian civilization.[24] Arno Clemens Gaebelein's bilious tract, *The Conflict of the Ages,* conjured a vision of an epic Jewish conspiracy stretching through history from the Illuminati to the

Bolsheviks. William Bell Riley, the founder of the World Christian Fundamentals Association, published *The Protocols and Communism,* which argued that the Bolshevik regime represented *The Protocols of the Elders of Zion* in action, that the Roosevelt administration was Jewish controlled, and that Jews were among "the most vicious atheists and most intolerable Communists I have met."[25] In the year following Hitler's accession to power, the influential fundamentalist magazine *Moody's Monthly* repeatedly printed letters from German pastors claiming that reports of anti-Semitic attacks by the Nazis had been fabricated by the social democratic and communist press.[26] Meanwhile, Riley praised Hitler for snatching "Germany from the very jaws of atheistic Communism."[27]

Typically, extreme fundamentalists contented themselves with circulating profascist, anti–New Deal, and anti-Semitic ideas in books and sermons, but a few sought to push Christian militancy onto the streets. The Kansas-based evangelical Gerald Winrod arguably moved the furthest toward establishing an openly fascist movement. His group, the Defenders of the Christian Faith, which had been set up as an antimodernist evangelical movement in the 1920s, praised Nazism and circulated an anti-Semitic newspaper, the *Defender,* to thousands of readers.[28] William Dudley Pelley, a failed Hollywood screenwriter and born-again Christian, led a similar group. The League for Liberation, typically known by its distinctive uniform as the Silver Shirts, dedicated itself to the establishment of a theocratic state and by the mid-1930s boasted a membership of around fifteen thousand.[29] Although he appealed to fundamentalist constituencies, Pelley's ideology was so bastardized—blending premillennialism with occult theories, theosophy, and spiritualism—that it hardly resembled traditional fundamentalism at all. Winrod also diverged wildly from orthodox fundamentalism; nevertheless, both figures were significant not only for representing indigenous versions of fascism, but also for drawing upon radical Protestantism to do so.[30]

It is tempting therefore to see Riley, Gaebelein, Winrod, and Pelley as evidence of a natural affinity between political extremism and religious fundamentalism, an instance of Sinclair Lewis's dictum that fascism would come to America brandishing the cross and the flag. People whose theologies centered around the belief in prophetic codes hidden in the Bible explaining the route to the end of the world would certainly seem to be a ripe audience for conspiratorial thinking. However, other fundamentalist leaders, many of them experiencing the same pressure of defeat, developed their politics and theology along different paths, while anti-Semitism and profascism were by no means limited to the Protestant world.[31] In many ways, Catholicism showed even greater fascist affinities, especially following the rapprochement between Mussolini and the Vatican in 1929. Even supportive, reform-minded Catholic New Dealers like

John A. Ryan believed that, if it came to a choice between communism and fascism, fascism was the preferable option. "Italian Fascism exhibits less disregard for individual rights than Russian Communism," he said, "and it shows more consideration for humanity's dearest possession; that is religion."[32]

Most American Catholic leaders found themselves in a better political position in the 1930s than in the past and thus had little reason to look for conspiracies to explain why the world was against them. However, a similar turn toward anti-Semitic anticommunism can be found among those who did experience setbacks analogous to those suffered by Protestant fundamentalists. The clearest case was the Radio Priest, Charles Coughlin, who became alienated from the New Deal when his support for Roosevelt failed to produce any political payoff. Together with a former Protestant preacher, Gerald L. K. Smith, and Francis Townsend, a rabble-rousing pension reformer from California, he launched a third-party movement called the National Union for Social Justice (NUSJ) in 1935, claiming the New Deal had been taken over by Moscow and that the only response was a new party built from the ground up according to Christian values. As Coughlin's newspaper, *Social Justice,* put it, "COMMUNISM OR SOCIAL JUSTICE: take your choice! There is no middle course. No other alternative can arise from the ruins of that modern capitalism which, throughout the world today, is visibly dissolving before our very eyes."[33]

Smith, in particular, was an interesting ally. A talented and charismatic evangelical Protestant, he—like Winrod—had not been involved with the scholastic disputes of the years immediately following World War I. Indeed, in the twenties, he worked with the AFL and denounced the Klan and in the early New Deal even sat on the Civil Works Administration Board. Nevertheless, he had no time for the reform ideas of the higher criticism, considering the essential truths of the Bible common, self-evident sense and became increasingly radical after he went to work for the notorious Louisiana caudillo Huey Long. Following Long's assassination in September 1935, Smith attempted to co-opt his base and began attacking the New Deal before audiences of thousands who came to witness his blistering oratory.[34]

Nevertheless, the NUSJ was a victim of poor timing, launched too late to contest the 1936 election.[35] The fractious egos of its leadership made meaningful cooperation impossible. Moderate support deserted the party in response to their aggressive attacks on Roosevelt, while the president undercut Townsend's proposals through his own Social Security measures.[36] John A. Ryan, who had praised Coughlin in 1932, wrote articles disputing the priest's claims to speak for the church. Even Bishop Michael Gallagher, Coughlin's closest friend, defender, and patron, publicly took issue with the Royal Oak pastor. "I do not consider the President a Communist," he said, "and it is not wise to call a man a liar because he may not agree with you." The NUSJ won fewer than nine hundred thousand votes. "When he first heard the [election] results," notes David Bennett, "Father Coughlin sat stunned in his Royal Oak office, the tears streaming down his cheeks. It was beyond comprehension."[37]

Even before the electoral disaster, Coughlin's exclusion from the halls of power had radicalized his politics and redirected his anger toward the Roosevelt administration rather than old enemies like Henry Ford and the Prohibitionists. After 1936, though, his diatribes were augmented by implicit, evasive allusions to an international Jewish conspiracy of which the New Deal was seen to be the American manifestation.[38] In the pages of *Social Justice* and on air, observations on European politics were tinged with approving comments about Nazi Germany. Hitler was praised for his stand against communism; the alignment of Hitler, Franco, Mussolini, and Hirohito was hailed as the "first open expression of a gigantic world-wide alignment against Russian communism."[39] German American propagandist George Sylvester Viereck, by this time a paid agent of the Nazis, was invited to write for *Social Justice.* In 1938, Coughlin began to call for the abandonment of "the inefficient system of parties" and the establishment instead of "corporate state elections."[40]

Even when it was justified by explicitly theological appeals, then, membership in the radical Right was as much a product of disposition as denomination. Secular countersubversives with attitudes as bloody minded as Riley's or Coughlin's exhibited similar behavior to the religious extremists, despite lacking their theological convictions. Indeed, the rise of Hitler was marked by a flowering of shirted movements in America, while dozens, perhaps hundreds, of other ultranationalist groups also emerged or developed from the patriotic organizations of the 1920s. Most were products of individual imaginations, frustrated careers, and personal failures, articulating visions of great conspiracies that served to affirm one's importance as a custodian of the truth in an otherwise indifferent world. A number of charismatic individuals attained something approaching celebrity. One of the most notorious, Elizabeth Dilling, acquired national fame after publishing *The Red Network* and *The Roosevelt Red Record,* which quickly became must-read books for radical countersubversives. Drawing upon ideas that had been developing since the Great Red Scare, and heavily influenced by the Christian fundamentalists, the books offered angry, detailed, and astonishingly wide-ranging assaults on liberalism and the left wing of American politics, alleging Jewish-Bolshevik influence in Washington, the churches, the media, and the universities. Unlike many other "professional patriots," Dilling never earned much money from her work, but she came to be in great demand as a speaker, touring the states giving polished speeches on the Red menace to rotary clubs, fraternal orders, and patriotic societies, building upon preexisting networks as well as cementing new links with other local groups. Later in the decade, she visited Nazi Germany and found it fine.[41]

The vast majority of America's borderline fascist associations had wretched memberships, comprising a founder, a family member, and perhaps a faithful pet. Only a small number attained followings even in the low thousands. The largest, a particularly vicious group calling itself the Black Legion that had formed from the broken remnants of the Ku Klux Klan in the Midwest, boasted somewhere between fifty and a hundred thousand members in Ohio, Michigan, Illinois, and Indiana, but after a spate of vigilante killings in the middle of the decade the Federal Bureau of Investigation (FBI, as the old Bureau of Investigation was now known) moved in to shut it down and arrest and prosecute its leaders.[42]

Together, the radical Right hardly amounted to anything that could reasonably be described as a national movement. They posed no risk to the integrity of the state, certainly not in the way fascist groups in Europe did. But the loose connections that were being established between them through networks of communication and travel did mean that the same theories could increasingly be found from New York to San Diego. Moreover, unlike the networks of the 1920s, these groups shared a more singular conception of the enemy. Rather than seeking to promote their own divergent policy objectives, hostility to the New Deal was the star from which extremists oriented themselves. Like Andrew Jackson a century before him, Roosevelt's impact on the political system was so pronounced that the opposition was defined and shaped by him as much as his supporters. By the mid-1930s, virtually every element of the radical right's fanaticism was directed either directly or indirectly at Roosevelt and his administration, which had come to symbolize all Jewish, internationalist, elite, liberal, Bolshevik, and modernist horrors in one. Anti-Semites claimed FDR stood for Franklin "Double-Crossing" Rosenfeld and that leading Jews such as Bernard Baruch and Henry Morgenthau Jr. really ran the government. Fundamentalists claimed the Blue Eagle was the mark of the beast referred to in Revelations 13, "that no man might buy or sell, save that had the mark, or the name of the beast, or the number of his name."[43] Dilling tastelessly anointed the administration the "Jew Deal." While each group built upon their respective theologies, philosophies, and personal ideologies, then, a shared rejection of the dominant political development of the times encouraged them to transcend their sectarian roots and become, in essence, an embryonic political community.

The Depression crisis and the rise of the New Deal thus both radicalized and undermined the former isolation of many extremists on the Right. Coughlin cooperated with Gerald L. K. Smith in the 1936 election campaign; Riley published articles by Dilling and other professional patriots in his newspaper and, in an astonishing reversal for a pronounced anti-Catholic of long standing, even defended Coughlin from attack; while Silver Shirts and other fascist groups worked together in the localities.[44] Indeed, many groups began distorting their former ideas to suit their new alliances. By the late 1930s, Winrod's philosophy had come to use *The International Jew* and *The Protocols of the Elders of Zion* more than orthodox fundamentalism. Even Gaebelein's book *The Conflict of the Ages* relied almost entirely upon secular conspiracy theories rather than the Bible to indict the modern world. His claims about the communist threat to America were taken from Overman Committee testimony, publications by professional patriots, and the controversies examined by Hamilton Fish in his hearings.[45] Only a final part of the book made any effort to integrate these ideas into classical dispensationalist thinking; only this section provided any real indication that the work was intended to be theological at all. The process of radicalization undermined the very thing that had formerly made fundamentalist ideology distinctive: the belief that moral truth could be obtained only from the Bible. Indeed, at every stage of the campaign against modernism, fundamentalists compromised with the very tendencies they opposed. Driven at first by a hostility to ecumenical consolidation, Riley's World Christian Fundamentals Association had been the first step in launching a major fundamentalist interdenominational movement, whereas in the longer term, opposition to liberals using the church as a lobby group ultimately forced fundamentalists to learn how to lobby for themselves.[46] In this manner, the reorientations of the 1930s created an extreme Right that was in a perverse way more plural, worldly, and politically minded than its progenitors.

The clearest indication of an emerging shared identity could be seen with the role played by Henry Ford. The Ford Motor Company's tremendous financial assets, Ford's by now national reputation as an anti-Semite, and his personal and corporate need to avoid being embroiled in any more costly lawsuits encouraged marriages of convenience with other extremists, where he provided the money while others acted.[47] Ford Motor Company in the thirties came to operate as a hub for the extreme Right. Nazi leader Fritz Kuhn was given jobs both at Ford Motor Company and the Henry Ford Hospital, while Harry Bennett dealt on Ford's behalf with Gerald L. K. Smith—who moved to Detroit in 1939 to be closer to Coughlin, Ford, and other sources of patronage—and with William Dudley Pelley.[48] According to Bennett, Ford paid Elizabeth Dilling five thousand dollars for six months' work in 1939, supposedly to investigate potential communist sympathies among the University of Michigan faculty but in practice as a stipend.[49] Astonishingly, even Father Coughlin began to work with his oldest enemy. Despite his history of attacking Ford as the chief source of communist influence in America, the Radio Priest—desperate for funds—now began to praise him as one of America's "industrial geniuses." *Social Justice* lauded the motor magnate, ringing in the new year in 1938 by printing an extended interview that focused on Ford's "fights for independence" from government and the communist-inspired unions. An ex-member of the Service

Department later claimed that in exchange, Ford bought thousands of copies of *Social Justice,* many of them never distributed.[50]

Ford was indulging freewheeling belligerents who were willing to act on the instincts he was no longer able to gratify personally. Nevertheless, his patronage also shifted the emphasis of the radical right-wing ideology espoused by his affiliates. Coughlin, for instance, marked the rapprochement with his former nemesis by more or less abandoning his traditional defense of the industrial worker. He launched a campaign against the CIO-sponsored United Auto Workers union, which had begun to make real headway in the battle to unionize Michigan industry. *Social Justice* claimed the CIO and its union members were financed by Moscow and that John L. Lewis had "turned turtle" by working with the Communist Party.[51] Lewis, Coughlin's writers claimed, was "a power-driven creature of a new age of dictators bent on invading the constitutional liberties of the American people," set upon using "the front of democratic labor organization to Sovietize American industry and bring about the success of the proletarian revolution in this country."[52] When organizing drives were launched in the Ford plants, Coughlin responded by forming a Gentile-only union for Ford workers, hoping to exploit working-class anti-Semitism to undermine support for the UAW.[53]

Under Ford's influence, the anti-Semitic messages in Coughlin's *Social Justice* also grew more strident. Black Hundred émigré Boris Brasol, who had authored many of the infamous *Dearborn Independent* anti-Semitic articles, was dispatched to write for Coughlin. Soon afterward, the paper reprinted *The Protocols* in entirety, something that Ford no longer dared to do.[54] Coughlin began calling for the formation of a militant Christian Front. "A Christian Front will not fear to be called 'anti-Semitic,' because it KNOWS the term 'anti-Semitic' is only another pet phrase of castigation in Communism's glossary of attack," *Social Justice* explained.[55] Attacks on Jews even began to make it onto Coughlin's radio hour. In early 1939, the *New York Post* revealed a public speech given by Coughlin was textually identical to one originally made by Joseph Goebbels. Reports emerged that Coughlin was involved with organizing a "Christian Index," through which Jewish stores in New York were boycotted.[56] Readers of *Social Justice* were treated to a reprinted address originally given by Adolf Hitler.[57] "We will never submit to Communism," Coughlin insisted in speeches, "cost what it may; for remember American Christians are and always will be as brave as Spanish Christians." Not one Jew had been killed in Germany, he claimed, while more than twenty million Christians had been "done to death under the Trotskys and Bela Kuns of Communism, both of whom are both [*sic*] Jews."[58]

Coughlin represented some of the most extreme tendencies toward fascist thought and action in 1930s America; certainly, few other figures of national prominence openly proposed abandoning electoral democracy altogether. He was also one of only a very small number of extremists capable of mobilizing militant groups across multiple cities, in no small part because of his more moderate early history. If new alliances were emerging among radical right-wingers in the New Deal decade, they were still conditioned by the uncompromising personalities that had pushed them into positions of opposition in the first place. Collaborations were often fractious affairs, often lasting only weeks or months before falling to pieces.[59] True to type, most leaders preferred to be big fish in small ponds than attain broader influence by compromise. It appears that a shared identity and political language were not enough to make a movement.

Taken together, the groups and individuals on the radical Right that might be reasonably described as fascist or cryptofascist, those that either openly supported fascist doctrine or articulated a close American variant, added up to a tiny fraction of the population: no more than a few hundred thousand people in a nation of 130 million. One plausible scholarly estimate counts around 250,000 men and women in fascist or protofascist groups, but even this cannot fully take into account the effect of multiple affiliations and potentially inflated rosters.[60] Such numbers suggest that the extreme Right was perhaps two to three times larger than the dues-paying membership of the CPUSA at its peak. On the other hand, the radical Right had little of the Communist Party's discipline, allies, political acuity, or capacity for strategic maneuver. Right-wing extremists could cause trouble in their localities, but were largely impotent on the national stage. Noxious as they were, they never presented a meaningful threat to American institutions or spoke for more than a tiny minority of American citizens. Despite the many conflicts and tensions of the 1930s, then, the political center of the United States held. The Depression crisis ultimately broadened the reach of American democracy and strengthened the relationship between the state and society, rather than giving rise to the kinds of political collapse and genocidal violence witnessed in parts of Europe, Asia, and Latin America.

Those who could be directly tied to Germany were fewer still. In 1933 Deputy Führer Rudolf Hess instructed a Nazi agent, Heinz Spanknoebel, to organize a group called the Friends of New Germany to promote Nazi foreign policy in the United States. The organization, later reconstituted as the German-American Bund, was dominated by foreign nationals and barely naturalized citizens. Because Nazi ideology was so strictly defined by a privileged ethnicity, it never succeeded in broadening its base to appeal to American citizens more generally. Indeed, even most German Americans tended to have little to do with the organization.[61] There were some other individuals who worked for the Nazis, of which George Sylvester Viereck was perhaps the most prominent. Multinational corporations continued to do business with the German government, and there were a small number of expatriate organizations that affiliated with the Nazi Party or received aid from them. But, not least because of Hitler's relative lack of interest in the United States in his early days of power, that was about the sum of America's direct links with Nazism.[62]

To the vast majority of Americans, fascism was like communism, simply and straightforwardly a "foreign" ideology. Endorsing it meant endorsing subservience to Berlin. The idea that fascist thinking in America might build upon indigenous traditions and concerns was as irrelevant to most people as the fact that communism had drawn strength from domestic revolutionary leftism.

Nevertheless, there were no clear lines dividing the radical Right from mainstream conservatism. Just as Communists were able to build alliances with groups whose values overlapped with theirs, shared beliefs on the Right—including a sense of alienation from modern industrial democracy; a strong commitment to home, family, church, and country; and a suspicion of unions, liberals, and international financiers—served to create opportunities for cooperation, and by extension damaging associations, between extremists and more mainstream conservatives.

Anti-Semitism provided one point of contact with mainstream society. Endemic to the times, even many New Dealers showed little concern about attacks on Jews in the early stages of Hitler's rise to power. Nevertheless, there were clear limits to the value of such rhetoric in public, in large part precisely because anti-Semitism quickly became so inextricably tied to German aggression. Geoffrey S. Smith surely goes too far in arguing that "with the possible exception of the candidacy of Alfred E. Smith in 1928, ethnic issues had never been a major divisive force in American politics."[63] But it was nevertheless true that, as Ford's experience in the 1920s revealed, vocal attacks on Jews were likely to attract costly lawsuits and tremendous negative publicity from an energetic and competent set of Jewish, liberal, and radical activists and lawyers, without offering much of a clear political upside. American anti-Semitism was also often moderated by a conception of civility that considered it acceptable to exclude Jews from polite society and treat them in discriminatory ways in employment and housing, but inappropriate to march in the streets and give poisonous public speeches about Jewish conspiracies. More Americans were indifferent to Jewish suffering in Germany than wanted it repeated in America, more were willing to tolerate antidemocratic tendencies in Europe than were eager for them at home. In this sense, the political utility of anti-Semitism, even in a society that remained deeply anti-Semitic, can easily be overstated.

Many fascist or quasi-fascist groups seemed to realize that whereas anti-Semitism could be used privately to cement links with potential allies, opposition to communism provided a more effective way of publicly defending their politics and building alliances with others on the Right. After all, most mainstream conservatives tended to be at most quietly anti-Semitic but noisily anticommunist. Ralph Easley, for instance, uttered anti-Semitic remarks to friends and associates in private discussion, but worked with conservative Jewish organizations in his various countersubversive projects. He was largely indifferent to the fate of German Jews, but felt strongly that Hitler was the only meaningful force in continental Europe capable of holding back the red tide from the East.[64] As he put it himself, "Many here say, if our country were in the same condition as Germany with reference to the Communists, we should say, Give us Hitler!"[65]

This tendency to excuse Nazism by downplaying or disregarding its anti-Semitic features while hailing it for its militant anticommunism was deftly exploited by its supporters.[66] In the fall of 1933, Viereck traveled to Germany to meet with Hitler. According to his account, he told the führer that Germany's reputation would be significantly strengthened if propaganda claimed anti-Semitic campaigns were directed at "internationalists" and Communists—what Viereck termed "bad" Jews—rather than the Jewish people as a whole.[67] Upon his return, Viereck began to put this policy into practice.

In one case, which would turn out to have deep ramifications for those involved, he introduced Ralph Easley to Ernst Schmitz, a Nazi agent ostensibly working for the German Tourist Board.[68] With Viereck's encouragement, Easley and Schmitz agreed to publish and distribute a book, *Communism in Germany*, to set the record straight about the Hitler regime. It would be written by German publicists but endorsed by Easley and his countersubversive allies. The book began with a quotation from Hitler—"At the beginning of the year there were weeks when we were within a hair's breadth of Bolshevist chaos"—and systematically presented German fascism as the only effective bulwark against communist internationalism, but effort was made to excise anti-Semitic comments from the text.[69] Germany was saved "solely by the followers of Adolf Hitler, the only factor of any real promise and strength in the great struggle in recent years," the book argued.[70] Ten thousand copies were printed, each set with a foreword signed by Easley, Hamilton Fish, Harry A. Jung, Walter S. Steele, Archibald Stevenson, and other leading countersubversives. Through Easley's connections, *Communism in Germany* was sent to dozens of organizations and influential individuals, from the president downward. A thousand copies were sent to the Better America Federation, four hundred to the American Coalition of Patriotic Societies, five hundred to the American Vigilant Intelligence Association, and several hundred to a half-dozen other patriotic groups—in all most of the informal network of professional patriots that spanned the nation.[71] The year 1933 marked the clash of "a renaissance and an insurrection," the book explained. "The decisive battle between faith and godlessness, between national consciousness and internationalism, between spirit, honor, and character on the one side and bestiality, dishonor and crime on the other, was fought on German soil."[72]

Anti-Semites and fascists thus used the language of countersubversion to cover their tracks and broaden their reach, just as segregationists of a later era would deploy the language of law and order as a substitute for white supremacist arguments when they ceased to be palatable in national debate. Communist-baiting lasted, in part at least, because it was a more secure rhetorical tool than anti-Semitism was. By the late 1930s, Coughlin had concluded that Jewish conspiracy was the key that linked the New Deal and the CIO to the Soviet Union, but it was anticommunism that allowed him to defend his changing commitments—opposition to unionization, anti-Semitism, friendship with Ford—as part of a consistent and long-held philosophy rather than a series of pragmatic shifts resulting from a shrinking popular base and the emergence of a new patron. Even as he reinvented himself, anticommunism remained the lynchpin of his self-definition.

In 1938 Coughlin began inserting his anti-Semitic ideas into radio addresses, producing a storm of protest from liberal, left-wing, and Jewish groups. The Radio Priest defended himself by claiming that he distinguished "most carefully between good Jews and bad Jews as well as I do between the good gentiles and bad gentiles." "There is no Jewish question in America," he argued. "Please God, may there never be one. However, there is a question of Communism in America. . . . Please God, we will solve it. If Jews persist in supporting Communism directly or indirectly, that will be regrettable." Through such evasive distinctions, Coughlin implied his critics were secret Bolsheviks. In a sermon entitled "Not Anti-Semitism but Anti-Communism," Coughlin asked, "Would not a dispassionate judge be inclined, then, to conclude that the effort on the part of my critics to assail my person and scoff at my presentation of facts—would he not conclude that this is related to their desire to protect Communism?"[73] In masterpieces of oblique reasoning, articles in *Social Justice* proudly proclaimed that they did not defend Nazism or attack Jews, only to follow up by pointing out that Nazism was a response by good German citizens to the threat of Red revolution and that Jewish Communists should be mercilessly assaulted.

Often, this kind of misdirection worked very effectively. Despite Coughlin's increasingly violent rhetoric, John Cogley, editor of the *Chicago Catholic Worker*, was still able to write to him at the end of the decade expressing fears that militant Coughlinites had "confused your anti-Communism campaign with an anti-Semitism campaign."[74] Weasel words helped the priest evade responsibility for his statements, especially when it came to avoiding sanction within the church. Following the death of Coughlin's immediate superior, Bishop Michael Gallagher, Archbishop Edward Mooney had been appointed to fill the role. Mooney was not only less sympathetic to Coughlin personally and ideologically than Gallagher, but he was also aware of the damage Coughlin was doing to the church's reputation. Nevertheless, like many in the hierarchy, he feared Coughlin's popularity and was not entirely free from lingering prejudices himself.[75] Msgr. Edward Hickey (a former chancellor of the Detroit Archdiocese) recollected in 1988 that many felt "Father Coughlin was in a stronger position probably at that time than Martin Luther had been centuries earlier."[76] In private letters, Mooney expressed his fear that if Coughlin were to lead a schismatic movement, he would take with him that "all too numerous type of Catholic," meaning the hundreds of thousands of poor, discontented, sometimes anti-Semitic Catholics who lived in the cities of the North.[77] Mooney complained that the articles in *Social Justice* were "so artfully gotten up, contain so many disclaimers of anti-Semitic feeling and put forward the communistic issue so cleverly that it [is] impossible to take issue with them to the point of refusing to pass the articles." "He is clever enough," Mooney continued, "to make his statements difficult to check . . . [and] clever enough as well to choose an issue on which many people are glad to have someone voice opinions which they themselves would prefer to guard in discreet silence."[78]

If the church muzzled Coughlin too comprehensively, they would appear as elitist enemies of the workingman, in league with the conspiratorial interests that Coughlin denounced. A combination of lingering anti-Semitism, class politics, and anticommunism therefore ensured the church leadership tolerated Coughlin's troublemaking long after it should have disciplined him. Used to thinking in epochs rather than years, the episcopacy opted to wait for Coughlin to hang himself rather than doing anything directly. In a note written shortly after taking office, Mooney wrote, "It will not be my policy to change anything or to inaugurate anything new. Everything must remain in status quo."[79] "Bland action now," he told the apostolic delegate, "might obviate the necessity of sterner measures later on when the movement has assumed definite shape and larger volume."[80] The church tinkered on the sidelines while Coughlin drove on. Christian Front groups were organized in several cities, the biggest of them in New York, and they began attacking Jewish shops and businesses and marching in fascist style in the streets.[81] "The Christian Front is no longer a dream," Coughlin told his audiences. "It is a reality—a reality that," as events polarized America, "grows stronger, more courageous and more determined."[82]

* * *

There was no single path to fascism in America. Explanations for the rising influence of anti-Semitic, conspiratorial, and antidemocratic ideas on the extreme Right in the 1930s often focus on the unique characteristics of particular subgroups: the conspiratorial methodology of Protestant fundamentalist Bible decoders, the corporatist traditions of the Catholic Church, the totalitarian ethic of big businessmen like Ford. But none of these explanations entirely satisfies, since other individuals in each of these communities did not respond in the same way. Political defeat clearly played its part in the formation of the rejectionist consciousness of extremists; again, though, other individuals experienced political exclusion without needing fascistic ideas to reconcile themselves to a hostile world. Although these were often important preconditions, then, they were not in themselves sufficient to explain an individual's decision to join the ranks of the radical Right. Ultimately, what united the hard-liners at the margins of American right-wing politics was a peculiar combination of character and community. Charles Coughlin, William Bell Riley, and Elizabeth Dilling differed greatly in personality and intelligence. None was insane, as their enemies often alleged, but all shared a tendency to "double down" on their beliefs in the face of setbacks, an inability to be self-critical, and an oppressive existence within introspective networks trading intricate and all-encompassing visions of conspiracy in Washington.

The danger of the cultural insularity produced by a closed community was clear, and many radical right-wingers were no less aware of the risks of political isolation than Browder-era Communists were. This was undoubtedly a reason extremists deployed anticommunist rhetoric to broaden their appeal, trading on shared values in the hope of ingratiating themselves with more powerful and influential conservatives. Although this tactic served the purposes of extremists, it was damaging for conservatives, who were already struggling with the damage done to their reputations by the Depression. When supporters of the New Deal responded to attacks against them in kind—putting in place a slow-burning antifascist campaign that ran almost from the beginning of the Roosevelt era until the end of the Second World War—conservatives found that now they were the ones facing accusations of disloyalty. Right-wing extremism had become more intense precisely because its members were marginalized. But it was tempting for the Left to present their aggression as evidence of strength. Before they knew it, the conservative Right was on the back foot, defending their patriotic credentials to the public as if they were no better than a pack of revolutionaries.

9

A Mirror Image

Anticommunists and Antifascists

By 1937 Henry Ford was the only major automobile manufacturer still refusing to negotiate with the United Auto Workers. Ford was at the forefront of resistance to the New Deal, not only on the union issue but also attacking plans to regulate the economy, increase taxes on the rich, and introduce other reforms that he saw as monopolistic or hostile to business. His example set the course for dozens of smaller manufacturers across the country. If reform was to succeed, a confrontation with Ford would have to take place, and almost inevitably at the River Rouge plant: the largest automobile factory in the world and the living symbol of Fordism.[1]

The drive to organize the Rouge began in the middle of 1937. UAW organizers printed leaflets declaring "Ford is Fascism" and "Unionism is Americanism." Offices were rented outside the city limits so Ford's controlling stake in the local police could not be used to disrupt their plans. Lawyers were readied, pressmen informed, each stage of the operation planned with care. Finally, at two o'clock on May 26, four leading UAW organizers—Richard T. Frankensteen, Walter Reuther, J. J. Kennedy, and Robert Kanter—arrived at Gate 4 of the plant to distribute leaflets, let the press take some photographs, and symbolically fire the starter pistol of the campaign.

Newspapermen turned up at the prearranged location early and spotted several cars with suspicious-looking men in dark suits and hats sitting in them, waiting. When asked what they were doing, the men told the journalists to leave. The four UAW organizers arrived a little late, approaching the site across an iron overpass over some rail tracks. At the request of the photographers, the four stopped at one end of the bridge to pose for shots in front of the large "Ford Motor Company" sign on the factory wall behind them. The men in the cars had left their vehicles and were milling around.

As the UAW organizers were having their photos taken, four of the suited men marched swiftly toward Dick Frankensteen. The first grabbed his jacket and pulled it over his head. Another, who had removed his own jacket and was wearing shirtsleeves and waistcoat, approached from the side and a little behind and started pummeling Frankensteen's ribs. Soon several more men joined in, until a small group was taking turns to punch him while he struggled to free himself from his jacket. He fell, and the group began kicking his body and head. A 250-pound former all-American college football star, Frankensteen summoned the energy to stand and lunge at his assailants, but as he rose he was grabbed and beaten back down. Two men held his legs apart while a third repeatedly kicked him in the groin.

Men set upon the other UAW activists. Reuther was punched in the face and stomach, back, and face again. After he fell down, his assailants picked his prone body off the floor and dropped him on the concrete at least a half-dozen times. They turned and dragged him to the end of the overpass, kicking and shouting, before throwing him down the steps. Kanter was pushed off the bridge, falling to the rails below.[2]

The attacks continued as the union men staggered away along the tracks. In a similar incident a couple of blocks away, another organizer's back was broken. A third clash came when a crew of female auxiliaries in green berets and armbands tried to get off a trolley car to distribute leaflets and were unceremoniously shoved back onto the carriage. In all, sixteen people, including seven of the auxiliaries, were injured in the fracas—kicked, pulled, choked, and beaten.[3]

All this was witnessed by the reporters. With the organizers driven off, the assailants began trying to destroy the evidence: attacking the journalists, ripping up notebooks, and breaking cameras. A Detroit News photographer, however, made it back to his car and stashed a set of exposed plates under the backseat before driving off. The images, printed in the national press and across the world over the next few days, are astonishing for the shamelessness of the attack as much as the violence itself. Taken together they offer a still slide show of the incident: the four UAW organizers standing on the overpass in front of the Ford sign, a slight camera blur catching the motion as Kanter and Reuther turn to face the men approaching from the left, Frankensteen's jacket pulled over his shoulders as his attackers lay into him. Cameramen lurk on the margins of the frame, revealing the hasty construction of the shots; punches are paused in midflight before plunging onto their targets; then the aftermath is revealed in an unidentified room, Reuther—blood running from his nose—holding Frankensteen's right hand almost tenderly as Frankensteen, sitting in a chair, his face crumpled and shirt and tie stained with blood, pulls back his hair with his left; and the next day, both men recovering in hospital beds with bruises and stitches all over their faces, smiling grimly for the cameras.

As people across the country looked at the images in their newspapers, the Ford Motor Company's public relations machine began rolling out denials. Press releases declared that there were no Service Men involved, that the attackers were ordinary Ford workers angry with the unionists, and that the unionists, who they called "raiders," had precipitated the violence by calling workers "scabs" as they tried to change shifts. Father Coughlin leaped to Ford's defense, *Social Justice* claiming that the UAW had provoked a riot.[4] "It was a staged, set-up affair," Harry Bennett told the press. "The union wanted the service men involved." But a photograph that showed handcuffs hanging from the waist of one of the attackers belied the suggestion that they lacked official sanction. Alongside the press corps, Reuther and Frankensteen had asked clergymen to come along, representatives of the Michigan Conference for the Protection of Civil Rights, and an agent working for Senator La Follette's newly created congressional committee investigating violations of civil liberties. UAW lawyers filed a complaint with the National Labor Relations Board, whose mandate under the recently passed Wagner Act required them to investigate cases of harassment of union organizers and, if necessary, empowered them to force companies to hold secret ballots on union affiliation. The *Chicago Daily Tribune* sourly noted that the UAW "had won a major propaganda victory at the cost of a few broken heads." The local Wayne County prosecutor's office began looking into possible criminal conduct by Ford staff. Resolutions calling for investigations were introduced into the Michigan state congress, while one of the witnesses, Rev. Raymond Prior Sanford, told journalists that local policemen had been looking on and had done nothing. "Before the U.A.W.A. [UAW of America] gets through with Harry Bennett and Ford's service department Dearborn will be a part of the United States and the workers will be able to enjoy their constitutional rights," Walter Reuther promised. Speaking before a mass meeting of Ford workers, UAW president Homer Martin announced, "The un-American tactics of the Ford Motor Company are at last being brought out into the open. The whole country, by this time, knows that 'Fordism' is really gangsterism, fascism and feudalism; in fact everything but Americanism."[5]

The shift in public mood toward support for federal activism and political reform in the 1930s reflected the failure of traditional politics to address the Depression crisis. However, public support for the New Deal was sustained through the efforts of liberals and left-wing activists to draw attention to the ways elites had traditionally used antiradical talk to maintain their dominance in American society. Reformers used the media and a set of newly created federal institutions to promote an ideal of American nationalism that rejected the antireform, "American plan" connotations of the 1920s. By keeping the opposition on the defensive, accusing elites and conservatives of being the real "un-Americans," liberal and left-wing activists formed a vital adjunct to the legislative and executive program put forth by the administration.

As a result of these endeavors, countersubversive thinking in the 1930s underwent an unprecedented reversal, as privileged elites found themselves accused of disloyalty. Although never quite as furious or as openly violent as the antiradical attacks that had come during the generation before, elite groups nevertheless began to experience what it was like to have their patriotism called into question. Voluntarist, extrajudicial tactics that had formerly been crucial methods of maintaining control at the local level now began to serve as evidence of injustice and exploitation in a national media conversation. Without any basic change in the way they were deployed, intimidation, abuse, and red-baiting suddenly became counterproductive, while attempts to introduce peacetime sedition laws and teacher-loyalty oaths, instead of cooling reformist zeal, were pointed to as evidence of the un-American tendencies of professional patriots afraid of a genuinely level playing field.[6] Formerly, as Ford employee Frank Hadas put it, organizations like the Service Department were "like the outbuilding in the backyard"—not to be talked about in polite company.[7] Now they became objects of national discussion, proof that "gangsterism" was hard at work in American corporations. Once the press began reporting these events, activists realized they could deliberately court violent responses, as with the Battle of the Overpass, knowing that the brutality of the reaction would legitimize their agenda, a strategy of creative tension later adopted to such great effect by the civil rights movement. As one union leader put it, "We could never organize a plant if it weren't for the cooperation of management."[8]

Because this took place in the context of a rising fascist movement at home and abroad, the language of antifascism came reflexively to inform these attempts to take control of the meaning of American nationalism. Ironically, such antifascist countersubversion was promoted particularly heavily by Communists and their Popular Front allies, many of whom had formerly been victims of countersubversive attack. Many on the Left understood fascism to be simply the extension of monopoly capitalism, the brutality of the existing order unmasked, and were therefore quick to question big businessmen's commitment to the republican order.[9] As Rossinow notes, many argued that "the Black Shirts of European fascism had their American counterparts not in William Dudley Pelley's Silver Shirts and other marginal groups but rather in the 'labor spy racket' and the large goon squads in Henry Ford's employ."[10]

In some cases, as with Ford and his continuing sponsorship of militant anti-Semites, there was indeed a case for saying that powerful interests were linked to fascist networks.[11] Not least because they shared a hostility to Communist politics and the New Deal, the borders between the radical Right and mainstream conservatives were never entirely clear. However, many antifascist accusations were exaggerated in traditional countersubversive fashion. Thus, even while it helped to support the New Deal agenda, loosely applying countersubversive smears to American conservatives also served to legitimize the language of loyalty that many liberals and left-wingers had in the previous generation condemned. This was the flip side to the Popular Front's liberal-left-wing alliance for reform. Ultimately, antifascism helped validate a more restrictive political space than had previously existed in the United States, and in this provided a crucial precedent for McCarthyism.[12]

* * *

The early years of Roosevelt's presidency were characterized by no small alarm at the growth of fascism in America. Almost immediately following Hitler's seizure of power, extremists organized military processions in various cities, Jews were abused in the streets, and the Nazi-sponsored Friends of New Germany held public demonstrations under flowing canopies of black swastikas on red-and-white backgrounds. Reports of assaults on American Jews in Germany encouraged a number of Jewish organizations to set up a boycott of German goods in America, and this in turn produced a backlash among German Americans, worried they would be tarred unfairly, as many had been during the First World War.

In Congress one of the most vocal antifascists was New York's Samuel Dickstein. Chair of the House Committee on Immigration and Naturalization and a Jewish American from a family of Lithuanian immigrants, Dickstein had earned his spurs as a Tammany Democrat in the New York state legislature, fighting socialism on the Lower East Side.[13] Throughout his political career, he had been a vocal antiradical, supporting the ejection of the New York Socialists in 1920, defeating the Socialist Meyer London to win his seat in the national House of Representatives in 1923, and conducting hearings into police commissioner Whalen's forged Amtorg documents in 1930.[14] But sensing the fading fortunes of antiradical politics during the Depression, he abandoned a plan to investigate the veterans' Bonus Expeditionary Force for suspected communist influence and by 1933 had refocused on the Far Right.[15] His official biographer, Dorothy Waring, explains, "The menacing shadow of Hitlerism appeared. . . . Rumbles of un-American propaganda reached Dickstein's ears. It was rumored Hitler was stretching his iron hand across the sea," and so, with "shears in hand, Dickstein set out to destroy the web of un-American propaganda spreading over the United States."[16]

In speeches, press releases, and radio addresses, Dickstein warned that a vast operation was being built in the United States with the ultimate goal of launching a fascist coup. A secret Nazi force funded by a war chest of more than 140 million marks sent from Munich, he claimed, had built cells in at least fifteen

states and was drilling storm troopers on American soil.[17] Over the previous
two years, ships coming from Germany had been filled with agents working
"under the direction of a Nazi leader who makes speeches to them all the way
across the ocean and prepares them for their propaganda work here."[18] With
them came reams of pro-Nazi material, booklets, pamphlets, and other propaganda subsequently circulated throughout the states. Three hundred agents
of the German Ministry of Propaganda had been smuggled into the country,
posing as employees of the German consulates, and a bureau had been set up
with instructions to spread more Nazi propaganda, "with the ultimate object
of overthrowing our government and installing in its place a dictatorship on
the Nazi model." Concluding that "insidious, well-planned and well-financed
Hitler propaganda is rapidly taking root," Dickstein announced that the Committee on Immigration would hold informal hearings during the congressional
recess and push for a formal investigation in 1934.[19]

Dickstein's allegations were quickly picked up by antifascists in the press corps.
The *American Hebrew* conjured a picture of a vast, disciplined cadre of Nazis
training for a seizure of power, a writer in *Harper's* asserted that secret meetings were being held to which the password for entry was "Let a Jew Die," and
the radical Jewish activist Samuel Untermyer claimed there were links between
Nazism and the Klan and that the German ambassador was "one of the most
destructive of propagandists."[20] There was truth to some of the less wild allegations: the year 1933 had seen a disturbing pattern of local conflicts provoked by
American Nazis patrolling the streets of American towns and cities, and the
Friends of New Germany had been explicitly encouraged by senior elements
within the Nazi Party. The Department of Justice issued a warrant for the arrest of Heinz Spanknoebel, leader of the Friends of New Germany, and he fled
the country rather than face charges under the Espionage Act.[21] But describing
these groups as a vast and menacing Nazi conspiracy set upon overthrowing the
American system was no more accurate than similar assertions about left-wing
revolutionaries had been in 1919. As with the abortive Bolshevik propaganda
bureau, the intention behind the limited German covert activity that did take
place was principally to earn a more positive hearing for Germany, not to overthrow the government of the United States. Claims about the imminent threat
posed by domestic shirted groups gave a shoddy array of fascist sympathizers
an aura of menace entirely out of proportion to reality.

The way in which a disproportionate vision of Nazi sedition was conjured via
the media in the buildup to Dickstein's investigation closely echoed the methodology of the Overman, Lusk, and Fish hearings, all of which Dickstein was
familiar with. Although he defended legitimate immigrants, many of whom
were his electors, Dickstein was entirely comfortable with the countersubversive assumption that right-wing political extremism was essentially a "foreign"

problem stemming from the covert activities of enemy states and that it there-fore could be solved through policing, investigations, and border controls.[22] The countersubversive rhetoric was more or less the same as ever, and the issues of concern—especially the baleful influence of propaganda—were directly lifted from prior political investigations against the Left. Replacing the word *Nazi* for *Bolshevik* would often suffice to make speeches and press releases more or less identical to ones given about radical influence in the past.

But if the rhetorical devices employed were the same, the shift from investi-gating one end of the political spectrum to the other shook up traditional politi-cal alignments in unexpected ways. For instance, among the first witnesses to appear before Dickstein's immigration subcommittee was Clarence Hathaway, the editor of the communist *Daily Worker,* whose principal target turned out to be the professional patriots who were normally the accusers at such hearings. To cries of outrage, Hathaway declared that Hamilton Fish, still probably the most well-known countersubversive in the country, was promoting Nazi pro-paganda in the United States.[23] Brandishing a copy of *Communism in Germany,* the book that Ralph Easley had helped assemble and distribute earlier in the year, which Fish and others had endorsed, Hathaway theatrically pointed to the first page: "This book has a foreword by Americans who read this book. This foreword is signed by a whole group of Americans, including Ralph M. Easley and Hamilton Fish, Jr., and a group of others. So that on one side you have the signature of Adolph Hitler on a quotation from him, and on the other side you have Congressman Fish and Easley."

Dickstein asked whether it was not possible that Fish signed the book "for the purpose of combating communism in the United States and for that pur-pose only . . . ?" "When one reads the foreword to a book devoted to Fascist propaganda and anti-Semitism, and against the working class generally," Ha-thaway replied, "one cannot state that he goes into this innocently. Congress-man Fish is not a child."[24] He also alleged that Fish had been seen at a meeting with Spanknoebel and other Nazi agents. This provoked a furious response, and Dickstein adjourned the hearings for two weeks to give the congressman a chance to respond.[25]

The antifascist hearings promised to "be a rather unpleasant experience for several professional patriots over here," an editorialist in the *Washington Post* noted. In the immediate aftermath of the publication of *Communism in Germany,* Easley had been criticized for naïveté, but Hathaway's allegations dramatically raised public interest in the affair, and, to Easley's frustration, other countersubversives among the coterie of signatories now began to shuffle away from the enterprise. Captain John B. Trevor of Walter S. Steele's American Coalition asked to have his name removed from the foreword, and Hamilton Fish also retracted his endorsement, he said, "in view of the attempt of the

Communists to make out that I am aligned with Nazi propaganda"—which, of course, he was.[26]

Never a man with a great capacity for self-criticism, Easley blamed "the Jews" for the sorry situation he found himself in.[27] As he watched his allies desert him, he wrote to associates that "d----- liars" at the *Jewish Daily Bulletin* "were having everybody deny that they ever signed the foreword or saw the book or heard of me."[28] He complained bitterly, "I have learned by experience in this matter that we cannot count upon the politicians doing anything that the Jews do not like, because those politicians have either received favors or expect to do so. While Hamilton Fish did what he did with his eyes wide open, he 'got cold feet' as soon as Untermyer got after him!"[29] Two weeks later, Fish appeared before the subcommittee and vigorously denied that he had ever met with Spanknoebel or supported anti-Semitic ideas. He was conspicuously silent about his name boldly sitting on the first page of *Communism in Germany*.

In summarizing his preliminary findings early in the new year, Dickstein declared he had uncovered evidence of Nazi influence in at least eighteen states and of between forty and fifty thousand dangerous illegal aliens smuggled into the country in the previous month alone—and that this only scratched the surface.[30] Although it was the Department of Justice rather than Dickstein that probably deserved the greater credit, Spanknoebel's decision to flee the country helped justify a fuller hearing. "In New York City," wrote the historian Sander A. Diamond, "the public's imagination transformed German waiters and beer-hall owners into Nazi spies. The Spanknöbel Affair gave Germany exactly the kind of adverse publicity it least desired."[31] By 168 votes to 31, the House endorsed Dickstein's proposal for a formal investigation into extremist propaganda in the United States. Principally this meant Nazi activities, though defining itself as investigating "un-Americanism" rather than "Nazism" in order to win crucial additional votes from conservatives, Communist, and other Far Left groups were also included within the committee's purview. In this way, in most unfamiliar circumstances to those who know only its later form, was born the original House Committee on Un-American Activities.[32]

Representative John McCormack of Massachusetts was put in charge. Dickstein claimed to have declined the chairmanship because he did not want the investigation to be seen as a Jewish plot.[33] Nevertheless, he ran the show. In hearings that stretched over the best part of a year, he took evidence from members and opponents of dozens of pro-Nazi groups, particularly the Friends of New Germany and William Dudley Pelley's Silver Shirts. Testimony revealed that American fascists were using Henry Ford's *The International Jew* to buttress their anti-Semitic claims, that a German American soldier had invited young Nazis with an interest in heavy weaponry to join the New York National Guard, and that a fascist boys' camp had been set up in New Jersey.[34] Violence broke out at several sessions when Nazi sympathizers and left-wing and Jewish groups clashed. Dickstein repeatedly lost his temper with contemptuous witnesses sporting swastika buttons and other offensive accoutrements who ridiculed Judaism and declared it to be part of a communist world conspiracy.[35]

The information was disturbing, the witnesses unpleasant, and the forays into the antiradical community embarrassing, but the evidence did not support the claim of an organized and powerful conspiracy against the American government, as Dickstein had suggested there was. The problem was not that authorities might need to deal with thugs bent on intimidating innocent American citizens because of their religion or that it should reserve the right to exclude or monitor noncitizens who were secretly in the pay of foreign agencies; it was that—just as with the committee's predecessors—Dickstein and his allies felt it constitutionally necessary to produce a contorted and overblown national security justification for such actions, and this served to distort the public understanding of the scale and nature of the threat. New Dealer Raymond Moley insisted to the committee that it was unimportant whether "an organic connection" with German fascism was proven in any particular case, because "if an organization in this country has the same ideals as that in Germany, it is a menace to this country."[36] Deploying the "dupe" analogy so often used by antiradicals in the past, Dickstein's biographer wrote, "Even those apparently pure Aryan organizations in the United States, which have grown up in every metropolitan center, had been duped into becoming the plaything and useful tools of the gigantic anti-Administration movement. Just as the master criminal will gather moronic henchmen to do his killing, so the Hidden Hand active on the American scene directed the energy of misguided American patriots."[37]

Dickstein offered a soapbox to figures of dubious credibility, giving conspiracy theories the stamp of congressional approval, just as his predecessors had done. Most famously, in November 1934, as the hearings were coming to a close, retired Marine Corps major general Smedley D. Butler testified that a number of Wall Street financiers, various army officers, and members of the American Legion were plotting a coup against President Roosevelt in order to install a fascist government.[38] A private army of five hundred thousand men was being built, largely from veterans' groups, and a Wall Street trader had offered Butler a huge sum of money to command it. Although an approach to Butler had indeed been made, subsequent investigations found no evidence of a genuine conspiracy. The trader who approached Butler was an admirer of the French Far Right Croix de Feu and had grandiose plans, but had apparently done nothing to put his ideas into action beyond trying (and failing) to recruit the major general. The story nevertheless received sweeping media coverage, and

Dickstein repeatedly and uncritically endorsed it.[39] "Butler has the evidence," he told journalists. "He's not going to make any serious charges unless he has something to back them up. We'll have men here with bigger names than his."[40]

The committee's final report stated that there was "no question that these attempts were discussed, were planned, and might have been placed in execution when and if the financial backers deemed it expedient." However, under the influence of the more sober-minded Chairman McCormack, the committee resisted calling the various nationally known figures who had been implicated without evidence, even excising their names from the record. John L. Spivak, an investigative journalist tied to the Communist Party, obtained an unredacted copy and wrote an article in the *New Masses* claiming that the decision to ignore America's power elite was a scandal of national proportions.[41] Spivak alleged that, like the characters in a dime-store novel, the committee had been diverted from their task when they realized how high up the conspiracy really went and had thus turned into "a close collaborator of the would-be fascist rulers of the country."[42] He was right that the committee was more cautious about defaming powerful conservatives than prior investigative committees had been toward less powerful radicals. Nevertheless, prior misdemeanors hardly justified present falsehoods.

Spivak's instincts were sounder when he complained that the committee had effectively given a pass to the National Civic Federation following the allegations about Fish's links to Nazi propaganda. Several witnesses told the committee that the Easleys had been the distributors of *Communism in Germany,* and when Ernst Schmitz and George Sylvester Viereck were called to testify they confirmed that they received several thousand dollars from Germany every month for public relations purposes.[43] There was a strong possibility Easley was paid for his services from this money. (Records of telephone conversations prior to the publication of the book indicate Easley not wishing to "do it" for less than "25"—presumably twenty-five thousand dollars—since "there is going to be a big fight and we shall have to get into the fight.")[44] It is conceivable, therefore, that a chain of cash linked the NCF to the German government, making them one of the few domestic groups that could actually be tied to Nazi operations in America. At one point, Spivak accosted Dickstein to ask him why he had not subpoenaed the federation's financial records after Hathaway's original allegations about *Communism in Germany.* The congressman was unable to provide a good answer.[45]

Actually, the reason was straightforward, if unedifying. The committee was using the federation as a source of information for its parallel hearings on communist activities, and it hardly made sense to be asking their "expert" advice at one moment and then accusing them of un-Americanism the next. In a deal behind the scenes, chief counsel Thomas Hardwick had reassured Easley that the NCF would not be investigated, and in exchange Easley promised to pull together his network of professional patriots to testify on the danger of left-wing revolutionaries in America.[46]

As strategies originally used to attack the Left were reapplied to the Far Right, antifascist countersubversives faced some of the tricky questions that antiradicals had struggled to answer. How much credit should be given to individual testimony, which was both an essential and yet unreliable component of any investigation into a closed community? What were the links between domestic extremists and foreign states, and to what purpose were foreign agents operating on American shores? Was there a meaningful difference between someone defending an unconscionable regime abroad and one advocating a replica of it at home? How far should an extremist movement be allowed to grow before it was considered a legitimate threat? What powers could the federal government assume without losing its republican character? And what relationship did moderates have with extremists who shared some of their preoccupations but little of their commitment to democracy?

The first incarnation of the House Un-American Activities Committee produced predictably ambivalent answers. On the one hand, Dickstein's investigations showed that Pelley's Silver Shirts had been talking about assassinating prominent Jews and helped to publicize the links between the Friends of New Germany and German Nazism.[47] Subsequently, the State Department issued a formal complaint to Berlin, and the German foreign ministry was forced to instruct all German nationals to leave the Friends of New Germany, contributing to its collapse shortly afterward. The movement was later resurrected in 1936 by Fritz Kuhn as the German-American Bund, this time notionally led by Americans—people with citizenship papers, if admittedly not very convincing accents. But it remained suspected and politically marginal throughout the decade, an outcome for which Dickstein's investigations can claim a share of credit.[48] On the other hand, the hearings circulated a number of unreliable theories about American fascism and helped reinforce the idea that American elites were an imminent threat to the nation's democratic institutions. Subsequently, Dickstein made a series of unsuccessful attempts to introduce new loyalty laws, including a peacetime sedition bill, a law banning from the mails any literature that incited racial or religious hatred, and another that gave broad latitude for the deportation of extremists.[49] Hindsight shows that none of these was urgently needed to preserve the Republic. But Dickstein's claims were sufficiently plausible to have real political traction. In 1934 President Roosevelt began reconstituting the Bureau of Investigation's political policing duties, re-creating the General Intelligence Division and instructing J. Edgar Hoover to investigate both radical Left and Right: in the words of one historian, this was "probably the most consequential decision" of the antifascist campaigns as a whole.[50] A year later, the bureau launched a comprehensive examination of both fascist and communist activities in America, and by the end of the decade it had reestablished itself as the principal domestic agency looking into political subversion. Rather than leading to an abandonment of smearing and political loyalty investigations, the shift of politics leftward during the 1930s caused it to metastasize.

Dickstein's hearings formed part of a complex and fractious public debate in which allegations of Nazism, fascism, Bolshevism, and communism were deployed uncritically by a wide range of individuals and groups. Like Bolshevism before it, fascism lost much of its historical specificity as it turned into a generalized term of abuse, a problem complicated by the fact that fascism was itself evolving into increasingly virulent forms in Germany. Nevertheless, it is possible to unpick different ways in which the language of antifascism was used. In particular, some individuals, like Dickstein, expressed hostility to both Bolshevism and fascism, while others, especially on the Left, used antifascist rhetoric to bolster their attacks on the right wing alone and to link American capitalist elites to Nazism. To these antifascist countersubversives, antiradicalism was not a precedent but a danger. As Roosevelt's secretary of the interior, Harold Ickes, put it, powerful men used fears of communism as "a wooden horse within the bowels of which fascism may enter the shrine of liberty."[51] For Ickes, fighting fascism therefore also required fighting the antiradical politics with which it was associated. This in turn opened the door to Popular Front cooperation. This division cut through the center of the Democratic Party, the New Deal coalition, and even through liberal organizations like the ACLU, which struggled to decide whether people on the Far Right should be entitled to the same constitutional protection as radicals on the Left.

The inversions that led the CPUSA to appear before a congressional investigative committee to denounce old countersubversives for disloyalty might seem more appropriate to a Lewis Carroll fable than American political history, but they did not end with the Dickstein hearings. In fact, the New Deal era saw a continuing pattern of looking-glass public investigations that challenged the patriotic credentials of right-wing antiradicals, vocally supported by former victims of government-sponsored loyalty hearings into the Left.[52] In 1935 trusted New Dealer Hugo Black chaired a committee looking into underhand lobbying practices by businessmen and raided the offices of several patriotic organizations.[53] Conservatives complained that they were being targeted by "an American Cheka" and that the committee was "spreading terror" through the "far-flung government agencies of espionage and intimidation." Demonstrating a remarkably selective memory, Republican senator Daniel D. Hastings of Delaware claimed, "Never outside Russia, Germany and Italy has intimidation on so vast a scale been attempted." Agents of the Black Committee, he said, were sweeping "down on the offices and homes of the victims, seiz[ing] books, documents, and correspondence," and innocent

Americans were being "dragged to Washington and pilloried on the witness stand by vengeful inquisitors," their names, addresses, and associations demanded and damned by association.[54]

Liberals and socialists seeking to support the New Deal agenda fed upon and strengthened this wave of hostility toward corporate elites and professional patriots, using "American fascism" as a generic designation for racists and enemies of labor. The *Nation* declared that the big corporations were engendering an American version of the *Führerprinzip*. Investigative journalist Raymond Gram Swing's *Forerunners to American Fascism* (1935) and Norman Thomas's *The Choice before Us* (1934), concluded the radical Right were dictators in waiting. In 1936 Warner Bros. released *Black Legion,* in which Humphrey Bogart was tricked into joining the noxious Klan offshoot that had recently been exposed and broken up by the FBI.[55] A year earlier, Doubleday had published Sinclair Lewis's *It Can't Happen Here,* which dripped with references to the previous decade's infelicitous history of antiradical snafus, in which a populist demagogue, Berzelius "Buzz" Windrip, comes to power and systematically constructs a fascist regime in the United States, only to be himself replaced by coup plotters who engineer a war with Mexico to exploit nationalist sentiment for personal benefit. In October 1936, theatrical versions were simultaneously performed in twenty cities across the country. The message was clear: the enemies of the New Deal may speak in the American vernacular, but their goal was European fascism. "If we ever have fascism in this country," Lewis told pressmen on the opening night of his play, "it will come as a result of the activities of the economic royalists whose minds are closed against anything that has happened since 1870."[56]

These arguments sought to reconcile traditional liberal and radical concerns—especially the power of capitalism and the effect of imperial expansion and militarization—with the discourse of countersubversion that had formerly been the preserve of antiradicals. In order to reinforce the claim that the Right rather than the Left was the real threat to American security, they added a new and powerful rhetorical component that had not been present in the previous generation. From around the mid-1930s, fascism was increasingly described as "totalitarian": a regime type that not only restricted the liberties of the individual but also reached into the deepest refuges of private life to utterly strip people of their humanity. The word had first been coined as a positive term of description by Mussolini, but it was left-wing reactions to Hitler that brought it chiefly into American public debate. Thus, before the term was applied to link extreme Left and Right, as it would be by anticommunists in later years, it was deployed to highlight the fundamental difference between fascist "totalitarianism" and Communist proletarian dictatorship. As Norman Thomas wrote in *The Choice before Us,* the "totalitarian state is infinitely more dangerous to the future than the acceptance of a temporary dictatorship for a transitional period. There are in the latter corrective elements, a conscious desire for a new social order freed from the exploitation of a profit-making class, and an economic program which are totally lacking in Fascism. The tendency of life in Russia is up, and not down, which is more than can be said for Germany."[57]

Antifascist pressure intensified in 1937 and 1938, as unions accelerated their organizing drives and reformist politicians looked to support them. Senator La Follette set up an investigative committee looking into violations of the Wagner Act, uncovering the tactics used by corporations to undermine legitimate unionism. La Follette's investigators, who included a range of reformers, veterans of the Interchurch World Movement's Steel Strike inquiry, and staff borrowed from the National Labor Relations Board, discovered that American industry was employing more than forty thousand labor spies to police its workforce, costing more than eighty million dollars a year.[58] Replete with photographs of an arsenal of weaponry used by corporate employers against their workers, the committee's investigations into dozens of industries produced jaw-dropping allegations of espionage, intimidation, beatings, provocation, and even murder, all to defend corporations' rights to manage.[59] Meanwhile, La Follette investigators coordinated their actions with union organizers to gather evidence firsthand, as when they attended the Battle of the Overpass at Ford's Rouge plant.

These revelations spurred on Popular Front reporters to make new claims about the dangers of American fascism. John Spivak offered an archetypal example of the wholesale adoption of countersubversive discourse for the pro-Communist Left; his 1939 book, *Secret Armies,* drew direct and explicit links (on the basis of evidence that, "by its very nature, naturally cannot be revealed") between French fascists, Nazi agents in preannexation Czechoslovakia, American fascists, and Henry Ford. "Underground armies in America," Spivak alleged, had learned the lessons of Germany's lack of preparation before World War I and now sought to built "an enormous propaganda machine and to draw into it as many native Americans as possible." Spivak argued it was "of vital importance . . . that preparations for fascist lawlessness be vigilantly uprooted. The Italian and German people made just this fatal mistake of tolerating the activities of Mussolini's and Hitler's gangs until they grew strong enough to seize power and crush every sign of democracy." Spivak demanded that Americans labor to "counteract such propaganda with greater and more intelligent propaganda to educate our people to the advantages of democracy"—a point that echoed almost word for word the conclusions of the Lusk Committee about the dangers of radicalism in 1919.[60]

In a characteristic Popular Front deployment of the old "dupe" analogy, A. B. Magil and Henry Stevens argued that Americans accustomed to hating fascism would nevertheless come to accept it if it was able to "masquerade under less objectionable names" and use the "cloak of '100 percent Americanism.'" For "Fascism takes on many disguises," and in America "in order to win popular support, it must appeal to the ideals and slogans in which most Americans still believe—to liberty and freedom. It must even pronounce itself antifascist."[61] In such a way, even open opposition to fascism was insufficient to clear capitalist elites of suspicion—for fascism was defined by the countersubversive Left simply as class hatred, and therefore an extension of capitalism's basically antagonistic relationship to democracy. In sum, only the elimination of capitalism could guarantee the end of fascism.

Earlier, Huxley had sought satiric bite by highlighting affinities between Fordism and communism. But the Left argued that Ford's complete control over every aspect of his corporate world more closely resembled "totalitarian" fascism. As a result, in the mid- to late-1930s, Ford's links to Nazism were discussed with a vigor that used to be reserved for his connections to Russia. Articles used details of Harry Bennett's reign of terror to point to the industrialists' un-American instincts. Readers learned how Ford had allowed the head of the Service Department to live in a mock castle, replete with towers, tunnels, hidden passageways, secret doors, and an underground den in which he kept lions and tigers as pets.[62] Bennett's idea must have been to use such outlandish ostentation to strengthen his authority in the plants. Now, exposed to the world, it was deeply damaging to the company's reputation. Whereas Ford had traditionally presented the independence of his fiefdom from government and Wall Street as evidence of his passionate commitment to American liberty, critics instead pointed to the absence of "industrial democracy." The power of these redefinitions ensured that by the time the UAW used the Wagner Act in 1941 to force an independent secret ballot on union membership, most of Ford's allies had deserted him. His old antagonist, Coughlin, stood virtually alone in defending Fordism as a "symbol of rugged individualism, 'Frontier Americanism' . . . of old-line American nationalism," free "from both banker and union control."[63] Of the fifty thousand votes cast by Ford workers in the ballot, more than 90 percent were for AFL- or CIO-affiliated unions.[64] After more than two decades of undeclared but persistent warfare, the Flivver King was forced to concede the principle of union bargaining, and the myth of a contented workforce at Ford was finally quashed. Coughlin's *Social Justice* described the event as "the fall of the Rock of Gibraltar."[65]

Between 1917 and 1933, the main challenges to the politics of countersubversion had come from northern liberals attached to the Al Smith wing of the Democratic Party and midwestern and western Republicans who held to a decentralized, Jeffersonian vision of American democracy. These groups, too, found their politics changing under the pressures of the New Deal and the Popular Front. As Roosevelt began to expand the reach of government, many questioned whether the president was a hero of reform or the architect of a Washington power grab. In keeping with the topsy-turvy climate of the time, this caused them to reevaluate their basic assumptions about the nature of subversion. Thus, even as efforts to purge America of fascism gained steam, the Right found itself winning new allies among some of its most trenchant critics.

The most visible opposition to the New Deal during Roosevelt's first term was the American Liberty League, established in the middle of 1934 by the businessmen and politicians who had formerly led the anti-Prohibition fight: Democrats such as Jouett Shouse, John Davis, and Al Smith, Republican James W. Wadsworth Jr., and funded from the deep pockets of the Du Pont family. As shown by the anti-Prohibition drive that gave birth to the organization, these figures were essentially antifederalists, but with Prohibition defeated their concerns refocused on the bureaucracies and federal agencies springing up under Roosevelt, as well as the growing alliance between the Democrats and the union movement. Quickly establishing itself as a leading political voice, the Liberty League raised comparable funds from wealthy private donors to the Democratic and Republican national campaigns, opened a Washington office with more than twice as many staff as Republican headquarters, and circulated more than five million pamphlets in the two years leading up to the 1936 election.[66] After efforts to deny Roosevelt the Democratic renomination in 1936 by supporting the southern conservative Eugene Talmadge fell flat, they threw their weight behind the Republican Party—while all the time claiming to be nonpartisan.

Given Al Smith's position as permanent bridesmaid to the presidency, many have focused on personal rivalries with Roosevelt as the reason behind his participation in the league. His animosity toward FDR was an open secret, and no doubt ego and frustrated opportunity played their part in his decision to break ranks with his party and president. His apparent defection from reformism did seem jarring: a man who had spoken out consistently for Catholics and immigrants as well as workers, who had led the resistance to the Red Scare in New York and stopped Palmer's march to the White House, who personified resistance to the Klan in the twenties and was considered wetter than virtually any other politician of his times seemed to have transformed overnight into a conservative of the worst order.

In truth, though, there was more consistency in Smith's politics than his critics were prepared to credit. He had always been hostile to what he considered to be excessive federal power, whether that meant Palmer in 1919, Prohibition in 1928, or Roosevelt in 1936, and this placed him closer to the old Bourbon Democrat tradition than it first seemed. What *was* inconsistent was his rhetoric. Formerly profoundly hostile to red-baiting, Smith now adopted the countersubversive language that had been used to attack him in the past. In one particularly famous speech in January 1936, Smith offered a barrage of misleading smears about the president, declaring that the New Deal's government by bureaucracy was destroying the foundations of law in America. "There can be only one capital, Washington or Moscow," he said. "There can be only the clear, pure, fresh air of free America, or the foul breath of communistic Russia. There can be only one flag, the Stars and Stripes, or the flag of the godless Union of the Soviets. There can be only one national anthem, The Star-Spangled Banner or the Internationale."[67] It might as well have been Palmer speaking. In response, Harold Ickes unearthed speeches from the 1928 campaign, when Smith had been attacked as a subversive, reading them to an audience at Washington's town hall to gales of laughter. Back in 1928, Smith had said that "the cry of socialism had always been raised by powerful interests that desired to put a damper upon progressive legislation" and was a charge he had been fighting for twenty-five years.[68]

While it sought to assume the mantle of popular democracy in its publications and press releases and boasted in Smith an old "friend of the working man," the Liberty League was dominated by the wealthy. It could influence public debate through the media and influence congressmen through donations and lobbying, but it struggled to build a mass membership.[69] Smith claimed that the president was privileging the South and West over his constituents in the urban Northeast, but the Second New Deal made such a complaint implausible. As a result, he took relatively few of his traditional supporters with him on his journey to the Right; most of his base stayed with Roosevelt.

Indeed, as the 1936 election approached, New Dealers found that the prominence of businessmen in the Liberty League was a boon. They opted to fight the reelection campaign as if they were running against the league rather than the broader-based Republican Party. Accusing businessmen of ingratitude, Roosevelt compared the league to an old man who had been saved from drowning only to complain that his silk hat had been lost. He joked that his enemies' newfound energy was a sign that his first term recovery program was working. The capitalist economy had been lying in intensive care, but now the patient was sufficiently recovered he could throw his crutches at the doctor. One leading Democrat renamed the organization the American Cellophane League since, he said, "first, it's a Du Pont product, and second, you can see right through it."[70]

The point was widely accepted by a supportive public and echoed in the words of other commentators. The favored term of the administration in attacking their opponents—*economic royalists*—was short of openly libelous but, with its allusion to Old Europe, implicitly cast doubt on Liberty Leaguers' commitment to republican democracy. Others were not so circumspect. "Sinclair Lewis has prepared us for orators like Mr. Smith and for organizations like the American

Liberty League," wrote one New Deal supporter. "We recognize the Fascist design and the Windrip oratory now." A letter in the *Washington Post* described the Liberty League as "the most dangerous Fascist lobby in America today," while Rabbi Stephen Wise declared that a vote for FDR was a vote against "Liberty League fascism in this country." That the founders of the league had only a few years earlier been hailed for their liberal opposition to the Prohibition amendment was long forgotten.[71]

The fight against Liberty League "fascism" helped ensure the president's victory in 1936, proving the popular adage of the time that a politician can be loved for the enemies he makes as much as his friends. Learning the lesson of defeat, the league moved into the background and by 1940 had wound down its public-facing activities entirely. Nevertheless, the league's emphasis on co-opting the language of Jeffersonian localism and individual autonomy for conservative ends would have a significant impact on right-wing politics in the 1940s and beyond. As Roosevelt set about winning urban working-class votes by hitching Jefferson's ideals to the methods of Hamilton, the Republican Party began to realize that fears over the power of the state could be used to paper over the fissures in the party that had been so painfully exposed in the 1920s. Gradually defecting from the New Deal orbit, old insurgents began to join conservatives like Michigan's senators, Arthur Vandenberg and Clare Hoffman, and Ohio's rising star, Robert Taft, in painting the president as a would-be dictator. This shift, which would see the progressive impulse in midwestern and western Republicanism almost completely replaced by an uncompromising conservatism, amounts to one of the most important structural changes in American politics in the early twentieth century and was an essential precondition for McCarthyism. The discourse of right-wing countersubversion was reinvigorated by being turned upside down. The state, rather than the margins of society, now became the presumed source of subversion, and the goal of countersubversives became policing Washington rather than empowering it.

At first, it was hard to imagine such a shift taking place—though perhaps no more inconceivable than the old warhorse of reform, Al Smith, transforming himself into a red-baiter. The progressive wing of the Republican party had greater claim than perhaps any group to have stopped federal countersubversion in its tracks after the Great Red Scare. Virtually all of the old insurgents who still lived had tacitly endorsed Roosevelt over Hoover in 1932, and many pundits anticipated a realignment that would bring them into formal alliance with the Roosevelt wing of the Democratic Party as part of a new liberal party. Senators Norris and La Follette, who represented both traditional rural voters and a growing industrial working class, played important roles in major New Deal programs: Norris provided the motor behind the Tennessee Valley

Authority (having spent much of the twenties fighting to ensure the Muscle Shoals dam did not fall into the hands of Henry Ford), and La Follette involved himself in a raft of labor and welfare laws before launching his Civil Liberties Committee. The insurgents even pushed the administration in a more radical direction on some issues, working with figures on the left of the New Deal such as Harold Ickes and Henry Wallace to accelerate the reform agenda.[72] Senator Borah had spoken out in defense of the Liberty League and against the National Industrial Recovery Act on antitrust grounds, but even he was by no means a blanket critic of the president's first-term program.[73] When he led an unsuccessful attempt to contest the Republican nomination for the presidency in 1936, Borah was as concerned with restraining conservatives within his own party as with defeating FDR. Meanwhile, the insurgents' Democratic ally from Montana, Senator Wheeler, attacked the NIRA and by 1935 was supporting alternative candidates to Roosevelt for the nomination.[74] But in the case of the president's controversial Revenue Act—the so-called soak-the-rich tax, which substantially raised income, corporate, estate, and gift taxes on America's wealthiest citizens—Wheeler was among its strongest supporters.[75]

After Roosevelt's reelection, though, opposition among the insurgents grew stronger, especially during the Supreme Court–packing battle, and many former allies began to deploy the same countersubversive rhetoric against the president that had previously been used against them. Wheeler led the opposition during the court fight, inflicting the first major political setback for the New Deal. Norris joined him in arguing that the executive challenge to judicial autonomy represented a step toward dictatorship. Even Hiram Johnson, the unofficial leader of the opposition to the Red Scare in 1919 and formerly a relatively close associate of the president, turned, in the words of one historian, into "one of the most vitriolic foes of the New Deal after 1936."[76] By 1939 "Young Bob" La Follette was the virtually the only Republican insurgent still working with the New Deal, largely because he, unlike his father, was more beholden to midwestern industrial workers than the rural voters who were at the core of his erstwhile collaborators' constituencies.

Whether outsmarted populists like Coughlin, disappointed progressives like Hiram Johnson, or alienated liberals like Al Smith, most of the leading figures who moved into opposition to Roosevelt nursed a history of personal frustrations, failed ambitions, and limited access to New Deal patronage. Supporters of the president were quick to point out that Al Smith and Burt Wheeler had both been left out in the cold. Self-interest seemed to explain why figures who had fought previous Republican administrations on progressive grounds were now fighting Roosevelt. Nevertheless, if many had personal grievances, all were animated by an abiding ideological hostility to the kind of bureaucratic United States that the New Deal was ushering in: an America of big labor, multinational corporations, professionalized interest groups, business lobbies, and deracinated, anonymous, soulless communities.

By defining its opposition to the president on countersubversive grounds, the Republican Party began to homogenize as the home of a new kind of antistatist anticommunism that stressed affinities between the New Deal and the authoritarian regimes of Europe. Antipathy remained strong between the different wings of the party, but it would weaken over time as Republicans benefited from a growing ideological coherence that had been starkly absent during the 1920s and fears of the power of big business declined in proportion to the growth of hostility to government.

Still, the backlash against the New Deal was not confined solely to traditional areas of Republican strength. A powerful strain of opposition to Roosevelt was also developing within the president's own party, as countersubversive thinking intertwined with southern fears for the future of white supremacy and concerns over the sanctity of the contract.

Although the primary focus of attention during the Great Red Scare of 1919 had been the European immigrant, especially if they were Jewish, suspicion about African Americans' loyalty had been an important strain of countersubversive thought from its inception. Labor shortages had kick-started the great migration of African American workers from the rural South to the industrial regions of the North, but blacks were often hired to displace higher-paid white workers or employed as strikebreakers. Migration thus contributed to a series of local racial conflicts that often concluded in violent white rampages against black neighborhoods. The period from 1917 to 1919 witnessed a near doubling in the frequency of lynching, which had formerly been in decline. More than twenty race riots broke out in the summer of 1919. General Leonard Wood used troops to reassert civil order in Omaha, Nebraska, in September, when a lynching escalated into an orgy of violence and the burning of the Douglas County courthouse. That same month, more than a hundred black Americans were killed in a mass lynching in Phillips County, Arkansas.[77]

Because the Red Scare coincided with these racial tensions, indeed was shaped by the same economic and social processes, older tropes about black people's supposedly flawed characters intertwined with newer fears over the subversive. The term *Black Bolshevism* was used to describe a fictive new generation of red Nat Turners and radical carpetbaggers: not protesters objecting to conditions of discrimination, but, in the words of the *New York Tribune*, people stirred up by "insidious IWW and Left Wing Socialist propaganda being disseminated among the negroes."[78] In fact, Communist recruitment among African Americans was minor; the movement remained principally the preserve of immigrants and white intellectuals. This neglect was reciprocal: as A. Philip Randolph famously stated, African Americans had enough trouble being black without also being red, while Marcus Garvey spent more time working with the Ku Klux Klan than left-wing radicals. Most African Americans in the 1920s were hostile not only to Communists, but to white working-class politics in general. Big business-men could afford to present themselves as enlightened on issues of race, as this increased competition for jobs and encouraged many African Americans to see their interests as aligned with employers rather than unions.[79] Henry Ford established himself as the largest employer of black workers in Detroit in the 1920s, hiring more than ten thousand African Americans by 1926. Ford funded African American community organizations like the NAACP and National Urban League and undertook the redevelopment of Inkster, a poor, predomi-nantly black town that lay on the outskirts of Detroit. Most black employees were segregated into the worst jobs, especially working the vast furnaces of the Rouge plant. Senior positions for African Americans only involved supervising other African Americans, and the Service Department was, if anything, more brutal in its treatment of black workers than whites.[80] But all-white unions failed to offer black workers a better deal. Rather than pushing for racial integration, the AFL had spent the late 1920s arguing for the extension of immigration re-striction to cover Mexican migrants who had been excluded by the National Origins Act. The NAACP's Walter White expressed a widely held view when he noted that the era of the open shop coincided with the period of blacks' "great-est industrial progress."[81]

None of this stopped countersubversives from associating African Ameri-cans with revolutionary politics. The Overman Committee's concern over the relationship between ethnicity and disloyalty allowed plenty of opportunities for witnesses and senators to cast doubt over "negro loyalty," while the Lusk Committee repeatedly complained of the danger Harlem supposedly posed to New York's security.[82] Despite, or perhaps even because of, its chairman's his-tory commanding an all-black unit during World War I, the Fish Committee was intensely interested in whether Communists had been making progress in black communities across the country. Several key members were southern-ers, and they had a disproportionate influence on the committee's direction. In hearings in Chattanooga, Memphis, New Orleans, Atlanta, and elsewhere, the congressmen repeated the same question, often verbatim, to virtually every witness: "How many of your Communists here are Negroes?"

Nowhere was there evidence of significant Communist inroads. Indeed, many witnesses who elsewhere overstated the danger of radicalism were eager to pres-ent the black community as loyal and conservative. The police commissioner of Memphis claimed that African Americans in his city were strongly opposed to Communist agitating, saying, "They just thought they were getting along so fine with our people down here that that was an effort on the part of others, who did not know them, or know their life or their habits, to confuse them, and they resented it."[83]

As with the dogmas of the old South, affirmations that black people were satisfied with their lot sat uneasily with the oversensitivity shown toward black protest. To reconcile these apparently conflicting claims, countersubversives suggested that blacks, while satisfied, were liable to exploitation by white radicals due to congenital mental weakness. As one witness before the Fish Committee put it, "The colored fellow, he is patriotic, he is loyal, but he is easily influenced."[84] J. Edgar Hoover, for one, believed that black protest was a result of Communist agitation among an otherwise contented populace. While such arguments effectively blamed outsiders for black anger, they offered a tacit admission that African Americans had the greatest reasons of all to feel alienated from a political system that had consistently failed them.

If countersubversives were sensitive to the danger of "Black Bolshevism" at a time when Jim Crow remained comparatively secure, it was unsurprising that the 1930s saw fears grow exponentially. During the Depression, cracks began to emerge in the solid wall separating black and white workers, and this in turn raised the possibility that the reformers and unions might seek to bring down the system of white supremacy. As they radicalized, black leaders began to attack older visions of a benign corporate liberalism as a paternalistic myth. Randolph's Brotherhood of Sleeping Car Porters challenged the NAACP's legalistic methods in favor of direct action, while some white unionists began to question the conventional wisdom of excluding potential allies on the basis of the color of their skin. By the end of the decade, even the relatively conservative-minded NAACP was supporting industrial organizing drives, even at the once-impregnable River Rouge plant.[85]

Moreover, the Communist Party reformed its own racial attitudes in the late 1920s, purging itself of what it called "white chauvinism," nominating black candidates for office, and declaring civil rights to be among its primary objectives. Following the Scottsboro defense and the efforts of black Communists to organize in Harlem and among southern textile workers and sharecroppers, the party made small but significant progress among African Americans. By the Popular Front era, Communists were using antifascist rhetoric to highlight the affinities between the anti-Semitism of Nazi Germany and the white supremacist culture of the American South.[86] When liberal unions and African American reformers came together to form the National Negro Congress in February 1936, representatives of the Communist Party were welcomed. Later, in Birmingham, Alabama, Communists cooperated with New Dealers and other civil rights activists to form the Southern Conference for Human Welfare. Stimulating a wave of fury among conservatives and confirming their assumptions that there were but a few steps from the Communist Party to the presidency, Eleanor Roosevelt accepted an invitation to attend the first meeting in 1938 and defiantly refused to sit in the "whites only" section of the hall.

If portents of a new racial liberalism were not worrying enough for southern patricians, their political influence was also eroding within the Democratic Party. The decision in 1936 to shift to a simple majority over a two-thirds vote for selecting the presidential nominee effectively removed the blocking mechanism southerners could exercise over any excessively liberal Democratic candidate proposed by the North. FDR tried hard to preserve his support in the South, employing many racists in his alphabet agencies and refusing to endorse calls for an antilynching law, but southern segregationists were not wrong in seeing the New Deal as a first step toward the collapse of the old order and their own party as an increasingly unreliable defender of white supremacy. Eleanor Roosevelt's vocal support for civil rights, the provision of work relief for African Americans, and the insistence by some of the more radical New Dealers that practical steps should be taken toward the equalization of conditions between white and black Americans all revealed that the New Deal and its allies in the labor movement were clearing the way for the civil rights movement to come.

Arguably the most visible spokesman for southern anticommunism in the 1930s was Martin Dies, a congressman from Orange Country, Texas. Originally elected in 1930, he had been a lukewarm supporter of Franklin Roosevelt at first, endorsing the administration's banking and business regulation bills but speaking out against wage and hour laws and Social Security policies that limited freedoms of contract.[87] Dies had something of the southern evangelical about him and was keen to present his opposition to the dictatorship of the proletariat as founded in a support for the "dictatorship of the Almighty."[88] On the congressional floor, he stressed that the fundamental incompatibility between communism and Americanism was a product of communism's denial of God's authority and, in his view, America's character as a Christian nation.[89] But if his rhetoric drew heavily upon a religious critique of Marxism-Leninism, it was CIO industrial militancy and the dangers of New Deal racial integration that became his chief targets, especially after the United Auto Workers occupied General Motors' manufacturing plant in Flint, Michigan, in 1936 and 1937. Michigan's governor, Frank Murphy, a loyal New Dealer, had refused to crush the strike: to Dies, this represented clear evidence of liberal acquiescence in the onrush of revolutionary radicalism.

In January 1937, Dies proposed a congressional resolution calling for an investigation into the sit-down strikes. However, it quickly became clear that New Dealers would make it impossible to gather the requisite votes for passage. Fortune intervened in the shape of Samuel Dickstein, who was struggling to revive his own investigative career. He had suffered a series of political setbacks driven by conservative opposition, and the laws he proposed to restrict political extremism had been universally rejected. A 1936 proposal to investigate links between the Black Legion and European fascism failed to win congressional support, and a resolution to reopen the investigation into un-American activities in early 1937 also failed.[90]

Both Dies and Dickstein were facing similar problems, albeit from different political angles. Dickstein's antifascist credentials ensured him strong support from the Left, and Dies enjoyed favor on the Right, but neither could boast sufficiently broad appeal to win a majority in a straight congressional vote. Recognizing this, the two agreed upon a Faustian pact, pushing for a shared investigation into "un-American" activities that would target both political extremes. Dickstein activated a liberal community in behalf of a right-wing, anti-labor Texan with a reputation for racism and anti-Semitism, including groups ranging from the Federal Council of Churches to local branches of the CIO and even the Communist-controlled American League for Peace and Democracy (the renamed American League against War and Fascism).[91] Meanwhile, Dies downplayed his concern with labor unions and racial liberalism and focused instead on the dangers of fascism. He argued that America was home to 480,000 Nazis and that the German-American Bund was planning to assassinate the president. Working together, Dickstein and Dies saw their proposal passed in the House by 191 votes to 41.[92] Aided once more by Communists and Popular Front antifascists, the investigation into un-American activities was revived—and would continue largely uninterrupted for the next thirty-seven years.

Dickstein, however, was outmaneuvered. Right-wingers on the House Rules Committee summarily refused him a seat on the committee and named Dies to the chairmanship. Alongside him were placed a couple of wobbly New Dealers, John J. Dempsey of New Mexico and Arthur Healey of Massachusetts, the latter of whom was virtually never present. The rest of the committee represented a microcosm of the emerging anti–New Deal coalition. Two Republicans, J. Parnell Thomas of New Jersey and Noah Mason of Illinois, were joined by two anti–New Deal Democrats, Joe Starnes of Alabama and Harold Mosier of Ohio.[93]

Samuel Dickstein's brief moment of political celebrity had ended. In a final irony, the man who made his name fighting socialism on the Lower East Side turned to Russia. Scholars analyzing declassified material at the end of the Cold War discovered that Dickstein had become an agent of the Soviet government in the House of Representatives and was paid more than twelve thousand dollars to denounce the Un-American Activities Committee he had been instrumental in forming. (Ultimately, the Soviets considered Dickstein, whom they nicknamed "Crook," to be singularly expensive and unproductive.)[94] Dickstein's investigations into un-Americanism had opened in 1934 with evidence provided by the

CPUSA. HUAC's resurrection in 1938 was supported by a Communist-front organization, the American League for Peace and Democracy, and an array of left-wing groups. And, as a final demonstration of quite how peculiar the politics of loyalty in the 1930s had become, the founding father of HUAC now ended up working as a paid Soviet agent of influence.

As a chaotic product of political realignment, the mirrored antifascist counter-subversion that emerged in the 1930s strengthened the New Deal reform project and forced right-wingers to reexamine their relationships with each other. At the same time, though, it strengthened support for the idea that individuals and groups should be challenged for their political loyalties, thus helping to restrict the boundaries of legitimate dissent. During Roosevelt's second term, pro- and antigovernment forces battled like Tweedledum and Tweedledee over who could challenge the other side's loyalty more effectively and which group was best placed to defend traditional liberties. Reformers attacked conservatives for fascism; conservatives responded by accusing the New Deal of being infiltrated by Communists. Both sides depicted themselves as defenders of democracy and their opponents as extremists who threatened it. All of this had the paradoxical effect of weakening faith in the system as a whole. Indeed, this was the truly worrying result of countersubversive politics in the 1930s, for it is through failures to accommodate disagreement that political systems genuinely run the risk of collapse.

10

The Big Truth
The New Anticommunist Politics

As the scandal over *Communism in Germany* unfolded, Ralph Montgomery Easley had remained blithely convinced of his innocence. Despite repeatedly making anti-Semitic and pro-Nazi comments, he did not believe himself to be an anti-Semite, on the grounds he was willing to associate with wealthy, privileged, or conservative Jews. During the 1920 controversy over Henry Ford's circulation of *The Protocols of the Elders of Zion*, Easley had written the industrialist to express sympathy, but pointed out that the NCF worked with "a number of very high-class important Jews" who could not possibly be party to such a program.[1] Although the auto manufacturer had published material "to cause a serious man of patriotic views to want the allegations thoroughly investigated," Easley warned that they should be careful, lest their claims produce "an indiscriminate anti-Semitic wave . . . which might lead to pogroms in this country."[2]

For Easley, class trumped ethnicity. And despite taking scandalously provocative actions in the early Depression years, he still saw himself as a peacemaker and a moderate rather than someone who stoked the flames of controversy, as if the conflict between Nazis and Jews was simply a misunderstanding in need of mediation. As allegations circulated that he and other countersubversives had been collaborating with fascists, Easley replied that his goal had simply been to bring together moderates from the German and Jewish communities. In mid-1934 he tried to organize a meeting between Morris Waldman of the American Jewish Committee (which had opposed the Jewish boycott of German goods), George Sylvester Viereck, and representatives of the Steuben Society, a major German American organization. In Easley's view, these were "the conservative elements in both groups," unlike the "radicals" in the American Jewish Congress and the Friends of New Germany, which he saw as broadly equivalent.[3] With tensions running high over the boycotts, the effort to get them together failed, but in June 1935 Easley convened a second meeting, at the Barclay Hotel in Midtown Manhattan, and this time members of the American Jewish Committee, the Steuben Society, and a number of other influential New Yorkers attended.[4]

Appearing as a voice of conciliation offered the head of the National Civic Federation a way of diverting attention from the fact that he had been caught cooperating with Nazism. At first this was probably just a matter of self-protection, but as the outrage over *Communism in Germany* died down, the strategic possibilities of such a position began to present themselves. Given the rivalries between the major Jewish organizations, Easley speculated privately that if the NCF set about countering the claim that communism was Jewish, it might count on support from conservative Jewish groups in the countersubversive campaigns that were its real priority.[5] Easley wrote Waldman to suggest that they "kill two birds with one stone" by creating a new countersubversive committee whose membership would be made up of at least one-third Jews and one-third German Americans. "Thus, in addition to helping to drive the Third International from our shores," Easley explained, "we should be helping also to dispel the anti-Semitic feeling which, unfortunately, is growing all too rapidly in the United States and which, if not soon curbed, may lead to serious consequences."[6]

Not all of those contacted by Easley were sympathetic, but the idea was not as outlandish as it might appear.[7] In the mid-1930s, Jewish Americans were deeply divided over how to respond to Nazism; many feared that an uncompromising approach might alienate powerful Christian allies. At the June 5 meeting, Waldman had attacked the Jewish boycott, criticized the Dickstein Committee for acting "indiscreetly, recklessly," and insisted that Jews stop "calling themselves a race. . . . After all, a man of the Jewish religion is a white man." Easley said that Waldman had indicated he "would greatly appreciate any effort on our part to help make clear to the American people the fundamental differences between the American Jewish Committee and the American Jewish Congress." For reasons of solidarity, Easley explained, the committee couldn't "very well make a campaign against another Jewish organization because that would invite criticism from uninformed Jews who think it is a crime for one Jew to attack another; but we can explain the situation and let anybody get mad who wants to."[8] The main thing, Easley believed, was "to provide a group comprising Americans who will view this whole issue as it involves the United States only."[9]

Over the next few months, these ideas evolved into a vague plan to revive the Department of National Unity, a branch of the National Civic Federation that had been set up at the height of the patriotic enthusiasm of the First World War. Writing to Pierre Du Pont, Easley explained that its goal would be to reconcile Jewish and German Americans through a combined effort to combat socialism, communism, anti-Semitism, Nazism, and fascism.[10] If the federation, "one of the leaders in the anti-Communist fight," were to defend the Jews from fascist smears, Easley said, it "would have a thousand times more influence than for all the Jews to do it."[11]

In the end, the plan never came to fruition: unsurprisingly, tensions only grew as Hitler accelerated his program of racial purification, and the federation had already suffered such loss of prestige in the early 1930s that many wanted nothing to do with it. But Easley nevertheless honored his pledge to stand up against anti-Semitism both publicly and privately.[12] Over the next few years, he circulated statements with titles like *Anti-Semitism and Nazi-ism Abhorrent to Americans,* wrote friends and associates to disagree with negative statements they made about Jews, and contacted newspapers and journalists to point out the differences between what he deemed honest anticommunism and libelous anti-Semitism. NCF counsel Archibald Stevenson even went so far as to argue that fallacious propaganda linking Jews to communism was "a serious threat to the equal freedom of all our citizens."[13] Easley seemingly abandoned his prior anti-Semitism, albeit by effectively rewriting his past. During the *Protocols* affair in 1920, Easley had felt that although he "ought to frown on any anti-Semitic movement in this country," it was "not a matter that The National Civic Federation can take up officially."[14] Now, however, it seemed the federation could act. Writing to George Cortelyou in mid-October 1934, Easley said, "Never have I done anything that I feel more proud of than what I did and am still trying to do in this German-Jewish controversy. We are the only people in the United States who are making any effort to bring these two warring elements together."[15]

The strategy was too little, too ill-informed, and too late. Bankrupted by the collapsed OGPU investigations, abandoned by former allies and patrons, and crushed under the weight of unpaid debts, Easley found himself increasingly submerged by events, until on September 7, 1939—six days after the German invasion of Poland—he died.[16] A stenographer seized the last furniture in the federation offices to count against unpaid wages; his wife admitted that she did not even know how she was going to pay for his funeral expenses.[17] In the obituaries, Gertrude Beeks Easley was quoted from the depths of her despair, saying that "Mr. Easley was the victim of his patriotism, having been attacked from every angle at the direct orders of Stalin who informed a labor delegation from the United States that The National Civic Federation was the greatest obstacle in his way."[18] To her at least, Easley died a martyr to the cause.

Easley's failure should not be used to conclude that his strategy was flawed. Despite its history of defeats, scandals, and setbacks, the politics of countersubversion still offered a viable method of bringing together a broad array of nationalist groups; the power of the antifascist campaigns of the 1930s had demonstrated both its endurance and its flexibility. Nevertheless, like Easley, many other countersubversives were struggling to escape the legacy of their past failures and the taint of fascism. To rebuild countersubversive politics on the Right, it would be necessary to establish a clear demarcation between nationalistic, conservative anticommunism and the right-wing extremism that had done so much damage to their reputation. Conservatives had a choice: continue to align with extremists in a "popular front of the right" that defended Nazi Germany as the last bastion against a red wave from the East, or turn to a novel formulation that argued the extreme Right and Left were two faces of the same evil and that hostility to Nazism therefore legitimated an equal hostility to communism.

Not all organizations made the same decisions when faced with this dilemma; the chance events of history and the varied characters of individuals resulted in divergent paths. Some, like Easley, learned painful political lessons only after first cooperating with fascists, while others headed in the wrong direction entirely. Some organizations swiftly eliminated the extremist elements in their midst and adopted the antitotalitarian formulation. Others aligned with fascism and faced shame, ignominy, and even prosecution as a result. Nevertheless, over time, through a combination of inclination, political positioning, and attrition, a new emphasis emerged within conservative politics, rejecting fascism as well as Bolshevism—and increasingly using popular hostility to Nazi Germany to justify a renewed emphasis on the dangers of communism.

In the world of American Protestantism, for instance, fundamentalists were seeking to rebuild after the setbacks of the twenties and at the same time resist the continued centralization of the churches under liberal auspices.[19] At first, under the influence of its editor, James M. Gray, the most important fundamentalist journal, *Moody's Monthly,* had taken a pro-Nazi line: printing letters from German pastors that described anti-Semitic incidents as Communist fabrications. Editorials claimed that "Jews in Germany are not being persecuted as a race, but that communism organized by Russian Jews is being punished by Hitler." However, the head of the Jewish Missions Department at *Moody's,* Solomon Birnbaum, gradually persuaded his colleagues that Jews were being persecuted because of their religion and ethnicity, not their politics, and that fundamentalists' Christian duty was to denounce such violence. A growing number of fundamentalist leaders began to distance themselves from the anti-Semitic utterances of figures such as Winrod, Gaebelein, and Riley. Keith Brooks, an associate of Winrod, broke with the Christian Defenders to set up the American Prophetic League, a California-based organization that explicitly disavowed Nazism. Brooks's 1938 "Manifesto to the Jews" described the *Protocols* as a malevolent forgery serving Nazi interests and denounced claims that Jews were disproportionately associated with communism.[20] The publicity that followed the manifesto's release scratched a line in the sand, and more than sixty other fundamentalist leaders soon came out in support. Elsewhere, the head of the

Pentecostal movement, Stanley H. Frodsham—who had spent the early 1920s denouncing "atheistic, anti-Christian Masonic Jewish conspiracy"—was persuaded to abandon his anti-Semitic views. Without accepting in the slightest that this amounted to a reversal of his former beliefs, Frodsham began to express righteous outrage when liberals claimed that fundamentalism was anti-Semitic.[21] Eventually, even Gray turned against the *Protocols*.[22]

Far from his triumphant role as founder of the World Christian Fundamentals Association, by the end of the 1930s William Bell Riley was left largely isolated. Although there is no evidence to suggest he abandoned his anti-Semitism, by 1941 even he had shifted his line on Nazism, comparing Hitler to Darwin as shared manifestations of a hated modernity.[23]

In this way, fundamentalists gradually distanced themselves from anti-Semitic sectarianism and Nazism. Interestingly, many chose to bury their anti-Catholic pasts at the same time. Abandoning attempts to work with Winrod, J. Frank Norris, for instance, pivoted toward a form of militant anticommunism that presented both Jews and Catholics as prophetic allies in the global struggle against atheistic internationalism. In the twenties, Norris had been an outspoken anti-Catholic as well as a Prohibitionist and supporter of immigration restriction; he had been instrumental in turning Texas Republican in the 1928 election, arguing that the papacy had, in the words of his biographer, "entered into an alliance with the Soviet Union, Italy, and Mexico and would [through Al Smith] seek to rule America, too." But in the 1930s, these attitudes almost completely vanished.[24] By the late 1940s, he was arguing that the pope was the only force on the global stage attuned to the danger of international communism.[25]

Realignment took distinctive forms in the Catholic world, yet the same underlying dilemma made its presence felt, as countersubversives within the church sought to purge themselves of fascist sympathies in the face of allegations of disloyalty. Support for fascism was well entrenched, not helped by the Vatican's example, and if anything, sympathy had grown during the Spanish Civil War, when many Catholics supported Franco's rebels over the anarchist-influenced and Comintern-aided republic. But the episcopacy in the United States nevertheless remained fearful of the damage fascist associations could do to the church's hard-won reputation for Americanism.

Detroit's Archbishop Mooney had studiously avoided a frontal assault on the church's most egregious anti-Semite, Charles Coughlin, fearing it would make him into a martyr, but as the Radio Priest's rhetoric intensified in the later 1930s Mooney became increasingly resigned to the necessity of action in order to defend the reputation of the church as a whole. Rather than targeting him directly, Mooney began to undercut the Royal Oak pastor's support by trying to build a personal reputation for the kind of prolabor anticommunism through which Coughlin had first rode to fame. He supported the Association of Catholic Trade Unionists (ACTU), an organization established in the early

1930s to bring together prolabor Catholics and as the UAW began its drives into the auto plants of Michigan insisted that good Catholics should support them.

There was a double benefit to such actions. Not only would the ACTU cement the church's credentials as a friend of the industrial worker, but it would also provide a disciplined phalanx capable of attacking Communist influence within the union movement.[26] The ACTU would echo concerns about employer malpractice raised by the La Follette Committee, support National Labor Relations Board complaints against manufacturers, attack racketeering and denounce fascism, but in the same breath criticize Communists as a grave menace to "sound unionism" and build alliances with other labor factions to isolate and exclude the radical Left at the grassroots.[27] Mooney invited ACTU leader Father Raymond Clancy to organize the Catholic Conference on Industrial Problems in Detroit, and over the next year Clancy repeatedly challenged Coughlin's claims that working with the CIO was equivalent to supporting communism. When Coughlin came out against a strike at the Chrysler plants, Clancy went on air to disagree.[28] Coughlin's claims to be the true friend of the laborer thus came to seem less convincing, and the risks of disciplining him began to recede.[29]

It was, however, the state that finally forced Mooney's hand. In the new year of 1940, the FBI caught seventeen members of the New York branch of the Coughlin-affiliated Christian Front with a cache of weapons and then arrested two hundred more amid stories that the group had planned to eliminate Jews, Communists, and a number of left-wing congressmen.[30] Mooney was told privately that the Department of Justice had taken pains to keep Coughlin's name out of the papers, but no such promises could be made when the cases went to trial.[31] Coughlin was forced into elaborate contortions to avoid being implicated.

In June Mooney ordered Coughlin to dissociate himself from *Social Justice*.[32] Meanwhile, the National Association of Broadcasters adopted a broadcasting standards code widely seen as written to get Coughlin off the air, and individual stations began dropping him (though occasional storms of protest were enough to make some think twice). By December 1941, he had been virtually silenced on the national stage. A couple of visitors to the Shrine Church, secretly sent by Mooney, reported back that Coughlin was as extreme as ever. "Masonry and Marxism rule the world today," Coughlin had told them over the last bottle of Italian vermouth from his cellar. "Willkie was the candidate of the Scottish Rite; Roosevelt of the Grand Orient, the Jews and the Yorkist Rite."[33] But rarely now were his theories circulated outside Royal Oak.

In both Protestant and Catholic denominations, then, religious leaders sought to isolate profascist and anti-Semitic elements in their midst and at the same time build new alliances outside their communities. This had the paradoxical effect of strengthening their anticommunist politics even as some of the most extreme countersubversives were purged.

Conservatives had begun to realize that anticommunism could operate as an effective ideology of countersubversion only if it ran parallel to American nationalism. The alliance struck by Texan congressman Martin Dies with Samuel Dickstein had been one of the most successful practical demonstrations of how the Right could use hostility to fascism to legitimate anticommunist politics rather than discredit it, and under Dies's chairmanship the resurrected House Un-American Activities Committee fought an increasingly effective public relations war against the New Deal on anticommunist grounds while largely avoiding crippling scandals of its own. HUAC echoed radical right-wingers' arguments that the New Deal was subversive, but stripped these arguments of their most overtly antidemocratic and extremist conclusions. The committee skated around allegations of fascism, ignored accusations of anti-Semitism, and achieved the unprecedented success—for a loyalty committee—of getting its annual mandate consistently renewed by Congress, by increased voting margins and with larger appropriations.

To maintain his distance from the radical Right, Dies devoted substantial chunks of committee time to investigating the activities of the German-American Bund, domestic fascists, and other extremist groups, earning the approbation of many centrists as well as conservatives in the process. By 1942 Dies could tell critics that he had examined 178 witnesses on Axis activities, filled four thousand printed pages of testimony, and issued seven reports on Nazi, fascist, and Japanese activities.[34] He framed his investigations in liberal language, presenting Hitler and Stalin as twin dictators and pointed to the New Deal investigative committees as precedents, saying, "People who applauded the methods and procedure of the La Follette and Black committees [should] find it hard to explain their willingness to 'strain at a gnat and swallow a camel.'"[35] As the mood began to turn against the Roosevelt administration, Dies's headline-grabbing investigations into Communist influence in the CIO, the La Follette Committee, and various New Deal agencies conjured a powerful image of governmental excesses, Communist infiltration, and liberal indifference. This catapulted Dies from a position of anonymity to one of substantial influence in the emerging conservative coalition. A December 1938 Gallup Poll gave him a 74 percent approval rating, 19 points higher than the president. More than three-quarters of the major newspapers were either fully or broadly supportive of his committee; even some of HUAC's harshest critics could not bring themselves to recommend doing away with it altogether.[36]

Unsurprisingly, radical right-wingers sought to affiliate themselves with Dies's highly popular investigations. *Social Justice* named the HUAC chairman "Man of the Week" in September 1938, offering "the applause of every honest, American-loving, ism-hating United States citizen, for his bravery and courage in attacking the thickening network of anti-American propaganda, which threatens true American democracy."[37] But Dies was always more popular with the radical Right than they were with him. In an ironic inversion of countersubversive tradition, claims that Dies was secretly working with William Dudley Pelley fell flat when the documents on which the allegations were based turned out to be forged.[38] Instead, Dies renewed Dickstein's attacks on the Silver Shirts, earning in the process an unlikely insult from Pelley for being a "Jew-lover from Texas."[39]

HUAC's investigations served an ill-concealed double purpose: explicitly to defend America from political subversion and implicitly to bring down the president. The 1938 midterms, following the Supreme Court–packing crisis, the "Roosevelt recession," and the backlash over the sit-down strikes, were a major opportunity for conservatives to pick up seats and a chance for the committee to flex its muscles. During the campaign, committeemen called for secretary of labor Frances Perkins's dismissal for her refusal to deport the Australian radical unionist Harry Bridges, a bête noire of the Right.[40] They launched investigations into the Works Progress Administration's Federal Theater Project, low-hanging fruit in political terms, as, Communist or not, many Americans had little sympathy for actors on the federal payroll. Dies paid particular attention to allegations that bohemian actors had been encouraging participants to engage in interracial relationships, knowing that such allegations would act like a red rag to the American white supremacist community. Committee members toured battleground states attacking various New Dealers for being soft on communism. And the strategy appeared to work. In a dramatic upset, Michigan's governor, Frank Murphy, who had refused to intervene against the sit-down strikers in Flint and had been a regular target of HUAC criticism, was thrown out of office. When it next came to voting on the committee's continuance, 152 congressman switched from neutrality to support. By 1940 only 6 congressmen were still willing openly to stand against it.[41]

With a Congress dominated by Republicans and conservative southern Democrats and support for countersubversion growing across the political spectrum, new countersubversive laws were passed for the first time since World War I. The Foreign Agents Registration Act of 1939 was designed to target figures like Viereck who had been paid by the Nazis to work for them in the United States, whereas the Hatch Act of August 1939 mandated the immediate dismissal of any federal employee found to be a member of a revolutionary or extremist group, reflecting the new focus on countersubversion within the state apparatus itself. Although they took place in the context of a looming war in Europe, these were nevertheless peacetime measures, making them largely unprecedented expansions of countersubversive legislative power.

HUAC's popularity left the administration in a quandary. Roosevelt had repeatedly expressed his antipathy to communism. He had renewed the FBI's powers to investigate extremist groups. Yet his administration was being criticized for Communistic tendencies. Quiet attempts to encourage Dies to focus only on Communists and avoid smearing liberals went nowhere. Appeals to party loyalty failed to restrain him. Tactical concessions—having anti-Dies appointees dismissed and offending programs terminated—only encouraged him. It was difficult to see what could be done without reinforcing Dies's claims that the administration was not serious about defending America from supposed hidden threats within.

Seeking to control HUAC's impact without appearing to be soft on communism, Roosevelt parachuted an ally onto the committee in early 1939 in the hope of moderating it. Congressman Jerry Voorhis was the scion of a privileged family with a background in socialist and progressive politics in California and a reputation for immense hard work. A self-proclaimed anticommunist, he was nevertheless one of the few to have voted against HUAC's continuance, on the grounds that it was targeting progressives rather than revolutionaries.[42] Roosevelt hoped his presence might help refocus the committee's efforts away from the New Deal.

Voorhis immediately began to push for a more rigorous focus on foreign covert action and a shift of initiative from Congress to the executive branch. The "real Soviet agents," he argued, welcomed any "blundering campaign . . . based on inconclusive evidence," as such campaigns served to discredit the politics of countersubversion altogether. The best means for rooting out Communists were not sweeping purges led by people with no real expertise, but investigations led by experts in the FBI.[43] Nevertheless, he defended the Dies Committee for some of the revelations it had made. "For a person to recognize the importance of the major facts brought about by the Dies Committee . . . is no indication that that person is not a progressive or a liberal," he maintained. "The Committee has some opponents who can see absolutely no good in its work and it has some supporters who can see absolutely no room for improvement." Instead, he concluded, the work of the committee should "be judged as nearly as possible on its merits and without passion."[44]

Despite receiving mailbags of supportive letters, Voorhis's attempts to find a middle way between Dies and his enemies were ultimately a failure. There was a basic incompatibility between the chairman's belief that public exposure was a vital tool to force reformers to distance themselves from Communists and Voorhis's view that the best way of dealing with Communists was by bureaucratic policing that would rigorously discriminate real foreign agents from the domestic liberal-Left. Indeed, arguably, Dies was closer to American countersubversive tradition, repeating Overman, Lusk, and Fish–style arguments that investigative committees had a crucial role in raising public awareness but stressing that patriotic individuals had to take responsibility to act to exclude political extremists in the localities. Proposals by Voorhis in 1939 to establish a working principle that the committee target organizations rather than individuals were ignored. The 1940 Voorhis Act, requiring the registration of all organizations controlled by foreign powers, forced the CPUSA to sever its formal ties with the Comintern but did nothing in practice to alter their relations with Moscow.[45] Efforts to establish weekly executive meetings, ban autonomous statements by individual congressmen (read: Dies) made in the committee's name, and apply judicial rules on the use of evidence were rejected by the conservative majority.[46]

Even when Voorhis succeeded, he failed. When a dispute developed over the committee's 1940 report, which Dies had laden with exaggerated language, Voorhis managed to coordinate an effort among committee members to moderate its tone.[47] But this served only to strengthen the committee's reputation. Noting that the report's release coincided with the twentieth anniversary of the Palmer Raids, a correspondent for *Time* observed that critics "cried that Martin Dies was leading a witch hunt, that he was emulating A. Mitchell Palmer, that he was a Fascist, that he relied on hearsay and innuendo and accused individuals of Communist activities without giving them a chance to reply," yet now the committee had issued "a document that no radical could have expected."[48] Rather than moderating Dies's attacks, it seemed that Voorhis was giving them a coat of respectability. In 1943 Voorhis was forced to submit a minority dissent after Dies published an annual report that had not even been circulated to the committee prior to issuance. Soon after, he quit—and by 1944 was voting against HUAC again.

As much as Dies's maneuvers immunized him from allegations of fascism, the popularity of the committee was not just a product of canny political positioning. Dies's successes were also informed by the CPUSA's failures. Events in the early Depression years had suggested that Communists had a meaningful role to play in American politics if they were willing to work sincerely with liberals and left-wingers. But although the Browder era was characterized by an effort to push the party away from its prior isolation, there remained strong tendencies in favor of keeping the movement small, disciplined, and pure. Behind the scenes, many leading Communists saw the Popular Front as tactical maneuver rather than a deeper challenge to their political philosophy. Even if the party's larger membership was transformed, its core remained unreformed.

Browderites argued they had successfully reconciled American nationalism with Communist internationalism. Since the United States was only part of a singular history tending toward one end, they argued there was no contradiction between being a Comintern signatory and an American party. In fact, they argued rather tendentiously, America's revolutionary tradition should make its citizens uniquely receptive to their message. "Precisely because we are Americans, and value and love our American revolutionary heritage, we are the enthusiastic supporters of the Soviet Union in its tremendous democratic achievements, including collectivization," Browder said in a speech at the New York Hippodrome in March 1938. "Precisely because we love and would protect the achievements of American democracy, we love and protect that higher form of democracy which is being surely and firmly established in the Soviet Union, showing the way to the whole world of the Twentieth Century, just as the United States was showing the way to the whole world in the Eighteenth Century."[49]

This reasoning may help to explain why the "Americanization" of the CPUSA during the Popular Front could take place at the same time as the party's covert activities were accelerating. The illegal apparatus had existed since the Communists were driven underground in 1920, but—as in many other countries—grew substantially in the 1930s.[50] Agents compiled lists of Communists with "suspicious" tendencies, examined the friends and families of unreliable members, and set up disciplinary commissions to train local branches on rooting out ideological imperfection among their members. If there was any greater freedom in being a Communist during the Popular Front, it was only because there were greater numbers of Communists to be disciplined.

The party's structure came to resemble something like the skins of an onion. At the center was the small paid bureaucracy: disciplined, more or less professional in outlook, and committed to the relationship of power stretching between the United States and Moscow. Browder estimated that there were perhaps 500 in the cadre with another 5,000 "close attachments."[51] Alongside this, the illegal apparatus, functionally independent of but supported by the party, included a small number of Soviet agents, handlers, and operatives, growing to several hundred at the peak of U.S.-Soviet engagement in the Second World War. It still remains unclear exactly how many "legal" party members were aware of and involved in these operations. Outside this small inner circle, there were a larger number of activists who joined and remained within the party, but who were not part of the core. These people—the vast bulk having joined since the Depression—were usually idealistic, romantic revolutionaries who accepted the principles of democratic centralism, followed orders from the center, and endorsed Soviet resolutions on international affairs, but were motivated primarily by either antifascism or questions of domestic social injustice. Beyond this were a still larger number of people who joined the party but left after a relatively short period of time, usually because they were unwilling to subject themselves to the disciplinary requirements demanded of them. At its peak, the CPUSA and the Young Communist League together had a little more than 100,000 members, but perhaps 250,000 to 300,000 people had been in the party at some point during the thirties.[52] Not all left in disgust; some continued to cooperate with the movement in shared enterprises of reform.

Finally, there were the "fellow travelers," an ambiguous and politically loaded category. Some closely followed the Comintern line but had been asked not to join for propaganda reasons: CPUSA leaders felt that well-known figures could have more influence by appearing independent, though such secrecy often proved to be counterproductive since the exposure of Communists in hiding was perfect evidence of party duplicity.[53] But by far the largest number were left-wingers who had come to accept the CPUSA as a legitimate political party and Bolshevik Russia as a legitimate player on the international stage, but did not see themselves as following the orders of either. Having witnessed the failures of countersubversive politics in the past and fearing fascism in the present, such individuals were willing to cooperate with organizations that Communists ran, like the American League against War and Fascism or the American Youth Congress; those in which Communists exercised a dominant influence, such as the National Negro Congress; or those in which Communists were influential minor partners, as in the Congress of Industrial Organizations. This group of allies—"dupes" working in "transmission belts" to their opponents, members of a "Popular" or "Democratic" Front to their friends—was the route through which the party exercised its greatest political influence, yet its control here was, by the same rationale, weakest. Browder commented that without a policy of "identifying ourselves with the American tradition, the cadre would have been powerless—absolutely powerless."[54] Popular Front allies were often privately regarded with contempt, but they were the party's greatest asset.

American communism had always presented a double image—one part revolutionary, the other part reformist—but the Popular Front took this to its logical extreme. Publicly, the movement appeared to be integrating itself with the New Deal political order; privately, Communists continued to be ready to defend the Soviet Union from capitalist assault. As a result, the image formed of the party depended in large part on which Communists one looked at, although many right-wing anticommunists sought to have their cake and eat it: focusing upon the margins of the party in order to highlight the biggest numbers—5 million Americans under Communist "influence," and so on—yet attributing to the outer reaches the disciplined and Moscow-oriented habits that were most characteristic of the core.

Nevertheless, there can be no doubt about who was really dominant within the party proper. Though representing the majority, ordinary members had no power to set policy. The average party activist could really influence the movement's political direction only through the individual decision of leaving or staying. Most Communists were committed to essentially enlightened projects of unionization, racial progress, and antifascism, and only a small proportion were directly involved in espionage, but this absolutely did not make the CPUSA a social democratic sheep in wolf's clothing. It was the party leadership that steered the ship, and, in the end, it would be the party leadership that destroyed the hard work done by rank-and-file Communists—by repeatedly prioritizing Stalin's interests over all other matters, both at home and abroad, even to the point of abandoning their allies at a moment's notice.

Throughout the 1930s, Soviet international policy made Nazism's job substantially easier. Despite presenting itself as implacably antifascist, the Comintern leadership acquiesced in the annihilation of the noncommunist Left in late-Weimar Germany and orchestrated the destruction of independent loyalism in Spain during the civil war. Both actions substantially weakened the forces of antifascism in Europe. Ironically, though, they reinforced Stalin's position; even major setbacks, such as local apparatuses being rooted out by fascist police operations, tended to the dictator's advantage. This was for two reasons. First, the destruction of large national Communist Parties, most notably Germany's—arguably the strongest source of alternative anti-Bolshevik variants of Marxist thought—reduced the likelihood of "deviationists" challenging Stalin's authority. Rather than powerful, independent Communist Parties, Stalin's instinctive preference was for small, semiclandestine organizations that were dependent on Soviet support. Second, the ease with which radicals were wiped out demonstrated beyond a doubt that the nineteenth-century world of barricades and spontaneous protests was over. Realistically, revolutionary Communists could expect to overthrow capitalism only if they had access to state power. By extension, the preservation of the Soviet Union took precedence over all else, for without its industrial and military capacity Bolshevik communism was doomed (as history would show). And because dictatorship was essential to the maintenance of Soviet power, Stalinist rule was considered no less vital than the survival of the Soviet Union. Anything was good communism if it was good for Stalin.

These arguments helped sustain the party's internal integrity, but they could do little about the growing number of former members who had been ejected from or had abandoned the party and subsequently spoke out against it. Because of its inability to transcend its factional habits, communism—in continually generating embittered yet well-trained ex-Communists—turned out to be its own worst enemy.

Dies swiftly recognized the value of putting former Communist witnesses on the stand. Ex-Communists offered detailed, personal, and (usually) coherent critiques of communism, sharply distinguished from old-style professional patriots. Among the most notable were Jay Lovestone and Benjamin Gitlow, senior party officials purged during the factional battles of the late 1920s; Benjamin Mandel, a typesetter from New York who also left the party during the Lovestone split; J. B. Matthews, onetime leader of the American League against War and Fascism; Fred Beal, a union organizer who had been convicted unfairly for murder during the North Carolina textile strikes of 1929, fled to Russia to avoid imprisonment, and subsequently returned, disillusioned, to serve out his sentence; Eugene Lyons, a fellow traveler who lived in Moscow in the late twenties and early 1930s before abandoning the party; Richard Krebs, a German-born Comintern agent who—as Jan Valtin—had traveled the world organizing Communist cells before being betrayed by his handlers and captured and tortured by the Nazis; and Walter Krivitsky, a senior official in Soviet military intelligence who defected in 1937 and would die under suspicious circumstances in Washington in February 1941. In the later 1930s and early 1940s, these individuals published dozens of articles and memoirs about their former lives as Communists, and most appeared before Dies to recount their past lives and denounce former associates.[55] Matthews, who was the least reliable, was also the most explosive witness, and after his testimony he was hired by the committee as chief investigator.[56] Matthews in turn employed Mandel to assist him. It even appeared at one point that Leon Trotsky might travel from Mexico to Washington to testify for Dies on Soviet military intelligence activities, though by the time of his assassination by Stalinist agents in May 1940 this had not taken place. They were aided, instructed, and sometimes stage-managed by a small number of old socialists and a few influential Russians living in exile, in particular émigrés George Sokolsky and Isaac Don Levine, who worked for the National Association of Manufacturers and the Hearst press, respectively; David J. Dallin, a New York–based Menshevik; and Max Eastman, the most articulate of Progressive Era revolutionary romantics, who lost his early enthusiasm for the Bolshevik experiment after a visit to Russia in 1923 and subsequently migrated rightward.[57]

Ex-Communists appeared as living proof of the coordinated international conspiracy that the countersubversives of the 1920s had believed existed but were unable to expose. Although the evidence they provided failed to indicate that communism posed a significant direct threat to the American political order, they did suggest that the American party was functionally inseparable from the Soviet system and that elements within it were participating in a transnational covert-operations network, two crucial claims that countersubversives had long failed to substantiate. Moreover, it was particularly notable how many sought to criticize the Bolshevik program for failing to live up to its own ideals. Max Eastman's theoretical work of 1926, *Marx, Lenin, and the Science of Revolution,* had been billed as a sympathetic critique of the Russian regime, but in fact attacked some of the foundational assumptions of Marxism-Leninism on broadly Marxist terms. By 1937 he was declaring that there was "not a hope left for the classless society in present-day Russia," that the wage differential in Russia was twice that of America, and that the Moscow Trials represented "the bloody punctuation of a twelve-year period of counter-revolution."[58] When Krebs came to speak to the Dies Committee, he revealed that he had been approached by Henry Ford to make a series of national radio broadcasts about communism. Krebs insisted that he would do so only on the condition he could make an equal number of anti-Nazi broadcasts, and as a result they never happened. In a similar vein, a supporter of Victor Kravchenko, a Soviet apparatchik who defected in 1944, wrote that he hoped "the stupid editors of the *New Republic,* the *Nation,* and *PM*—(whose support of the USSR is sickening) will see [his memoir] and be forced to take cognizance of what goes on under Stalin as reported by a man who is *not* a reactionary."[59]

As later critics noted, there were strong incentives for a former Communist not only to recant but to cast his or her former life in the blackest terms.[60] Partly, this was psychological: breaking with the party was a traumatic experience, and people often responded as if they had been converted—envisioning a previous life of sin followed by a journey into the light. Many who joined the Communist movement tended to see history and politics in Manichaean terms, and so upon departure veered from one extreme to the other. There were also practical, even financial, advantages to be had from establishing oneself as an expert on party wrongdoing: publishing contracts, speaking engagements, congressional retainers, even naturalization papers for foreign defectors facing deportation proceedings might result from a particularly startling piece of testimony. The speed with which a former Communist was welcomed into American society depended on how he or she reflected upon the past. There were therefore certain difficulties in taking at face value an individual's insistence that the public accept their wise assessment of past foolishness.

Nevertheless, with the mounting volume of personal testimony, it became harder and harder to sustain a belief in Stalinist innocence. Even the *Nation* and the *New Republic,* which had little good to say about Dies, accepted the memoirs written by several of his ex-Communist witnesses.[61] Not just conservatives and former Communists but liberals and Socialists spoke out against the perversion of the Soviet ideal. Progressives including John Dos Passos, Sidney Hook, Edmund Wilson—all of whom had endorsed the CPUSA presidential candidate in 1932—Lutheran socialist Reinhold Niebuhr, and the ACLU's Roger Baldwin turned against Russia in the mid- to late 1930s, rejecting the claims of Trotskyite conspiracy that were being used to justify Stalin's purges. In March 1937, a commission under John Dewey traveled to Mexico to interview Trotsky and pronounced unfounded the allegations made against him by Stalin's apparatchiks. Led by Dewey and Hook, anticommunist liberals joined together in May 1939 to form the Committee for Cultural Freedom (CCF) in the hope of further distancing left-of-center politics from communism. Pressure from the CCF was in turn important in forcing the ACLU, among others, to begin to purge its pro-Communist members, beginning with Harry F. Ward.

For as long as the Popular Front persisted, the CPUSA could argue that progressivism, not communism, was the target of right-wing countersubversive attacks. This strategy was the most powerful and persuasive of the party's defenses, far more valuable than its Leninist organizational structure, its devoted membership, or the orders it received from Moscow—not least because often it was true. Earl Browder repeatedly warned that red-baiting served to "split open the progressive and democratic forces, and set them to fighting one another so that the reactionaries may slip back into power," a claim that was repeated time and again in party publications.[62] People needed to look only to the history of the Great Red Scare to see how the fragmentation of the Left almost inevitably led to an extended period of reaction. When right-wing countersubversives attacked, say, the CIO for being communistic, many non-communist CIO members would respond with anger and draw closer to their Communist allies in defensive solidarity. In response to the formation of the Committee for Cultural Freedom, party apologists declared that by "turning antifascist feeling against the Soviet Union they have encouraged the fantastic falsehood that the USSR and the totalitarian states are basically alike. By this strategy they hope to create dissension among the progressive forces whose united strength is a first necessity for the defeat of fascism."[63]

In his retirement, Browder reflected upon this maneuver. He observed that under Martin Dies, whom he described as "the ablest chairman it ever had," HUAC found itself "year after year in the frustrating position of furnishing the Communists with some of their most effective ammunition," whereas in later years "under chairmen compared to whom Martin Dies was a giant, the same Committee has been relatively successful and the Communists unable to make any effective counter-attack." Why was this? Browder noted that, "by creating a new class of 'security suspects,' composed of all the seven or eight million persons who had engaged in organizations that also included the Communists in the years after 1930, the government automatically created a dissatisfied and disaffected group which . . . necessarily has a vested interest in halting the anti-communist crusade." But, with the collapse of the Popular Front, the CPUSA lost this ability to "stimulate and rally broad circles of allies" because it had "driven [its] allies away."[64]

With the signing and enactment of the Molotov-Ribbentrop Pact during August and September 1939 and the carving up of independent Poland between Nazi- and Communist-controlled zones, then, the most effective tool available to the CPUSA to resist a resurgent countersubversive politics on the Right vanished. Though Communists continued to make the claim, it was no longer persuasive to say that anticommunists were aiding the cause of fascism by attacking a party that had just signed a treaty with Hitler.

The speed with which the leadership adjusted to the realignment was remarkable and the party's abandonment of the Popular Front shocking. It was not just a matter of reluctant defeatism. As leading party activist John Gates recalled, "We attacked the Roosevelt administration once again as we had done back in 1933, calling it dictatorial and profascist. Although we said we supported neither side, in effect our main attack was against the West."[65] When Germany invaded

Russia in June 1941, policy reversed once again, and by the time of Pearl Harbor Communist newspapers were pledging loyalty to the American government.[66] But the damage had been done: the Americanization of the party had been shown to be a hollow and only half-completed process.

Having spent years defending Russia as the only force willing to stand against Germany and criticizing the West for appeasement, the CPUSA's volte-face was politically disastrous. Earl Browder later sought to downplay the significance of the twenty-two months of Nazi-Soviet collaboration, saying that membership was quickly rebuilt after the CPUSA began supporting the war effort. At the time, a reported 15 percent decline in membership was explained as a response to fears of attack, not a principled opposition to the pact with Hitler.[67] It was true that some Americans responded favorably to the new anti-interventionist line.[68] Communist opposition matched the views of John L. Lewis and others in the CIO unions who opposed U.S. engagement overseas. But others were angered and alienated: after breaking with the National Negro Congress after it endorsed an anti-interventionist resolution sponsored by both CPUSA and CIO elements, A. Philip Randolph refused to cooperate not only with Communists in his planned March on Washington, but with their Popular Front allies as well.[69] Here, as elsewhere, it was not just the decision to oppose the war that was so damaging, but the way in which policy lines had so clearly shifted in response to the demands of Moscow.

Meanwhile, the Roosevelt administration toughened its stance toward the party. Browder was arrested for passport fraud, tried, and in February 1941 given a four-year prison sentence. The FBI ratcheted up its covert investigations of the radical Left. Congress passed the Alien Registration Act, or Smith Act: a peacetime sedition law criminalizing advocacy of the overthrow of the Republic by force or violence—something that had not been passed even at the height of the Red Scare. In the past, opposition on civil liberties grounds would have derailed such a measure; now, however, the bill passed the Senate by acclamation and sailed through the House with only four opposing votes.[70] Ironically, after it became clear that the first target would be Trotskyites, even the CPUSA praised the law—further testament, if needed, of the degree to which the antifascist campaigns and reformed anticommunism of the 1930s had decisively shifted the debate over civil liberties and federal power.[71]

More than any other event in the 1930s, the pact powerfully reinforced the conservative claim that fascism and communism were indistinguishable forms of totalitarianism. As the *Wall Street Journal* argued in June 1941, despite the opening of the eastern front, "the American people know that the principal difference between Mr. Hitler and Mr. Stalin is the size of their respective mustaches."[72]

* * *

Not everyone was converted to a crusading anticommunism between 1936 and 1941, and even the most anticommunist liberals struggled to muster enthusiasm for Dies. An alternate narrative of events spoke too loudly for him to be seen as a trustworthy ally, one that traced anticommunism's history back through the failures, abuses, racism, and violence of the countersubversive movement of the 1910s and 1920s, that recalled the contributions made by Communists to American reform during the New Deal, that noticed Congressman Dies's conspicuous popularity among segregationists and reactionaries and his barely concealed efforts to bring down Roosevelt. "We have been through the whole thing several times before," the *New Republic* reminded its readers, "in the Lusk inquiry, the Fish investigations and the Dickstein probe."[73]

Certainly, Dies showed as little regard for congressional procedure as his predecessors. The chairman gave broad latitude to unreliable witnesses. Rarely were accused parties given an opportunity to rebut allegations, which quickly became established as fact thanks to verbatim media reporting. Congressional privilege ensured Dies was free from the restraining effect of libel suits, and committee members repeatedly demonstrated their palpable lack of expert knowledge of revolutionary radicalism.[74] To much liberal hilarity, at various points it was suggested that Shirley Temple, a number of ancient Greek dramatists, and the Elizabethan playwright Christopher Marlowe might all be under Bolshevik influence. "By attributing to the Communists a following of 2,000,000 and in a host of other ways," James A. Weschler wrote in the *Nation*, "Mr. Dies has thrown sand in democratic eyes." The Nazis are often credited with developing, as a disinformation strategy, the idea of "the big lie"—couching significant false information within a dense network of accurate statements in order to heighten its plausibility. HUAC stumbled upon the opposite policy: proffering a litany of inaccuracies and misdirection that served to obscure "the big truth" of Stalinist repression from much of liberal America. "Some of the things Mr. Dies says about the Communist Party's influence on avowedly independent groups are true," accepted Weschler. "But truth must be read in context," and in this context "the facts are too often indistinguishable from the fraud to be useful."[75] The point could have been made about virtually any moment in the long history of countersubversion between 1917 and 1945; for this, only countersubversives deserved the blame.

Nevertheless, critics of the committee were equally wrong when they argued, for instance, that American Communists were "so committed to the policy of coöperation with all democratic forces that one can hardly tell them from the New Deal Democrats," as the *New Republic* said in August 1938.[76] And complaints about HUAC's sweeping inaccuracies might have been better served had they not so often been followed by sweeping smears in the other direction. In a savage indictment in the *Nation,* Paul Y. Anderson described the Dies Committee as the "central agency" for the spread of fascism in America and its spiritual godfather to be Joseph Goebbels.[77] Harold Ickes argued that "Mussolini rose to absolute power in Italy as a result of a 'communist' hunt; that Hitler did the same thing in Germany; that Japan invaded China in order to suppress 'communism'; that England has grovelled on its belly before Hitler because it is afraid of communism," and that the inevitable result of anticommunism in America therefore "will be fascism."[78] Weschler, who believed Dies was intentionally ignoring the threat posed by "business men whose links to fascism are real and ominous," darkly speculated that Dies's high jinks might be a prelude to a planned assault on power.[79]

However, the chief, overriding, reason for resisting the new anticommunism remained the more immediate fear of Nazi Germany and, after Operation Barbarossa, the knowledge that the Soviet Union was essential to Hitler's defeat. Perhaps the single most common complaint raised by critics of HUAC under Dies was not that it was violating civil liberties, but that it had focused too little attention on the extreme Right and too much on the Left.[80] In the context of a growing anti-interventionist movement, which sought to resist all efforts to push America into war, liberals feared the defeat of the president could lead to fascism at home. In this context, the activities of a tiny Communist Party seemed irrelevant.

In fact, for most anti-interventionists, neutrality had nothing to do with fascism.[81] As with World War I, nonintervention was presented as a defense of popular democracy, not an assault upon it. They expressed the same opposition to American involvement in Europe that they had in 1917, well before Nazism appeared on the international stage. Following his part in fighting the Supreme Court–packing plan, Senator Wheeler played a major role in organizing political opposition to intervention, as did Borah until his death in January 1940 and Senator La Follette Jr.—figures who in the past had been attacked as Bolsheviks but were now denounced as fascists or dupes of fascism. Senator Gerald Nye, who was best known for chairing an investigation into the role of munitions manufacturers in World War I, became another thorn in the administration's side, while Borah's and Wheeler's wives took on leading roles in the anti-interventionist America First, which amassed some 850,000 members by the middle of 1941.

Undoubtedly, some anti-interventionists were influenced by genealogical connections with Germany, and others were sympathetic to fascism's *volkisch* language. Many were anti-Semitic. Nevertheless, most claimed to be defending the republican tradition of proud exclusion from the entangling alliances of Europe. As had been the case in World War I, anti-interventionists pointed to the close link between crusading foreign policies and the centralization of political power, suggesting that aiding the Allies would exacerbate the tendencies already shown by the Roosevelt administration to disregard the Constitution. In this context, the president's decision to seek an unprecedented third term in 1940 was considered another step toward dictatorship, a point, it might be noted, that was echoed from the Left by the pacifist and deeply antifascist *Christian Century.*[82]

That said, one did not have to look very hard to find unsavory anti-interventionists capable of justifying liberal fears of fascism on the march. For a substantial minority, hatred of Bolshevism still outweighed any concerns over cooperating with Nazism. Celebrity aviator Charles Lindbergh declared that he would "a hundred times rather see my country ally herself with England, or even with Germany with all her faults, than with the cruelty, the godlessness, and the barbarism that exist in Soviet Russia." Hamilton Fish argued that any condemnation of Japanese or German expansionism would serve only to strengthen Soviet Russia's hand. Fish, who had begun to move toward the anti-interventionists during the 1936 campaign when he had acted as an adviser to Senator Borah, established himself as a leading critic of the administration's foreign policy, opposing Roosevelt's Lend Lease proposals and joining America First. Apparently failing to learn his lesson from the Dickstein hearings, Fish even agreed to appear at a "German Day" rally organized by Bundists at Madison Square Garden in September 1938. Sitting on the podium before a large swastika, Fish listened attentively as a marching band played the "Horst Wessel Song" and contentedly looked on as an audience of thousands gave the Nazi salute.[83] Rumors began to circulate that Fish was using his office to print copies of *The Protocols of the Elders of Zion;* it later transpired that Viereck had been using his long-standing association with the congressman to insert anti-interventionist speeches into the *Congressional Record.*[84] In an astonishing breach of diplomatic protocol, Fish even traveled to Europe two weeks before war broke out to meet with the Nazi leadership. In his autobiography, he recollected that he had "an exclusive and unique interview with Joachim von Ribbentrop," whom he described as "a gracious and charming host," at his mountain villa, near Salzburg, Austria. In "over twenty years of politics," Fish believed he had "never spoken with anyone in a more informal and open manner." With an eye on the likely reaction at home, he was forced to decline Ribbentrop's offer to arrange a meeting with Hitler himself. But in retrospect, Fish wrote, "I am ashamed I did not do so. I would have urged him not to attack Poland, but to use every means within the law to recover the city of Danzig and a land corridor to the Baltic Sea—thereby ending German resentment over the Versailles Treaty."[85] In Fish's world, despite the policy's failure for nearly a decade, appeasing the Nazis required only one further concession. "I think the time has come to make a careful check-up on Mr. Fish," FDR wrote to Cordell Hull, secretary of state, upon the congressman's return.[86]

As well as including figures whose anticommunism had not yet been tempered with antifascism, then, the anti-interventionist movement offered an opportunity for down-at-the-heel domestic extremists to reintegrate themselves to the mainstream. They duly clutched at their newfound allies like an unpopular child finally allowed to join the ball game. Bundists praised Senator Nye as an outstanding leader, and Coughlinites extolled the virtues of Senators Wheeler and Borah.[87] The National Legion of Mothers of America (NLMA), an organization that sought to use gendered ideas of maternal privilege to oppose America's "boys" going off to war, discovered local branches of their organization had been infiltrated by both Bundists and Coughlinites. Chapters in Boston and Cleveland had to be expelled entirely, as they became completely dominated by extremist groups; eventually the president, Kathleen Norris, resigned in protest at the direction the membership was taking. At one point, Fish attended an NLMA meeting and gave an antiwar speech in which he stated that he would abide by any congressional vote to go to war. He was booed by the crowd; one mother got up and shouted at him that she would "be willing to be shot for treason rather than fight on the side of Soviet Russia"—a phrase that almost perfectly inverted Eugene Debs's refusal to go to war for Wall Street back in 1918.[88]

If this brought extremists some advantage, it was extraordinarily damaging to the anti-interventionist movement, for it allowed their opponents to depict them all as fascistic.[89] Applying traditional countersubversive logic, Roosevelt took to the radio to argue that the leaders of the America First Committee were "unwitting aids of the agents of Nazism."[90] Although this convoluted phrase showed that isolationists were generally at least twice removed from Germany, Attorney General Francis Biddle admitted privately that the president was "not much interested . . . in the constitutional right to criticize the government in wartime," and many of Roosevelt's allies—especially Harold Ickes—began deploying countersubversive language to denounce America First.[91] FBI surveillance of anti-interventionists was initiated. Roosevelt began authorizing domestic wiretaps, and in early 1941 the administration began grand-jury investigations looking into whether anti-interventionists, including Fish, had violated the Espionage Act. Seeking to enhance its bureaucratic authority, FBI director Hoover fed reports about America First to the president.[92] Unperturbed, Fish appeared on the radio to tell the public that "there is one thing worse [than Nazism] and that is the bloody hand of communism."[93]

Following Pearl Harbor, America First collapsed, and most anti-interventionists came to support the war effort. Nevertheless, the administration continued to settle scores in a series of countersubversive actions that historian Leo Ribuffo has called the "Brown Scare." These matched the World War I loyalty trials in purpose, although not in scale or intensity. By contrast, the wholly unprecedented decision to imprison tens of thousands of Japanese Americans on the

West Coast not only reprised the loyalty campaigns but far exceeded them in terms of the deployment of raw state power. In 1942 the Treasury Department instituted proceedings against the Ford Motor Company, which had continued to do business with the Nazis, under the Trading with the Enemy Act.[94] In May 1942, *Social Justice* was formally denied mailing privileges by the postmaster general. Hamilton Fish's clerk, George Hill, was imprisoned for perjury after denying links with Viereck. Viereck, meanwhile, was jailed as an agent of a foreign power. Subsequently, Fish was called before a grand jury and quizzed at length on his links to Viereck and other German agents, only narrowly avoiding indictment.[95]

The culmination of Roosevelt's antifascist assault came with the so-called Great Sedition Trial, in which around two dozen right-wing extremists were indicted en masse for conspiracy. Viereck, Dilling, Pelley, Winrod, and a series of less well-known figures were accused of participating in an international fascist plot to cause chaos in the armed forces, something that was both inaccurate and practically impossible given the marginality of the figures involved. The trial was badly conceived, the allegations unpersuasive, and the case mishandled, dragging on inconclusively before collapsing, a show trial, but one so inept that it could have been organized only in a democracy.[96] Nevertheless, well-known interventionist advocates like Walter Winchell (later a vocal supporter of McCarthy) and Drew Pearson praised the action, circulating expansive justifications for the policing of political loyalty based on exaggerated accounts of the fascist menace within. Countersubversive thinking was stronger than it had ever been.

With a war against fascism in which Soviet Russia was a vital ally, much of the steam had been taken out of Dies's investigations. Sailing as ever with the winds of American nationalism, Dies began targeting America First and within three days of Pearl Harbor declared that HUAC would hold hearings into Japanese conspiracies. In 1942, looking into the internment-camp system on the West Coast, he began criticizing the guards for treating the inmates too well. Meanwhile, for at least as long as the United States underwrote the Red Army's campaign in the East, the Roosevelt administration had no interest in stoking a conflict with Stalin.[97] Browder was released from prison, and Whittaker Chambers, a still-unknown Communist Party defector who had warned Adolf Berle, a close ally of Roosevelt, about Communist influence in Washington, was ignored.

The CPUSA temporarily returned to its former position as loyal ally of the government. Indeed, Communists went further than they had during the Popular Front era: endorsing a no-strike pledge for the length of the war, condemning

A. Philip Randolph's "Double V" campaign for pushing desegregation in the army and war industries, and in 1944 formally dissolving the CPUSA entirely and replacing it by the more innocuous-sounding Communist Political Association.[98] The party threw itself into patriotic drives, fund-raising efforts, and publicity campaigns; by January 1943, one-fifth of its membership had enlisted, many serving with bravery.[99] In one of the more surreal events of the war, Earl Browder, whom Roosevelt released from prison in May 1942, offered to shake the hand of J. P. Morgan as a gesture of national unity.

But the party's efforts never dissolved the stigma of the Ribbentrop-Molotov period, and efforts to be more capitalist than the capitalists hardly helped the party strengthen its influence among workers. Over the next four years, the blood of twenty million soldiers went a long way toward improving Russia's image in the American mind. Russian dances and folk songs became popular among patriots grateful for the sacrifices made by their ally. Ambassador Joseph E. Davies's *Mission to Moscow,* which recounted his experiences in Moscow in 1937–38 and as unofficial liaison between Roosevelt and Stalin during the war, lauded the conduct of the Russians and dismissed criticisms of the Moscow Trials. It became a best-seller and was later turned into a movie. But Russophilia did not put down enduring roots, nor did it lead to a changed perspective toward communism. As Ford's publicists had done in the later 1920s, Davies defended Russia on the grounds that Stalin had abandoned the revolutionary politics that had previously defined his nation; meanwhile, the *New York Times* commented in late 1943 that the best thing American Communists could do for "America and for Russo-American relations is to follow the example set in Moscow and disappear."[100]

By the end of the war, many of the radical and anti-interventionist critics of the New Deal had been silenced by a wave of loyalty campaigns that marked the culmination of more than a decade's worth of antifascist attacks. Alongside the damage to his reputation, the array of legal proceedings against his company, and the victory of the United Auto Workers, Henry Ford was devastated by the premature death of his son and heir, Edsel, in 1943, and largely retreated from public life.[101] William Dudley Pelley's newspaper was removed from the mails, and he was charged with sedition. At his trial, he attempted to recant—calling Hitler an "enemy of America"—but was convicted within four hours and sentenced to fifteen years.[102] Accusations of Nazi collaboration continued to dog Hamilton Fish until he was gerrymandered out of his seat by his own party in 1944. And after an off-the-record warning from President Roosevelt in April 1942, Archbishop Mooney finally issued Coughlin with a formal reprimand, holding up the possibility of expulsion from the church in the case of any future disobedience. In November, as a final act of muzzling, Mooney instructed Coughlin that every circular he sent out be submitted to the chancery for approval.[103] Coughlin retired to his priestly duties. It had been a long fight—lasting in some cases for more than a decade—but many of the most disreputable members of the countersubversive movement had been consigned to the ash heap of history.

To the Left, this seemed like a victory. But antifascism had helped to reinvigorate the politics of countersubversion as a whole, and as the Left and center-Left lobbied for campaigns to root out supposedly disloyal right-wing enemies within the United States, much of the traditional resistance to countersubversive crusading disappeared. With Dies and other members of the conservative coalition co-opting the language of antifascism to justify their hostility to communism, augmented by a new antistatist rhetoric that presented their investigations as part of a general resistance to totalitarian power, the war against Nazi Germany led to a far more tightly restricted realm of political debate than in the past and more universal acceptance among the American people that domestic extremists needed to be investigated, monitored, and, if necessary, repressed—even if no direct lines of agency could be found between them and foreign powers and if no immediate threat to national security could be identified. Roosevelt's third triumphant reelection in 1944 made it hard for many to imagine the possibility that the nation would ever return to the conservative politics of the past, when liberals and conservatives had competed to outdo each other in their assault upon "radical subversion." But for the perspicacious observer, it was nevertheless already possible to identify the stirrings of a new anticommunism that would emerge with terrifying force during the McCarthy era.

Conclusion
Toward McCarthy

As the Second World War drew to an end, the U.S. economy was booming and the memories of the longest depression in the nation's history had begun to fade. The war drew a line between a new America built in the forge of conflict and the struggling and self-critical nation that had preceded it, home to tens of millions of unemployed and tens of thousands of revolutionaries. Doubts about the wisdom of American overseas engagement had been silenced by Pearl Harbor, Auschwitz, and Bergen-Belsen. Doubts about the wisdom of democratic governance in a world dominated by totalitarian states had been vindicated by military triumph.

Yet Franklin Delano Roosevelt, the man who had presided over a transformation in the American state more far reaching than any since the Civil War, was dead. With a new, untested president in the White House and tensions running high over the disposition of Germany and Eastern Europe, the future of the grand alliance was in doubt. Even as the nation drove toward a brighter future, not everyone found their positions were as secure as they might have hoped.

Three dismissals in particular symbolized the end of an era in countersubversive politics and the beginning of something new. The first to lose his job was Earl Russell Browder, the longest-serving and most successful leader of the CPUSA. Under Browder's leadership, the party had climbed to its greatest peaks of influence and stooped to a new low in publicly defending an unconscionable pact with the Nazis. In later life, Browder would define his legacy in terms of the policy of constructive engagement: a shift toward the center that saw American communism moderate its revolutionary ambitions in public and carve out a progressive role within the broader reform movement. More recent historians on the Right have associated his time in office with a less inspiring story, identifying the Browder era as the moment when core elements of the CPUSA began to act as an adjunct to Soviet military intelligence in the construction of its American espionage networks. Both of these narratives are true, and it speaks to the contradictions of American communism that they took place more or less side by side.

Browder was too closely associated with the Popular Front for Moscow to consider keeping him in charge as relations between East and West froze over. In 1944 the cadre had proclaimed the dissolution of the CPUSA and the inauguration of an era of peaceful engagement between Russia and the United States, but this lasted less than a year. In April 1945, Jacques Duclos, an important French Communist, published an article in *Cahiers du Comunisme* that denounced the American party's accommodationist stance.[1] The next month, the article was translated into English and reprinted in American journals. Recognizing a message from Moscow when they saw it, the party abandoned its line in short order.[2]

At first several senior American Communists defended the Browder position, but following high-level discussions in May, June, and July the leadership opted to admit their "errors" and move to an oppositional stance. The aging William Z. Foster exploited this for maximum personal benefit. His allies and supporters launched a wave of purges in which activists across the country were instructed to root out "Browderism" and prepare for an extended period of hostility between communist and capitalist worlds.[3] But since the party had almost unanimously supported the dissolution of the CPUSA a year earlier, the stench of disloyalty could be found everywhere—even within. John Gates later commented that he was constantly "plagued by the fear that I might be reverting to Browderite weakness."[4] Another party member, Junius Scales, recalled, "I would have liked to forget Browderism, but every party resolution, directive, or article spoke of the need to root it out. Every weakness in Party work, collective or individual, was adroitly traced to that cardinal sin."[5] This was the genius of the system of "self-criticism" that maintained party discipline without force: because all were complicit in decisions, no one was free from guilt when they were reversed. Like gangsters forced to commit a crime of initiation, Communists were locked in by a system of mutual implication.

The new head of the party, Eugene Dennis, a tall Irish Norwegian from Seattle, nevertheless found himself presiding over a divided party.[6] Anti-Foster Communists began to coalesce around Dennis and the offices of the *Daily Worker*, while Fosterites continued rooting out suspected Browderites.[7] Aware that he was being written out of the party's history, Browder defended his old policies with growing determination. Whether one agreed with him or not, it was clear that he posed a risk to party unity and had to go. On February 6, 1946, he was expelled.[8]

Americans who joined the Communist Party usually did so because they hoped to improve the society in which they lived. With the daily experience of unemployment, low wages, racial inequality, and police repression, it seemed that the only solution was a wholesale replacement of the Republic. Once they joined the party, the factors that had alienated them from the constitutional order were augmented by new ones. They could expect public scorn, government-sanctioned violence, arrest, even deportation as a result of their political beliefs. Exclusion, harassment, and abuse became a form of masochistic evidence of the wisdom of their philosophy, for if history was not with them, why did they provoke so much capitalist hatred?

As the values espoused by the international movement diverged from its daily conduct, Communists were forced to make difficult choices: to abandon the party on the basis of an ambiguous commitment to personal ethics—a worryingly "bourgeois" concept—or to reaffirm the rhetorical commitment to internationalism, enlightenment, and Marx while abandoning all of them in practice. Articulated through a language of self-discipline that stressed the necessity of solidarity in the face of reactionary assault, the controlling elements of the Communist Party were able to pull moderates away from a course that might have confounded their critics. American Communists proved unable to question Stalin on fundamental issues of international policy, despite the fact that the Russian dictator had repeatedly demonstrated his determination to manipulate the international movement for national and personal motives. As a result, the party never earned more than a narrow appeal. The great mass of workers, rarely charmed by elegant theoretical models, responded unfavorably to a organization that appeared irrelevant and dogmatic, untrustworthy and foreign. This effectively continued until the party's functional demise in the mid-1950s, all efforts to break away from its suicidal political course proving fruitless.

During the first decade of the Cold War, countersubversives would take advantage of the party's rejectionist drift to accelerate their war on American communism. Truman instituted new loyalty programs in the effort to uncover federal employees with radical affiliations who had previously been ignored by the Roosevelt administration.[9] FBI monitoring of the CPUSA grew. The Department of Justice, encouraged by HUAC, used the Smith Act to prosecute more than a hundred leading party members, though the trials remained plagued by constitutional challenges, doubtful testimony, and allegations of impropriety.[10] In 1949 the largest single trial of CPUSA members saw eleven Communist leaders charged with violating the ban on membership in a revolutionary organization. The Communists' lawyers resorted to contemptuous tactics of disruption and denunciation, but the prosecution behaved no better—manipulating evidence to suit their claims—and the judge rarely intervened to stop them. To make their case, prosecutors brought forward a series of government spies and agents who had been operating within the party, confirming Communist fears of infiltration and stimulating further internal purges. After a nine-month trial, all the defendants were found guilty, each receiving at least three years in prison; as repression continued, the CPUSA continued to shrink in size.[11]

During his term in Atlanta Penitentiary, John Gates took the opportunity to study the history of radical protest in America. He read how Socialist leader Eugene Debs had run for president in 1920 while locked up in the very same prison in which he was now residing. The United States had just passed through the Great Red Scare, the labor movement had been smashed, Debs had been declared an enemy of the state, yet he still won nearly a million votes from the Left and held the sympathy of a large swath of Americans who believed the repression of political dissent was anathema to the traditions of American constitutional history. These Americans would not only fight to get Debs released from prison, but in 1921 succeed in winning it—and had in the interim more or less halted the antiradical tide that swept across the country in 1919. Despite widespread objections to the Smith Act trials on civil liberties grounds, the crowds defending the party were far smaller today, and there were no queues of Americans waiting at polling booths to vote for Communist candidates in elections. "The contrast with our case was painful," he acknowledged.[12]

The experiences of the previous decade had dramatically reduced Americans' hostility to the politics of loyalty, their sensitivity to violations of traditional liberties, and their support for outsiders. Many anticommunists had cleaned up their act, distancing themselves from extremists and using antifascist and antistatist rhetoric to justify a more general war on the "totalitarianism" of the extreme Left and Right. The war on domestic fascists—none of whom could reasonably be said to have posed a genuine threat to national security—helped adjust many to the need for limits on radical political advocacy even in the absence of an immediate threat to America's political institutions. Those who applauded the prosecutions of Pelley, Viereck, and Dilling would struggle to explain their opposition to the trials of Foster, Dennis, and Gates.

Nevertheless, deep divisions remained over the best way of dealing with communism. Reprising the theme that had run throughout the history of countersubversion, anticommunists struggled to balance their geopolitical opposition to the Soviet Union with a desire to preserve the domestic liberties that they believed made the United States worth fighting for. Liberals continued to argue that the only prophylactic against revolution was reform. Conservatives responded that "softness" on communism was a sign of weakness. They instead turned to the tried-and-trusted methods of countersubversion, working closely with the Federal Bureau of Investigation to gain information on the party and its allies and using congressional investigations to call upon the people across the country to wage a personal, local war on the Red Menace in their midst.

A second individual to lose his job in the early years of the Cold War was Congressman Jerry Voorhis, who had struggled unsuccessfully to push HUAC in a more moderate direction, tried to promote bureaucratic anticommunism over the populist crusading of Martin Dies, and epitomized liberals' difficulties with resurgent anticommunist politics in the later 1930s: unsure whether to praise conservatives for their moments of clarity or condemn them for their errors. Unexpectedly, in the 1946 elections, Voorhis was turned out of office by a young, unknown Republican named Richard Milhous Nixon. The result, the *Washington Post* noted, was "a surprise, even to Nixon's staunchest backers."[13] Fighting an uphill battle against an entrenched incumbent, Nixon had pursued the political strategy that he would subsequently refine to a fine art. Drawing attention to Voorhis's history in the socialist movement prior to joining the New Deal Democrats, and presenting him as the candidate of the CIO, Nixon smeared this former member of HUAC and author of countersubversive legislation with allegations of radicalism and insinuations of disloyalty. Voorhis distanced himself from groups associated even indirectly with the CPUSA—taking out a paid ad in every newspaper in his district insisting that the progressive movement "cannot be mixed with Communist influences" and declaring in speeches that the "one great obstacle" to international peace was "the attitude of Soviet Russia"—but this made little difference in the face of Nixon's concerted campaign of red-baiting, and Voorhis was defeated.[14] Voorhis remained bitter about his defeat for many years, publishing a book denouncing his successor in 1972, just as Nixon was about to win one of the most sweeping landslides in American history and, as the ringing voice of the supposedly silent majority, begin a second term in the White House.[15]

After his defeat of Voorhis, Nixon continued his red-baiting, defeating a Democratic rival for the Senate, Helen Gahagan Douglas, and making it onto the Eisenhower ticket as vice president through his reputation as an anticommunist bulldog. In no small part due to Nixon's successes, many other Republican politicians began to wake up to the value of red-baiting. The crucial discovery was that the strategy no longer threatened to split the Republican Party between conservatives and progressives, as it had in the 1920s—in fact, quite the opposite. Both the antistatist instincts of the midwestern and western Republican wings and the conservative instincts of the East were united in fighting a singular enemy—"New Deal Communism"—whereas such attacks deeply divided the Democrats. During the 1948 election, Roosevelt's former vice president and the unelected leader of the liberal Left broke away from the Democratic Party to launch a new Progressive Party, an effort that proved no more successful than "Fighting Bob" La Follette's bolt from the Republicans had been in 1924. Henry Wallace and his supporters rejected the confrontational drift Russo-American relations had taken under Truman and pushed for an ambitious reform program in combination with a rapprochement with the Soviets. For this Wallace progressives were attacked as stooges of communism and humiliated in the election. Political opponents highlighted Communist endorsements of the Progressives even as Wallace tried to distance himself from his unpopular supporters. Ultimately, instead of the 4 or 5 million votes Wallace had expected to win, he received less than 1.2 million: approximately 2.5 percent of the vote, and slightly fewer than the number who in the same election deserted the Democrats to vote for the staunchly segregationist and militantly anticommunist Dixiecrats.[16] In the 1920s, the power of countersubversion had been dramatically curtailed by the fact that both Democrats and Republicans were divided over the issue of loyalty crusading; in the 1940s, however, red-baiting served to bring the Republicans together and fragment the New Deal coalition. Now, political self-interest could accelerate and intensify the politics of anticommunism.

Nixon's persistent exploitation of red-baiting rhetoric to attack his enemies can obscure his equally distinctive record as also perhaps the most effective congressional countersubversive investigator of the early Cold War period, achieving a success that figures such as Overman, Lusk, and Fish—even Dies—would have dreamed of. After winning Voorhis's congressional seat, Nixon headed straight for HUAC. A health scare had forced Dies into retirement in 1944, but his spirit lived on in the committee he had turned into a national institution. On the opening day of Congress in January 1945, Mississippi's John E. Rankin, who had been heavily involved with HUAC since the beginning, proposed an amendment to change HUAC into a standing committee, so that it would no longer be necessary to win votes for continuance every year. Narrowly defeated at first, Rankin asked for a public roll call. Politicians being politicians, a second vote passed comfortably, supported by a strong coalition of Republicans and southern Democrats who preferred a swift change of heart to the risk of publicly appearing to protect Communists.[17]

The pattern of truths mixed with falsehoods and exaggerations that characterized the Dies-era hearings continued. In October 1946, former Communist Party member Louis Budenz appeared before the committee to detail his role in building secret Soviet espionage networks. Among others, Budenz named Gerhart Eisler, a German who had moved to New York in the late 1930s, as a Soviet agent. Eisler was subsequently subpoenaed, and the committee was able to antagonize him sufficiently to have him cited for contempt. The citation became the subject of Richard Nixon's maiden speech in Congress; soon after, Eisler fled the country, helping convince the public of his guilt, just as fleeing had done for Ludwig Martens and Heinz Spanknoebel. In July 1948, another defector, Elizabeth Bentley, named a series of senior New Deal officials as having passed secrets to the Soviets, including Lauchlin Currie, a White House assistant to FDR; Harry Dexter White, second in command at the Treasury; and a number of other less prominent administrators.[18] Shortly after, a second ex-Communist witness, Whittaker Chambers, corroborated the claims for Nixon and HUAC, before adding a new name: Alger Hiss, a clean-shaven young New Dealer from the highest echelons of the State Department who had been prominently involved in setting up the United Nations and now headed the Carnegie fund.

Chambers was extremely careful about the details of his allegations, asserting that Hiss was, at one time, a Communist, and saying nothing about espionage. Nevertheless, Hiss had indeed been a spy.

Coming as the revelations did among a series of more general attacks on the legacy of the New Deal, many liberals were understandably inclined to dismiss them as fabrications designed to destroy the memory of Roosevelt. Hiss aggressively denied the allegations against him, drawing upon a reservoir of distinguished political references and depicting the attacks as smears on the New Deal. Liberals who wanted to defend the New Deal thus found themselves defending Hiss. Of course, this was not new; it was simply a variant on the same strategy that Communists had used to defend themselves during the Popular Front era. Instead of arguing that an attack on Communists was an attack on all progressives, Hiss simply denied he was a Communist at all and claimed that the effort was nothing but an effort to destroy the memory of the New Deal.

Under Nixon's watchful eye, Hiss eventually goaded Chambers into making his allegations outside the protective arena of HUAC and then aggressively launched a libel suit against the ex-Communist to clear his name. It was this hubristic strategy that forced Chambers to declare that Hiss was not only a Communist but a spy, proven through documents taken from Hiss during the thirties and kept as an insurance policy. With the statute of limitations on es-pionage expired, it was Hiss's own claims of innocence that provided the crime of perjury for which he could be prosecuted. In December he was indicted and after a series of tortuous trials found guilty, subsequently spending forty-four months in jail.[19] The public trial of Hiss, however, has never ended, with both sides continuing to litigate the issues to this day. Perhaps more than any other domestic event in the early Cold War period, the Hiss prosecution reignited fears of subversion and marked out the divisions of the McCarthy era. But it also expressed the complexity of countersubversive politics, with Nixon's vis-ceral hostility to the New Deal blue blood expressing in graphic form the way in which cold geopolitical calculations regarding the security of the nation had become inextricably tied to populist hostility toward political elites.

But what of the old insurgents, the individuals who had played such a major role in resisting the expansion of the national security state between the wars, who had been attacked as Bolsheviks in the 1920s before adopting countersub-versive language themselves in the 1930s to criticize the New Deal, and who had, in a final twist, been denounced as fascists during the war with Hitler for opposing American intervention? Most of them were dead: Borah in January 1940, Norris three years later, Hiram Johnson in August 1945—on the same day the atomic bomb was dropped on Hiroshima. Midwestern Republican politics was no longer a home for progressivism. Instead, it was dominated by antistatist conservatives such as Robert Taft and Arthur Vandenberg, who inherited the old progressives' suspicion of Washington but abandoned pretty much everything else.

Anti-interventionists who had reluctantly acquiesced to the war after Pearl Harbor nursed bitter memories of the abuse they had received from New Deal liberals, and some would come to see anticommunism as a way to get even.[20] Burton Wheeler continually complained about Roosevelt's softness toward Stalin, arguing that "our biggest mistake was in helping to build up one totalitarian menace—communism—in order to conquer the other, Nazism." At the war's end, Wheeler traveled to Europe to speak to Churchill and Eisenhower about communism and came to the conclusion that the United States had deliberately allowed Russia to take Berlin. Shortly before the Potsdam summit, Wheeler met with Truman to pass on his concerns. "Mr. President," he told him, "you'd better stand up to Russia."[21]

America's countersubversive politics between 1917 and 1945 was shaped above all by the continuing struggle to balance the nation's localistic and libertarian traditions with the machinery necessary to push American influence into the world and protect the nation from the covert operations of its rivals. Countersubversion was alien to American traditions, which argued that political policing was a habit of Old World empires, not the free American Republic. With substantial opposition across the political spectrum to anything that seemed to limit the rights of American citizens to dissent, politicians from Wilson onward sought to limit the size of federal bureaucracies and augment them with calls for vigilant public action to protect the country and engineer a spirit of patriotism. Instead of investigating claims about radical subversion neutrally and carefully, bureaucracies overshot and then were shut down in disgrace. As a result, the countersubversive project was left in the hands of true believers in the private sector, professional patriots who tended to be either self-interested, corrupt, or incompetent. By the time of the Depression, countersubversive politics had racked up a generation's worth of misdemeanors, all of which seemed to confirm the view that countersubversion was nothing more than restriction on liberty designed to entrench the position of elites and undermine the interests of the common people.

However, the changes that took place during the 1930s produced a resurgence of countersubversive politics that would be hard to explain if one were to look at its history of failure alone. There were three main developments. First, the Communist Party generated fractions, splits, and exiles who were willing and able to speak up for the necessity of countersubversion more effectively than professional patriots had in the past. To at least this extent, anticommunism's ability to emerge from the ashes of a failed antiradicalism was a product of communism's continuing failure to live up to its claimed ideals. Second, the New Deal administration set about building a countersubversive infrastructure capable of developing real expertise and largely replacing old-style countersubversive activities in the private sector and the legislature. This new machinery offered the potential of rigorously investigating subversion, while new laws dramatically lowered the burden of proof needed to prosecute revolutionary radicals. With an ideologue as blinkered as J. Edgar Hoover in charge, the new FBI was never going to abandon its obsessions with repressing unions and destroying the civil rights movement. But at least when compared to the blundering efforts of the professional patriots of the 1920s, it was hard to deny that the FBI was competent at what it did. In this sense, the resurgence of anticommunism from the 1930s onward was an ironic testament to the importance of "big government" bureaucracies when constructing the national security state (not that many of Hoover's most enthusiastic supporters would have admitted it). Third, countersubversion itself came to mean something new and more persuasive. Although the term never shed its history of failure, individuals began to change their arguments to fit a new audience and new times. Countersubversive discourse on the Left used fears of fascism to conduct an effective campaign against radical populists and conservatives, but in the process helped legitimate the idea of repressing domestic political extremists in general. Martin Dies and his successors learned that to be effective, they would have to use antifascist arguments to justify their own anticommunism. As threats began to emerge to the racial status quo, Dixie's patrician elite began to accuse civil rights activists of communism. And in hostility to the New Deal and anger at their own political exclusion, the antistatists who had done so much to frustrate the politics of countersubversion between 1917 and 1933 began to argue that the "Red Menace" not only was real, but had arrived in Washington. Their fear of excessively centralized power had initially encouraged them to fight the red-baiters; now it led them to join their former opponents in a shared struggle against Roosevelt and his legacy, a struggle that arguably still continues today. Indeed, it is this basic understanding—one that concerns itself only marginally with the agency of rival nation-states, the technicalities of institutional loyalties, or the complexities of ideology, but sees "communism" simply as a matter of big-state politics, to be resisted by grassroots organizations reasserting the local traditions of America—that shapes modern conservatism in the twenty-first century. To repeat the point, it was deeply ironic that in the 1920s, the strongest voices for this form of politics, figures like Borah, Norris, Hiram Johnson, and Robert La Follette, had been themselves accused of Bolshevism.

And it was here that the third and final dismissal of the new Cold War era took place. By 1945 the sole remaining voice of the old Republican insurgents was Wisconsin's "Young Bob" La Follette. Despite voicing an anti-interventionism during the war that earned him contempt from liberals as a fascist stooge—just as his father had been attacked in 1917 and 1918—La Follette had been slower to question his alliance with the New Deal than the other midwestern and western progressives. The senator had been running Wisconsin politics as a more or less independent fiefdom for years, and Roosevelt swapped federal patronage for La Follette's support. Meanwhile, the Wisconsin senator's electoral strength had increasingly come to depend upon union votes in Wisconsin's industrial zones. This had worked as long as the New Deal had been in the ascendant, but with the tide turning against the Democrats La Follette had no choice but to return to his Republican roots. This alienated him from many of his working-class supporters who saw their loyalties with Roosevelt's coalition, but his family's long history of putting personality before party hardly endeared him to the Republican faithful, either. In the 1946 primary, La Follette found himself challenged by a Republican outsider with relatively little political experience yet a surprising degree of support, a man who in the year that La Follette first entered the Senate had been a seventeen-year-old running a chicken-breeding business in Grand Chute, Outagamie County. La Follette was attacked for his anti-interventionism, accused of being a war profiteer and of being unpatriotic. And despite the power of the La Follette machine, by the slimmest of margins he was defeated.

Observing this unexpected upset, Howard J. McMurray, who would be the Democrats' candidate for the Senate seat in the fall, declared, "La Follette's defeat was not a defeat for liberalism in Wisconsin, it was a defeat for isolationism, Republicanism and political opportunism."[22] It was indeed a defeat for isolationism; however, gaining, as he did, only half the number of votes as his Republican rival when the election came around, it seemed McMurray was mistaken on the second and third counts. Others mourned Senator La Follette's political passage more eloquently, noting his long service for liberalism hidden behind the smears against his loyalty. A correspondent in the *New Republic* reminded readers, "For two generations, terrorization by employers had been the common practice, and this largely accounted for the slow growth of the organized labor movement." La Follette's Civil Liberties Committee "caused the industrial terrorists to run to cover and in many cases stopped their practices." His defeat was "more than just the removal from the Senate of a dependable fighter for the common good. It is a sad commentary on the lack of appreciation of some of our liberals and some of organized labor for those who served the people's cause faithfully and tirelessly."[23] Indeed, La Follette's defeat truly marked the end of an era.

And the name of the man who put the final nail into the coffin of the old midwestern Republican order by ousting Senator La Follette, who showed no fear in attacking one of Washington's most established political personalities on grounds of lack of patriotic spirit, the man who would be entering as a freshman senator in 1947 just as the Cold War picked up steam? It was Joseph McCarthy.

Notes

Introduction

1. For general accounts of political repression prior to the McCarthy era, see Robert Justin Goldstein, *Political Repression in Modern America: From 1870 to the Present;* Michael J. Heale, *American Anticommunism: Combating the Enemy Within, 1830–1970;* Richard Gid Powers, *Not without Honor: The History of American Anticommunism;* Markku Ruotsila, *British and American Anticommunism before the Cold War;* and Ted Morgan, *Reds: McCarthyism in Twentieth-Century America.*

2. Daniel Yergin, *Shattered Peace: The Origins of the Cold War and the National Security State;* Melvyn P. Leffler, "The American Conception of National Security and the Beginnings of the Cold War, 1945–1948"; Douglas M. Charles, *J. Edgar Hoover and the Anti-interventionists: FBI Political Surveillance and the Rise of the Domestic Security State, 1939–1945.*

3. Alan Brinkley, "The Problem of American Conservatism," 415.

4. Michael Kazin, *The Populist Persuasion: An American History,* 2; Merle Curti, *The Roots of American Loyalty,* 231.

5. Daniel Bell, ed., *The Radical Right;* Robert Murray, *The Great Red Scare: A Study in National Hysteria, 1919–1920;* Richard Hofstadter, *The Paranoid Style in American Politics, and Other Essays;* Murray B. Levin, *Political Hysteria in America: The Democratic Capacity for Repression;* David Brion Davis, ed., *The Fear of Conspiracy: Images of Un-American Subversion from the Revolution to the Present;* Joel Kovel, *Red-Hunting in the Promised Land: Anticommunism and the Making of America.* Important precursors to these arguments can be found in the writings of Charles Beard, William F. Ogburn, Sigmund Freud, and Theodor Adorno, not to mention several of the civil liberties activists discussed in this book.

6. Stanley Coben, "A Study in Nativism: The American Red Scare of 1919–20," 53–57. As Michael Rogin notes, this kind of argument practiced exactly the kind of status politics that it attacked. Rogin, *Ronald Reagan, the Movie, and Other Episodes in Political Demonology,* 277.

7. See Gail Bederman, *Manliness and Civilization: A Cultural History of Gender and Race in the United States, 1880–1917.*

8. Alan Brinkley, *Voices of Protest: Huey Long, Father Coughlin, and the Great Depression;* Leo D. Ribuffo, *The Old Christian Right: The Protestant Far Right from the Great Depression to the Cold War.*

9. Conservatives have sought to emphasize the degree to which the Communist Party USA (CPUSA) supported Soviet espionage in the United States, particularly during the Second World War. See in particular Harvey Klehr, John Earl Haynes, and Fridrikh Igorevich Firsov, *The Secret World of American Communism;* Harvey Klehr, John Earl Haynes, and Kyrill M. Anderson, *The Soviet World of American Communism;* and Harvey Klehr, John Earl Haynes, and Alexander Vassiliev, *Spies: The Rise and Fall of the KGB in America.* Historians on the Left have argued that radicals often challenged entrenched hierarchies of class, race, and gender. For instance, see Kim E. Nielsen, *Un-American Womanhood: Antiradicalism, Antifeminism, and the First Red Scare;* Kate Weigand, *Red Feminism: American Communism and the Making of Women's Liberation;* Glenda Elizabeth Gilmore, *Defying Dixie: The Radical Roots of Civil Rights, 1919–1950;* and Beverley Gage, *The Day Wall Street Exploded: A Story of America in Its First Age of Terror.*

10. Alan Wald, *The New York Intellectuals: The Rise and Decline of the Anti-Stalinist Left from the 1930s to the 1980s;* Markku Ruotsila, "Neoconservatism Prefigured: The Social Democratic League of America and the Anticommunists of the Anglo-American Right, 1917–21"; Steve Rosswurm, *The FBI and the Catholic Church, 1935–1962;* Jennifer Luff, *Commonsense Anticommunism: Labor and Civil Liberties between the World Wars.*

11. Benjamin L. Alpers, *Dictators, Democracy, and American Public Culture: Envisioning the Totalitarian Enemy, 1920s–1950s;* Michael Kimmage, *The Conservative Turn: Lionel Trilling, Whittaker Chambers, and the Lessons of Anti-Communism;* Patrick Allitt, *The Conservatives: Ideas and Personalities throughout American History;* Jennifer Burns, "In Search of a Usable Past: Conservative Thought in America."

12. Regin Schmidt, *Red Scare: FBI and the Origins of Anticommunism in the United States, 1919–1943,* 9.

13. Richard Gid Powers uses the term quite differently. See Powers, *Not without Honor;* historiographical discussion in Michael J. Heale, "Beyond the 'Age of McCarthy': Anticommunism and the Historians"; and Larry Ceplair, *Anti-communism in Twentieth Century America: A Critical History,* 18.

14. Theda Skocpol, Marshall Ganz, and Ziad Munson, "A Nation of Organizers: The Institutional Origins of Civic Voluntarism in the United States," 527.

15. Gerald Horne, *Black Liberation/Red Scare: Ben Davis and the Communist Party;* Michael Denning, *The Cultural Front: The Laboring of American Culture in the Twentieth Century;* Gilmore, *Defying Dixie.*

16. William F. Buckley Jr. and L. Brent Bozell, *McCarthy and His Enemies: The Record and Its Meaning,* 285.

17. Gary Gerstle, "Race and the Myth of the Liberal Consensus"; Elizabeth Fones-Wolf, *Selling Free Enterprise: The Business Assault on Labor and Liberalism, 1945–1960;*

Thomas Sugrue, *The Origins of the Urban Crisis: Race and Inequality in Postwar Detroit;* Rick Perlstein, *Before the Storm: Barry Goldwater and the Unmaking of the American Consensus;* George Lewis, *The White South and the Red Menace: Segregationists, Anticommunism, and Massive Resistance, 1945–1965;* Kim Phillips-Fein, *Invisible Hands: The Businessmen's Crusade against the New Deal.*

Chapter 1. Policing Politics

1. State of the Union address, December 4, 1917, in *The Papers of Woodrow Wilson* edited by Arthur S. Link, 45:199 (hereafter cited as WWP).

2. Shelton Stromquist, *Re-inventing "the People": The Progressive Movement, the Class Problem, and the Origins of Modern Liberalism.*

3. Herbert Croly, *The Promise of American Life,* 1; Jeanette Keith, "The Politics of Southern Draft Resistance, 1917–1918: Class, Race, and Conscription in the Rural South," 1336–37, 1355.

4. *Atlanta Constitution,* May 31, 1917; *New York Tribune,* October 25, 1919; Keith, "Politics of Southern Draft Resistance," 1343.

5. Curti, *Roots of American Loyalty,* 224, 232.

6. See discussion in Forrest Revere Black, "*Debs vs. The United States:* A Judicial Milepost on the Road to Absolutism."

7. Francis Newton Thorpe, *The Constitutional History of the United States,* 2:343.

8. Max Eastman, *Love and Revolution: My Journey through an Epoch,* 34. See also Curti, *Roots of American Loyalty,* 228.

9. For a detailed overview over the debates surrounding the use of treason and espionage laws, see David M. Rabban, *Free Speech in Its Forgotten Years,* chap. 6.

10. Joan Jensen, *The Price of Vigilance,* 14.

11. *New York Times,* February 25, June 9, 1915.

12. Brett Gary, *The Nervous Liberals: Propaganda Anxieties from World War I to the Cold War,* 10.

13. Ellen Schrecker, *Many Are the Crimes: McCarthyism in America,* 53; William Preston Jr., *Aliens and Dissenters: Federal Suppression of Radicals, 1903–1933,* 189; Anthony Gaughan, "Woodrow Wilson and the Rise of Militant Interventionism in the South," 780–84; I. A. Newby, "States' Rights and Southern Congressmen during World War I," 41.

14. Geoffrey R. Stone, "Judge Learned Hand and the Espionage Act of 1917: A Mystery Unraveled."

15. *New York Times,* April 19, 1917.

16. James Weinstein, *The Decline of Socialism in America, 1912–1925,* 130.

17. *New York Times,* May 19, 1917.

18. "Whose War?," *Masses,* April 1917, in *Shaking the World: John Reed's Revolutionary Journalism,* edited by John Newsinger, 93.

19. J. Weinstein, *Decline of Socialism in America,* 126.

20. *New York Times,* June 16, 26, September 29, 30, 1917, April 15, September 15, 1918.

21. Stewart Halsey Ross, *Propaganda for War: How the United States Was Conditioned to Fight the Great War of 1914–1918,* 265, 267; Preston, *Aliens and Dissenters,* 146; Stone, "Learned Hand and the Espionage Act," 357.

22. Henry A. Turner, "Woodrow Wilson and Public Opinion," 518; Robert W. Dunn, ed., *The Palmer Raids,* 12; Daniel Bell, *Marxian Socialism in the United States,* 106.

23. Patrick Renshaw, "The IWW and the Red Scare, 1917–1924," 67.

24. H. C. Peterson and Gilbert C. Fite, *Opponents of War, 1917–1918,* 155; Stone, "Learned Hand and the Espionage Act," 339–41; Ross, *Propaganda for War,* 265.

25. Peterson and Fite, *Opponents of War,* 251; Gage, *Day Wall Street Exploded,* 116.

26. Woodrow Wilson, *The State: Elements of Practical and Historical Politics,* 633; Christopher Wolfe, "Woodrow Wilson: Interpreting the Constitution"; Scott J. Zentner, "Liberalism and Executive Power: Woodrow Wilson and the American Founders."

27. Jensen, *The Price of Vigilance,* 38.

28. Turner, "Wilson and Public Opinion," 515–17.

29. Ross, *Propaganda for War,* 245, 248, 249. See also Daniel M. Smith, "Authoritarianism and American Policy Making in Two World Wars."

30. Jensen, *The Price of Vigilance,* 17, 22, 25, 45–50.

31. Peterson and Fite, *Opponents of War,* 19.

32. Jensen, *The Price of Vigilance,* 60–61, 63.

33. Peterson and Fite, *Opponents of War,* 231–32.

34. *Atlanta Constitution,* June 12, 1917.

35. *New York Tribune,* January 13, 1918.

36. In April 1918 alone, tarring and featherings took place in Louisiana, Oklahoma, Wisconsin, Colorado, Michigan, Oregon, Nevada, Alabama, Kansas, Florida, New York, Texas, Pennsylvania, and Arkansas. *New York Tribune,* April 4, 1918; *New York Times,* April 11, 12, 14, 1918; *Washington Post,* April 14, 9, 1918; *New York Tribune,* April 24, 1918; *Atlanta Constitution,* April 24, 1918; *New York Tribune,* April 25, 1918; *Atlanta Constitution,* April 28, 1918; *Washington Post,* April 28, 1918; *Chicago Daily Tribune,* April 30, 1918.

37. Richard Slotkin, *Gunfighter Nation: The Myth of the Frontier in Twentieth-Century America,* 173–74; Richard Maxwell Brown, *Strains of Violence: Historical Studies of American Violence and Vigilantism,* 93–94.

38. Stephen H. Norwood, *Strikebreaking and Intimidation: Mercenaries and Masculinity in Twentieth-Century America.*

39. *New York Tribune,* January 13, 1918; *Atlanta Constitution,* February 14, 1918; *Chicago Daily Tribune,* February 13, 1918.

40. *Washington Post,* April 24, 1918.

41. *Atlanta Constitution,* July 25, 1918; *Chicago Daily Tribune,* November 13, 1920.

42. *New York Times,* June 2, 1918.

43. *Chicago Daily Tribune,* March 23, 1918; *Washington Post,* March 24, 1918.

44. *Atlanta Constitution,* June 5, 1918.

45. *Chicago Daily Tribune,* March 26, 1918.

46. *Chicago Daily Tribune,* April 6, 1918.

47. *New York Tribune,* January 13, 1918; *Washington Post,* February 14, 1918.

48. *New York Times,* June 2, 1918.

49. *Chicago Daily Tribune,* February 16, 1918; *New York Tribune,* January 13, April 6, 1918.

50. J. Weinstein, *Decline of Socialism in America,* 161.

51. U.S. Senate, *Report and Hearings: Brewing and Liquor Interests and German and Bolshevik Propaganda,* 2:2661–67 (hereafter cited as Overman Committee).

52. *New York Times,* February 25, 1918.

53. *New York Times,* December 26, 1917, August 12, 1918.

54. *New York Times,* November 1, June 4, 1914, January 7, 1915, March 10, 1919, January 27, September 15, 20, 1918.

55. *New York Times,* February 28, 1919.

56. Goldstein, *Political Repression in Modern America,* 110; Preston, *Aliens and Dissenters,* 81, 182–83.

57. *New York Times,* April 15, 17, May 3, 5, 11, 13, 15, 16, 1917, February 8, 1918.

58. *New York Times,* May 9, 13, 20, 1918; Peterson and Fite, *Opponents of War,* 217.

59. Peterson and Fite, *Opponents of War,* 220. In all, twenty-six Republican senators opposed the Sedition Act. *New York Times,* May 5, 1918.

60. Gaughan, "Rise of Militant Interventionism in the South," 793; David Sarasohn, "The Insurgent Republicans: Insurgent Image and Republican Reality," 254; Peterson and Fite, *Opponents of War,* 6, 22, 217–18.

61. *New York Times,* November 2, 1917.

62. *New York Times,* April 6, 1918.

63. *New York Times,* June 3, 1917.

64. Peterson and Fite, *Opponents of War,* 215. See Attorney General Gregory's comments in Zechariah Chafee Jr., "Free Speech in Wartime," 936.

65. George Creel to Woodrow Wilson, November 8, 1918, WWP, 51:645; John A. Thompson, *Reformers and War: American Progressive Publicists and the First World War,* 228.

66. WWP, 44:420, 273, 48:208.

67. Woodrow Wilson to Albert Sidney Burleson, October 19, 30, 1917, WWP, 44:397, 473; Preston, *Aliens and Dissenters,* 128; Ross, *Propaganda for War,* 269; Peterson and Fite, *Opponents of War,* 19.

68. Osward Garrison Villard to Joseph Patrick Tumulty, September 26, 1917; Walter Lippman to Edward House, October 17, 1917; Herbert Croly to Wilson, October 19, 1917; Upton Sinclair to Wilson, October 22, 1917; John Spargo to Wilson, November 1, 1917; Roger Nash Baldwin to Wilson, February 27, 1918; Amos Pinchot to Wilson, May 24, 1918; Edward Prentiss Costigan to Wilson, May 29, 1918, WWP, 44:272, 393–94, 420, 468–71, 492, 46:481, 48:146, 150.

69. *New Republic,* September 22, 1917.

70. *Nation,* October 19, 1918.

71. Thompson, *Reformers and War,* 224–26, 230–31.

72. *New Republic,* December 1, 1917.

73. *Nation,* January 17, 1919.

74. George Jean Nathan and H. L. Mencken, *The American Credo: A Contribution toward the Interpretation of the National Mind,* 16–17.

75. Rabban, *Free Speech in Its Forgotten Years,* chap. 7.

76. *Nation,* October 20, 1920.

77. Eastman, *Love and Revolution,* 45; Peterson and Fite, *Opponents of War,* 251.

Chapter 2. War and Peace

1. Theodore Draper, *The Roots of American Communism*, 161–63.

2. New York State Legislature, Joint Legislative Committee to Investigate Seditious Activities, *Revolutionary Radicalism: Its History, Purpose, and Tactics, Report of the New York State Investigative Committee*, 2:639–47 (hereafter cited as Lusk Committee).

3. *New York Times*, June 13, 1919.

4. Lincoln Steffens, *The Autobiography of Lincoln Steffens*, 761.

5. David S. Foglesong, *America's Secret War against Bolshevism: U.S. Intervention in the Russian Civil War*; Christopher Lasch, *The American Liberals and the Russian Revolution*; State of the Union address, December 4, 1917, WWP, 45:199 (see chap. 1, n. 1).

6. Memorandum by Franklin Knight Lane, November 5, 1918, WWP, 51:604; Melvyn P. Leffler, *The Specter of Communism: The United States and the Origins of the Cold War, 1917–1953*, 7–11.

7. James R. Mock and Cedric Larson, *Words That Won the War: The Story of the Committee on Public Information, 1917–1919*, 304; Claude E. Fike, "The Influence of the Creel Committee and the American Red Cross on Russian-American Relations, 1917–1919," 100.

8. State of the Union address, December 4, 1917, WWP, 45:199; Wilson to Fourth All-Russia Congress of Soviets, March 11, 1918, WWP, 46:598. See also Lasch, *American Liberals and the Russian Revolution*, 84–86.

9. George Kennan, "The Sisson Documents"; *Chicago Daily Tribune*, September 15, 1918; *New York Tribune*, September 22, 1918; diary of Colonel House, September 24, 1918, cited in WWP, 51:4, 104.

10. Sisson later claimed that he had never said Lenin and Trotsky were *merely* German agents. In fact, the CPI explicitly stated that the Bolshevik government was "a German government acting *solely* in the interests of Germany and . . . for the benefit of the Imperial German Government *alone*" (emphasis added). Edgar Sisson, *One Hundred Red Days: A Personal Chronicle of the Bolshevik Revolution*, 381; Committee on Public Information, "The German-Bolshevik Conspiracy," introduction to *Documents of Soviet-American Relations*, vol. 2, *Propaganda, Economic Affairs, Recognition, 1917–1933*, edited by Harold J. Goldberg; Robert Lansing to Edgar Sisson, September 14, 1918.

11. *New York Tribune*, September 22, October 3, 1918.

12. *Atlanta Constitution*, September 22, 1918; David W. McFadden, *Alternative Paths: Soviets and Americans, 1917–1920*, 170.

13. *Chicago Daily Tribune*, September 24, 1918.

14. *New York Tribune*, November 12, 1918; *New York Times*, November 12, 1918; Lasch, *American Liberals and the Russian Revolution*, 114.

15. Morris Hillquit, *Loose Leaves from a Busy Life*, 279.

16. *New York Times*, January 2, 1919; *Washington Post*, February 18, 1919.

17. *New Republic*, April 6, 1918; *New York Tribune*, January 8, 1919; *Washington Post*, January 8, 1919.

18. Dmitri S. von Mohrenschildt, "Lincoln Steffens and the Bolshevik Revolution," 35–37.

19. Norman E. Saul, *War and Revolution: The United States and Russia, 1914–1921*, 275.

20. "Bolshevism in America," *Revolutionary Age*, December 18, 1918, in *Shaking the World*, edited by Newsinger, 170–71.

21. Overman Committee, 3:23 (see chap. 1, n. 51).

22. *New York Times*, April 7, 1919.

23. Todd Pfannestiel, "The Soviet Bureau: A Bolshevik Strategy to Secure U.S. Diplomatic Recognition through Economic Trade," 173, 178; *Soviet Russia* 1, no. 1 (1919): 1; McFadden, *Alternative Paths*, 291–93. See also Auvo Kostiainen, "Santeri Nuorteva and the Origins of Soviet-American Relations."

24. *Atlanta Constitution*, September 17, 1918; *Washington Post*, September 17, 1918.

25. Roy Talbert, *Negative Intelligence: The Army and the American Left, 1917–1941*, 141–42, 145–46.

26. Overman Committee, 2:2701–2, 2712.

27. Ibid., 2729.

28. Gage, *Day Wall Street Exploded*, 117–18.

29. Overman Committee, 1:xli, xxix, 2778, 2:2751, 2771.

30. Arthur M. Schlesinger Jr. and Roger Bruns, ed., *Congress Investigates: A Documented History, 1792–1974*, 2987.

31. *New York Times*, February 6, 1919.

32. *Washington Post*, February 4, 1919.

33. *Washington Post*, February 5, 1919; *New York Times*, February 5, 1919; *Atlanta Constitution*, February 5, 1919; *New York Tribune*, February 5, 1919.

34. *Atlanta Constitution*, February 1, 1919; *Chicago Daily Tribune*, February 5, 1919; *New York Tribune*, February 5, 1919; Talbert, *Negative Intelligence*, 148–49; Walter Goodman, *The Committee: The Extraordinary Career of the House Committee on Un-American Activities*, 5.

35. *New York Times*, February 18, 1919; *New York Tribune*, February 18, 1919; Overman Committee, 2:2777. See also *New Republic*, March 15, 1919.

36. Overman Committee, 2:2777, 3:147.

37. This process would continue throughout the 1920s, to great effect. See Stanley Lemons, *The Woman Citizen: Social Feminism in the 1920s*; Weigand, *Red Feminism*, chap. 1; and Nielsen, *Un-American Womanhood*.

38. Overman Committee, 1:xxxi–ii.

39. *New York Times*, February 18, 1919.

40. Overman Committee, 3:224.

41. Ibid., 2:2780.

42. Ibid., 3:112, 136, 138.

43. Ibid., 358, 387.

44. *New York Times*, January 30, 1919.

45. *New York Times*, February 15, 1919.

46. *New York Times*, January 26, February 11, 1919.

47. *New York Times*, March 8, 1919.

48. Overman Committee, 3:826, 828.

49. Peter G. Filene, *Americans and the Soviet Experiment, 1917–1933*, 30–37.

50. *New York Times,* August 8, 1916.

51. Overman Committee, 3:502.

52. Ibid., 465, 532.

53. Ibid., 2:2761, 3:468.

54. Ibid., 621.

55. Ibid., 1:xlii.

56. *New York Times,* April 7, February 26, 1919.

57. Speech by Harry Winitsky, executive secretary of the Communist Party of New York, December 22, 1919, http://www.marxists.org.

58. J. Weinstein, *Decline of Socialism in America,* 243–46.

59. Draper, *Roots of American Communism,* 130, 137–38, 147, 190; Doug Rossinow, *Visions of Progress: The Left-Liberal Tradition in America,* 90; Ted Morgan, *A Covert Life: Jay Lovestone, Communist, Anti-Communist, and Spymaster,* 13.

60. James Weinstein, "Anti-war Sentiment and the Socialist Party, 1917–1918," 225–29.

61. *New York Tribune,* April 30, May 1, 1919.

62. *New York Tribune,* March 14, 1919.

63. *New York Tribune,* April 11, 1919.

64. *Atlanta Constitution,* April 29, 1919; Morgan, *Reds,* 69.

65. *Atlanta Constitution,* April 30, 1919; *Chicago Daily Tribune,* April 30, 1919.

66. *Chicago Daily Tribune,* May 1, 1919.

67. *Atlanta Constitution,* May 1, 1919.

68. *Atlanta Constitution,* May 2, 1919.

69. Dunn, *The Palmer Raids,* 16; *New York Times,* May 2, 1919.

70. Dunn, *The Palmer Raids,* 18, 17.

71. John Bruce Mitchell, "'Reds' in New York's Slums."

72. *New York Tribune,* May 8, 1919.

73. *New York Tribune,* April 30, May 1, 1919.

74. For a fuller exploration of the Lusk Committee investigations, see Todd Pfannestiel, *Rethinking the Red Scare: The Lusk Committee and New York's Crusade against Radicalism, 1919–1923.*

75. *New Republic,* July 9, 1919; *New York Times,* June 22, July 17, 22, 1919; Lawrence H. Chamberlain, *Loyalty and Legislative Action,* 32–34; Levin, *Political Hysteria in America,* 101.

76. *New York Times,* June 24, 1919.

77. T. E. Vadney, "The Politics of Repression: A Case Study of the Red Scare in New York"; Chamberlain, *Loyalty and Legislative Action,* 50–51.

78. *New York Tribune,* May 2, 1919.

79. Chamberlain, *Loyalty and Legislative Action,* 11–13, 16.

80. *New York Times,* June 13, 1919.

Chapter 3. Red Scare

1. John Higham, *Strangers in the Land: Patterns of American Nativism,* 223; Goldstein, *Political Repression in Modern America,* 140.

2. *Washington Post,* April 5, 1919.

3. *New York Tribune,* March 29, 1919.

4. Levin, *Political Hysteria in America,* 3; Goldstein, *Political Repression in Modern America,* 139.

5. Harold Underwood Faulkner, *American Economic History,* 586.

6. Henry A. Gemery, "Immigrants and Emigrants: International Migration and the US Labor Market in the Great Depression," in *Migration and the International Labor Market, 1850–1939,* edited by Timothy J. Hatton and Jeffrey G. Williamson, 175–202.

7. Kazin, *Populist Persuasion,* 64.

8. Charles W. Toth, "Samuel Gompers, Communism, and the Pan American Federation of Labor," 274.

9. Kazin, *Populist Persuasion,* 62, 70.

10. *New York Times,* January 8, 1919.

11. Coben, "Study in Nativism," 68; Philip Taft, *Organized Labor in American History,* 341; Luff, *Commonsense Anticommunism,* 4.

12. Harvey O'Connor, *Revolution in Seattle,* 1, 127; *New York Tribune,* January 20, 1919; Robert L. Friedheim, *The Seattle General Strike,* 26–27.

13. One story held that this information reached the Metal Trades Council, the labor union, when a Western Union messenger boy confused it with the Metal Trades Association and delivered the owners' private mail directly to the workers. O'Connor, *Revolution in Seattle,* 127.

14. Friedheim, *The Seattle General Strike,* 16–17.

15. *New Republic,* April 5, 1919.

16. Friedheim, *The Seattle General Strike,* 101.

17. Corey Robin, *The Reactionary Mind,* 5.

18. O'Connor, *Revolution in Seattle,* 138; *New York Times,* February 7, 1919.

19. *Chicago Daily Tribune,* February 7, 1919.

20. Taft, *Organized Labor in American History,* 342.

21. *New York Times,* February 8, 1919.

22. Ibid.

23. The deportees were also widely described by a sloppy press as Russians. In fact, according to former immigration commissioner Frederick Howe, one was a U.S. citizen, and twenty-seven were from England, Scotland, Ireland, Denmark, Norway, and Finland. The rest were from Poland, Russia, and Austro-Hungary. *Nation,* February 14, 1920.

24. *New York Times,* February 11, 9, 1919.

25. *New Republic,* November 12, 1919.

26. Robert K. Murray, "Communism and the Great Steel Strike of 1919," 447.

27. Higham, *Strangers in the Land,* 226; *Nation,* November 15, 1919; Murray, "Communism and the Great Steel Strike," 458.

28. *New York Times,* October 16, 8, 1919.

29. Taft, *Organized Labor in American History,* 358.

30. *New Republic,* November 12, 1919.

31. Samuel Gompers and William English Walling, *Out of Their Own Mouths: A Revelation and Indictment of Sovietism;* Samuel Gompers, *The Truth about Soviet Russia and Bolshevism.*

32. Richard L. Lyons, "The Boston Police Strike of 1919," 156, 160, 165.

33. Coeur d'Alene address, WWP, 63:216 (see chap. 1, n. 1).

34. See, for instance, William M. Dick, *Labor and Socialism in America: The Gompers Era*, 156–58.

35. Allen Wakstein, "The Origins of the Open Shop Movement, 1919–1920," 460–69.

36. William Pencak, *For God and Country: The American Legion, 1919–1941;* Thomas A. Rumer, *The American Legion: An Official History, 1919–1989.*

37. Rumer, *American Legion,* 44, 93.

38. Ibid., 94.

39. *New Republic,* April 14, 1920; *Atlanta Constitution,* November 13, 1919.

40. Richard Crossman, ed., *The God That Failed: Six Studies in Communism,* 26–42.

41. Morgan, *Reds,* 73; Michal R. Belknap, "Uncooperative Federalism: The Failure of the Bureau of Investigation's Intergovernmental Attack on Radicalism," 26. Interestingly, William J. Flynn, head of the bureau, stated that the "agitation is purely domestic and has no foreign connection, although there may be some foreigners active in it." *Atlanta Constitution,* June 19, 1919.

42. Gage, *Day Wall Street Exploded,* 178; Morgan, *Reds,* 75.

43. Frank J. Donner, *The Age of Surveillance: The Aims and Methods of America's Political Intelligence System,* 36.

44. The wartime American Protective League was also temporarily resurrected. APL veterans were given three-day commissions to help in the roundups. Jensen, *The Price of Vigilance,* 283.

45. Robert Strauss Feuerlicht, *America's Reign of Terror: World War One, the Red Scare, and the Palmer Raids,* 2.

46. Ibid.

47. Dunn, *The Palmer Raids,* 26–27, 50.

48. Estimates of the total number arrested vary. See Talbert, *Negative Intelligence,* 195; Stanley Coben, *A. Mitchell Palmer: Politician,* 227; Feuerlicht, *America's Reign of Terror,* 92; and Dunn, *The Palmer Raids,* 32.

49. Dunn, *The Palmer Raids,* 32–33, 40; Feuerlicht, *America's Reign of Terror,* 95.

50. *Nation,* February 14, 1920.

51. Feuerlicht, *America's Reign of Terror,* 3–5.

52. Dunn, *The Palmer Raids,* 40.

53. Feuerlicht, *America's Reign of Terror,* 6.

54. Ibid., 96.

55. Dunn, *The Palmer Raids,* 33–40; Schmidt, *Red Scare,* 293.

56. *Nation,* April 10, 1920.

57. Dunn, *The Palmer Raids,* 34–35.

58. Samuel Flagg Bemis, *A Diplomatic History of the United States,* 723.

59. Secretary of State Bainbridge Colby to Italian Ambassador, August 10, 1920, reprinted in Goldberg, *Documents of Soviet-American Relations,* vol. 2. See also Joan Hoff-Wilson, *Ideology and Economics: US Relations with the Soviet Union, 1918–1933,* 16.

60. Pfannestiel, "Soviet Bureau," 190–91.

61. *New York Times,* January 30, 1920.

62. *New York Times*, January 15, 1920.

63. U.S. Senate, *Russian Propaganda: Hearings before a Subcommittee of the Committee on Foreign Relations Pursuant to S. Res. 263, Directing the Committee on Foreign Relations to Investigate the Status and Activities of Ludwig C. A. K. Martens, Who Claimed to Be a Representative of the Russian Socialist Soviet Republic*, 53–59, 153–58, 172–77, 202, 216 (hereafter cited as Martens Investigation).

64. Hughes press release, March 21, 1923, in Goldberg, *Documents of Soviet-American Relations*, vol. 2; Warren I. Cohen, *Empire without Tears: America's Foreign Relations, 1921–1933*, 84; Hoff-Wilson, *Ideology and Economics*, 14; Douglas Little, "Antibolshevism and American Foreign Policy, 1919–1939: The Diplomacy of Self-Delusion," 378; Malbone W. Graham, "Russian-American Relations, 1917–1933: An Interpretation," 398.

65. Filene, *Americans and the Soviet Experiment*, 66.

66. Billings address, WWP, 63:174–75.

67. Des Moines address, WWP, 63:76–77.

68. George E. Mowry, *The California Progressives*; Richard Coke Lower, "Hiram Johnson: The Making of an Irreconcilable," 506; *New York Times*, July 4, September 12, 1919.

69. *Atlanta Constitution*, September 17, 1919.

70. Anti-Saloon League of America, *Proceedings of the Nineteenth National Convention*, 136–38.

71. Ralph Lord Roy, *Communism and the Churches*, 13.

72. *Atlanta Constitution*, February 23, 1919. See also *New York Times*, February 11, 1923.

73. Roy A. Haynes, *Prohibition Inside Out*, 176–77.

74. William D. Upshaw, *Bombshells for Wets and Reds: The Twin Devils of America*, 13.

75. Higham, *Strangers in the Land*, 300.

76. Ibid., 306, 309.

77. W. Chapin Huntington, *The Homesick Million: Russia-Out-of-Russia*, 19–20.

78. Richard Abraham, *Alexander Kerensky: The First Love of the Revolution*, 360.

79. Mark Raeff, *Russia Abroad: A Cultural History of the Russian Emigration, 1919–1939*, 5.

80. Norman L. Zucker, *George W. Norris: Gentle Knight of American Democracy*, 28.

81. Sean Dennis Cashman, *America in the Twenties and Thirties: The Olympian Age of Franklin Delano Roosevelt*, 47.

Chapter 4. Divided Loyalties

1. *Forum*, February 1920, 63173–80.

2. John D. Hicks, *Republican Ascendancy, 1921–1933*, 16; Woodrow C. Whitten, "Criminal Syndicalism and the Law in California, 1919–1927," 3–4.

3. *New York Times*, January 11, 1920, June 15, 1921, June 25, 1922; David H. Bennett, *The Party of Fear: From Nativist Movements to the New Right in American History*, 213.

4. *New York Times*, December 21, 1919.

5. Louis F. Post, *The Ethics of Democracy*, 323, 325.

6. Feuerlicht, *America's Reign of Terror*, 101.

7. Louis F. Post, *The Deportations Delirium of Nineteen-Twenty*.

8. U.S. Senate, *Charges of Illegal Practices of the Department of Justice: Hearings before a Subcommittee of the Committee on the Judiciary*, 6 (hereafter cited as Senate Palmer Investigation), 10.

9. Ibid., 195.

10. Gage, *Day Wall Street Exploded*, 181.

11. Chafee, "Free Speech in Wartime."

12. Peter H. Irons, "'Fighting Fair': Zechariah Chafee, Jr., the Department of Justice, and the 'Trial at the Harvard Club.'"

13. Gage, *Day Wall Street Exploded*, 239.

14. Allitt, *Conservatives*, 142.

15. *New Republic*, November 26, 1919.

16. Sidney Howard, *The Labor Spy*, 12, 178, 198–99; Heale, *American Anticommunism*, 75.

17. Higham, *Strangers in the Land*, 233.

18. David R. Colburn, "Governor Al Smith and the Red Scare, 1919–1920," 427, 433, 436, 443.

19. Ibid., 423–44; *New York Times*, January 18, 1920.

20. *Atlanta Constitution*, March 29, 1920; *New York Times*, April 18, 1920.

21. J. Leonard Bates, "The Teapot Dome Scandal and the Election of 1924," 305.

22. Earland I. Carson, "Franklin D. Roosevelt's Post-mortem of the 1928 Election," 298.

23. *New York Times*, June 15, October 18, 1919.

24. *New York Times*, January 19, April 6, 1920.

25. *New York Times*, April 2, 14, 1920.

26. *New York Times*, December 31, 1919, May 2, 1920.

27. *New York Times*, April 10, 1920.

28. George B. Lockwood, *Americanism*, 109–10, 117, 150–51.

29. LeRoy Ashby, *The Spearless Leader: Senator Borah and the Progressive Movement in the 1920s*, 111; Richard Lowitt, *George W. Norris: The Persistence of a Progressive, 1913–1933*, 143–44.

30. *New York Times*, December 21, 1919.

31. *New York Times*, March 28, April 8, 19, 30, 1920.

32. *New York Times*, June 7, 1920.

33. *New York Times*, June 13, 1920.

34. *New York Times*, June 18, 1920.

35. Sarasohn, "Insurgent Republicans," 259.

36. Ray Tucker and Frederick R. Barkley, *Sons of the Wild Jackass*, 4.

37. Clinton W. Gilbert, *You Takes Your Choice*, 164. See also Burton K. Wheeler, "Reminiscences," 92.

38. Margaret Leslie Davis, *Dark Side of Fortune: Triumph and Scandal in the Life of Oil Tycoon Edward L. Doheny*, 126; James M. Giglio, *H. M. Daugherty and the Politics of Expediency*, 129; Harry M. Daugherty, *The Inside Story of the Harding Tragedy*, 63.

39. Giglio, *Daugherty and the Politics of Expediency*, 168–70.

40. *Washington Post,* March 28, 1924.

41. Wheeler, "Reminiscences," 93; U.S. Senate, *Hearings before the Select Committee on the Investigation of the Attorney General* (hereafter cited as Daugherty Investigation), 1:75, 3:2901; Giglio, *Daugherty and the Politics of Expediency,* 171–74, 229, 232.

42. Daugherty, *Inside Story of the Harding Tragedy,* 287.

43. *Chicago Daily Tribune,* September 22, 1924; *Washington Post,* September 22, 1924; Daugherty, *Inside Story of the Harding Tragedy,* 168, 222; Burton K. Wheeler with Paul F. Healy, *Yankee from the West,* 255.

44. Giglio, *Daugherty and the Politics of Expediency,* 207, 214.

45. Wheeler, *Yankee from the West,* 229.

46. Daugherty Investigation, 3:2452.

47. Belknap, "Uncooperative Federalism," 31–38, 42.

48. *Chicago Daily Tribune,* July 5, 1924.

49. *Chicago Daily Tribune,* May 29, August 2, July 19, 1924; Fred E. Haynes, "The Significance of the Latest Third Party Movement," 180.

50. *Chicago Daily Tribune,* May 17, 1924; *Wall Street Journal,* June 5, 1924.

51. Wheeler, *Yankee from the West,* 254. See also *Chicago Daily Tribune,* February 2, March 9, November 22, 1923, September 15, 1924.

52. *Los Angeles Times,* October 18, 1924.

53. *Chicago Daily Tribune,* March 29, 1923, September 2, 1924.

54. *New Republic,* April 9, 1924.

55. Robert H. Ferrell and Howard H. Quint, eds., *The Talkative President: The Off-the-Record Press Conferences of Calvin Coolidge,* 19, 255–56.

56. Heale, *American Anticommunism,* 91.

57. *Chicago Daily Tribune,* November 6, 1924.

58. Ralph M. Easley (hereafter cited as RME) to J. D. Battle, November 24, 1934, Box 435, Folder 1, "Subversive Activities Files—General Correspondence, A–E," National Civic Federation Papers (hereafter cited as NCF Papers).

59. Fred Marvin quoted in Norman Hapgood, ed., *Professional Patriots,* 92–93; and *New Republic,* September 3, 1924.

60. Giglio, *Daugherty and the Politics of Expediency,* 228.

61. R. M. Whitney, *Reds in America,* 41.

62. RME to Alton B. Parker, May 25, 1920, Box 449, Folder 2, "Midday Club Luncheon, Brearley Plan, 1920 Socialism Inquiry," NCF Papers.

63. Christopher J. Cyphers, *The National Civic Federation and the Making of a New Liberalism, 1900–1915,* 6.

64. Taft, *Organized Labor in American History,* 228; Philip Taft, *The A. F. of L. in the Time of Gompers,* 226.

65. J. Weinstein, *Decline of Socialism in America,* 131.

66. Hapgood, *Professional Patriots,* 98.

67. *Washington Post,* July 26, 1925.

68. RME to Grover Whalen, August 28, 1933, Box 435, Folder 5, "Subversive Activities Files—General Correspondence, U–Z," NCF Papers.

69. Paul Murphy, "Sources and Nature of Intolerance in the 1920s," 66, 67.

70. Donner, *Age of Surveillance*, 43.

71. Rosswurm, *FBI and the Catholic Church*, 12–13, 18.

72. Cohen, *Empire without Tears*, 88.

73. Louis Gallagher, *Edmund A. Walsh, S.J.: A Biography*, 81; Edmund A. Walsh, *The Last Stand: An Interpretation of the Soviet Five-Year Plan*, 184.

74. *Los Angeles Times*, May 23, 1920.

75. *Los Angeles Times*, January 28, 1922; Edwin Layton, "The Better America Federation: A Case Study of Superpatriotism," 137, 146, 147.

76. Peter H. Amman, "A 'Dog in the Nighttime' Problem: American Fascism in the 1930s," 567.

77. *Los Angeles Times*, June 15, 26, 27, 30, 1923, November 17, 1924.

78. Fred R. Marvin, *Underground with the Reds*, 1, 21.

79. Jensen, *The Price of Vigilance*, 289.

80. Murphy, "Sources and Nature of Intolerance," 68. For a more comprehensive recent examination of the Klan, see Nancy MacLean, *Behind the Mask of Chivalry: The Making of the Second Ku Klux Klan*.

81. Pencak, *For God and Country*, 22, 26, 44.

82. Martin Zanger, "Politics of Confrontation: Upton Sinclair and the Launching of the ACLU in Southern California," 387.

83. Pencak, *For God and Country*, 84; Murphy, "Sources and Nature of Intolerance," 72–75.

84. *New Republic*, August 15, 1928, August 20, October 8, 1924.

85. *Nation*, July 20, 1927.

Chapter 5. Red Herrings

1. Eric Hobsbawm, *The Age of Extremes: The Short Twentieth Century, 1914–1991*, 58.

2. Preston, *Aliens and Dissenters*, 141–42; Harvey Klehr and John Earl Haynes, *The American Communist Movement: Storming Heaven Itself*, chap. 2.

3. J. Weinstein, *Decline of Socialism*, 255, 268; Irving Howe and Lewis Coser, *The American Communist Party: A Critical History (1919–1957)*, 70–72; Theodore Draper, *American Communism and Soviet Russia*, 27; *New York Times*, May 8, 1920.

4. Cohen, *Empire without Tears*, 84.

5. Constance Ashton Myers, *The Prophet's Army: Trotskyists in America, 1928–1941*.

6. James Gilbert Ryan, *Earl Browder: The Failure of American Communism*, 47.

7. *New York Times*, July 9, 1929, June 27, 1930.

8. *New York Times*, August 15, September 8, October 1, 1929.

9. J. Weinstein, *Decline of Socialism*, 335.

10. Antonio Gramsci, "Freedom and Discipline," in *Pre-prison Writings*, 26.

11. Klehr, Haynes, and Anderson, *Soviet World of American Communism*, app. B, 334–35.

12. Harvey Klehr, *The Heyday of American Communism: The Depression Decade*, 4.

13. Joseph R. Starobin, *American Communism in Crisis, 1943–1957*, 43.

14. "Browder Interview III," June 16, 1953, Box 01, Folder 03, Browder Interviews, Theodore Draper Papers, 3.

15. Klehr and Haynes, *American Communist Movement*, 52–53; "Browder Interview III," June 16, 1953, Box 01, Folder 03, Browder Interviews, Draper Papers, 3.

16. Ryan, *Earl Browder*, 45.

17. *New York Times*, March 4, 1930.

18. Little, "Antibolshevism and American Foreign Policy," 380; Evan E. Young, "The Attitude of the United States Government Toward the Soviet Régime," 75.

19. Claudius O. Johnson, *Borah of Idaho*, 354; William Appleman Williams, *The Tragedy of American Diplomacy*, 124.

20. Reinhard H. Luthin, "Smith Wildman Brookhart of Iowa: Insurgent Agrarian Politician," 191.

21. Wheeler, *Yankee from the West*, 200–202.

22. *Chicago Daily Tribune*, September 12, 1923.

23. Filene argues, however, that Borah's knowledge of Russia and strategic choices limited his success on the Senate Foreign Relations Committee. Filene, *Americans and the Soviet Experiment*, 91–92.

24. Cohen, *Empire without Tears*, 87.

25. James D. Mooney, vice president of General Motors, speech reported in *Economic Review of the Soviet Union* 6, no. 10 (1931), reprinted in *From Isolation to Containment, 1921–1952: Three Decades of American Foreign Policy from Harding to Truman*, edited by Richard D. Challener, 36.

26. Walter Lippmann was the only voice of dissent. Robert D. Schulzinger, *The Wise Men of Foreign Affairs: The History of the Council of Foreign Relations*, 15.

27. *Washington Post*, November 25, 1930.

28. Schulzinger, *Wise Men of Foreign Affairs*, 20.

29. George D. Beelen, "The Harding Administration and Mexico: Diplomacy by Economic Persuasion," 177.

30. Supporters included William F. Buckley, father of the postwar conservative intellectual; Edward L. Doheny, the principal source of bribes during the Teapot Dome affair; conservative Republicans such as Henry Cabot Lodge, Albert Fall, and Overman Committee member William Henry King; and Wilson Democrat veterans of the wartime loyalty campaigns, including former secretary of state Robert Lansing, former secretary of the treasury William Gibbs McAdoo, former attorney general Thomas Watt Gregory, and former secretary of the interior Franklin Lane. McAdoo and Gregory were already on retainer. Lane would within a year become vice president of one of Doheny's many oil companies. And Fall's involvement with Doheny would become clear with the Teapot Dome scandal. Clifford W. Trow, "Woodrow Wilson and the Mexican Interventionist Movement of 1919," 54, 64.

31. Daniela Spenser, *The Impossible Triangle: Mexico, Soviet Russia, and the United States in the 1920s*, ix.

32. Wheeler, *Yankee from the West*, 263.

33. Richard V. Salisbury, "Mexico, the United States, and the 1926–1927 Nicaraguan Crisis," 320.

34. Spenser, *Impossible Triangle*, 78, 84; W. Dirk Raat and William H. Beezley, eds., *Twentieth Century Mexico*, 59–60; Little, "Antibolshevism and American Foreign Policy," 381.

35. Testimony of Arthur Bliss Lane in U.S. Senate, *Hearings before a Special Committee to Investigate Propaganda or Money Alleged to Have Been Used by Foreign Governments to Influence United States Senators* (hereafter cited as Reed Committee), pt. 5, 344; "Walter Le Mat," Box 443, Folder 16, NCF Papers; interview with Walter Le Mat, April 16, 1931, ibid.; notes, "Diaries of Gaston Means, 1931 Jan–Aug," Box 445, Folder 5, NCF Papers.

36. Spenser, *Impossible Triangle*, 26–27.

37. On Hearst documents, see testimony of Robert H. Murray and David E. Smiley, Reed Committee, pt. 2; Mrs. Fremont Older, *William Randolph Hearst: American*, 434; Ian Mugridge, *The View from Xanadu: William Randolph Hearst and United States Foreign Policy*, 137. On the German conspiracy, see *Atlanta Constitution*, March 3, 1929; and *New York Times*, March 3, 1930, March 4, 5, 6, July 2, 4, 11, 12, 1929.

38. Quoted in Ashby, *Spearless Leader*, 210; Spenser, *Impossible Triangle*, 130; Marian C. McKenna, *Borah*, 231.

39. Spenser, *Impossible Triangle*, 84.

40. Reed Committee, 16; Patrick J. Maney, *"Young Bob" La Follette: A Biography of Robert M. La Follette, Jr., 1895–1953*, 51.

41. Lowitt, *George W. Norris*, 370–71; George W. Norris, *Fighting Liberal: The Autobiography of George W. Norris*, 375.

42. *Nation*, June 3, 1931.

43. McKenna, *Borah*, 295.

44. Matthew Woll to Herbert Hoover, May 14, 1929, "Series X. Subversive Activities Files, General Correspondence F–L," Box 435, Folder 2, NCF Papers.

45. Ralph M. Easley (hereafter cited as RME) to General Samuel McRoberts, June 30, 1930, Box 437, Folder 6, NCF Papers.

46. Statement by Gertrude Beeks Easley, June 22, 1932, "Diaries of Gaston Means, 1932 Apr–Dec," Box 446, Folder 4, NCF Papers.

47. See detailed diary, Box 445, Folder 3, NCF Papers.

48. Lucien C. Wheeler (hereafter cited as LCW) to A. J. Bulwinkle, December 11, 1929, "Gastonia Trial—Correspondence 1929," Box 441, Folder 6, NCF Papers. See also correspondence between Easley and Means, Box 445, Folder 3, NCF Papers.

49. LCW to RME, October 12, 1929, Box 441, Folder 6, NCF Papers; Gertrude Beeks Easley (hereafter cited as GBE) to C. C. Huitt, November 28, 1931, "Personal Correspondence, Gertrude Beeks Easley, 1930–1949," Folder n.d., NCF Papers; Edwin P. Hoyt, *Spectacular Rogue: Gaston B. Means*, 223.

50. LCW to RME, January 5, 1930; RME to LCW, January 6, 1930; LCW to RME, January 28, 1930; RME to LCW, January 29, 1930, Box 441, Folder 6, NCF Papers.

51. RME to Edmund A. Walsh (hereafter cited as EAW), February 1, 1930, "OGPU, Means and Weitz [sic] Confidential, Correspondence, J–W," Box 450, Folder 4, NCF Papers.

52. See "Subversive Activities Files—Amtorg Trading Corp." La Salle Report, Box 436, Folder 6, NCF Papers.

53. See extensive coverage in *New York Times* from March 7 to March 9, 1939. See also Herbert Mitgang, *Once upon a Time in New York: Jimmy Walker, Franklin Roosevelt, and the Last Great Battle of the Jazz Age*, 20; Grover Whalen, *Mr. New York*, 156; Ryan, *Earl Browder*, 40.

54. *New York Times,* March 19, 25, 23, 1930.

55. *New York Times,* May 10, 1930. Easley said nothing about their true origin. "I realized, of course," Easley wrote to Hamilton Fish, "that I must not weaken Whalen's position because he had put them out as if he had secured them." RME to Hamilton Fish (hereafter cited as HF), September 19, 1930, "OGPU, Means and Weitz [*sic*] Confidential, Correspondence E–G," Box 450, Folder 1, NCF Papers.

56. Anthony C. Troncone, "Hamilton Fish Sr. and the Politics of American Nationalism, 1912–1945," 134.

57. *New York Times,* May 23, 1930.

58. Goodman, *Committee,* 8.

59. *New York Times,* July 1, 5, August 29, September 5, 19, 29, November 1, 1929.

60. Goodman, *Committee,* 6. There has been some speculation that the documents were planted by the Soviet Union as a measure to embarrass the American government, but this view has been persuasively discredited. See Klehr, Haynes, and Firsov, *Secret World of American Communism,* 126; Klehr, Haynes, and Vassiliev, *Spies,* 161–62.

61. Troncone, "Hamilton Fish Sr.," 136. In an unsent mea culpa to Fish, Easley later held himself "entirely responsible" for the affair.

62. Ibid., 140.

63. Fish and Easley collaborated closely in organizing the hearings. RME to Mrs. William Sherman Walker, May 16, 1930, Box 436, Folder 6, NCF Papers; RME to HF, June 2, 1930, "Fish Investigating Committee," Box 441, Folder 2, NCF Papers; U.S. House of Representatives, *Hearings: Investigation of Communist Propaganda,* pt. 3, 2:3–47 (hereafter cited as Fish Committee).

64. Fish Committee, pt. 1, 4:206–18; pt. 3, vol. 3; pt. 3, 4:173–88.

65. *New York Times,* May 24, July 28, 1930.

66. *New Republic,* July 23, 1930.

67. *New York Times,* July 14, 15, 1930.

68. Notes of meeting, August 21, 1930, "Diaries of Gaston Means, 1930," Box 445, Folder 4, NCF Papers.

69. RME to Herbert Hoover, September 1931, Box 437, Folder 6, NCF Papers.

70. RME to Gaston B. Means, August 8, 1930, "[Gaston] Means Affair, Correspondence," Box 445, Folder 1, NCF Papers.

71. The Bureau of Investigation had declined an offer to participate. Troncone, "Hamilton Fish Sr.," 164.

72. RME to Herbert Hoover, September 1931, Box 437, Folder 6, NCF Papers.

73. RME interview with M. [Means], June 23, 1931, Box 445, Folder 5, NCF Papers.

74. Powers, *Not without Honor,* 90. See also Richard Kay Hanks, "Hamilton Fish and American Isolationism, 1920–1944," 34.

75. RME to HF, November 25, 1930, Box 437, Folder 6, NCF Papers.

76. RME interview with M. [Means], June 23, 1931, Box 445, Folder 5, NCF Papers.

77. Notes of conversation, August 4, 1931, ibid.

78. RME to HF, June 22, 1931, Box 437, Folder 6, NCF Papers.

79. HF to Woll, July 6, 1931, Box 445, Folder 5, NCF Papers.

80. Richard Current, "Hamilton Fish: Crusading Isolationist," in *Public Men in and out of Office,* edited by John Thomas Salter, 215.

81. *New Republic,* January 28, 1931.

82. Goodman, *Committee,* 12.

83. RME to Finley J. Shepard, May 27, 1938, Box 488, Folder 2, NCF Papers.

84. GBE to Mrs. Finley J. Shepard, August 19, 1932, "German Propaganda Samples," Box 442, Folder 7, NCF Papers; RME to Wheeler P. Bloodgood, October 17, 1930, "OGPU, Means & Weitz [*sic*] Confidential, Correspondence Bl–D," Box 449, Folder 10, NCF Papers; A. H. Laidlow to RME, August 16, 1929, Box 450, Folder 4, NCF Papers; Maude Wetmore to RME, October 1, 1929, March 2, 1930, Box 488, Folder 2, NCF Papers; RME to John Hays Hammond, February 13, 1929; RME to Hammond, April 4, 1929, "OGPU, Means and Weitz [*sic*] Confidential, Correspondence H–I," Box 450, Folder 2, NCF Papers. For the considerable pressure applied by the Easleys to potential donors, see "Personal Correspondence, GBE, 1917–1929," Box 495, Folder 5, NCF Papers; and "Personal Correspondence, GBE, 1920–1929," Box 495, Folder 8, NCF Papers.

85. Hoyt, *Spectacular Rogue,* 290. See also "Diaries of Gaston Means, 1931 Sep," Box 446, Folder 1, NCF Papers. Means publicly denied the claims about the Shepards when they reached the press. *Washington Post,* May 12, 1932; *New York Times,* May 12, 1932.

86. RME to Mrs. Finley J. Shepard, April 15, 1933, Box 445, Folder 1, NCF Papers.

87. To minimize the damage to himself and his anonymous donors, Easley lodged no criminal complaint against Means, although he did manage to pressure the con man's wife into returning around twenty thousand dollars. In a later article on Means, J. Edgar Hoover discussed the investigation but notably did not mention Easley. J. Edgar Hoover and Courtney Ryler Cooper, "The Amazing Mr. Means."

88. RME to Samuel McRoberts, June 30, 1930, Box 437, Folder 6, NCF Papers.

89. Hoyt, *Spectacular Rogue,* 48; *New York Times,* September 9, 13, 19, November 29, December 17, 1917.

90. Hoyt, *Spectacular Rogue,* 115–27. See also May Dixon Thacker, *The Strange Death of President Harding: From the Diaries of Gaston B. Means;* and Robert H. Ferrell, *The Strange Deaths of Warren G. Harding.*

91. Hoyt, *Spectacular Rogue,* 9.

92. RME to J. Kemp Bartlett, November 26, 1931, Box 437, Folder 6, NCF Papers.

93. RME to Charles L. Edgar, October 30, 1931, ibid.

94. Hoyt, *Spectacular Rogue,* 285.

95. Statement by GBE, June 22, 1932, Box 446, Folder 4, NCF Papers.

96. For more on Wheeler, see M. Davis, *Dark Side of Fortune,* 232.

97. Notes, June 21, 1932, Box 443, Folder 15, NCF Papers.

98. RME to Albert K. Stebbins, October 27, 1931, Box 437, Folder 6, NCF Papers; "Montgomery" [RME] to "M." [Means], March 17, 1932, Box 445, Folder 1, NCF Papers; Hoyt, *Spectacular Rogue,* 299.

99. Memorandum, July 26, 1938, Box 493, Folder 20, NCF Papers.

100. *New York Times,* September 16, 1934.

101. *New York Times,* August 11, 1936, December 13, 1938.

102. Hoover and Cooper, "The Amazing Mr. Means."

103. Ibid.

104. Dallek, *Roosevelt and American Foreign Policy,* 79–80.

105. Bemis, *Diplomatic History of the United States*, 725.

106. Dallek, *Roosevelt and American Foreign Policy*, 81.

107. Litvinov organized a special meeting to reassure American Communists that nothing would change. "It's a scrap of paper which will soon be forgotten in the realities of Soviet-American relations," he said. Gary Kern, *A Death in Washington: Walter G. Krivitsky and the Stalin Terror*, 42.

108. For instance, Graham, "Russian-American Relations," 409.

Chapter 6. Subversive Capitalism

1. Wayne Lewchuck, "Fordism and the Moving Assembly Line: The British and American Experience, 1895–1930," in *On the Line: Essays in the History of Auto Work*, by Nelson Lichtenstein and Stephen Meyer III; Allan Nevins, *Ford: The Times, the Man, the Company*; Stephen Meyer III, *The Five Dollar Day: Labor Management and Social Control in the Ford Motor Company, 1908–1921*.

2. Henry Ford, in collaboration with Samuel Crowther, *My Life and Work*, 113.

3. Nevins, *Ford*, 554.

4. Ford, *My Life and Work*, 129; Lewchuck, "Fordism and the Moving Assembly Line," 23.

5. Lewchuck, "Fordism and the Moving Assembly Line," 17, 19; Frank Marquart, *An Auto Worker's Journal: The UAW from Crusade to One-Party Union*, 9, 14.

6. David L. Lewis, *The Public Image of Henry Ford: An American Folk Hero and His Company*, 72, 535.

7. Meyer, *Five Dollar Day*, 1.

8. James D. Norris, *Advertising and the Transformation of American Society, 1865–1920*, 165.

9. Albert Lee, *Henry Ford and the Jews*, 3.

10. Nevins, *Ford*, 558.

11. Meyer, *Five Dollar Day*, 129–30.

12. Ford, *My Life and Work*, 127.

13. Quoted in William Adams Simonds, *Henry Ford: A Biography*, 132.

14. Ford, *My Life and Work*, 262.

15. Meyer, *Five Dollar Day*, 114, 183.

16. Ibid., 40.

17. "Ford Motor Co. * Labor * Radical and Union Activity * 1919"; "Labor * Espionage—Agencies Active in Detroit—1919," Greenleaf Notes, Box 6, Accession 81, Allan Nevins Research Papers.

18. Roger Keeran, *The Communist Party and the Auto Workers Union*, 34.

19. Ford, *My Life and Work*, 170.

20. Bennett and Sorensen both claimed credit for closing the Sociological Department. Harry Bennett, as told to Paul Marcus, *We Never Called Him Henry*, 33; Leo D. Ribuffo, *Right Center Left: Essays in American History*, 75; W. C. Klann, "Reminiscences," 155.

21. Arthur J. Kuhn, *GM Passes Ford, 1918–1938: Designing the General Motors Performance-Control System*, 257.

22. John McCarten, "The Little Man in Henry Ford's Basement—Part I," 9.

23. David L. Lewis, *Detroit Magazine,* June 18, 1972.

24. H. Bennett, *We Never Called Him Henry,* 65; Keith Sward, *The Legend of Henry Ford,* 297.

25. H. Bennett, *We Never Called Him Henry,* 68.

26. Klann, "Reminiscences," 103; A. M. Wibel, "Reminiscences," 351; H. Bennett, *We Never Called Him Henry,* 68; Larry Engelman, *Intemperance: The Lost War against Liquor,* 146; Sward, *Legend of Henry Ford,* 300.

27. Irving R. Bacon, "Reminiscences," 85–86.

28. H. S. Ablewhite, "Reminiscences," 68; McCarten, "Little Man in Henry Ford's Basement," 200.

29. McCarten, "Little Man in Henry Ford's Basement," 201.

30. John H. O'Brien, "Henry Ford's Commander in Chief," 70.

31. McCarten, "Little Man in Henry Ford's Basement," 200; Ford R. Bryan, *Henry's Lieutenants,* 30.

32. "Labor * IWW in Detroit Area—1919–1920"; "Labor * Union Wrecking by Labor Spies—1919—IAM #82," Greenleaf Notes, Box 6, Nevins Research Papers.

33. "Labor * Radicals * Socialist Party in Detroit—1919–1920," ibid.

34. "Labor * Radicals * Socialist Party Branches in Detroit—1919–1920," ibid.

35. "Ford Motor Co. * Labor * Attitude toward 1919 Coal and Steel Strikes and Wadsworth"; "Labor * Radicals * Socialist Party in Detroit—1919–1920," ibid.

36. Nevins, *Ford,* 452.

37. Federico Bucci, *Albert Kahn: Architect of Ford,* 43.

38. Simonds, *Henry Ford: A Biography,* 104; Nevins, *Ford,* 455.

39. Albert Kahn, speech on the twentieth anniversary of the American Concrete Institute (1924?), Albert Kahn Papers, 8–9.

40. Ford, *My Life and Work,* 17.

41. Booton Herndon, *Ford: An Unconventional Biography of the Two Henry Fords and Their Times,* 155.

42. Ford, *My Life and Work,* 5, 99–100, 262.

43. Quoted in Nevins, *Ford,* 494.

44. Simonds, *Henry Ford: A Biography,* 6.

45. Engelman, *Intemperance,* 6; *New York Times,* July 9, 1916, October 19, 1923.

46. *New York Times,* June 29, 1923.

47. *New York Times,* February 10, 1927, June 21, 1928.

48. *New York Times,* July 25, 1929.

49. Antonio Gramsci, *Prison Notebooks,* 2:218. On Ford's Puritanical streak, see H. Bennett, *We Never Called Him Henry,* 21.

50. Gramsci, *Prison Notebooks,* 2:217.

51. Perhaps unsurprisingly, given its subsequent notoriousness, many differing accounts of the origins of the anti-Semitic campaign can be found. See Lee, *Ford and the Jews,* 18; Ribuffo, *Right Center Left,* 77; W. J. Cameron, "Reminiscences," 10.

52. Lee, *Ford and the Jews,* 28.

53. It seems Ford failed to equate his evangelical anti-Semitism with hatred for Albert Kahn, who, for his part, never expressed disapproval in return. Reinhold Niebuhr was

scathing about Ford's architect, who, he reported, said yes all the time so as not to upset his "lucrative position." Lee, *Ford and the Jews*, 33; Ford, *My Life and Work*, 251–52; Reinhold Niebuhr, "Reminiscences," 49.

54. Lee, *Ford and the Jews*, 14, 24–25, 29, 47, 59.

55. Henry Ford, in collaboration with Samuel Crowther, *Today and Tomorrow*, 24.

56. Ford, *My Life and Work*, 250.

57. Ribuffo, *Right Center Left*, 55.

58. John Dos Passos, *U.S.A.*, 773.

59. Ford, *My Life and Work*, 251.

60. Ribuffo, *Right Center Left*, 88.

61. Cameron, "Reminiscences," 15.

62. Henry Ford, *The International Jew*, 215, 216.

63. *Dearborn Independent*, August 15, 1925.

64. Ribuffo, *Right Center Left*, 90.

65. Lee, *Ford and the Jews*, 64–70.

66. Ribuffo, *Right Center Left*, 105.

67. H. Bennett, *We Never Called Him Henry*, 18.

68. The deal amounted to only a few hundred tractors, in the end. Edward Jay Epstein, *Dossier: The Secret History of Armand Hammer*, 74.

69. With Henry Ford as a potential customer, Hammer "was able to sign up scores of other American companies." Hammer claimed Ford underwent a Pauline conversion—"from a frothing, anti-Bolshevik into a wise advocate of trade with the Soviet Union." Ibid., 88; Joseph Finder, *Red Curtain*, 31.

70. *Dearborn Independent*, January 11, February 1, 1919.

71. *Dearborn Independent*, February 15, 1919.

72. Cameron, "Reminiscences," 26.

73. *Dearborn Independent*, June 13, 1925.

74. *Dearborn Independent*, October 26, 1926, 11.

75. *Dearborn Independent*, November 6, 1926, 10.

76. Finder, *Red Curtain*, 51; Mira Wilkins and Frank Earnest Hill, *American Business Abroad: Ford on Six Continents*, 216.

77. Lichtenstein and Meyer, *On the Line*, 3.

78. Wilkins and Hill, *American Business Abroad*, 220.

79. In the end, more than five hundred designs by Kahn and his company were used in the country, some reproduced in their entirety many times over. Ibid., 90.

80. Ibid., 222.

81. Albert Kahn, speech to Cleveland Engineering Society, December 16, 1930, Kahn Papers.

82. Wilkins and Hill, *American Business Abroad*, 217.

83. Bucci, *Albert Kahn*, 90.

84. Fish Committee, pt. 1, 4:59–79; pt. 5, 1:10–26, 29–39, 78–81, 108, 180–96 (see chap. 5, n. 63).

85. Walsh, *Last Stand*, 147.

86. *Chicago Daily Tribune*, September 25, 1930; *New York Times*, July 26, August 23, 1930; *Chicago Daily Tribune*, August 24, 1930; *Washington Post*, August 25, 1930.

87. Fish Committee, pt. 1, 4:23, 5:39; pt. 3, 3:109–264, 4:78–173.

88. Marquart, *Auto Worker's Journal,* 33.

89. Keeran, *Communist Party and the Auto Workers Union,* 28, 59.

90. Sidney Fine, *The Automobile under the Blue Eagle: Labor, Management, and the Automobile Manufacturing Code,* 5.

91. Keeran, *Communist Party and the Auto Workers Union,* 41.

92. Peter Gavrilovich and Bill McGraw, *Detroit Almanac,* 45.

93. *Detroit Times,* April 6, 1933.

94. Gavrilovich and McGraw, *Detroit Almanac,* 289.

95. Lichtenstein and Meyer, *On the Line,* 1.

96. Thomas King, "Employers' Strategies in the Detroit Labor Market, 1900–1929," in ibid., 43.

97. See chart 2, "The Dynamics of Automobile Demand," in *Auto Industry: Prices,* Joe Brown Collection, 8.

98. Fine, *Automobile under the Blue Eagle,* 20.

99. Keeran, *Communist Party and the Auto Workers Union,* 62.

100. Simonds, *Henry Ford: A Biography,* 226.

101. Keeran, *Communist Party and the Auto Workers Union,* 80.

102. Simonds, *Henry Ford: A Biography,* 192.

103. Keeran, *Communist Party and the Auto Workers Union,* 72–73.

104. Sward, *Legend of Henry Ford,* 238.

105. Keeran, *Communist Party and the Auto Workers Union,* 73.

106. Simonds, *Henry Ford: A Biography,* 239, 240.

107. Charles E. Coughlin, *Father Coughlin's Radio Discourses, 1931–1932,* 227.

108. Simonds, *Henry Ford: A Biography,* 193.

109. See "Edsel Ford: Artistic Industrialist," *Dearborn Herald,* 8, no. 2 (1979); Linda Bank Downs, *Diego Rivera: The Detroit Industry Murals.*

110. Diego Rivera, *My Art, My Life: An Autobiography,* 112–13, 115.

111. *Detroit Free Press,* March 17, 1933.

112. Alex Goodall, "The Battle of Detroit and Anticommunism in the Depression Era."

113. Allitt, *Conservatives,* 137.

114. David E. Nye, *Henry Ford, "Ignorant Idealist,"* 3.

Chapter 7. Troubled Spirits

1. George Sylvester Viereck, "Henry Ford and Reincarnation."

2. E. L. Doctorow, *Ragtime,* 116.

3. *Detroit Free Press,* March 17, 1919 (emphasis added).

4. Ford, *My Life and Work,* 9 (emphasis added).

5. *New York Times,* July 25, 1929.

6. John Abernathy Smith, "Ecclesiastical Politics and the Founding of the Federal Council of Churches," 365; Paul A. Carter, *The Decline and Revival of the Social Gospel: Social and Political Liberalism in American Protestant Churches, 1920–1940,* 60.

7. George M. Marsden, *Fundamentalism and American Culture: The Shaping of Twentieth-Century Evangelicalism, 1870–1925,* 206–7.

8. Ibid., 142, 147.

9. Ferenc Morton Szasz, *The Divided Mind of Protestant America, 1880–1930*, 86; Joel A. Carpenter, *Revive Us Again: The Reawakening of American Fundamentalism*, 7.

10. Szasz, *Divided Mind of Protestant America*, 86.

11. Marsden, *Fundamentalism and American Culture*, 66.

12. J. Gresham Machen, *Christianity and Liberalism*, 2, 10–11.

13. Marsden, *Fundamentalism and American Culture*, 143.

14. David O. Beale, *In Pursuit of Purity: American Fundamentalism since 1850*, 106.

15. Carter, *Decline and Revival of the Social Gospel*, 92.

16. Robert Moats Miller, *American Protestantism and Social Issues, 1919–1939*, 42–43; Carter, *Decline and Revival of the Social Gospel*, 26; Miller, *American Protestantism and Social Issues*, 188–93; Commission of Inquiry, Interchurch World Movement, *Report on the Steel Strike of 1919*, 27–28, 33, 43.

17. William Z. Foster, *The Great Steel Strike and Its Lessons*, i.

18. *New York Times*, May 3, 1920.

19. E. Victor Bigelow, *Mistakes of the Interchurch Steel Report, Address by Rev. E. Victor Bigelow, Minister South Church, Andover, MA, November 22, 1920, before Boston Ministers Meeting, Pilgrim Hall*, 16, 22.

20. Machen, *Christianity and Liberalism*, 13–14n2, 65; C. Allyn Russell, *Voices of American Fundamentalism: Seven Biographical Studies*, 150.

21. Roy, *Communism and the Churches*, 9. The only American bishop ever to hold membership in the Communist Party was Bishop William Montgomery Brown, an eccentric who styled himself *Episcopus in partibus Bolshevikium et Infidelium*. "Bad" Bishop Brown claimed his mission was to "banish Gods from skies and capitalists from earth" by integrating Marx and Darwin into a reformed Christianity. He was tried for heresy and deposed by the Episcopal order in 1925. William Montgomery Brown, *Communism and Christianity*, 16; Roy, *Communism and the Churches*, 9, 21–28; Marsden, *Fundamentalism and American Culture*, 178.

22. *New York Times*, July 15, 1920.

23. *New York Times*, March 22, 1920.

24. Marshall Olds, *Analysis of the Interchurch World Movement Report on the Steel Strike*, 209; *New York Times*, August 22, 1920.

25. *Detroit Free Press*, February 17, 1919.

26. Carter, *Decline and Revival of the Social Gospel*, 21; Szasz, *Divided Mind of Protestant America*, 89; William Vance Trollinger, *God's Empire: William Bell Riley and Midwestern Fundamentalism*, 53.

27. Dwight Wilson, *Armageddon Now! The Premillennarian Response to Russia and Israel since 1917*, 55.

28. Arno Clemens Gaebelein, *The Conflict of the Ages: The Mystery of Lawlessness; Its Origin, Historic Development, and Coming Defeat*, 103.

29. Roy, *Communism and the Churches*, 43.

30. Gaebelein, *Conflict of the Ages*, 144; D. Wilson, *Armageddon Now!*, 16–17; Marsden, *Fundamentalism and American Culture*, 144.

31. Robert Mapes Anderson, *Visions of the Disinherited: The Making of American Pentecostalism*, 84, 215–16.

32. For instance, see the wry remark in Arno Clemens Gaebelein, *Half a Century: The Autobiography of a Servant*, 91.

33. Bruce Barton, *The Man Nobody Knows*, 22, 23, 87, 104; Miller, *American Protestantism and Social Issues*, 26.

34. Miller, *American Protestantism and Social Issues*, 24.

35. Trollinger, *God's Empire*, 43.

36. Szasz, *Divided Mind of Protestant America*, 93; Barry Hankins, *God's Rascal: J. Frank Norris and the Beginnings of Southern Fundamentalism*, 4.

37. Trollinger, *God's Empire*, 42.

38. *New Republic*, August 15, 1928

39. Carpenter, *Revive Us Again*, xi, 13.

40. Elizabeth Fones-Wolf and Ken Fones-Wolf, "Lending a Hand to Labor: James Myers and the Federal Council of Churches, 1926–1947," 69n20, 70–71.

41. June Bingham, *Courage to Change: An Introduction to the Life and Thought of Reinhold Niebuhr*, 129.

42. Reinhold Niebuhr, *Leaves from the Notebook of a Tamed Cynic*, 99, 180. Estimates suggest perhaps forty thousand employees were sacked, with a further twenty thousand affected upstream in the production process. Kuhn, *GM Passes Ford*, 305.

43. Niebuhr, "Reminiscences," 85.

44. Ibid., 28–29, 85.

45. Carter, *Decline and Revival of the Social Gospel*, 155, 159.

46. Keeran, *Communist Party and the Auto Workers Union*, 42, 90; Carter, *Decline and Revival of the Social Gospel*, 49, 65, 127, 133; Szasz, *Divided Mind of Protestant America*, 94.

47. *Detroit Labor News*, May 10, 1929.

48. Carter, *Decline and Revival of the Social Gospel*, 147.

49. Ibid., 151.

50. Harry F. Ward, *In Place of Profit: Social Incentives in the Soviet Union*, 18, 19, 25.

51. Miller, *American Protestantism and Social Issues*, 70, 98.

52. Ibid., 64.

53. Carter, *Decline and Revival of the Social Gospel*, 203.

54. *Detroit Free Press*, March 19, 1919.

55. John Patrick Diggins, "American Catholics and Italian Fascism," 55.

56. Wilson D. Miscamble, "The Limits of Catholic Antifascism: The Case of John A. Ryan," 531–32.

57. Rosswurm, *FBI and the Catholic Church*, 1–3.

58. Ronald W. Schatz, "American Labor and the Catholic Church, 1919–1950," 180.

59. Brinkley, *Voices of Protest*, 82. See also Sheldon Marcus, *Father Coughlin: The Tumultuous Life of the Priest of the Little Flower*.

60. Charles E. Coughlin, *A Series of Lectures on Social Justice, April 1936*, 64. On Coughlin and Mexico, see Geoffrey S. Smith, *To Save a Nation: American Countersubversives, the New Deal, and the Coming of World War II*, 30.

61. Charles E. Coughlin, *Father Coughlin's Radio Sermons Complete*, 156, 238, 246; Charles E. Coughlin, *A Series of Lectures on Social Justice, March 1935*, 124; *Social Justice*, March 13, 1936; Ruth Mugglebee, *Father Coughlin and the Shrine of the Little Flower*, 223.

62. See testimony of Charles E. Coughlin before the Fish Committee (see chap. 5, n. 63).

63. Mugglebee, *Coughlin and the Shrine of the Little Flower*, 208.

64. Kazin, *Populist Persuasion*, 113.

65. Coughlin, *Father Coughlin's Radio Discourses*, 39.

66. Engelman, *Intemperance*, xii.

67. *New York Times*, December 14, 1919.

68. Engelman, *Intemperance*, 140–43.

69. Ibid., 77–78, 126, 136.

70. Engelman, *Intemperance*, 6, 201–2; *New York Times*, November 3, July 3, 1919; *Detroit Free Press*, July 4, 11, 1919.

71. *Detroit Free Press*, July 4, 11, 1919.

72. For his stance, the senator was "virtually excommunicated by the Methodist church." *New York Times*, July 28, 1923.

73. George Wolfskill, *The Revolt of the Conservatives: A History of the American Liberty League, 1934–1940*, 46.

74. *New York Times*, September 24, 1931.

75. *New York Times*, September 21, 1931.

76. *New York Times*, September 22, 25, 1931.

77. *New York Times*, September 25, 1931.

78. *Washington Post*, September 29, 1931.

79. Coughlin, *Father Coughlin's Radio Discourses*, 34, 223.

Chapter 8. American Fascism

1. Fine, *Automobile under the Blue Eagle*, 36.

2. Oz Frankel, "Whatever Happened to 'Red Emma'? Emma Goldman, from Alien Rebel to American Icon," 909–911.

3. Heale, *American Anticommunism*, 101.

4. Richard H. Pells, *Radical Visions and American Dreams: Culture and Social Thought in the Depression Years*, 65.

5. Von Mohrenschildt, "Lincoln Steffens and the Bolshevik Revolution," 38–39.

6. Pells, *Radical Visions and American Dreams*, 76.

7. Roger Baldwin, "Freedom in the US and USSR" (original emphasis removed).

8. See, for instance, Lasch, *American Liberals and the Russian Revolution*; Filene, *Americans and the Soviet Experiment*; Frank A. Warren, *Liberals and Communism: The "Red Decade" Revisited*; Denning, *Cultural Front*; and Mary E. Glantz, *FDR and the Soviet Union: The President's Battles over Foreign Policy*.

9. Rossinow, *Visions of Progress*, 2–3.

10. "Report on Cases Handled by the International Labor Defense to the Fourth National Conference," December 29–31, 1929, International Labor Defense Records.

11. Fine, *Automobile under the Blue Eagle*, 407; J. R. Prickett, "Communists and the Communist Issue in the American Labor Movement, 1920–1950," 112, 129; Keeran, *Communist Party and the Auto Workers Union*, 140.

12. Schrecker, *Many Are the Crimes*, 32.

13. Robin D. G. Kelley, *Hammer and Hoe: Alabama Communists during the Great Depression*, 95.

14. Mark Naison, *Communists in Harlem during the Depression*, xvii.

15. Ryan, *Earl Browder*, 1.

16. "Browder Interview," June 28, 1955, Box 01, Folder 07, Browder Interviews, Draper Papers.

17. "Browder Interview," October 10, 1955, Box 01, Folder 08, Browder Interviews, Draper Papers, 28.

18. Denning, *Cultural Front*.

19. "Browder Interview III," June 16, 1953, Box 01, Folder 03, Browder Interviews, Draper Papers, 2–3.

20. "Statement of Earl Browder to the McNaboe Committee, June 29, 1938," Box 02, Folder 32, McNaboe Committee, Draper Papers, 3.

21. John Gates, *The Story of an American Communist*, 38–39.

22. "'The American Communist Party under Attack': A Memorandum by Earl Browder. Prepared for Theodore Draper," December 9, 1955, Box 01, Folder 16, Browder Memorandum, Draper Papers, 4, 12, 14.

23. Wolfskill, *Revolt of the Conservatives*, 108, 165.

24. Neither anti-Semitism nor anticommunism was, of course, new to fundamentalists. Many had endorsed the *Protocols* during the Ford controversy in the early 1920s, and the language of "apostate Jews" was in many ways a dispensationalist creation. But individuals who in the 1930s would be deeply bound up in anti-Semitic politics, such as William Bell Riley, nevertheless seem to have only made intermittent anti-Semitic remarks in the twenties, whereas it became their defining feature in the 1930s. Carpenter, *Revive Us Again*, 103.

25. Ibid., 99; Trollinger, *God's Empire*, 62. See also Matthew Avery Sutton, "Was FDR the Antichrist? The Birth of Fundamentalist Antiliberalism in a Global Age."

26. Carpenter, *Revive Us Again*, 98–99.

27. Trollinger, *God's Empire*, 73.

28. Amman, "A 'Dog in the Nighttime' Problem," 568.

29. See Scott Beekman, *William Dudley Pelley: A Life in Right-Wing Extremism and the Occult*.

30. Ribuffo, *Old Christian Right*, 107.

31. Ribuffo points out that most fundamentalist congregations, as southerners, would in fact have voted for Roosevelt during the 1930s. However, it is something of a leap to suggest this made them enthusiastic New Dealers. Ibid., 181.

32. Miscamble, "Limits of Catholic Antifascism," 533. Of course, Ryan was not saying that either was desirable.

33. *Social Justice*, May 1, 1936.

34. Ribuffo, *Old Christian Right*, 133, 136.

35. James P. Shenton, "The Coughlin Movement and the New Deal," 353–54, 357; Wallace Stegner, "The Radio Priest and His Flock," 238; David H. Bennett, *Demagogues in the Depression: American Radicals and the Union Party, 1932–1936*, 80; Brinkley, *Voices of Protest*, 126.

36. See, for instance, the changing patterns of letter writing referred to in Brinkley, *Voices of Protest*, 258; D. Bennett, *Demagogues in the Depression*, 223, 225; Coughlin, *Series of Lectures, April 1936*, 69.

37. D. Bennett, *Demagogues in the Depression*, 254, 263.

38. David Bennett argues that in the early 1930s, Coughlin's close associates knew him as "personally anti-Semitic and a possessor of an elaborate library on the subject." But before his 1936 defeat, he had sought to reach out to non-Catholic supporters, including Jews. Before the Fish Committee, Coughlin had stated, "In this country the communists are not the Jews. I think that it is a libel on the Jewish race to say that only Jews are Communists," and in 1936 he had declared that the NUSJ was open to "black and white, Catholic, Protestant and Jew—all who love social justice." Ibid., 52. See also Rodger Streitmatter, *Mightier than the Sword: How the New Media Have Shaped American History*, 127; testimony of Charles E. Coughlin, Fish Committee (see chap. 5, n. 63); Coughlin, *Series of Lectures, April 1936*, 13.

39. *Social Justice*, December 9, 1936, June 27, 1938.

40. Charles E. Coughlin, *Sixteen Radio Lectures: 1938 Series*, 92.

41. Glen Jeansonne, *Women of the Far Right: The Mothers' Movement and World War II*, 15, 73.

42. Amman, "A 'Dog in the Nighttime' Problem," 567.

43. Carpenter, *Revive Us Again*, 93–94.

44. Trollinger, *God's Empire*, 74–75; Ribuffo, *Old Christian Right*, 66.

45. Gaebelein, *Conflict of the Ages*, 61, 95–96, 100, 109, 115.

46. Beale, *In Pursuit of Purity*, 103.

47. Lee, *Henry Ford and the Jews*, 100.

48. H. Bennett, *We Never Called Him Henry*, 129; Lee, *Henry Ford and the Jews*, 110.

49. H. Bennett, *We Never Called Him Henry*, 126–27. Apparently, Ford also provided Dilling with her office furniture. Jeansonne, *Women of the Far Right*, 18.

50. *Social Justice*, November 9, 1936, January 10, 1938; Max Wallace, *The American Axis: Henry Ford, Charles Lindbergh, and the Rise of the Third Reich*, 141–42.

51. *Social Justice*, May 3, 1937.

52. *Social Justice*, January 11, 18, 1937.

53. The union proved a dead loss and barely existed except on paper. Lee, *Henry Ford and the Jews*, 104.

54. *Social Justice*, July 18, 1938.

55. *Social Justice*, July 25, 1938.

56. D. Bennett, *Demagogues in the Depression*, 280.

57. *Social Justice*, February 20, 1929.

58. Charles E. Coughlin, *Why Leave Our Own? 13 Addresses on Christianity and Americanism*, 47–49.

59. See, for instance, Beekman, *William Dudley Pelley*, 98–99.

60. Amman, "A 'Dog in the Nighttime' Problem," 570.

61. Ronald H. Bayer, *Neighbors in Conflict: The Irish, Germans, Jews, and Italians of New York City, 1929–1941*, 60.

62. Manfred Jonas, *The United States and Germany: A Diplomatic History*, 212, 216.

63. G. Smith, *To Save a Nation*, 4.

64. Ralph M. Easley (hereafter cited as RME) to George Sylvester Viereck (hereafter cited as GSV), April 25, 1933, Box 441, Folder 13, NCF Papers.

65. RME and Gertrude Beeks Easley interview with Emil [*sic*] Schmitz, September 17, 1933, Box 439, Folder 9, NCF Papers.

66. Arnold A. Offner, *American Appeasement: United States Foreign Policy and Germany, 1933–1938*, 57.

67. Testimony of GSV, *Hearings before Special Committee on Un-American Activities: Investigation of Nazi Propaganda Activities and Investigation of Certain Other Propaganda Activities* (hereafter cited as McCormack-Dickstein Committee), 90–91.

68. Viereck was working on a number of similar projects at the time. See Niel M. Johnson, *George Sylvester Viereck: German-American Propagandist*, 178–79; Leland Bell, *In Hitler's Shadow: The Anatomy of American Nazism*, 8; Sander A. Diamond, *The Nazi Movement in the United States, 1924–1941*, 108–10; interview with Walter Kappe, n.d., Box 442, Folder 6, NCF Papers.

69. Only three references to Jews remained in the book: an allusion to the "front of Marxism, Judaism and Pacifism," another about "the old Russian Jewish revolution," and a description of the German Communist Party as a "Jewish-Marxistic mortal enemy of the German nation." Adolf Ehrt, *Communism in Germany: The Truth about the Communist Conspiracy on the Eve of the National Revolution*, 28, 31, 59.

70. Ibid., 155.

71. International Committee to Combat the World Menace of Communism, Box 443, Folder 12, NCF Papers.

72. Ehrt, *Communism in Germany*, 177.

73. Charles E. Coughlin, *"Am I an Anti-Semite?": Addresses from November 1938 to January 1939*, 94, 97, 64, 71.

74. Quoted in Charles J. Tull, *Father Coughlin and the New Deal*, 209.

75. Privately, Mooney observed, "I am not blind to the fact that these addresses have produced some good effects. They may well incite conservative Jews to react more energetically against their co-nationals who are, out of all proportion to their number in the population, active in the cause of communism." Edward Mooney to apostolic delegate, December 18, 1938, Coughlin Case, Box 1, Edward Mooney Papers.

76. Interview for *The American Experience: The Radio Priest* (PBS, 1988).

77. Mooney to apostolic delegate, December 18, 1938, Coughlin Case, Box 1, Mooney Papers.

78. Ibid., November 26, 1938.

79. Note, June 2, 1937, ibid.

80. Mooney to apostolic delegate, October 29, 1937, ibid. For more details of the duel between Mooney and Coughlin, see "A Summary of Facts in the Father Coughlin Incident, October 5th, 1937 to January 9th, 1938" and Mooney to apostolic delegate, December 4, 1937, ibid.

81. Brinkley, *Voices of Protest*, 267.

82. Excerpts recorded in Box 1, Coughlin Case, Mooney Papers.

Chapter 9. A Mirror Image

1. *Chicago Daily Tribune,* May 19, 1937; *New York Times,* May 23, 1937.

2. *Detroit News,* August 7, October 22, 1997; *Atlanta Daily World,* May 28, 1937.

3. *New York Times,* May 27, 1937.

4. *Social Justice,* June 7, 1937; *Washington Post,* May 28, 1937.

5. *Chicago Daily Tribune,* May 28, 1937; *Atlanta Constitution,* May 27, 1937; *New York Times,* May 30, 27, 1937; *Washington Post,* May 27, 1937; "Speech, Ford Mass Meeting, 5 June 1937," Box 3, UAW President's Office—Homer Martin Collection.

6. *New York Times,* August 11, April 25, May 13, 1935.

7. Frank Hadas, "Reminiscences," 107.

8. Herndon, *Ford,* 171.

9. Larry Ceplair, *Under the Shadow of War: Fascism, Antifascism, and Marxists, 1918–1939,* 4.

10. Rossinow, *Visions of Progress,* 166.

11. Allegations have been made that Ford was funneling money to the Nazis. It is impossible to prove with any certainty whether there was substance in such allegations. Albert Lee, in his study of Henry Ford's anti-Semitism, concluded—on what evidence it is not clear—that it was "likely." Simonds, *Henry Ford: A Biography,* 202; Lee, *Henry Ford and the Jews,* 57. For circumstantial claims, see Wallace, *American Axis,* 50–51.

12. Ribuffo, *Old Christian Right,* xiii.

13. Thomas M. Henderson, *Tammany Hall and the New Immigrants: The Progressive Years,* 224–25.

14. Dickstein's biography of 1935 claims that he voted against the bill to bar the Socialists from the assembly. However, in reminiscences during the McCarthy era, he said, "I voted to oust them." Dorothy Waring, *American Defender,* 76; Samuel Dickstein, "Reminiscences," 17, 91.

15. Dickstein, "Reminiscences," 28.

16. Waring, *American Defender,* 120–22.

17. *New York Times,* October 17, 18, 12, 1933.

18. *Washington Post,* November 1, 1933; *New York Times,* November 14, 1933.

19. *New York Times,* October 10, 11, 1933; *Washington Post,* October 11, 1933.

20. *New York Times,* October 13, 27, 1933; *Atlanta Constitution,* October 24, 1933; *New York Times,* November 3, 1933.

21. L. Bell, *In Hitler's Shadow,* 13; *New York Times,* October 28, 29, 31, 1933.

22. *New York Times,* March 14, 1932; *Washington Post,* March 21, 22, 1932; *New York Times,* May 5, April 19, August 14, 1932; *Washington Post,* January 5, 1935.

23. U.S. House of Representatives, *Hearings before a Subcommittee of the Committee on Immigration and Naturalization: Nazi Propaganda Activities by Aliens in the United States,* 21 (hereafter cited as Dickstein Immigration Hearings).

24. Ibid., 23.

25. *Chicago Daily Tribune,* November 16, 1933; *New York Times,* November 16, 1933; *Washington Post,* November 16, 1933.

26. *Washington Post,* November 16, 1933; Morris D. Waldman to Ralph M. Easley (hereafter cited as RME), October 18, 1933, Box 441, Folder 13, NCF Papers; Joseph M.

Proskauer to RME, November 1, 1933, Box 441, Folder 11, "German Anti-Semitism, Correspondence M–R," NCF Papers; RME to Capt. John B. Trevor, December 12, 1933; Capt. John B. Trevor to RME, December 13, 1933; Viereck to RME, November 17, 1933, Box 441, Folder 13, NCF Papers; Hamilton Fish (hereafter cited as HF) to RME, November 22, 1933, Box 441, Folder 10, NCF Papers.

27. RME to HF, November 25, 1933, Box 441, Folder 10, NCF Papers.

28. RME to Brig-Gen. John R. Delafield, November 28, 1933, Box 441, Folder 9, NCF Papers.

29. RME to Finley J. Shepard, November 29, 1933, Box 441, Folder 12, "German Anti-Semitism, Correspondence S," NCF Papers.

30. *New York Times,* January 24, 21, 1934.

31. Diamond, *Nazi Movement in the United States,* 125.

32. The committee is commonly known as the McCormack-Dickstein Committee. In one sense, this adds clarity, since the HUAC of the 1940s was technically a different body. But it also downplays the links between McCormack-Dickstein, Dies, and the postwar HUAC and by extension the degree to which legislative investigations into un-Americanism were revivified in the 1930s by antifascist groups.

33. *Washington Post,* April 6, 1934.

34. *Washington Post,* June 7, 1934; *New York Times,* June 8, 1934; *Washington Post,* June 8, August 24, 1934.

35. *Chicago Daily Tribune,* October 18, December 6, 1934.

36. *Chicago Daily Tribune,* July 10, 1934.

37. Waring, *American Defender,* 132.

38. *Chicago Daily Tribune,* November 21, 1934; *New York Times,* November 21, 1934.

39. Arthur M. Schlesinger Jr., *The Age of Roosevelt: The Politics of Upheaval,* 83.

40. *Chicago Daily Tribune,* November 22, 1934; *New York Times,* November 22, 1934; *Washington Post,* November 26, 1934; *Chicago Daily Tribune,* November 27, 1934.

41. On Spivak's Communist links, see Klehr, Haynes, and Vassiliev, *Spies,* 160–61.

42. *New Masses,* January 29, 1935.

43. McCormack-Dickstein Committee, 61 (see chap. 8, n. 67).

44. The outcome of the financial negotiations is not clear. Telephone conversations between RME and Ernst Schmitz, September 21, 30, 1933, Box 442, Folder 4, NCF Papers.

45. *New Masses,* January 29, 1935.

46. RME to Matthew Woll, June 30, 1934, Box 435, Folder 5, NCF Papers.

47. Beekman, *William Dudley Pelley,* 104.

48. L. Bell, *In Hitler's Shadow,* 15–22, 57, 106.

49. *New York Times,* July 24, May 17, 1935.

50. Ribuffo, *Old Christian Right,* 184; Charles, *Hoover and the Isolationists,* 31–34.

51. *New York Times,* December 9, 1937.

52. *New York Times,* July 15, 1934.

53. *Chicago Daily Tribune,* February 1, 1936.

54. *Chicago Daily Tribune,* February 9, March 7, 13, 1936. Black's supposedly ruthless "Cheka" failed to get any bill through Congress. *Washington Post,* July 23, 1935; *New*

York Times, July 24, 1935; *Washington Post,* July 24, 1935; *Chicago Daily Tribune,* August 2, 1935.

55. Ribuffo, *Old Christian Right,* 21, 182.

56. *New York Times,* October 4, 1936.

57. Norman Thomas, *The Choice before Us: Mankind at the Crossroads,* 67.

58. Jerold Auerbach, "The La Follette Committee: Labor and Civil Liberties in the New Deal," 440. See also Jerold Auerbach, *Labor and Liberty: The La Follette Committee and the New Deal.*

59. Leo Huberman, *The Labor Spy Racket.*

60. John L. Spivak, *Secret Armies: The New Technique of Nazi Warfare,* 8, 131, 159–60.

61. A. B. Magil and Henry Stevens, *The Peril of Fascism,* 11.

62. O'Brien, "Ford's Commander in Chief," 71; H. Bennett, *We Never Called Him Henry,* 82.

63. *Social Justice,* March 31, 1941.

64. Sward, *Legend of Henry Ford,* 417.

65. *Social Justice,* June 2, 1941.

66. Wolfskill, *Revolt of the Conservatives,* 57, 63, 67.

67. *Chicago Daily Tribune,* January 26, 1936.

68. Wolfskill, *Revolt of the Conservatives,* 157–58.

69. Frederick Rudolph, "The American Liberty League, 1934–1940," 26.

70. Phillips-Fein, *Invisible Hands,* 13.

71. Wolfskill, *Revolt of the Conservatives,* 211, 217, 218; *New York Times,* September 3, 1934; *Chicago Daily Tribune,* January 30, 1936; *Washington Post,* August 12, 1936; *New York Times,* October 25, 1936.

72. Rossinow, *Visions of Progress,* 118.

73. *New York Times,* September 25, 1934.

74. Schlesinger, *Age of Roosevelt,* 141; Marian C. McKenna, "Prelude to Tyranny: Wheeler, FDR, and the 1937 Court Fight," 408.

75. McKenna, "Prelude to Tyranny," 410.

76. James T. Patterson, "A Conservative Coalition Forms in Congress, 1933–1939," 758; McKenna, "Prelude to Tyranny," 408.

77. For a fuller account of the relationship between race and countersubversion, see Mark Ellis, "J. Edgar Hoover and the 'Red Summer' of 1919"; Mark Ellis, *Race, War, and Surveillance: African Americans and the United States Government during World War I;* Eric Arnesen, "No 'Graver Danger': Black Anticommunism, the Communist Party, and the Race Question"; Jan Voogd, *Race Riots and Resistance: The Red Summer of 1919.*

78. Ibid., 46.

79. Meier and Rudwick argue that Ford's decision to employ black workers on a large scale stemmed from a principled belief in the necessity of fair treatment of African Americans. But the racial tensions stimulated by this policy were extremely helpful in managing employee-management disputes. Indeed, almost as soon as Ford was defeated over union representation in 1941, the corporation began to implement restrictions on black employment. "You will have little difficulty in figuring out the reason," Donald Marshall wrote to his former assistant Willis Ward. August Meier and Elliott Rudwick,

Black Detroit and the Rise of the UAW, 11; Donald Marshall to Willis Ward, July 5, 1941, Willis Ward personal papers.

80. Ablewhite, "Reminiscences," 70–71; Willis F. Ward, "Reminiscences," 12–13. See also Meier and Rudwick, *Black Detroit and the Rise of the UAW,* 39.

81. Ibid., 31.

82. J. M. Pawa, "The Search for Black Radicals: American and British Documents Relative to the 1919 Red Scare."

83. Fish Committee, pt. 3, 1:248, 251–59; pt. 3, 4:199–204; pt. 5, 3:282–86 (see chap. 5, n. 63).

84. Ibid., pt. 6, 1:67, 243, 302.

85. The Detroit office of the NAACP remained a more or less wholly owned subsidiary of the Ford empire, though, and both it and local black church leaders refused to endorse the national policy in favor of the AFL and CIO. Ralph Bunche, *The Political Status of the Negro in the Age of FDR,* 587–88.

86. Rossinow, *Visions of Progress,* 166–72.

87. George N. Green, *The Establishment in Texas Politics: The Primitive Years, 1938–1957,* 70; Michael Wreszin, "The Dies Committee, 1938," in *Congress Investigates,* edited by Schlesinger and Bruns, 2927.

88. Schlesinger and Bruns, *Congress Investigates,* 2963.

89. Alan D. Harper, "The Antired Decade Remembered," 131; Green, *Establishment in Texas Politics,* 74.

90. *Washington Post,* May 27, 1936.

91. L. Bell, *In Hitler's Shadow,* 67; Goodman, *Committee,* 19.

92. Ibid., 23.

93. Ibid., 22–23.

94. Allen Weinstein and Alexander Vassiliev, *The Haunted Wood: Soviet Espionage in America—the Stalin Era,* 142–43.

Chapter 10. The Big Truth

1. Ralph M. Easley (hereafter cited as RME) to Ford, September 14, 1920, Box 441, Folder 10, NCF Papers.

2. RME to William J. Cameron, October 29, 1920, Box 441, Folder 19, NCF Papers; RME to Isaac Landman, September 24, 1920, Box 441, Folder 10, NCF Papers.

3. RME to Samuel McCrea Cavert, May 22, 1934, Box 441, Folder 9, "German Anti-Semitism, Correspondence A–D," NCF Papers.

4. RME speech before dinner, June 5, 1934, Box 441, Folder 10, NCF Papers.

5. Confidential memorandum by RME, Chairman Executive Council, National Civic Federation (Tentative Draft), Box 437, Folder 5, "Anti-Communist Campaign," NCF Papers.

6. RME to Morris D. Waldman, April 10, 1934, Box 441, Folder 13, NCF Papers.

7. RME to Wilbur K. Thomas, October 20, 1934; Thomas to RME, November 12, 1934; RME to Thomas, November 30, 1934; Thomas to RME, December 6, 1934, Box 441, Folder 13, NCF Papers.

8. RME to William Phillips, June 6, 1934, Box 441, Folder 11, NCF Papers.

9. Untitled note, June 18, 1934, Box 441, Folder 9, NCF Papers.

10. RME to Pierre S. Du Pont, October 20, 1934, ibid.

11. RME to William Green, October 10, 1936, Box 441, Folder 10, NCF Papers.

12. Herman C. Kudlich to RME, October 30, 1934; RME to Kudlich, November 1, 1934 (unsent until December 5); RME to Kudlich, December 5, 1934, Box 441, Folder 10, NCF Papers; RME to Waldman and Viereck, June 19, 1938, Lambert Fairchild to RME, June 30, 1938, Box 442, Folder 4, NCF Papers.

13. RME to Green, November 5, 1934, Box 441, Folder 10, NCF Papers; Archibald E. Stevenson to James N. Rosenberg, October 20, 1936, Box 435, Folder 4, "General Correspondence, P–T," NCF Papers. For NCF interventions against Nazism and anti-Semitism, see RME to Samuel Dickstein, October 16, 1934, Box 441, Folder 9, NCF Papers; Maud S. De Land to Gertrude Beeks Easley (hereafter cited as GBE), October 29, 1934; GBE to De Land, November 16, 1934, Box 442, Folder 6, NCF Papers; Box 439, Folder 13, "Communist Domination of the Works Project Administration," NCF Papers; *New York Tribune*, August 19, 1935; RME to Mrs. Robert Lehman, October 13, 1936, Box 441, Folder 10, NCF Papers; RME to Waldman, October 21, 1936, Box 441, Folder 13, NCF Papers. Easley claimed the federation lost fifteen hundred dollars in donations because of its stance against anti-Semitism. RME to Waldman, October 19, 1934, November 15, 1936, Box 441, Folder 13, NCF Papers.

14. RME to V. Everit Macy, September 1, 1920, Box 331, Folder 11, "German Anti-Semitism, Correspondence M–R," NCF Papers.

15. RME to George B. Cortelyou, October 16, 1934, Box 441, Folder 9, NCF Papers.

16. William O. Lucas to GBE, January 7, 1938, Box 444, Folder 1, "Lucas, William O.," NCF Papers; Box 444, Folder 4, "Matthews, Frederick C.," NCF Papers; Norman T. Whitaker to RME, March 13, 1937, Box 434, Folder 4, "Whitaker vs. Easley," NCF Papers; RME to Finley J. Shepard, May 27, 1938, Box 488, Folder 2, NCF Papers; RME to Shepard, July 19, 1938, Box 434, Folder 4, NCF Papers; GBE to Mrs. Edward B. McLean, July 24, 25, 1938, Box 445, Folder 1, NCF Papers; and the extensive correspondence between Harold Kaplan and GBE, dating until the end of October 1939, Box 434, Folder 3, "Whitaker vs. Easley," NCF Papers. Archibald Stevenson, too, was in dire financial straits. Stevenson to GBE, March 24, 1939, Box 445, Folder 1, NCF Papers.

17. Mack W. Beeks to Harold Kaplan, October 10, 1939; GBE to Harold Kaplan, October 26, 1939, Box 434, Folder 3, NCF Papers.

18. *Rye Chronicle*, September 15, 1939.

19. Carter, *Decline and Revival of the Social Gospel*, 184.

20. Carpenter, *Revive Us Again*, 98–99; William R. Glass, "Fundamentalism's Prophetic Vision of the Jews: The 1930s," 68–70.

21. Anderson, *Visions of the Disinherited*, 218–19.

22. Carpenter, *Revive Us Again*, 105.

23. Trollinger, *God's Empire*, 79.

24. Hankins, *God's Rascal*, 66.

25. Russell, *Voices of American Fundamentalism*, 28, 43–44; Hankins, *God's Rascal*, 6.

26. John A. Donovan to editor of *Brooklyn Tablet*, November 14, 1937, Coughlin Case, Box 1, Mooney Papers.

27. See, for example, Social Action Leaflet no. 2, "Communism 1930s and 1940s," Box 8, Raymond Clancy Collection. For ACTU internal politics, see Douglas P. Seaton, *Catholics and Radicals: The Association of Catholic Trade Unionists and the American Labor Movement, from Depression to Cold War*, 75–97.

28. Clancy statement on Radio WMBC, November 15, 1939, Box 4, Clancy Collection.

29. *Social Justice*, July 8, August 26, 1940.

30. Lee, *Henry Ford and the Jews*, 105; Brinkley, *Voices of Protest*, 267. For more details of Mooney's actions, see Leslie Woodcock Tentler, *Seasons of Grace: A History of the Catholic Archdiocese of Detroit*.

31. Mooney to apostolic delegate, March 8, 1940, Coughlin Case, Box 1, Mooney Papers.

32. Ibid., June 5, 1940, Box 2.

33. "Report of Arnold Lunn's Visit with Fr. Coughlin, Dec. 14, 1940," ibid.

34. Speech ca. 1941, Box 158, Folder 1, "Speeches—HUAC, c. 1941," Martin Dies Collection. See also Martin Dies, *The Trojan Horse in America: A Report to the Nation*.

35. Statement by Congressman Martin Dies for the American Forum, Box 157, Folder 24, "Speeches—HUAC c. 1940," Dies Collection.

36. Kenneth Heineman, "Media Bias in Coverage of the Dies Committee on Un-American Activities," 38; Goodman, *Committee*, 53.

37. *Social Justice*, September 12, 1938.

38. *Time*, February 19, 1940.

39. Ribuffo, *Old Christian Right*, 74–75.

40. Goodman, *Committee*, 25, 47; Schrecker, *Many Are the Crimes*, 28, 94, 97–98, 112; Stanley I. Kutler, *The American Inquisition*, chap. 5.

41. Goodman, *Committee*, 49, 117.

42. Claudius O. Johnson, "Jerry Voorhis: What Is Right Rather than What Is Expedient," in *Public Men in and out of Office*, edited by Salter, 331n.

43. Speech by Jerry Voorhis (about 1940), Box 53, Folder 18, "Articles and Speeches Relating to HUAC," H. Jerry Voorhis Collection, 1–2.

44. Speech by Jerry Voorhis (about 1939 or 1940), ibid., 2.

45. Klehr, Haynes, and Firsov, *Soviet World of American Communism*, 7.

46. Goodman, *Committee*, 87.

47. Schlesinger and Bruns, *Congress Investigates*, 3018.

48. *Time*, January 15, 1940.

49. Earl Browder, "Lessons of the Moscow Trials," speech delivered at the Hippodrome, New York, March 18, 1938, Draper Papers.

50. Thomas Sakmyster, *Red Conspirator: J. Peters and the American Communist Underground*.

51. "Browder Interview," June 28, 1955, Box 1, Folder 7, Draper Papers. See also Harvey Klehr, *Communist Cadre: The Social Background of the American Communist Party Elite*.

52. "Browder Interview," October 10, 1955, Box 1, Folder 8, Draper Papers.

53. Schrecker, *Many Are the Crimes*, 26, 38.

54. "Browder Interview," June 28, 1955, Box 1, Folder 7, Draper Papers, 26.

55. Eugene Lyons, *Moscow Carrousel*; Eugene Lyons, *Assignment in Utopia*; Fred Beal, *Proletarian Journey: New England, Gastonia, Moscow*; *Time*, October 30, 1939; Walter G. Krivitsky, *In Stalin's Secret Service: An Expose of Russia's Secret Policies by the Former Chief of the Soviet Intelligence in Western Europe*; Benjamin Gitlow, *I Confess: The Truth about American Anticommunism*; Eugene Lyons, *Stalin, Czar of All the Russias*; Eugene Lyons, *The Red Decade: The Stalinist Penetration of America*; Richard Krebs, *Out of the Night*. For Lovestone's engagement with the anticommunist apparatus during this period, see Morgan, *Covert Life*, chap. 9.

56. Schrecker, *Many Are the Crimes*, 44.

57. Sokolsky introduced Matthews to the Dies Committee, while Dallin helped orchestrate the defection of the senior Bolshevik Victor Kravchenko in 1944. Levine ghostwrote Jan Valtin's, Walter Krivitsky's, and Oksana Kasenkina's books. Sokolsky had also been a vehement critic of protofascist groups. John V. Fleming, *The Anti-Communist Manifestos: Four Books That Shaped the Cold War*, 185; Victor Kravchenko, *I Chose Freedom: The Personal and Political Life of a Soviet Official*; Kern, *Death in Washington*, 177–78; G. Smith, *To Save a Nation*, 67.

58. Max Eastman, *Marx, Lenin, and the Science of Revolution*; Max Eastman, *The End of Socialism in Russia*, 9, 30, 40, 46.

59. Fleming, *Anti-Communist Manifestos*, 140, 206.

60. For instance, see Harold Josephson, "Ex-Communists in Crossfire: A Cold War Debate"; Herbert L. Packer, *Ex-Communist Witnesses: Four Studies in Fact-Finding*.

61. *Nation*, January 6, 1940, 24, January 18, 1941; *New Republic*, January 22, 27, 1941.

62. Browder, "Lessons of the Moscow Trials."

63. Committee of 400 statement, cited in Kern, *Death in Washington*, 210.

64. "The American Communist Party under Attack," a memorandum by Earl Browder, prepared for Theodore Draper, December 9, 1955, Draper Papers, 7–8.

65. Gates, *Story of an American Communist*, 76.

66. *Communist*, December 1941.

67. *Communist*, August 1940.

68. Schrecker, *Many Are the Crimes*, 16–17.

69. Rossinow, *Visions of Progress*, 157.

70. Schrecker, *Many Are the Crimes*, 96, 97.

71. Goodman, *Committee*, 65–67, 99n3.

72. Les K. Adler and Thomas G. Patterson, "Red Fascism: The Merger of Nazi Germany and Soviet Russia in the American Image of Totalitarianism, 1930s–1950s," 1051. See Thomas R. Maddux, "Red Fascism, Brown Bolshevism: The American Image of Totalitarianism in the 1930s."

73. *New Republic*, August 31, 1938.

74. Heineman, "Media Bias in Coverage of the Dies Committee," 45.

75. *Nation*, November 23, 1940.

76. *New Republic*, August 31, 1938.

77. *Nation*, August 27, 1938.

78. Harold L. Ickes, *The Secret Diary of Harold L. Ickes*, 574.

79. *Nation*, November 23, 1940.

80. *New Republic,* August 26, 1940, 264; April 22, 1940, 532–33.

81. Wayne S. Cole, *America First: The Battle against Intervention, 1940–1941,* 8.

82. Carter, *Decline and Revival of the Social Gospel,* 212.

83. Cole, *America First,* 85; Troncone, "Hamilton Fish Sr.," 193, 231, 296.

84. Jeansonne, *Women of the Far Right,* 31; Charles, *Hoover and the Isolationists,* 92–93.

85. Hamilton Fish, *Memoirs of an American Patriot,* 79–86.

86. Troncone, "Hamilton Fish Sr.," 325.

87. L. Bell, *In Hitler's Shadow,* 62.

88. Jeansonne, *Women of the Far Right,* 50–51, 54.

89. Cole, *America First,* 107.

90. Ribuffo, *Old Christian Right,* 185.

91. Jeansonne, *Women of the Far Right,* 152; Cole, *America First,* 108.

92. Charles, *Hoover and the Isolationists,* 62.

93. Fish, *Memoirs of an American Patriot,* 79.

94. Wallace, *American Axis,* 344.

95. Troncone, "Hamilton Fish Sr.," 403–4.

96. Beekman, *William Dudley Pelley,* 141.

97. Cole, *America First,* 118; Wreszin, "The Dies Committee," in *Congress Investigates,* edited by Schlesinger and Bruns, 2950–53; Ribuffo, *Old Christian Right,* 187.

98. Guenter Lewy, *The Cause That Failed: Communism in American Political Life,* 72; Schrecker, *Many Are the Crimes,* 102. On the Soviet roots of the decision to dissolve the CPUSA, see Starobin, *American Communism in Crisis,* 53–55, 64–66; Maurice Isserman, *Which Side Were You On? The American Communist Party during the Second World War,* 1–2.

99. Schrecker, *Many Are the Crimes,* 17. Communists in the military found it very difficult to see active service. Gates, *Story of an American Communist,* chap. 6; Junius Irving Scales and Richard Nickson, *Cause at Heart: A Former Communist Remembers,* chap. 9.

100. Lewy, *Cause That Failed,* 67, 70.

101. H. Bennett, *We Never Called Him Henry,* 168.

102. Ribuffo, *Old Christian Right,* 79.

103. Edward Mooney to Coughlin, November 29, 1942, Coughlin Case, Box 2, Mooney Papers.

Conclusion

1. Schrecker, *Many Are the Crimes,* 18.

2. Starobin, *American Communism in Crisis,* 83; Ryan, *Earl Browder,* 247.

3. Draper, *Roots of American Communism,* 314.

4. Gates, *Story of an American Communist,* 108.

5. Scales and Nickson, *Cause at Heart,* 161.

6. Starobin, *American Communism in Crisis,* 12–13, 51.

7. Gates, *Story of an American Communist,* 107.

8. *New York Times,* February 7, 1946.

9. See David Caute, *The Great Fear: The Anti-Communist Purge under Truman and Eisenhower,* 25.

10. Kutler, *The American Inquisition,* 153.

11. Harper, "The Antired Decade Remembered," 129.

12. Gates, *Story of an American Communist,* 141.

13. *Washington Post,* December 18, 1946.

14. Jerry Voorhis to National Citizens Political Action Campaign, September 18, 1946, Box 58, Folder 5, "Notes for Debate with Nixon," Voorhis Collection.

15. Jerry Voorhis, *The Strange Case of Richard Milhous Nixon.*

16. Schrecker, *Many Are the Crimes,* 36.

17. Goodman, *Committee,* 161, 167–73.

18. A. Weinstein and Vassiliev, *Haunted Wood,* 106.

19. Allen Weinstein, *Perjury: The Hiss-Chambers Case,* xv.

20. Ribuffo, *Old Christian Right,* 193.

21. Wheeler, *Yankee from the West,* 388, 397.

22. *New Republic,* August 26, 1946.

23. *New Republic,* September 9, 1946.

Bibliography

Newspapers, Current Affairs Journals, and Magazines

American Magazine
American Mercury
Atlanta Constitution
Atlanta Daily World
Chicago Daily Tribune
Daily Worker
Dearborn Herald
Dearborn Independent
Detroit Free Press
Detroit Magazine
Detroit News
Detroit Times
Forbes
Forum
Liberty
Los Angeles Times
Michigan Catholic
Mystic Triangle
Nation
National Review
New Masses
New Republic
New York Review of Books
New York Times
New York Tribune
Social Justice

Southern Patriot
Soviet Russia Today
Time
Wall Street Journal
Washington Post

Archival Material

Ablewhite, H. S. "Reminiscences." Accession 65. Benson Ford Research Center, the Henry Ford, Dearborn, Mich.

Bacon, Irving R. "Reminiscences." Accession 65. Benson Ford Research Center, the Henry Ford, Dearborn, Mich.

Brown, Joe. Collection. Archives of Labor and Urban Affairs, Walter P. Reuther Library, Wayne State University, Detroit.

Cameron, W. J. "Reminiscences." Draft, 1952. Accession 65. Benson Ford Research Center, the Henry Ford, Dearborn, Mich.

Clancy, Raymond. Collection. Walter P. Reuther Library, Wayne State University, Detroit.

Dickstein, Samuel. "Reminiscences." 1949–50. Columbia Oral History Project, Columbia University, New York.

Dies, Martin. Collection. Sam Houston Center, Texas State Library and Archives Commission, Liberty.

Draper, Theodore. Papers. Robert Woodruff Library, Emory University, Atlanta.

Hadas, Frank. "Reminiscences." Draft. Accession 65. Benson Ford Research Center, the Henry Ford, Dearborn, Mich.

International Labor Defense. Records. Schomberg Center for Research in Black Culture, New York Public Library.

Kahn, Albert. Papers. Bentley Ford Historical Library, University of Michigan, Ann Arbor.

Klann, W. C. "Reminiscences." Accession 65. Benson Ford Research Center, the Henry Ford, Dearborn, Mich.

Mooney, Edward. Papers. Archdiocese of Detroit.

National Civic Federation. Papers. New York Public Library.

Nevins, Allan. Research Papers. Accession 81. Benson Ford Research Center, the Henry Ford, Dearborn, Mich.

Niebuhr, Reinhold. "Reminiscences." 1954. Columbia Oral History Project, Columbia University, New York.

UAW President's Office—Homer Martin Collection. Walter P. Reuther Library, Wayne State University, Detroit.

Voorhis, H. Jerry. Collection. Honnald Library of the Claremont Colleges, St. Clara, Calif.

Ward, Willis F. Personal papers. Accession 527. Benson Ford Research Center, the Henry Ford, Dearborn, Mich.

———. "Reminiscences." Accession 65. Benson Ford Research Center, the Henry Ford, Dearborn, Mich.

Wheeler, Burton K. "Reminiscences." 1968. Columbia Oral History Project, Columbia University, New York.

Wibel, A. M. "Reminiscences." First draft. Accession 65. Benson Ford Research Center, the Henry Ford, Dearborn, Mich.

Government Documents, Reports, and Hearings

New York State Legislature, Joint Legislative Committee to Investigate Seditious Activities. *Revolutionary Radicalism: Its History, Purpose, and Tactics, Report of the New York State Investigative Committee.* 4 vols. 1920. Reprint, New York: Da Capo, 1971.

U.S. House of Representatives. *Hearings: Investigation of Communist Propaganda* ["Fish Committee"]. July 1930.

———. *Hearings and Reports before House Special Committee on Un-American Activities* ["Dies Committee"]. 1938–44.

———. *Hearings before a Subcommittee of the Committee on Immigration and Naturalization: Nazi Propaganda Activities by Aliens in the United States* ["Dickstein Immigration Hearings"]. November–December 1933.

———. *Hearings before Special Committee on Un-American Activities: Investigation of Nazi Propaganda Activities and Investigation of Certain Other Propaganda Activities* ["McCormack-Dickstein Committee"]. April–December 1934.

U.S. Senate. *Charges of Illegal Practices of the Department of Justice: Hearings before a Subcommittee of the Committee on the Judiciary* ["Senate Palmer Investigation"]. January–March 1921.

———. *Hearings before a Special Committee to Investigate Propaganda or Money Alleged to Have Been Used by Foreign Governments to Influence United States Senators* ["Reed Committee"]. December 1927.

———. *Hearings before the Select Committee on the Investigation of the Attorney General* ["Daugherty Investigation"]. March–June 1924.

———. *Report and Hearings: Brewing and Liquor Interests and German and Bolshevik Propaganda* ["Overman Committee"]. 1918–19. Washington, D.C.: U.S. Government Printing Office, 1919.

———. *Russian Propaganda: Hearings before a Subcommittee of the Committee on Foreign Relations Pursuant to S. Res. 263, Directing the Committee on Foreign Relations to Investigate the Status and Activities of Ludwig C. A. K. Martens, Who Claimed to Be a Representative of the Russian Socialist Soviet Republic* ["Martens Investigation"]. January–March 1920. Washington, D.C.: U.S. Government Printing Office, 1920.

Other Sources

Abraham, Richard. *Alexander Kerensky: The First Love of the Revolution.* London: Sidgwick and Jackson, 1987.

Adler, Les K., and Thomas G. Patterson. "Red Fascism: The Merger of Nazi Germany and Soviet Russia in the American Image of Totalitarianism, 1930s–1950s." *American Historical Review* 75 (April 1970): 1046–64.

Alexander, Robert J. *The Right Opposition: The Lovestoneites and the International Communist Opposition of the 1930s.* Westport, Conn.: Greenwood Press, 1981.

Allitt, Patrick. *The Conservatives: Ideas and Personalities throughout American History.* New Haven, Conn.: Yale University Press, 2009.

Alpers, Benjamin L. *Dictators, Democracy, and American Public Culture: Envisioning the Totalitarian Enemy, 1920s–1950s.* Chapel Hill: University of North Carolina Press, 2002.

Amman, Peter H. "A 'Dog in the Nighttime' Problem: American Fascism in the 1930s." *History Teacher* 19, no. 4 (1986): 559–84.

Anderson, Robert Mapes. *Visions of the Disinherited: The Making of American Pentecostalism.* New York: Oxford University Press, 1979.

Anti-Saloon League of America. *Proceedings of the Nineteenth National Convention.* Westerville, Ohio: American Issue, 1919.

Arnesen, Eric. "No 'Graver Danger': Black Anticommunism, the Communist Party, and the Race Question." *Labor* 3 (2006): 13–52.

Ashby, LeRoy. *The Spearless Leader: Senator Borah and the Progressive Movement in the 1920s.* Urbana: University of Illinois Press, 1972.

Auerbach, Jerold. *Labor and Liberty: The La Follette Committee and the New Deal.* Indianapolis: Bobbs-Merrill, 1966.

———. "The La Follette Committee: Labor and Civil Liberties in the New Deal." *Journal of American History* 51, no. 3 (1964): 435–59.

Baldwin, Roger. "Freedom in the US and USSR." *Soviet Russia Today* (1934).

Barton, Bruce. *The Man Nobody Knows.* 1925. Reprint, London: Constable, 1927.

Bates, J. Leonard. "The Teapot Dome Scandal and the Election of 1924." *American Historical Review* 60, no. 2 (1955): 303–22.

Bayer, Ronald H. *Neighbors in Conflict: The Irish, Germans, Jews, and Italians of New York City, 1929–1941.* Baltimore: Johns Hopkins University Press, 1978.

Beal, Fred. *Proletarian Journey: New England, Gastonia, Moscow.* New York: Hillman-Curl, 1937.

Beale, David O. *In Pursuit of Purity: American Fundamentalism since 1850.* Greenville, S.C.: Unusual Publications, 1986.

Bederman, Gail. *Manliness and Civilization: A Cultural History of Gender and Race in the United States, 1880–1917.* Chicago: University of Chicago Press, 1998.

Beekman, Scott. *William Dudley Pelley: A Life in Right-Wing Extremism and the Occult.* Syracuse, N.Y.: Syracuse University Press, 2005.

Beelen, George D. "The Harding Administration and Mexico: Diplomacy by Economic Persuasion." *Americas* 41, no. 2 (1984): 177–89.

Belknap, Michal R. "Uncooperative Federalism: The Failure of the Bureau of Investigation's Intergovernmental Attack on Radicalism." *Publius* 12, no. 2 (1982): 25–47.

Bell, Daniel. *Marxian Socialism in the United States.* 1952. Reprint, Princeton, N.J.: Princeton University Press, 1967.

———, ed. *The Radical Right.* New York: Criterion, 1955.

Bell, Leland V. *In Hitler's Shadow: The Anatomy of American Nazism.* New York: Kennikat, 1973.

Bemis, Samuel Flagg. *A Diplomatic History of the United States.* 3rd ed. New York: Henry Holt, 1950.

Bennett, David H. *Demagogues in the Depression: American Radicals and the Union Party, 1932–1936.* New Brunswick, N.J.: Rutgers University Press, 1969.

———. *The Party of Fear: From Nativist Movements to the New Right in American History.* Chapel Hill: University of North Carolina Press, 1988.

Bennett, Harry, as told to Paul Marcus. *We Never Called Him Henry.* New York: Fawcett, 1951.

Bigelow, E. Victor. *Mistakes of the Interchurch Steel Report, Address by Rev. E. Victor Bigelow, Minister South Church, Andover, MA, November 22, 1920, before Boston Ministers Meeting, Pilgrim Hall.* Andover, Mass.: n.p., 1921.

Bingham, June. *Courage to Change: An Introduction to the Life and Thought of Reinhold Niebuhr.* New York: Charles Scribner's Sons, 1961.

Black, Forrest Revere. "*Debs vs. The United States*: A Judicial Milepost on the Road to Absolutism." *University of Pennsylvania Law Review and American Law Register* 81, no. 2 (1932): 160–75.

Brinkley, Alan. "The Problem of American Conservatism." *American Historical Review* 99, no. 2 (1994): 409–29.

———. *Voices of Protest: Huey Long, Father Coughlin, and the Great Depression.* New York: Alfred A. Knopf, 1982.

Brown, Richard Maxwell. *Strains of Violence: Historical Studies of American Violence and Vigilantism.* New York: Oxford University Press, 1975.

Brown, William Montgomery. *Communism and Christianism.* 1920. Reprint, Galion, Ohio: Bradford-Brown Educational, 1923.

Bryan, Ford R. *Henry's Lieutenants.* Detroit: Wayne State University Press, 1993.

Bucci, Federico. *Albert Kahn: Architect of Ford.* New York: Princeton Architectural Press, 1993.

Buckley, William F., Jr., and L. Brent Bozell. *McCarthy and His Enemies: The Record and Its Meaning.* Chicago: Regnery, 1954.

Bunche, Ralph. *The Political Status of the Negro in the Age of FDR.* Chicago: University of Chicago Press, 1973.

Burns, Jennifer. "In Search of a Usable Past: Conservative Thought in America." *Modern Intellectual History* 7, no. 2 (2010): 479–94.

Carpenter, Joel A. *Revive Us Again: The Reawakening of American Fundamentalism.* New York: Oxford University Press, 1997.

Carson, Earland I. "Franklin D. Roosevelt's Post-mortem of the 1928 Election." *Midwest Journal of Political Science* 8, no. 3 (1964): 298–308.

Carter, Paul A. *The Decline and Revival of the Social Gospel: Social and Political Liberalism in American Protestant Churches, 1920–1940.* Ithaca, N.Y.: Cornell University Press, 1954.

Cashman, Sean Dennis. *America in the Twenties and Thirties: The Olympian Age of Franklin Delano Roosevelt.* New York: New York University Press, 1989.

Caute, David. *The Great Fear: The Anti-Communist Purge under Truman and Eisenhower.* London: Secker and Warburg, 1978.

Ceplair, Larry. *Anti-Communism in Twentieth-Century America: A Critical History.* Santa Barbara, Calif.: ABC-CLIO, 2011.

———. *Under the Shadow of War: Fascism, Antifascism, and Marxists, 1918–1939.* New York: Columbia University Press, 1987.

Chafee, Zechariah, Jr. "Free Speech in Wartime." *Harvard Law Review* 32, no. 8 (1919): 932–73.

Challener, Richard D., ed. *From Isolation to Containment, 1921–1952: Three Decades of American Foreign Policy from Harding to Truman.* London: Edward Arnold, 1970.

Chamberlain, Lawrence H. *Loyalty and Legislative Action.* Ithaca, N.Y.: Cornell University Press, 1951.

Charles, Douglas M. *J. Edgar Hoover and the Anti-interventionists: FBI Political Surveillance and the Rise of the Domestic Security State, 1939–1945.* Columbus: Ohio State University Press, 2007.

Coben, Stanley. *A. Mitchell Palmer: Politician.* New York: Columbia University Press, 1963.

———. "A Study in Nativism: The American Red Scare of 1919–20." *Political Science Quarterly* 79, no. 1 (1964): 52–75.

Cohen, Warren I. *Empire without Tears: America's Foreign Relations, 1921–1933.* New York: Alfred A. Knopf, 1987.

Colburn, David R. "Governor Al Smith and the Red Scare, 1919–1920." *Political Science Quarterly* 88, no. 3 (1973): 423–44.

Cole, Wayne S. *America First: The Battle against Intervention, 1940–1941.* Madison: University of Wisconsin Press, 1953.

Commission of Inquiry, Interchurch World Movement. *Report on the Steel Strike of 1919.* New York: Harcourt, Brace, and Howe, 1920.

Coughlin, Charles E. *"Am I an Anti-Semite?": Addresses from November 1938 to January 1939.* Detroit: Condon, 1939.

———. *Father Coughlin's Radio Discourses, 1931–1932.* Royal Oak, Mich.: Radio League of the Little Flower, 1932.

———. *Father Coughlin's Radio Sermons Complete.* Baltimore: Knox and O'Leary, 1931.

———. *A Series of Lectures on Social Justice, April 1936.* Royal Oak, Mich.: Radio League of the Little Flower, 1936.

———. *A Series of Lectures on Social Justice, March 1935.* Royal Oak, Mich.: Radio League of the Little Flower, 1935.

———. *Sixteen Radio Lectures: 1938 Series.* Detroit: Condon, 1938.

———. *Why Leave Our Own? 13 Addresses on Christianity and Americanism.* Detroit: Inland, 1939.

Croly, Herbert. *The Promise of American Life.* 1909. Reprint, Cambridge, Mass.: Harvard University Press, 1965.

Crossman, Richard. *The God That Failed: Six Studies in Communism.* London: Hamish Hamilton, 1950.

Curti, Merle. *The Roots of American Loyalty.* New York: Columbia University Press, 1946.

Cyphers, Christopher J. *The National Civic Federation and the Making of a New Liberalism, 1900–1915.* Westport, Conn.: Praeger, 2002.

Dallek, Robert. *Franklin D. Roosevelt and American Foreign Policy, 1932–1945.* Oxford: Oxford University Press, 1979.

Daugherty, Harry M. *The Inside Story of the Harding Tragedy.* New York: Churchill, 1932.

Davis, David Brion, ed. *The Fear of Conspiracy: Images of Un-American Subversion from the Revolution to the Present.* Ithaca, N.Y.: Cornell University Press, 1971.

Davis, Margaret Leslie. *Dark Side of Fortune: Triumph and Scandal in the Life of Oil Tycoon Edward L. Doheny.* Berkeley: University of California Press, 1998.

Denning, Michael. *The Cultural Front: The Laboring of American Culture in the Twentieth Century.* New York: Verso, 1996.

Diamond, Sander A. *The Nazi Movement in the United States, 1924–1941.* Ithaca, N.Y.: Cornell University Press, 1974.

Dick, William M. *Labor and Socialism in America: The Gompers Era.* Port Washington, N.Y.: Kennikat, 1972.

Dies, Martin. *The Trojan Horse in America: A Report to the Nation.* New York: Dodd, Mead, 1940.

Diggins, John Patrick. "American Catholics and Italian Fascism." *Journal of Contemporary History* 2, no. 4 (1967): 51–68.

Dilling, Elizabeth. *The Red Network: A "Who's Who" and Handbook of Radicalism for Patriots.* Kenilworth, Ill.: Dilling, 1934.

Doctorow, E. L. *Ragtime.* 1975. Reprint, London: Macmillan, 1976.

Donner, Frank J. *The Age of Surveillance: The Aims and Methods of America's Political Intelligence System.* New York: Alfred A. Knopf, 1980.

Dos Passos, John. *U.S.A.* 1938 (as a trilogy). Reprint, London: Penguin, 2001.

Downs, Linda Bank. *Diego Rivera: The Detroit Industry Murals.* New York: W. W. Norton, 1999.

Draper, Theodore. *American Communism and Soviet Russia.* London: Macmillan, 1960.

———. *The Roots of American Communism.* New York: Viking, 1957.

Drucker, Peter. *Max Shachtman and His Left: A Socialist's Odyssey through the "American Century."* Atlantic Highlands, N.J.: Humanities Press, 1994.

Dunn, Robert W., ed. *The Palmer Raids.* New York: International, 1948.

Eastman, Max. *The End of Socialism in Russia.* London: Martin Secker and Warburg, 1937.

———. *Love and Revolution: My Journey through an Epoch.* 1942. Reprint, New York: Random House, 1964.

———. *Marx, Lenin, and the Science of Revolution.* London: Allen and Unwin, 1926.

Ehrt, Adolf. *Communism in Germany: The Truth about the Communist Conspiracy on the Eve of the National Revolution.* Berlin: General League of Germany Anti-Communist Associations, 1933.

Ellis, Mark. "J. Edgar Hoover and the 'Red Summer' of 1919." *Journal of American Studies* 28, no. 1 (1994): 39–59.

———. *Race, War, and Surveillance: African Americans and the United States Government during World War I.* Bloomington: Indiana University Press, 2001.

Engelman, Larry. *Intemperance: The Lost War against Liquor.* New York: Free Press, 1979.

Epstein, Edward Jay. *Dossier: The Secret History of Armand Hammer.* London: Orion Business Books, 1996.

Faulkner, Harold Underwood. *American Economic History.* 1924. Reprint, New York: Harper and Brothers, 1954.

Ferrell, Robert H. *The Strange Deaths of Warren G. Harding.* Columbia: University of Missouri Press, 1996.

Ferrell, Robert H., and Howard H. Quint, eds. *The Talkative President: The Off-the-Record Press Conferences of Calvin Coolidge.* New York: Garland Press, 1979.

Feuerlicht, Robert Strauss. *America's Reign of Terror: World War One, the Red Scare, and the Palmer Raids.* New York: Random House, 1971.

Fike, Claude E. "The Influence of the Creel Committee and the American Red Cross on Russian-American Relations, 1917–1919." *Journal of Modern History* 31, no. 2 (1959): 93–109.

Filene, Peter G. *Americans and the Soviet Experiment, 1917–1933.* Cambridge, Mass.: Harvard University Press, 1967.

Finder, Joseph. *Red Curtain.* New York: New Republic, 1983.

Fine, Sidney. *The Automobile under the Blue Eagle: Labor, Management, and the Automobile Manufacturing Code.* Ann Arbor: University of Michigan Press, 1963.

Fish, Hamilton. *Memoirs of an American Patriot.* Washington, D.C.: Regnery Gateway, 1991.

Fleming, John V. *The Anti-Communist Manifestos: Four Books That Shaped the Cold War.* New York: W. W. Norton, 2009.

Foglesong, David S. *America's Secret War against Bolshevism: U.S. Intervention in the Russian Civil War.* Chapel Hill: University of North Carolina Press, 1995.

Fones-Wolf, Elizabeth. *Selling Free Enterprise: The Business Assault on Labor and Liberalism, 1945–1960.* Urbana: University of Illinois Press, 1994.

Fones-Wolf, Elizabeth, and Ken Fones-Wolf. "Lending a Hand to Labor: James Myers and the Federal Council of Churches, 1926–1947." *Church History* 68, no. 1 (1999): 62–86.

Ford, Henry. *The International Jew.* Vol. 1. Dearborn, Mich.: Dearborn Publishing, 1920.

Ford, Henry, in collaboration with Samuel Crowther. *My Life and Work.* London: Heinemann, 1922.

———. *Today and Tomorrow.* London: Heinemann, 1926.

Foster, William Z. *The Great Steel Strike and Its Lessons.* New York: B. W. Huebsch, 1920.

Frankel, Oz. "Whatever Happened to 'Red Emma'? Emma Goldman, from Alien Rebel to American Icon." *Journal of American History* 83, no. 3 (1996): 903–42.

Friedheim, Robert L. *The Seattle General Strike.* Seattle: University of Washington Press, 1964.

Gaebelein, Arno Clemens. *The Conflict of the Ages: The Mystery of Lawlessness; Its Origin, Historic Development, and Coming Defeat.* 1933. Reprint, London: Pickering and Inglis, 1934.

———. *Half a Century: The Autobiography of a Servant.* 1930. Reprint, New York: Garland, 1988.

Gage, Beverley. *The Day Wall Street Exploded: A Story of America in Its First Age of Terror.* New York: Oxford University Press, 2008.

Gallagher, Louis. *Edmund A. Walsh, S.J.: A Biography.* New York: Benziger Brothers, 1962.

Gary, Brett. *The Nervous Liberals: Propaganda Anxieties from World War I to the Cold War.* New York: Columbia University Press, 1999.

Gates, John. *The Story of an American Communist.* New York: Thomas Nelson and Sons, 1958.

Gaughan, Anthony. "Woodrow Wilson and the Rise of Militant Interventionism in the South." *Journal of Southern History* 65, no. 4 (1999): 771–808.

Gavrilovich, Peter, and Bill McGraw. *Detroit Almanac.* Detroit: Detroit Free Press, 2001.

Gerstle, Gary. "Race and the Myth of the Liberal Consensus." *Journal of American History* 82, no. 2 (1995): 579–86.

Giglio, James M. *H. M. Daugherty and the Politics of Expediency*. Kent, Ohio: Kent State University Press, 1978.

Gilbert, Clinton W. *You Takes Your Choice*. New York: G. P. Putnam's Sons, 1924.

Gilmore, Glenda Elizabeth. *Defying Dixie: The Radical Roots of Civil Rights, 1919–1950*. New York: W. W. Norton, 2008.

Gitlow, Benjamin. *I Confess: The Truth about American Anticommunism*. New York: E. P. Dutton, 1940.

Glantz, Mary E. *FDR and the Soviet Union: The President's Battles over Foreign Policy*. Lawrence: University Press of Kansas, 2005.

Glass, William R. "Fundamentalism's Prophetic Vision of the Jews: The 1930s." *Jewish Social Studies* 47, no. 1 (1985): 63–76.

Goldberg, Harold J., ed. *Documents of Soviet-American Relations*. Vol. 2, *Propaganda, Economic Affairs, Recognition, 1917–1933*. Gulf Breeze, Fla.: Academic International Press, 1995.

Goldstein, Robert Justin. *Political Repression in Modern America: From 1870 to the Present*. Cambridge, Mass.: Schenkman, 1978.

Gompers, Samuel. *The Truth about Soviet Russia and Bolshevism*. Washington, D.C.: American Federation of Labor, 1920.

Gompers, Samuel, and William English Walling. *Out of Their Own Mouths: A Revelation and Indictment of Sovietism*. New York: E. P. Dutton, 1921.

Goodall, Alex. "The Battle of Detroit and Anticommunism in the Depression Era." *Historical Journal* 51, no. 2 (2008): 457–80.

Goodman, Walter. *The Committee: The Extraordinary Career of the House Committee on Un-American Activities*. London: Secker and Warburg, 1964.

Graham, Malbone W. "Russian-American Relations, 1917–1933: An Interpretation." *American Political Science Review* 28, no. 3 (1934): 387–409.

Gramsci, Antonio. *Pre-prison Writings*. Edited by Richard Bellamy. Cambridge: Cambridge University Press, 1994.

———. *Prison Notebooks*. Edited by Joseph A. Buttigieg. New York: Columbia University Press, 1975.

Green, George N. *The Establishment in Texas Politics: The Primitive Years, 1938–1957*. London: Greenwood Press, 1979.

Griffith, Robert. *The Politics of Fear: Joseph McCarthy and the Senate*. Lexington: University Press of Kentucky, 1970.

Griffith, Robert, and Athan Theoharis, eds. *The Specter: Original Essays on the Cold War and the Origins of McCarthyism*. New York: New Viewpoints, 1974.

Hankins, Barry. *God's Rascal: J. Frank Norris and the Beginnings of Southern Fundamentalism*. Lexington: University Press of Kentucky, 1996.

Hanks, Richard Kay. "Hamilton Fish and American Isolationism, 1920–1944." Ph.D. diss., University of California, Riverside, 1971.

Hapgood, Norman, ed. *Professional Patriots*. New York: Albert and Charles Boni, 1927.

Harper, Alan D. "The Antired Decade Remembered." *Reviews in American History* 7, no. 1 (1979): 128–33.

Hatton, Timothy J., and Jeffrey G. Williamson, eds. *Migration and the International Labor Market, 1850–1939*. London: Routledge, 1994.

Haynes, Fred E. "The Significance of the Latest Third Party Movement." *Mississippi Valley Historical Review* 12, no. 2 (1925): 177–86.

Haynes, John Earl. *Red Scare or Red Menace? American Communism and Anticommunism in the Cold War Era.* Chicago: Ivan R. Dee, 1996.

Haynes, Roy A. *Prohibition Inside Out.* London: T. Fisher Unwin, 1924.

Heale, Michael J. *American Anticommunism: Combating the Enemy Within, 1830–1970.* Baltimore: Johns Hopkins University Press, 1990.

———. "Beyond the 'Age of McCarthy': Anticommunism and the Historians." In *The State of U.S. History,* edited by Melvyn Stokes. Oxford: Berg, 2002.

Heineman, Kenneth. "Media Bias in Coverage of the Dies Committee on Un-American Activities." *Historian* 55, no. 1 (1992): 37–52.

Henderson, Thomas M. *Tammany Hall and the New Immigrants: The Progressive Years.* New York: Arno Press, 1976.

Herndon, Booton. *Ford: An Unconventional Biography of the Two Henry Fords and Their Times.* London: Cassell, 1969.

Hicks, John D. *Republican Ascendancy, 1921–1933.* New York: Harper and Row, 1963.

Higham, John. *Strangers in the Land: Patterns of American Nativism.* New Brunswick, N.J.: Rutgers University Press, 1955.

Hillquit, Morris. *Loose Leaves from a Busy Life.* New York: Macmillan, 1934.

Hobsbawm, Eric. *The Age of Extremes: The Short Twentieth Century, 1914–1991.* London: Penguin, 1994.

Hoff-Wilson, Joan. *Ideology and Economics: US Relations with the Soviet Union, 1918–1933.* Columbia: University of Missouri Press, 1974.

Hofstadter, Richard. *The Paranoid Style in American Politics, and Other Essays.* New York: Alfred A. Knopf, 1965.

Hoover, J. Edgar, and Courtney Ryler Cooper. "The Amazing Mr. Means." *American Magazine,* December 1936.

Horne, Gerald. *Black Liberation/Red Scare: Ben Davis and the Communist Party.* Newark: University of Delaware Press, 1994.

Howard, Sidney. *The Labor Spy.* New York: Republic, 1924.

Howe, Irving, and Lewis Coser. *The American Communist Party: A Critical History (1919–1957).* Boston: Beacon Press, 1957.

Hoyt, Edwin P. *Spectacular Rogue: Gaston B. Means.* New York: Bobbs-Merrill, 1963.

Huberman, Leo. *The Labor Spy Racket.* New York: Modern Age Books, 1937.

Huntington, W. Chapin. *The Homesick Million: Russia-Out-of-Russia.* Boston: Stratford, 1933.

Ickes, Harold L. *The Secret Diary of Harold L. Ickes.* Vol. 2, *The Inside Struggle, 1936–1939.* New York: Simon and Schuster, 1954.

Irons, Peter H. "'Fighting Fair': Zechariah Chafee, Jr., the Department of Justice, and the 'Trial at the Harvard Club.'" *Harvard Law Review* 94, no. 6 (1981): 1205–36.

Isserman, Maurice. *Which Side Were You On? The American Communist Party during the Second World War.* Middletown, Conn.: Wesleyan University Press, 1982.

Jeansonne, Glen. *Women of the Far Right: The Mothers' Movement and World War II.* Chicago: University of Chicago Press, 1996.

Jensen, Joan. *The Price of Vigilance*. Chicago: Rand McNally, 1968.

Johnson, Claudius O. *Borah of Idaho*. New York: Laymans, Green, 1936.

Johnson, Niel M. *George Sylvester Viereck: German-American Propagandist*. Urbana: University of Illinois Press, 1972.

Jonas, Manfred. *The United States and Germany: A Diplomatic History*. Ithaca, N.Y.: Cornell University Press, 1984.

Josephson, Harold. "Ex-Communists in Crossfire: A Cold War Debate." *Historian* 44, no. 1 (1981): 69–83.

Kazin, Michael. *The Populist Persuasion: An American History*. Rev. ed. Ithaca, N.Y.: Cornell University Press, 1995.

Keeran, Roger. *The Communist Party and the Auto Workers Union*. Bloomington: Indiana University Press, 1980.

Keith, Jeanette. "The Politics of Southern Draft Resistance, 1917–1918: Class, Race, and Conscription in the Rural South." *Journal of American History* 87, no. 4 (2001): 1335–61.

Kelley, Robin D. G. *Hammer and Hoe: Alabama Communists during the Great Depression*. Chapel Hill: University of North Carolina Press, 1990.

Kennan, George. "The Sisson Documents." *Journal of Modern History* 28, no. 2 (1956): 130–54.

Kern, Gary. *A Death in Washington: Walter G. Krivitsky and the Stalin Terror*. New York: Enigma, 2003.

Kimmage, Michael. *The Conservative Turn: Lionel Trilling, Whittaker Chambers, and the Lessons of Anti-Communism*. Cambridge, Mass.: Harvard University Press, 2009.

Klehr, Harvey. *Communist Cadre: The Social Background of the American Communist Party Elite*. Stanford, Calif.: Hoover Institution Press, 1978.

———. *The Heyday of American Communism: The Depression Decade*. New York: Basic Books, 1984.

Klehr, Harvey, and John Earl Haynes. *The American Communist Movement: Storming Heaven Itself*. New York: Twayne, 1992.

Klehr, Harvey, John Earl Haynes, and Kyrill M. Anderson. *The Soviet World of American Communism*. New Haven, Conn.: Yale University Press, 1998.

Klehr, Harvey, John Earl Haynes, and Fridrikh Igorevich Firsov. *The Secret World of American Communism*. New Haven, Conn.: Yale University Press, 1995.

Klehr, Harvey, John Earl Haynes, and Alexander Vassiliev. *Spies: The Rise and Fall of the KGB in America*. New Haven, Conn.: Yale University Press, 2009.

Kostiainen, Auvo. "Santeri Nuorteva and the Origins of Soviet-American Relations." *American Studies in Scandinavia* 15 (1983): 1–13.

Kovel, Joel. *Red Hunting in the Promised Land: Anticommunism and the Making of America*. 1994. Reprint, London: Cassell, 1997.

Kravchenko, Victor. *I Chose Freedom: The Personal and Political Life of a Soviet Official*. New York: Charles Scribner's Sons, 1946.

Krebs, Richard. *Out of the Night*. London: W. Heinemann, 1941.

Krivitsky, Walter G. *In Stalin's Secret Service: An Expose of Russia's Secret Policies by the Former Chief of the Soviet Intelligence in Western Europe*. New York: Harper, 1939.

Kuhn, Arthur J. *GM Passes Ford, 1918–1938: Designing the General Motors Performance-Control System.* University Park: Pennsylvania State University Press, 1986.

Kutler, Stanley I. *The American Inquisition.* New York: Hill and Wang, 1982.

Lasch, Christopher. *The American Liberals and the Russian Revolution.* New York: Columbia University Press, 1962.

Latham, Earl. *The Communist Controversy in Washington: From the New Deal to Mc-Carthy.* Cambridge, Mass.: Harvard University Press, 1966.

Layton, Edwin. "The Better America Federation: A Case Study of Superpatriotism." *Pacific Historical Review* 30, no. 2 (1961): 137–47.

Lee, Albert. *Henry Ford and the Jews.* New York: Stein and Day, 1980.

Leffler, Melvyn P. "The American Conception of National Security and the Beginnings of the Cold War, 1945–1948." *American Historical Review* 89, no. 2 (1984): 346–81.

———. *The Specter of Communism: The United States and the Origins of the Cold War, 1917–1953.* New York: Hill and Wang, 1994.

Lemons, Stanley. *The Woman Citizen: Social Feminism in the 1920s.* Urbana: University of Illinois Press, 1973.

Levin, Murray B. *Political Hysteria in America: The Democratic Capacity for Repression.* New York: Basic Books, 1971.

Lewis, David L. *The Public Image of Henry Ford: An American Folk Hero and His Company.* Detroit: Wayne State University Press, 1976.

Lewis, George. *The White South and the Red Menace: Segregationists, Anticommunism, and Massive Resistance, 1945–1965.* Gainesville: University Press of Florida, 2004.

Lewis, Sinclair. *Babbitt.* 1922. Reprint, London: Vintage, 1994.

Lewy, Guenter. *The Cause That Failed: Communism in American Political Life.* Oxford: Oxford University Press, 1990.

Lichtenstein, Nelson, and Stephen Meyer III. *On the Line: Essays in the History of Auto Work.* Urbana: University of Illinois Press, 1989.

Liebich, André. *From the Other Shore: Russian Social Democracy after 1921.* Cambridge, Mass.: Harvard University Press, 1997.

Link, Arthur S., ed. *The Papers of Woodrow Wilson.* 69 vols. Princeton, N.J.: Princeton University Press, 1966–94.

Little, Douglas. "Antibolshevism and American Foreign Policy, 1919–1939: The Diplomacy of Self-Delusion." *American Quarterly* 35, no. 4 (1983): 376–90.

Lockwood, George B. *Americanism.* 3rd ed. Washington, D.C.: National Republican Publishing, 1921.

Lower, Richard Coke. "Hiram Johnson: The Making of an Irreconcilable." *Pacific Historical Review* 41, no. 4 (1972): 505–26.

Lowitt, Richard. *George W. Norris: The Persistence of a Progressive, 1913–1933.* Urbana: University of Illinois Press, 1971.

Luff, Jennifer. *Commonsense Anticommunism: Labor and Civil Liberties between the World Wars.* Chapel Hill: University of North Carolina Press, 2012.

Luthin, Reinhard H. "Smith Wildman Brookhart of Iowa: Insurgent Agrarian Politician." *Agricultural History* 25, no. 4 (1951): 187–97.

Lyons, Eugene. *Assignment in Utopia.* New York: Harcourt, Brace, 1937.

——. *Moscow Carrousel*. New York: Alfred A. Knopf, 1936.

——. *The Red Decade: The Stalinist Penetration of America*. Indianapolis: Bobbs-Merrill, 1941.

——. *Stalin, Czar of All the Russias*. Philadelphia: Lippincott, 1940.

Lyons, Richard L. "The Boston Police Strike of 1919." *New England Quarterly* 20, no. 2 (1947): 147–68.

Machen, J. Gresham. *Christianity and Liberalism*. New York: Macmillan, 1923.

MacLean, Nancy. *Behind the Mask of Chivalry: The Making of the Second Ku Klux Klan*. New York: Oxford University Press, 1994.

Maddux, Thomas R. "Red Fascism, Brown Bolshevism: The American Image of Totalitarianism in the 1930s." *Historian* 70, no. 1 (1977): 85–103.

Magil, A. B., and Henry Stevens. *The Peril of Fascism*. New York: International, 1938.

Maney, Patrick J. *"Young Bob" La Follette: A Biography of Robert M. La Follette, Jr., 1895–1953*. Columbia: University of Missouri Press, 1978.

Marcus, Sheldon. *Father Coughlin: The Tumultuous Life of the Priest of the Little Flower*. Boston: Little, Brown, 1973.

Marquart, Frank. *An Auto Worker's Journal: The UAW from Crusade to One-Party Union*. University Park: Pennsylvania State University Press, 1975.

Marsden, George M. *Fundamentalism and American Culture: The Shaping of Twentieth-Century Evangelicalism, 1870–1925*. 1980. Reprint, Oxford: Oxford University Press, 1982.

Marvin, Fred R. *Underground with the Reds*. New York: Commercial Newspaper, 1923.

McCarten, John. "The Little Man in Henry Ford's Basement—Part I." *American Mercury*, May 1940.

McFadden, David W. *Alternative Paths: Soviets and Americans, 1917–1920*. New York: Oxford University Press, 1993.

McKenna, Marian C. *Borah*. Ann Arbor: University of Michigan Press, 1961.

——. "Prelude to Tyranny: Wheeler, FDR, and the 1937 Court Fight." *Pacific Historical Review* 62, no. 4 (1993): 405–31.

Meier, August, and Elliott Rudwick. *Black Detroit and the Rise of the UAW*. Oxford: Oxford University Press, 1979.

Meyer, Stephen, III. *The Five Dollar Day: Labor Management and Social Control in the Ford Motor Company, 1908–1921*. Albany: State University of New York Press, 1981.

Miller, Robert Moats. *American Protestantism and Social Issues, 1919–1939*. Chapel Hill: University of North Carolina Press, 1958.

Miscamble, Wilson D. "The Limits of Catholic Antifascism: The Case of John A. Ryan." *Church History* 59, no. 4 (1990): 523–38.

Mitchell, John Bruce. "'Reds' in New York's Slums." *Forum*, April 1919.

Mitgang, Herbert. *Once upon a Time in New York: Jimmy Walker, Franklin Roosevelt, and the Last Great Battle of the Jazz Age*. New York: Free Press, 2000.

Mock, James R., and Cedric Larson. *Words That Won the War: The Story of the Committee on Public Information, 1917–1919*. Princeton, N.J.: Princeton University Press, 1939.

Morgan, Ted. *A Covert Life: Jay Lovestone, Communist, Anti-Communist, and Spymaster*. New York: Random House, 1999.

———. *Reds: McCarthyism in Twentieth-Century America.* New York: Random House, 2003.

Mowry, George E. *The California Progressives.* Berkeley: University of California Press, 1951.

Mugglebee, Ruth. *Father Coughlin and the Shrine of the Little Flower.* Garden City, N.Y.: Doubleday, 1933.

Mugridge, Ian. *The View from Xanadu: William Randolph Hearst and United States Foreign Policy.* Montreal: McGill-Queen's, 1995.

Murphy, Paul. "Sources and Nature of Intolerance in the 1920s." *Journal of American History* 51, no. 1 (1964): 60–76.

Murray, Robert K. "Communism and the Great Steel Strike of 1919." *Mississippi Valley Historical Review* 38, no. 3 (1951): 445–66.

———. *The Great Red Scare: A Study in National Hysteria, 1919–1920.* Minneapolis: University of Minnesota Press, 1955.

Myers, Constance Ashton. *The Prophet's Army: Trotskyists in America, 1928–1941.* Westport, Conn.: Greenwood Press, 1977.

Naison, Mark. *Communists in Harlem during the Depression.* Urbana: University of Illinois Press, 1983.

Nathan, George Jean, and H. L. Mencken. *The American Credo: A Contribution toward the Interpretation of the National Mind.* New York: Alfred A. Knopf, 1920.

Nevins, Allan. *Ford: The Times, the Man, the Company.* New York: Charles Scribner's Sons, 1954.

Newby, I. A. "States' Rights and Southern Congressmen during World War I." *Phylon (1960–)* 24, no. 1 (1963): 34–50.

Newsinger, John, ed. *Shaking the World: John Reed's Revolutionary Journalism.* London: Bookmarks, 1998.

Niebuhr, Reinhold. *Leaves from the Notebook of a Tamed Cynic.* 1957. Reprint, New York: World, 1970.

Nielsen, Kim E. *Un-American Womanhood: Antiradicalism, Antifeminism, and the First Red Scare.* Columbus: Ohio State University Press, 2001.

Norris, George. *Fighting Liberal: The Autobiography of George W. Norris.* New York: Macmillan, 1945.

Norris, James D. *Advertising and the Transformation of American Society, 1865–1920.* New York: Greenwood, 1990.

Norwood, Stephen H. *Strikebreaking and Intimidation: Mercenaries and Masculinity in Twentieth-Century America.* Chapel Hill: University of North Carolina Press, 2002.

Nye, David E. *Henry Ford, "Ignorant Idealist."* London: Kennikat Press, 1999.

O'Brien, John H. "Henry Ford's Commander in Chief." *Forum,* February 1938.

O'Connor, Harvey. *Revolution in Seattle.* New York: Monthly Review Press, 1964.

Offner, Arnold A. *American Appeasement: United States Foreign Policy and Germany, 1933–1938.* Cambridge, Mass.: Belknap, 1969.

Older, Mrs. Fremont. *William Randolph Hearst: American.* New York: D. Appleton-Century, 1936.

Olds, Marshall. *Analysis of the Interchurch World Movement Report on the Steel Strike.* 1923. Reprint, New York: Da Capo Press, 1971.

Packer, Herbert L. *Ex-Communist Witnesses: Four Studies in Fact-Finding.* Stanford, Calif.: Stanford University Press, 1962.

Patterson, James T. "A Conservative Coalition Forms in Congress, 1933–1939." *Journal of American History* 52, no. 4 (1966): 757–72.

Pawa, J. M. "The Search for Black Radicals: American and British Documents Relative to the 1919 Red Scare." *Labor History* 16, no. 2 (1975): 272–84.

Pells, Richard H. *Radical Visions and American Dreams: Culture and Social Thought in the Depression Years.* New York: Harper and Row, 1973.

Pencak, William. *For God and Country: The American Legion, 1919–1941.* Boston: Northeastern University Press, 1989.

Perlstein, Rick. *Before the Storm: Barry Goldwater and the Unmaking of the American Consensus.* New York: Hill and Wang, 2001.

Peterson, H. C., and Gilbert C. Fite. *Opponents of War, 1917–1918.* 1957. Reprint, Seattle: University of Washington Press, 1967.

Pfannestiel, Todd. *Rethinking the Red Scare: The Lusk Committee and New York's Crusade against Radicalism, 1919–1923.* New York: Routledge, 2003.

———. "The Soviet Bureau: A Bolshevik Strategy to Secure U.S. Diplomatic Recognition through Economic Trade." *Diplomatic History* 27, no. 2 (2003): 171–92.

Phillips-Fein, Kim. *Invisible Hands: The Businessmen's Crusade against the New Deal.* New York: W. W. Norton, 2009.

Post, Louis F. *The Deportations Delirium of Nineteen-Twenty.* Chicago: C. H. Kerr, 1923.

———. *The Ethics of Democracy.* 1903. Reprint, Indianapolis: Bobbs-Merrill, 1916.

Powers, Richard Gid. *Not without Honor: The History of American Anticommunism.* New York: Free Press, 1995.

Preston, William, Jr. *Aliens and Dissenters: Federal Suppression of Radicals, 1903–1933.* Cambridge, Mass.: Harvard University Press, 1963.

Prickett, J. R. "Communists and the Communist Issue in the American Labor Movement, 1920–1950." Ph.D. diss., University of California, Los Angeles, 1975.

Raat, W. Dirk, and William H. Beezley, eds. *Twentieth-Century Mexico.* Lincoln: University of Nebraska Press, 1986.

Rabban, David M. *Free Speech in Its Forgotten Years.* Cambridge: Cambridge University Press, 1997.

Raeff, Mark. *Russia Abroad: A Cultural History of the Russian Emigration, 1919–1939.* New York: Oxford University Press, 1990.

Renshaw, Patrick. "The IWW and the Red Scare, 1917–1924." *Journal of Contemporary History* 3, no. 4 (1968): 63–72.

Ribuffo, Leo P. *The Old Christian Right: The Protestant Far Right from the Great Depression to the Cold War.* Philadelphia: Temple University Press, 1983.

———. *Right Center Left: Essays in American History.* New Brunswick, N.J.: Rutgers University Press, 1992.

Rivera, Diego. *My Art, My Life: An Autobiography.* New York: Dover, 1945.

Robin, Corey. *The Reactionary Mind.* Oxford: Oxford University Press, 2011.

Rogin, Michael Paul. *The Intellectuals and McCarthy: The Radical Specter.* Cambridge, Mass.: MIT Press, 1967.

———. *Ronald Reagan, the Movie, and Other Episodes in Political Demonology.* Berkeley: University of California Press, 1987.

Ross, Stewart Halsey. *Propaganda for War: How the United States Was Conditioned to Fight the Great War of 1914–1918.* Jefferson, N.C.: McFarland, 1996.

Rossinow, Doug. *Visions of Progress: The Left-Liberal Tradition in America.* Philadelphia: University of Pennsylvania Press, 2008.

Rosswurm, Steve. *The FBI and the Catholic Church, 1935–1962.* Amherst: University of Massachusetts Press, 2009.

Roy, Ralph Lord. *Communism and the Churches.* New York: Harcourt, Brace, 1960.

Rudolph, Frederick. "The American Liberty League, 1934–1940." *American Historical Review* 56, no. 1 (1950): 19–33.

Rumer, Thomas. *The American Legion: An Official History, 1919–1989.* New York: M. Evans, 1990.

Ruotsila, Markku. *British and American Anticommunism before the Cold War.* London: Frank Cass, 2001.

———. "Neoconservatism Prefigured: The Social Democratic League of America and the Anticommunists of the Anglo-American Right, 1917–21." *Journal of American Studies* 40, no. 2 (2006): 327–45.

Russell, C. Allyn. *Voices of American Fundamentalism: Seven Biographical Studies.* Philadelphia: Westminster Press, 1976.

Ryan, James Gilbert. *Earl Browder: The Failure of American Communism.* Tuscaloosa: University of Alabama Press, 1997.

Sakmyster, Thomas. *Red Conspirator: J. Peters and the American Communist Underground.* Urbana: University of Illinois Press, 2011.

Salisbury, Richard V. "Mexico, the United States, and the 1926–1927 Nicaraguan Crisis." *Hispanic American Historical Review* 66, no. 2 (1986): 319–39.

Salter, John Thomas, ed. *Public Men in and out of Office.* New York: Da Capo, 1972.

Sarasohn, David. "The Insurgent Republicans: Insurgent Image and Republican Reality." *Social Science History* 3, nos. 3–4 (1979): 245–61.

Saul, Norman E. *War and Revolution: The United States and Russia, 1914–1921.* Lawrence: University Press of Kansas, 2001.

Scales, Junius Irving, and Richard Nickson. *Cause at Heart: A Former Communist Remembers.* Athens: University of Georgia Press, 1987.

Schatz, Ronald W. "American Labor and the Catholic Church, 1919–1950." *U.S. Catholic Historian* 3, no. 3 (1983): 178–90.

Schlesinger, Arthur M., Jr. *The Age of Roosevelt: The Politics of Upheaval.* 1960. Reprint, Boston: Houghton Mifflin, 1966.

Schlesinger, Arthur M., Jr., and Roger Bruns, eds. *Congress Investigates: A Documented History, 1792–1974.* Vol. 4. New York: Chelsea House, 1975.

Schmidt, Regin. *Red Scare: FBI and the Origins of Anticommunism in the United States, 1919–1943.* Copenhagen: Museum Tusculanum Press, University of Copenhagen, 2000.

Schrecker, Ellen. *Many Are the Crimes: McCarthyism in America.* Boston: Little, Brown, 1998.

Schulzinger, Robert D. *The Wise Men of Foreign Affairs: The History of the Council of Foreign Relations.* New York: Columbia University Press, 1984.

Seaton, Douglas P. *Catholics and Radicals: The Association of Catholic Trade Unionists and the American Labor Movement, from Depression to Cold War.* London: Associated University Presses, 1981.

Shenton, James P. "The Coughlin Movement and the New Deal." *Political Science Quarterly* 73, no. 3 (1958): 352–73.

Simonds, William Adams. *Henry Ford: A Biography.* London: Michael Joseph, 1946.

Sisson, Edgar. *One Hundred Red Days: A Personal Chronicle of the Bolshevik Revolution.* 1931. Reprint, Westport, Conn.: Hyperion Press, 1977.

Skocpol, Theda, Marshall Ganz, and Ziad Munson. "A Nation of Organizers: The Institutional Origins of Civic Voluntarism in the United States." *American Political Science Review* 94, no. 3 (2000): 527–46.

Slotkin, Richard. *Gunfighter Nation: The Myth of the Frontier in Twentieth-Century America.* New York: HarperPerennial, 1993.

Smith, Daniel M. "Authoritarianism and American Policy Makers in Two World Wars." *Pacific Historical Review* 43, no. 3 (1974): 303–23.

Smith, Geoffrey S. *To Save a Nation: American Counter-subversives, the New Deal, and the Coming of World War II.* New York: Basic Books, 1973.

Smith, John Abernathy. "Ecclesiastical Politics and the Founding of the Federal Council of Churches." *Church History* 43, no. 3 (1974): 350–65.

Spenser, Daniela. *The Impossible Triangle: Mexico, Soviet Russia, and the United States in the 1920s.* Durham: Duke University Press, 1999.

Spivak, John L. *Secret Armies: The New Technique of Nazi Warfare.* New York: Modern Age, 1939.

Starobin, Joseph R. *American Communism in Crisis, 1943–1957.* Cambridge, Mass.: Harvard University Press, 1972.

Steffens, Lincoln. *The Autobiography of Lincoln Steffens.* New York: Harcourt, Brace, 1931.

Stegner, Wallace. "The Radio Priest and His Flock." In *The Aspirin Age, 1919–1941,* edited by Isabel Leighton. London: Simon and Schuster, 1950.

Stone, Geoffrey R. "Judge Learned Hand and the Espionage Act of 1917: A Mystery Unraveled." *University of Chicago Law Review* 70, no. 1 (2003): 335–58.

Streitmatter, Rodger. *Mightier than the Sword: How the New Media Have Shaped American History.* Boulder, Colo.: Westview Press, 1997.

Stromquist, Shelton. *Re-inventing "the People": The Progressive Movement, the Class Problem, and the Origins of Modern Liberalism.* Urbana: University of Illinois Press, 2006.

Sugrue, Thomas. *The Origins of the Urban Crisis: Race and Inequality in Postwar Detroit.* Princeton, N.J.: Princeton University Press, 1996.

Sutton, Matthew Avery. "Was FDR the Antichrist? The Birth of Fundamentalist Antiliberalism in a Global Age." *Journal of American History* 98, no. 4 (2012): 1052–74.

Sward, Keith. *The Legend of Henry Ford.* Toronto: Rinehart, 1948.

Swing, Raymond Gram. *Forerunners of American Fascism.* 1935. Reprint, Freeport, N.Y.: Books for Libraries Press, 1962.

Szasz, Ferenc Morton. *The Divided Mind of Protestant America, 1880–1930.* Tuscaloosa: University of Alabama Press, 1982.

Taft, Philip. *The A. F. of L. in the Time of Gompers.* New York: Harper and Brothers, 1957.

———. *Organized Labor in American History.* New York: Harper and Row, 1964.

Talbert, Roy. *Negative Intelligence: The Army and the American Left, 1917–1941.* Jackson: University Press of Mississippi, 1991.

Taylor, Gregory S. *The History of the North Carolina Communist Party.* Columbia: University of South Carolina Press, 2009.

Tentler, Leslie Woodcock. *Seasons of Grace: A History of the Catholic Archdiocese of Detroit.* Detroit: Wayne State University Press, 1990.

Thacker, May Dixon. *The Strange Death of President Harding: From the Diaries of Gaston B. Means.* New York: Guild, 1930.

Thomas, Norman. *The Choice before Us: Mankind at the Crossroads.* New York: Macmillan, 1934.

Thompson, John A. *Reformers and War: American Progressive Publicists and the First World War.* Cambridge: Cambridge University Press, 1987.

Thorpe, Francis Newton. *The Constitutional History of the United States.* 2 vols. Chicago: Callaghan, 1901.

Toth, Charles W. "Samuel Gompers, Communism, and the Pan American Federation of Labor." *Americas* 23, no. 3 (1967): 273–78.

Trollinger, William Vance. *God's Empire: William Bell Riley and Midwestern Fundamentalism.* Madison: University of Wisconsin Press, 1990.

Troncone, Anthony C. "Hamilton Fish Sr. and the Politics of American Nationalism, 1912–1945." Ph.D. diss., Rutgers University, 1993.

Trow, Clifford W. "Woodrow Wilson and the Mexican Interventionist Movement of 1919." *Journal of American History* 58, no. 1 (1971): 46–72.

Tucker, Ray, and Frederick R. Barkley. *Sons of the Wild Jackass.* 1932. Reprint, Freeport, N.Y.: Books for Libraries Press, 1969.

Tull, Charles J. *Father Coughlin and the New Deal.* Syracuse, N.Y.: Syracuse University Press, 1965.

Turner, Henry A. "Woodrow Wilson and Public Opinion." *Public Opinion Quarterly* 21, no. 4 (1957–58): 505–20.

Upshaw, William D. *Bombshells for Wets and Reds: The Twin Devils of America.* Cincinnati: God's Bible School, 1936.

Vadney, T. E. "The Politics of Repression: A Case Study of the Red Scare in New York." *New York History* (1968): 58–74.

Viereck, George Sylvester. "Henry Ford and Reincarnation." *Mystic Triangle* (1928): 641–64.

von Mohrenschildt, Dmitri S. "Lincoln Steffens and the Bolshevik Revolution." *Russian Review* 5, no. 1 (1945): 31–41.

Voogd, Jan. *Race Riots and Resistance: The Red Summer of 1919.* New York: Peter Lang, 2008.

Voorhis, Jerry. *The Strange Case of Richard Milhous Nixon.* New York: Paul S. Erikson, 1972.

Wakstein, Allen. "The Origins of the Open Shop Movement, 1919–1920." *Journal of American History* 51, no. 3 (1964): 460–75.

Wald, Alan M. *The New York Intellectuals: The Rise and Decline of the Anti-Stalinist Left from the 1930s to the 1980s.* Chapel Hill: University of North Carolina Press, 1987.

Wallace, Max. *The American Axis: Henry Ford, Charles Lindbergh, and the Rise of the Third Reich.* New York: St. Martin's Press, 2003.

Walsh, Edmund A. *The Last Stand: An Interpretation of the Soviet Five-Year Plan*. Boston: Little, Brown, 1931.

Ward, Harry F. *In Place of Profit: Social Incentives in the Soviet Union*. New York: Charles Scribner's Sons, 1933.

Waring, Dorothy. *American Defender*. New York: Robert Speller, 1935.

Warren, Frank A. *Liberals and Communism: The "Red Decade" Revisited*. Bloomington: Indiana University Press, 1966.

Weigand, Kate. *Red Feminism: American Communism and the Making of Women's Liberation*. Baltimore: Johns Hopkins University Press, 2001.

Weinstein, Allen. *Perjury: The Hiss-Chambers Case*. New York: Random House, 1997.

Weinstein, Allen, and Alexander Vassiliev. *The Haunted Wood: Soviet Espionage in America—the Stalin Era*. New York: Random House, 1999.

Weinstein, James. "Anti-war Sentiment and the Socialist Party, 1917–1918." *Political Science Quarterly* 74, no. 2 (1959): 215–39.

———. *The Decline of Socialism in America, 1912–1925*. New York: Monthly Review Press, 1967.

Whalen, Grover. *Mr. New York*. New York: G. P. Putnam's Sons, 1955.

Wheeler, Burton K., with Paul F. Healy. *Yankee from the West*. New York: Doubleday, 1962.

Whitney, R. M. *Reds in America*. New York: Berkwith Press, 1924.

Whitten, Woodrow C. "Criminal Syndicalism and the Law in California, 1919–1927." *Transactions of the American Philosophical Society* 59, no. 2 (1969): 3–73.

Wilkins, Mira, and Frank Ernest Hill. *American Business Abroad: Ford on Six Continents*. Detroit: Wayne State University Press, 1964.

Williams, William Appleman. *The Tragedy of American Diplomacy*. 1959. Reprint, New York: Delta, 1972.

Wilson, Dwight. *Armageddon Now! The Premillennarian Response to Russia and Israel since 1917*. Grand Rapids, Mich.: Baker Book House, 1977.

Wilson, Woodrow. *The State: Elements of Practical and Historical Politics*. Boston: D. C. Heath, 1898.

Wolfe, Christopher. "Woodrow Wilson: Interpreting the Constitution." *Review of Politics* 41, no. 1 (1979): 121–42.

Wolfskill, George. *The Revolt of the Conservatives: A History of the American Liberty League, 1934–1940*. Boston: Riverside, 1962.

Yergin, Daniel. *Shattered Peace: The Origins of the Cold War and the National Security State*. Boston: Houghton Mifflin, 1977.

Young, Evan E. "The Attitude of the United States Government toward the Soviet Régime." *Annals of the American Academy of Political and Social Science* 114 (July 1924): 70–75.

Zanger, Martin. "Politics of Confrontation: Upton Sinclair and the Launching of the ACLU in Southern California." *Pacific Historical Review* 38, no. 4 (1969): 383–406.

Zentner, Scott J. "Liberalism and Executive Power: Woodrow Wilson and the American Founders." *Polity* 26, no. 4 (1994): 579–99.

Zucker, Norman L. *George W. Norris: Gentle Knight of American Democracy*. Urbana: University of Illinois Press, 1966.

Index

ALEX GOODALL is a lecturer in modern history at the University of York, where he specializes in the history of revolutionary and counterrevolutionary politics in the Americas.